October 30–November 3, 2017
Dallas, TX, USA

**Association for
Computing Machinery**

Advancing Computing as a Science & Profession

CCS'17

Proceedings of the 2017 ACM SIGSAC Conference on

Computer and Communications Security

Sponsored by:

ACM SIGSAC

**Association for
Computing Machinery**

Advancing Computing as a Science & Profession

The Association for Computing Machinery
2 Penn Plaza, Suite 701
New York, New York 10121-0701

Notice to Past Authors of ACM-Published Articles
ACM intends to create a complete electronic archive of all articles and/or other material previously published by ACM. If you have written a work that has been previously published by ACM in any journal or conference proceedings prior to 1978, or any SIG Newsletter at any time, and you do NOT want this work to appear in the ACM Digital Library, please inform permissions@acm.org, stating the title of the work, the author(s), and where and when published.

ISBN: 978-1-4503-4946-8 (Digital)

ISBN: 978-1-4503-5685-5 (Print)

Additional copies may be ordered prepaid from:

ACM Order Department
PO Box 30777
New York, NY 10087-0777, USA

Phone: 1-800-342-6626 (USA and Canada)
+1-212-626-0500 (Global)
Fax: +1-212-944-1318
E-mail: acmhelp@acm.org
Hours of Operation: 8:30 am – 4:30 pm ET

ACM CCS 2017 General Chair's Welcome

It is our great pleasure to welcome you to the 2017 ACM Conference on Computer and Communications Security (CCS) in Dallas, Texas. We are honored to organize ACM CCS 2017 in Dallas this year and extend our welcome to attendees from around the globe to this exciting city. We hope that you enjoy what the conference has to offer this year, both for the scientific discussions, and for the social events.

Dallas is one of the fastest growing urban area in America, with one million residents coming to the region every seven years. It is also one of the most demographically diverse and young cities in the country, which imbues the city with a friendly, outgoing sense of hospitality and genuine civic pride. Here you will find a large collection of international corporations, nationally recognized sports teams, and world class shopping. The Dallas Arts District and the many parks and gardens throughout Dallas will provide you with opportunities to enjoy the local culture while you are here.

ACM CCS is the flagship annual conference of the Special Interest Group on Security, Audit and Control (SIGSAC) of the Association for Computing Machinery. CCS brings together information security researchers, practitioners, developers, and users from all over the world to explore cutting-edge ideas and results. It provides an environment to conduct intellectual discussions. From its inception, CCS has established itself as a high standard research conference in its area. Its reputation continues to grow and is reflected in the prestigious technical program of high quality papers, workshops, tutorials, panel discussion and prestigious keynote addresses.

CCS 2017 would not have been possible without the help of numerous volunteers. We first want to thank all the authors who have submitted their work to CCS – without their commitment CCS 2017 would never have been possible. We also thank the program chairs, the program committee and the entire ACM organization and SIGSAC steering committee for their dedication and commitment. Special thanks go to Ms. Rhonda Walls and her team for the wonderful handling of the organization. Last but not least, we would like to express our gratitude to our generous sponsors of the conference, listed in the program, for their valuable support.

We hope that you will find this program interesting and thought-provoking and that the conference will provide you with a valuable opportunity to share ideas with other researchers and practitioners from institutions around the world. We wish you a pleasant and enjoyable stay in Dallas, Texas.

Dr. Bhavani Thuraisingham
CCS 2017 General Chair
The University of Texas at Dallas
Richardson, Texas

Program Chairs' Welcome

Welcome to the 24th ACM Conference on Computer and Communications Security!

Since 1993, CCS has been the ACM's flagship conference for research in all aspects of computing and communications security and privacy. This year's conference attracted a record number of 836 reviewed research paper submissions, of which a record number of 151 papers were selected for presentation at the conference and inclusion in the proceedings.

The papers were reviewed by a Program Committee of 146 leading researchers from academic, government, and industry from around the world. Reviewing was done in three rounds, with every paper being reviewed by two PC members in the first round, and additional reviews being assigned in later rounds depending on the initial reviews. Authors had an opportunity to respond to reviews received in the first two rounds. We used a subset of PC members, designated as the Discussion Committee, to help ensure that reviewers reconsidered their reviews in light of the author responses and to facilitate substantive discussions among the reviewers. Papers were discussed extensively on-line in the final weeks of the review process, and late reviews were requested from both PC members and external reviewers when additional expertise or perspective was needed to reach a decision. We are extremely grateful to the PC members for all their hard work in the review process, and to the external reviewers that contributed to selecting the papers for CCS.

Before starting the review process, of the 842 submissions the PC chairs removed six papers that clearly violated submission requirements or were duplicates, leaving 836 papers to review. In general, we were lenient on the requirements, only excluding papers that appeared to deliberately disregard the submission requirements. Instead of excluding papers which carelessly deanonymized the authors, or which abused appendices in the opinion of the chairs, we redacted (by modifying the submitted PDF) the offending content and allowed the papers to be reviewed, and offered to make redacted content in appendices available to reviewers upon request.

Our review process involved three phases. In the first phase, each paper was assigned two reviewers. Following last year's practice, we adopted the Toronto Paper Matching System (TPMS) for making most of the review assignments, which were then adjusted based on technical preferences declared by reviewers. Each reviewer had about 3 weeks to complete reviews for around 12 papers. Based on the results of these reviews, an additional reviewer was assigned to every paper that had at least one positive-leaning review. Papers where both initial reviews were negative, but with low confidence or significant positive aspects, were also assigned additional reviews. At the conclusion of the second reviewing round, authors had an opportunity to see the initial reviews and to submit a short rebuttal. To ensure that all the authors' responses were considered seriously by the reviewers, the Discussion Committee members worked closely with the reviewers to make sure that they considered and responded to the authors' rebuttals. When reviewers could not reach an agreement, or additional expertise was needed, we solicited additional reviews. The on-line discussion period was vibrant and substantive, and at the end of this process the 151 papers you find here were selected for CCS 2017.

We are grateful to all the PC members and external reviewers for their hard work and thoughtful discussions; to the General Chair, Bhavani Thuraisingham, for saving us from having to deal with anything other than the program and answering all our questions promptly and helpfully; to the Proceedings Chairs, Matthew Wright and Apu Kapadia, for all their efforts working with the publisher to produce the proceedings; to Hui Lu for managing the submission server and its interface with TPMS; and to all the authors who submitted papers to CCS.

We hope everyone finds the conference engaging, enlightening, and inspiring!

David Evans

University of Virginia

Tal Maklin

Columbia University

Dongyan Xu

Purdue University

ACM CCS 2017 Program Committee Co-Chairs

Table of Contents

CCS 2017 Conference Organization xxii

Keynote Talk

- **Security and Machine Learning** 1
  David Wagner *(University of California, Berkeley)*

Session A1: Multi-Party Computation 1

- **DUPLO: Unifying Cut-and-Choose for Garbled Circuits** 3
  Vladimir Kolesnikov *(Bell Labs)*, Jesper Buus Nielsen, Mike Rosulek, Ni Trieu *(Oregon State University)*,
  Roberto Trifiletti *(Aarhus University)*

- **Authenticated Garbling and Efficient Maliciously Secure Two-Party Computation** 21
  Xiao Wang *(University of Maryland)*, Samuel Ranellucci *(University of Maryland & George Mason University)*,
  Jonathan Katz *(University of Maryland)*,

- **Global-Scale Secure Multiparty Computation** 39
  Xiao Wang *(University of Maryland)*, Samuel Ranellucci *(University of Maryland & George Mason University)*,
  Jonathan Katz *(University of Maryland)*

Session A2: Human Authentication

- **Hearing Your Voice is Not Enough: An Articulatory Gesture Based Liveness Detection
  for Voice Authentication** 57
  Linghan Zhang, Sheng Tan, Jie Yang *(Florida State University)*

- **VibWrite: Towards Finger-input Authentication on Ubiquitous Surfaces
  via Physical Vibration** 73
  Jian Liu, Chen Wang, Yingying Chen *(Rutgers University)*,
  Nitesh Saxena *(University of Alabama at Birmingham)*

- **Presence Attestation: The Missing Link in Dynamic Trust Bootstrapping** 89
  Zhangkai Zhang *(Beihang University)*, Xuhua Ding *(Singapore Management University)*,
  Gene Tsudik *(University of California, Irvine)*, Jinhua Cui *(Singapore Management University)*,
  Zhoujun Li *(Beihang University)*

Session A3: Adversarial Machine Learning

- **DolphinAttack: Inaudible Voice Commands** 103
  Guoming Zhang, Chen Yan, Xiaoyu Ji, Tianchen Zhang, Taimin Zhang, Wenyuan Xu *(Zhejiang University)*

- **Evading Classifiers by Morphing in the Dark** 119
  Hung Dang, Yue Huang, Ee-Chien Chang *(National University of Singapore)*

- **MagNet: A Two-Pronged Defense against Adversarial Examples** 135
  Dongyu Meng *(ShanghaiTech University)*, Hao Chen *(University of California, Davis)*

Session A4: Browsers

- **Hindsight: Understanding the Evolution of UI Vulnerabilities in Mobile Browsers** 149
  Meng Luo, Oleksii Starov, Nima Honarmand, Nick Nikiforakis *(Stony Brook University)*

- **Deterministic Browser** 163
  Yinzhi Cao, Zhanhao Chen, Song Li, Shujiang Wu *(Lehigh University)*

- **Most Websites Don't Need to Vibrate: A Cost-Benefit Approach to Improving
  Browser Security** 179
  Peter Snyder, Cynthia Taylor, Chris Kanich *(University of Illinois at Chicago)*

Session A5: Cryptocurrency

- **Be Selfish and Avoid Dilemmas: Fork After Withholding (FAW) Attacks on Bitcoin**.............. 195
  Yujin Kwon, Dohyun Kim, Yunmok Son *(Korea Advanced Institute of Science and Technology)*,
  Eugene Vasserman *(Kansas State University)*, Yongdae Kim *(Korea Advanced Institute of Science and Technology)*

- **Betrayal, Distrust, and Rationality: Smart Counter-Collusion Contracts
  for Verifiable Cloud Computing** 211
  Changyu Dong, Yilei Wang, Amjad Aldweesh *(Newcastle University)*,
  Patrick McCorry *(University College London)*, Aad van Moorsel *(Newcastle University)*

- **Zero-Knowledge Contingent Payments Revisited: Attacks and Payments for Services** 229
  Matteo Campanelli *(City University of New York Graduate Center)*,
  Rosario Gennaro *(City College of New York)*, Steven Goldfeder *(Princeton University)*,
  Luca Nizzardo *(IMDEA Software Institute & Universidad Politécnica de Madrid)*

Session B1: Multi-Party Computation 2

- **Pool: Scalable On-Demand Secure Computation Service Against Malicious Adversaries** 245
  Ruiyu Zhu, Yan Huang *(Indiana University)*, Darion Cassel *(Carnegie Mellon University & Indiana University)*

- **A Framework for Constructing Fast MPC over Arithmetic Circuits with Malicious
  Adversaries and an Honest-Majority** 259
  Yehuda Lindell, Ariel Nof *(Bar-Ilan University)*

- **Efficient, Constant-Round and Actively Secure MPC: Beyond the Three-Party Case** 277
  Nishanth Chandran *(Microsoft Research India)*, Juan A. Garay *(Texas A&M University & Yahoo Research)*,
  Payman Mohassel *(Visa Research)*, Satyanarayana Vusirikala *(Microsoft Research India)*

Session B2: Passwords

- **Let's Go in for a Closer Look: Observing Passwords in Their Natural Habitat** 295
  Sarah Pearman, Jeremy Thomas, Pardis Emami Naeini, Hana Habib, Lujo Bauer, Nicolas Christin,
  Lorrie Faith Cranor *(Carnegie Mellon University)*, Serge Egelman *(International Computer Science Institute)*,
  Alain Forget *(Google, Inc.)*

- **Why Do Developers Get Password Storage Wrong? A Qualitative Usability Study** 311
  Alena Naiakshina, Anastasia Danilova, Christian Tiefenau, Marco Herzog, Sergej Dechand,
  Matthew Smith *(University of Bonn)*

- **The TypTop System: Personalized Typo-Tolerant Password Checking** 329
  Rahul Chatterjee *(Cornell University & Cornell Tech)*, Joanne Woodage *(Royal Holloway, University of London)*,
  Yuval Pnueli *(Technion – Israel Institute of Technology)*, Anusha Chowdhury *(Cornell University)*,
  Thomas Ristenpart *(Cornell University & Cornell Tech)*

Session B3: Investigating Attacks

- **Rise of the HaCRS: Augmenting Autonomous Cyber Reasoning Systems
  with Human Assistance** 347
  Yan Shoshitaishvili *(Arizona State University)*, Michael Weissbacher *(Northeastern University)*,
  Lukas Dresel, Christopher Salls, Ruoyu Wang, Christopher Kruegel,
  Giovanni Vigna *(University of California, Santa Barbara)*

- **Neural Network-based Graph Embedding for Cross-Platform Binary Code
  Similarity Detection** 363
  Xiaojun Xu *(Shanghai Jiao Tong University)*, Chang Liu *(University of California, Berkeley)*,
  Qian Feng *(Samsung Research America)*, Heng Yin *(University of California, Riverside)*,
  Le Song *(Georgia Institute of Technology)*, Dawn Song *(University of California, Berkeley)*

- **RAIN: Refinable Attack Investigation with On-demand Inter-Process Information
  Flow Tracking** 377
  Yang Ji, Sangho Lee, Evan Downing, Weiren Wang, Mattia Fazzini, Taesoo Kim, Alessandro Orso,
  Wenke Lee *(Georgia Institute of Technology)*

Session B4: Privacy Policies

- **Synthesis of Probabilistic Privacy Enforcement** 391
  Martin Kučera, Petar Tsankov, Timon Gehr, Marco Guarnieri, Martin Vechev *(ETH Zurich)*

- **A Type System for Privacy Properties** 409
  Véronique Cortier *(CNRS, LORIA)*, Niklas Grimm *(TU Wien)*, Joseph Lallemand *(Inria, LORIA)*,
  Matteo Maffei *(TU Wien)*

- **Generating Synthetic Decentralized Social Graphs with Local Differential Privacy** 425
  Zhan Qin *(State University of New York at Buffalo & Hamad Bin Khalifa University)*,
  Ting Yu, Yin Yang, Issa Khalil *(Hamad Bin Khalifa University)*,
  Xiaokui Xiao *(Nanyang Technological University)*,
  Kui Ren *(State University of New York at Buffalo & Qatar Computing Research Institute)*

Session B5: Blockchains

- **Revive: Rebalancing Off-Blockchain Payment Networks** 439
  Rami Khalil, Arthur Gervais *(ETH Zurich)*

- **Concurrency and Privacy with Payment-Channel Networks** 455
  Giulio Malavolta *(Friedrich-Alexander-University Erlangen-Nürnberg)*,
  Pedro Moreno-Sanchez, Aniket Kate *(Purdue University)*, Matteo Maffei *(TU Wien)*,
  Srivatsan Ravi *(University of Southern California)*

- **Bolt: Anonymous Payment Channels for Decentralized Currencies** 473
  Matthew Green, Ian Miers *(Johns Hopkins University)*

Session C1: Oblivious RAM

- **S3ORAM: A Computation-Efficient and Constant Client Bandwidth Blowup ORAM
  with Shamir Secret Sharing** 491
  Thang Hoang, Ceyhun D. Ozkaptan, Attila A. Yavuz *(Oregon State University)*,
  Jorge Guajardo *(Robert Bosch RTC)*, Tam Nguyen *(Oregon State University)*

- **Deterministic, Stash-Free Write-Only ORAM** 507
  Daniel S. Roche, Adam Aviv, Seung Geol Choi, Travis Mayberry *(United States Naval Academy)*

- **Scaling ORAM for Secure Computation** 523
  Jack Doerner, Abhi Shelat *(Northeastern University)*

Session C2: World Wide Web of Wickedness

- **Don't Let One Rotten Apple Spoil the Whole Barrel: Towards Automated Detection
  of Shadowed Domains** 537
  Daiping Liu *(University of Delaware)*, Zhou Li *(ACM Member)*, Kun Du *(Tsinghua University)*,
  Haining Wang *(University of Delaware)*, Baojun Liu, Haixin Duan *(Tsinghua University)*

- **Herding Vulnerable Cats: A Statistical Approach to Disentangle Joint Responsibility
  for Web Security in Shared Hosting** 553
  Samaneh Tajalizadehkhoob *(Delft University of Technology)*,
  Tom Van Goethem *(imec-DistriNet, KU Leuven)*,
  Maciej Korczyński, Arman Noroozian *(Delft University of Technology)*,
  Rainer Böhme *(Innsbruck University)*, Tyler Moore *(University of Tulsa)*,
  Wouter Joosen *(imec-DistriNet, KU Leuven)*,
  Michel van Eeten *(Delft University of Technology)*

- **Hiding in Plain Sight: A Longitudinal Study of Combosquatting Abuse** 569
  Panagiotis Kintis *(Georgia Institute of Technology)*, Najmeh Miramirkhani *(Stony Brook University)*,
  Charles Lever, Yizheng Chen, Rosa Romero-Gómez *(Georgia Institute of Technology)*,
  Nikolaos Pitropakis *(London South Bank University)*, Nick Nikiforakis *(Stony Brook University)*,
  Manos Antonakakis *(Georgia Institute of Technology)*

Session C3: Machine Learning Privacy

- **Machine Learning Models that Remember Too Much** 587
  Congzheng Song *(Cornell University)*, Thomas Ristenpart, Vitaly Shmatikov *(Cornell Tech)*

- **Deep Models Under the GAN: Information Leakage from Collaborative Deep Learning** 603
  Briland Hitaj *(Stevens Institute of Technology & University of Rome - La Sapienza)*,
  Giuseppe Ateniese, Fernando Perez-Cruz *(Stevens Institute of Technology)*

- **Oblivious Neural Network Predictions via MiniONN Transformations** 619
  Jian Liu, Mika Juuti, Yao Lu, N. Asokan *(Aalto University)*

Session C4: From Verification to ABE

- **Verifying Security Policies in Multi-agent Workflows with Loops** 633
  Bernd Finkbeiner *(CISPA, Saarland University)*,
  Christian Müller, Helmut Seidl, Eugen Zălinescu *(Technische Universität München)*

- **Attribute-Based Encryption in the Generic Group Model: Automated Proofs
  and New Constructions** 647
  Miguel Ambrona *(IMDEA Software Institute & Universidad Politecnica de Madrid)*,
  Gilles Barthe *(IMDEA Software Institute)*, Romain Gay *(ENS)*, Hoeteck Wee *(CNRS & ENS)*

- **FAME: Fast Attribute-based Message Encryption** 665
  Shashank Agrawal *(Visa Research & Microsoft Research)*, Melissa Chase *(Microsoft Research)*

Session C5: Using Blockchains

- **Practical UC-Secure Delegatable Credentials with Attributes and Their
  Application to Blockchain** 683
  Jan Camenisch *(IBM Research - Zurich)*, Manu Drijvers *(IBM Research - Zurich & ETH Zurich)*,
  Maria Dubovitskaya *(IBM Research - Zurich)*

- **Solidus: Confidential Distributed Ledger Transactions via PVORM** 701
  Ethan Cecchetti, Fan Zhang, Yan Ji *(Cornell University; IC3)*, Ahmed Kosba *(University of Maryland; IC3)*,
  Ari Juels *(Cornell Tech, Jacobs Institute; IC3)*, Elaine Shi *(Cornell University; IC3)*

- **Fairness in an Unfair World: Fair Multiparty Computation from Public Bulletin Boards** 719
  Arka Rai Choudhuri, Matthew Green, Abhishek Jain, Gabriel Kaptchuk, Ian Miers
  (Johns Hopkins University)

Session D1: Functional Encryption and Obfuscation

- **5Gen-C: Multi-input Functional Encryption and Program Obfuscation
  for Arithmetic Circuits** 747
  Brent Carmer *(Oregon State University & Galois, Inc.)*, Alex J. Malozemoff *(Galois, Inc.)*,
  Mariana Raykova *(Yale University)*

- **IRON: Functional Encryption using Intel SGX** 765
  Ben Fisch *(Stanford University)*, Dhinakaran Vinayagamurthy *(University of Waterloo)*,
  Dan Boneh *(Stanford University)*, Sergey Gorbunov *(University of Waterloo)*

- **Implementing BP-Obfuscation Using Graph-Induced Encoding** 783
  Shai Halevi *(IBM Research)*, Tzipora Halevi *(CUNY Brooklyn College)*,
  Victor Shoup *(IBM Research & New York University)*,
  Noah Stephens-Davidowitz *(New York University)*

Session D2: Vulnerable Mobile Apps

- **AUTHSCOPE: Towards Automatic Discovery of Vulnerable Authorizations
  in Online Services** 799
  Chaoshun Zuo, Qingchuan Zhao, Zhiqiang Lin *(University of Texas at Dallas)*

- **Mass Discovery of Android Traffic Imprints through Instantiated Partial Execution** 815
  Yi Chen *(Institute of Information Engineering, Chinese Academy of Sciences
  & University of Chinese Academy of Sciences)*, Wei You, Yeonjoon Lee *(Indiana University, Bloomington)*,
  Kai Chen *(Institute of Information Engineering, Chinese Academy of Sciences & University
  of Chinese Academy of Sciences)*, XiaoFeng Wang *(Indiana University, Bloomington)*,
  Wei Zou *(Institute of Information Engineering, Chinese Academy of Sciences & University
  of Chinese Academy of Sciences)*

- **Unleashing the Walking Dead: Understanding Cross-App Remote Infections
  on Mobile WebViews** 829
  Tongxin Li *(Peking University & Indiana University, Bloomington)*,
  Xueqiang Wang *(Indiana University, Bloomington)*,
   Mingming Zha, Kai Chen *(Institute of Information Engineering & Chinese Academy of Sciences
  & University of Chinese Academy of Sciences)*, XiaoFeng Wang, Luyi Xing *(Indiana University, Bloomington)*,
  Xiaolong Bai *(Tsinghua University)*, Nan Zhang *(Indiana University, Bloomington)*,
  Xinhui Han *(Peking University)*

Session D3: Logical Side Channels

- **May the Fourth Be With You: A Microarchitectural Side Channel Attack on Several
  Real-World Applications of Curve25519**.. 845
  Daniel Genkin *(University of Pennsylvania & University of Maryland)*, Luke Valenta *(University of Pennsylvania)*,
  Yuval Yarom *(University of Adelaide & Data61)*

- **STACCO: Differentially Analyzing Side-Channel Traces for Detecting SSL/TLS
  Vulnerabilities in Secure Enclaves**... 859
  Yuan Xiao, Mengyuan Li, Sanchuan Chen, Yinqian Zhang *(Ohio State University)*

- **Precise Detection of Side-Channel Vulnerabilities using Quantitative Cartesian
  Hoare Logic** 875
  Jia Chen, Yu Feng, Isil Dillig *(University of Texas at Austin)*

Session D4: Crypto Primitives

- **Better Than Advertised: Improved Collision-Resistance Guarantees for MD-Based
  Hash Functions** 891
  Mihir Bellare, Joseph Jaeger, Julia Len *(University of California, San Diego)*

- **Generic Semantic Security against a Kleptographic Adversary** 907
  Alexander Russell *(University of Connecticut)*, Qiang Tang *(New Jersey Institute of Technology)*,
  Moti Yung *(Snap.Inc & Columbia University)*, Hong-Sheng Zhou *(Virginia Commonwealth University)*

- **Defending Against Key Exfiltration: Efficiency Improvements for Big-Key
  Cryptography via Large-Alphabet Subkey Prediction** 923
  Mihir Bellare, Wei Dai *(University of California, San Diego)*

Session D5: Network Security

- **Client-side Name Collision Vulnerability in the New gTLD Era: A Systematic Study** 941
  Qi Alfred Chen *(University of Michigan)*, Matthew Thomas, Eric Osterweil *(Verisign Labs)*,
  Yulong Cao, Jie You, Z. Morley Mao *(University of Michigan)*

- **The Wolf of Name Street: Hijacking Domains Through Their Nameservers**............................ 957
  Thomas Vissers *(imec-DistriNet, KU Leuven)*, Timothy Barron *(Stony Brook University)*,
  Tom Van Goethem, Wouter Joosen *(imec-DistriNet, KU Leuven)*, Nick Nikiforakis *(Stony Brook University)*

- **Faulds: A Non-Parametric Iterative Classifier for Internet-Wide OS Fingerprinting**................ 971
  Zain Shamsi, Daren B.H. Cline, Dmitri Loguinov *(Texas A&M University)*

Session E1: Hardening Crypto

- **T/Key: Second-Factor Authentication From Secure Hash Chains**.. 983
  Dmitry Kogan, Nathan Manohar, Dan Boneh *(Stanford University)*

- **Practical Graphs for Optimal Side-Channel Resistant Memory-Hard Functions**.................... 1001
  Joel Alwen *(IST Austia)*, Jeremiah Blocki, Ben Harsha *(Purdue University)*

- **Better Bounds for Block Cipher Modes of Operation via Nonce-Based Key Derivation** 1019
  Shay Gueron *(University of Haifa and Amazon Web Services)*, Yehuda Lindell *(Bar-Ilan University)*

Session E2: Securing Mobile Apps

- **The ART of App Compartmentalization: Compiler-based Library Privilege Separation on Stock Android**... 1037
  Jie Huang, Oliver Schranz, Sven Bugiel, Michael Backes *(Saarland University)*

- **Vulnerable Implicit Service: A Revisit**.. 1051
  Lingguang Lei *(Chinese Academy of Sciences & Institute of Information Engineering, Chinese Academy of Sciences)*,
  Yi He *(Tsinghua University)*, Kun Sun *(George Mason University)*,
  Jiwu Jing, Yuewu Wang *(Chinese Academy of Sciences & Institute of Information Engineering,
  Chinese Academy of Sciences)*,
  Qi Li *(Tsinghua University)*, Jian Weng *(Jinan University)*

- **A Stitch in Time: Supporting Android Developers in WritingSecure Code** 1065
  Duc Cuong Nguyen *(Saarland University)*, Dominik Wermke, Yasemin Acar *(Leibniz University, Hannover)*,
  Michael Backes *(Saarland University)*, Charles Weir *(Lancaster University)*,
  Sascha Fahl *(Leibniz University, Hannover)*

Session E3: Physical Side Channels

- **Exploiting a Thermal Side Channel for Power Attacks in Multi-Tenant Data Centers** 1079
  Mohammad A. Islam, Shaolei Ren *(University of California, Riverside)*,
  Adam Wierman *(California Institute of Technology)*

- **Watch Me, but Don't Touch Me! Contactless Control Flow Monitoring via Electromagnetic Emanations** 1095
  Yi Han, Sriharsha Etigowni, Hua Liu, Saman Zonouz, Athina Petropulu *(Rutgers University)*

- **Viden: Attacker Identification on In-Vehicle Networks** 1109
  Kyong-Tak Cho, Kang G. Shin *(University of Michigan)*

Session E4: Adversarial Social Networking

- **Practical Attacks Against Graph-based Clustering**.. 1125
  Yizheng Chen, Yacin Nadji, Athanasios Kountouras *(Georgia Institute of Technology)*,
  Fabian Monrose *(University of North Carolina at Chapel Hill)*, Roberto Perdisci *(University of Georgia)*,
  Manos Antonakakis *(Georgia Institute of Technology)*, Nikolaos Vasiloglou *(Symantec CAML Group)*

- **Automated Crowdturfing Attacks and Defenses in Online Review Systems** 1143
  Yuanshun Yao, Bimal Viswanath, Jenna Cryan, Haitao Zheng, Ben Y. Zhao *(University of Chicago)*

- **POISED: Spotting Twitter Spam Off the Beaten Paths** 1159
  Shirin Nilizadeh *(University of California, Santa Barbara)*,
  Francois Labrèche, Alireza Sedighian *(Ecole Polytechnique de Montréal)*,
  Ali Zand *(University of California, Santa Barbara)*, José Fernandez *(Ecole Polytechnique de Montréal)*,
  Christopher Kruegel *(University of California, Santa Barbara)*, Gianluca Stringhini *(University College London)*,
  Giovanni Vigna *(University of California, Santa Barbara)*

Session E5: Privacy-Preserving Analytics

- **Practical Secure Aggregation for Privacy-Preserving Machine Learning**.................................. 1175
  Keith Bonawitz, Vladimir Ivanov, Ben Kreuter *(Google Inc.)*, Antonio Marcedone *(Cornell Tech)*,
  H. Brendan McMahan, Sarvar Patel, Daniel Ramage, Aaron Segal, Karn Seth *(Google Inc.)*

- **Use Privacy in Data-Driven Systems: Theory and Experiments with Machine Learnt Programs**... 1193
  Anupam Datta, Matthew Fredrikson, Gihyuk Ko, Piotr Mardziel, Shayak Sen *(Carnegie Mellon University)*

- **SGX-BigMatrix: A Practical Encrypted Data Analytic Framework With Trusted Processors** 1211
  Fahad Shaon, Murat Kantarcioglu, Zhiqiang Lin, Latifur Khan *(University of Texas at Dallas)*

Session F1: Private Set Intersection

- **Malicious-Secure Private Set Intersection via Dual Execution** 1229
  Peter Rindal, Mike Rosulek *(Oregon State University)*

- **Fast Private Set Intersection from Homomorphic Encryption** 1243
  Hao Chen, Kim Laine *(Microsoft Research)*, Peter Rindal *(Oregon State University)*

- **Practical Multi-party Private Set Intersection from Symmetric-Key Techniques** 1257
  Vladimir Kolesnikov *(Bell Labs)*, Naor Matania, Benny Pinkas *(Bar-Ilan University)*,
  Mike Rosulek, Ni Trieu *(Oregon State University)*

Session F2: Insights from Log(in)s

- **Detecting Structurally Anomalous Logins Within Enterprise Networks** 1273
  Hossein Siadati, Nasir Memon *(New York University)*

- **DeepLog: Anomaly Detection and Diagnosis from System Logs through Deep Learning** 1285
  Min Du, Feifei Li, Guineng Zheng, Vivek Srikumar *(University of Utah)*

- **RiskTeller: Predicting the Risk of Cyber Incidents** 1299
  Leyla Bilge, Yufei Han, Matteo Dell'Amico *(Symantec Research Labs)*

Session F3: Crypto Pitfalls

- **Key Reinstallation Attacks: Forcing Nonce Reuse in WPA2** 1313
  Mathy Vanhoef, Frank Piessens *(imec-DistriNet, KU Leuven)*

- **CCCP: Closed Caption Crypto Phones to Resist MITM Attacks,
  Human Errors and Click-Through** 1329
  Maliheh Shirvanian, Nitesh Saxena *(University of Alabama at Birmingham)*

- **No-Match Attacks and Robust Partnering Definitions – Defining Trivial Attacks
  for Security Protocols is Not Trivial** 1343
  Yong Li *(Huawei Technologies Düsseldorf)*, Sven Schäge *(Ruhr-Universität Bochum)*

Session F4: Private Queries

- **Querying for Queries: Indexes of Queries for Efficient and Expressive IT-PIR** 1361
  Syed Mahbub Hafiz, Ryan Henry *(Indiana University)*

- **PeGaSus: Data-Adaptive Differentially Private Stream Processing** 1375
  Yan Chen, Ashwin Machanavajjhala *(Duke University)*, Michael Hay *(Colgate University)*,
  Gerome Miklau *(University of Massachusetts, Amherst)*

- **Composing Differential Privacy and Secure Computation:
  A Case Study on Scaling Private Record Linkage** 1389
  Xi He, Ashwin Machanavajjhala *(Duke University)*, Cheryl Flynn, Divesh Srivastava *(AT&T Labs-Research)*

Session F5: Understanding Security Fails

- **Where the Wild Warnings Are: Root Causes of Chrome HTTPS Certificate Errors** 1407
  Mustafa Emre Acer, Emily Stark, Adrienne Porter Felt *(Google Inc.)*,
  Sascha Fahl *(Leibniz University Hannover)*, Radhika Bhargava *(Purdue University)*,
  Bhanu Dev *(International Institute of Information Technology, Hyderabad)*,
  Matt Braithwaite, Ryan Sleevi, Parisa Tabriz *(Google Inc.)*

- **Data Breaches, Phishing, or Malware? Understanding the Risks of Stolen Credentials** 1421
  Kurt Thomas *(Google)*, Frank Li *(University of California, Berkeley)*,
  Ali Zand, Jacob Barrett, Juri Ranieri, Luca Invernizzi, Yarik Markov, Oxana Comanescu,
  Vijay Eranti, Angelika Moscicki, Daniel Margolis *(Google)*,
  Vern Paxson *(University of California, Berkeley & International Computer Science Institute)*,
  Elie Bursztein *(Google)*

- **Certified Malware: Measuring Breaches of Trust in the Windows Code-Signing PKI** 1435
  Doowon Kim, Bum Jun Kwon, Tudor Dumitraş *(University of Maryland)*

Session G1: Searchable Encryption

- **Forward Secure Dynamic Searchable Symmetric Encryption with Efficient Updates** 1449
  Kee Sung Kim, Minkyu Kim, Dongsoo Lee, Je Hong Park, Woo-Hwan Kim *(National Security Research Institute)*

- **Forward and Backward Private Searchable Encryption from Constrained Cryptographic Primitives** 1465
  Raphaël Bost *(Direction Générale de l'Armement & Université de Rennes 1)*,
  Brice Minaud *(Royal Holloway, University of London)*, Olga Ohrimenko *(Microsoft Research)*

Session G2: Bug-Hunting Risks and Rewards

- **Economic Factors of Vulnerability Trade and Exploitation** 1483
  Luca Allodi *(Eindhoven University of Technology)*

- **Quantifying the Pressure of Legal Risks on Third-party Vulnerability Research** 1501
  Alexander Gamero-Garrido, Stefan Savage, Kirill Levchenko, Alex C. Snoeren
  (University of California, San Diego)

Session G3: Crypto Standards

- **Identity-Based Format-Preserving Encryption** 1515
  Mihir Bellare *(University of California, San Diego)*, Viet Tung Hoang *(Florida State University)*

- **Standardizing Bad Cryptographic Practice: A Teardown of the IEEE Standard for Protecting Electronic-design Intellectual Property** 1533
  Animesh Chhotaray, Adib Nahiyan, Thomas Shrimpton, Domenic Forte,
  Mark Tehranipoor *(University of Florida)*

Session G4: Voting

- **New Techniques for Structural Batch Verification in Bilinear Groups with Applications to Groth–Sahai Proofs** 1547
  Gottfried Herold *(Ecole Normale Supérieure)*, Max Hoffmann *(Ruhr-Universität Bochum)*,
  Michael Klooß *(Karlsruhe Institute of Technology)*, Carla Ràfols *(Universitat Pompeu Fabra)*,
  Andy Rupp *(Karlsruhe Institute of Technology)*

- **Practical Quantum-Safe Voting from Lattices** 1565
  Rafaël del Pino, Vadim Lyubashevsky, Gregory Neven, Gregor Seiler *(IBM Research - Zurich)*

Session G5: Hardening Hardware

- **A Touch of Evil: High-Assurance Cryptographic Hardware from Untrusted Components** ... 1583
  Vasilios Mavroudis, Andrea Cerulli *(University College London)*, Petr Svenda *(Masaryk University)*,
  Dan Cvrcek, Dusan Klinec *(EnigmaBridge)*, George Danezis *(University College London)*

- **Provably-Secure Logic Locking: From Theory To Practice** 1601
  Muhammad Yasin *(New York University)*, Abhrajit Sengupta *(New York University)*,
  Mohammed Thari Nabeel, Mohammed Ashraf *(New York University Abu Dhabi)*,
  Jeyavijayan (JV) Rajendran *(University of Texas at Dallas & Texas A&M University)*,
  Ozgur Sinanoglu *(New York University Abu Dhabi)*

Session H1: Crypto Attacks

- **The Return of Coppersmith's Attack: Practical Factorization of Widely Used RSA Moduli** .. 1631
  Matus Nemec *(Masaryk University, Ca' Foscari University of Venice)*,
  Marek Sys, Petr Svenda *(Masaryk University)*, Dusan Klinec *(EnigmaBridge, Masaryk University)*,
  Vashek Matyas *(Masaryk University)*

- **Algorithm Substitution Attacks from a Steganographic Perspective** 1649
  Sebastian Berndt, Maciej Liśkiewicz *(University of Lübeck)*

- **On the Power of Optical Contactless Probing: Attacking Bitstream Encryption of FPGAs** ... 1661
  Shahin Tajik, Heiko Lohrke, Jean-Pierre Seifert, Christian Boit *(Technische Universität Berlin)*

Session H2: Code Reuse Attacks

- **The Dynamics of Innocent Flesh on the Bone: Code Reuse Ten Years Later** 1675
  Victor van der Veen, Dennis Andriesse, Manolis Stamatogiannakis *(Vrije Universiteit Amsterdam)*,
  Xi Chen *(Vrije Universiteit Amsterdam & Microsoft)*,
  Herbert Bos, Cristiano Giuffrdia *(Vrije Universiteit Amsterdam)*

- **Capturing Malware Propagations with Code Injections and Code-Reuse Attacks** 1691
  David Korczynski *(University of Oxford)*, Heng Yin *(University of California, Riverside)*

- **Code-Reuse Attacks for the Web: Breaking Cross-Site Scripting Mitigations
  via Script Gadgets** 1709
  Sebastian Lekies, Krzysztof Kotowicz *(Google)*, Samuel Groß *(SAP)*,
  Eduardo A. Vela Nava *(Google)*, Martin Johns *(SAP)*

Session H3: Web Security

- **Tail Attacks on Web Applications** 1725
  Huasong Shan, Qingyang Wang *(Louisiana State University)*, Calton Pu *(Georgia Institute of Technology)*

- **Rewriting History: Changing the Archived Web from the Present** 1741
  Ada Lerner *(Wellesley College)*, Tadayoshi Kohno, Franziska Roesner *(University of Washington)*

- **Deemon: Detecting CSRF with Dynamic Analysis and Property Graphs** 1757
  Giancarlo Pellegrino *(CISPA, Saarland University)*, Martin Johns *(SAP SE)*,
  Simon Koch, Michael Backes, Christian Rossow *(CISPA, Saarland University)*

Session H4: Formal Verification

- **A Comprehensive Symbolic Analysis of TLS 1.3** 1773
  Cas Cremers *(University of Oxford)*, Marko Horvat *(MPI-SWS)*,
  Jonathan Hoyland, Sam Scott, Thyla van der Merwe *(Royal Holloway, University of London)*

- **HACL*: A Verified Modern Cryptographic Library** 1789
  Jean-Karim Zinzindohoué, Karthikeyan Bhargavan *(INRIA)*, Jonathan Protzenko *(Microsoft Research)*,
  Benjamin Beurdouche *(INRIA)*

- **Jasmin: High-Assurance and High-Speed Cryptography** 1807
  José Bacelar Almeida *(INESC TEC and Universidade do Minho)*,
  Manuel Barbosa *(INESC TEC and FCUP Universidade do Porto)*, Gilles Barthe *(IMDEA Software Institute)*,
  Arthur Blot *(ENS Lyon)*, Benjamin Grégoire *(Inria Sophia-Antipolis)*, Vincent Laporte *(IMDEA Software Institute)*,
  Tiago Oliveira *(INESC TEC and FCUP Universidade do Porto)*, Hugo Pacheco *(INESC TEC and Universidade do Minho)*,
  Benedikt Schmidt *(Google Inc.)*, Pierre-Yves Strub *(École Polytechnique)*

Session I1: Post-Quantum

- **Post-Quantum Zero-Knowledge and Signatures from Symmetric-Key Primitives** 1825
  Melissa Chase *(Microsoft Research)*, David Derler *(Graz University of Technology)*,
  Steven Goldfeder *(Princeton University)*, Claudio Orlandi *(Aarhus University)*,
  Sebastian Ramacher *(Graz University of Technology)*,
  Christian Rechberger *(Graz University of Technology & Denmark Technical University)*,
  Daniel Slamanig *(AIT Austrian Institute of Technology)*, Greg Zaverucha *(Microsoft Research)*

- **To BLISS-B or not to be - Attacking strongSwan's Implementation
  of Post-Quantum Signatures** 1843
  Peter Pessl *(Graz University of Technology)*, Leon Groot Bruinderink *(Technische Universiteit Eindhoven)*,
  Yuval Yarom *(University of Adelaide and Data61)*

- **Side-Channel Attacks on BLISS Lattice-Based Signatures: Exploiting Branch Tracing
  against strongSwan and Electromagnetic Emanations in Microcontrollers** 1857
  Thomas Espitau *(UPMC)*, Pierre-Alain Fouque *(Université de Rennes I)*, Benoît Gérard *(DGA.MI)*,
  Mehdi Tibouchi *(NTT Corporation)*

Session I2: Information Flow

- **Nonmalleable Information Flow Control** 1875
  Ethan Cecchetti, Andrew C. Myers *(Cornell University)*,
  Owen Arden *(University of California, Santa Cruz & Harvard University)*

- **Cryptographically Secure Information Flow Control on Key-Value Stores** 1893
  Lucas Waye, Pablo Buiras *(Harvard University)*, Owen Arden *(University of California, Santa Cruz)*,
  Alejandro Russo *(Chalmers University of Technology)*, Stephen Chong *(Harvard University)*

- **Object Flow Integrity** 1909
  Wenhao Wang, Xiaoyang Xu, Kevin W. Hamlen *(University of Texas at Dallas)*

Session I3: Personal Privacy

- **BBA+: Improving the Security and Applicability of Privacy-Preserving Point Collection** 1925
  Gunnar Hartung *(Karlsruhe Institute of Technology)*, Max Hoffmann *(Ruhr-Universität Bochum)*,
  Matthias Nagel, Andy Rupp *(Karlsruhe Institute of Technology)*

- **walk2friends: Inferring Social Links from Mobility Profiles** 1943
  Michael Backes *(Saarland University)*, Mathias Humbert *(ETH Zurich and EPFL)*,
  Jun Pang *(University of Luxembourg)*, Yang Zhang *(Saarland University)*

- **Back to the Drawing Board: Revisiting the Design of Optimal Location
  Privacy-preserving Mechanisms** 1959
  Simon Oya *(University of Vigo)*, Carmela Troncoso *(IMDEA Software Institute)*,
  Fernando Pérez-González *(University of Vigo)*

Session I4: Verifying Crypto

- **Certified Verification of Algebraic Properties on Low-Level Mathematical Constructs
  in Cryptographic Programs** 1973
  Ming-Hsien Tsai, Bow-Yaw Wang, Bo-Yin Yang *(Academia Sinica)*

- **A Fast and Verified Software Stack for Secure Function Evaluation** 1989
  José Bacelar Almeida *(INESC TEC & Universidade do Minho)*,
  Manuel Barbosa *(INESC TEC & FCUP Universidade do Porto)*, Gilles Barthe *(IMDEA Software Institute)*,
  François Dupressoir *(University of Surrey)*, Benjamin Grégoire *(Inria Sophia-Antipolis)*,
  Vincent Laporte *(IMDEA Software Institute)*, Vitor Pereira *(INESC TEC & FCUP Universidade do Porto)*

- **Verified Correctness and Security of mbedTLS HMAC-DRBG** 2007
  Katherine Q. Ye *(Princeton University & Carnegie Mellon University)*,
  Matthew Green *(Johns Hopkins University)*, Naphat Sanguansin, Lennart Beringer *(Princeton University)*,
  Adam Petcher *(Oracle)*, Andrew W. Appel *(Princeton University)*

Session I5: Communication Privacy

- **How Unique is Your .onion? An Analysis of the Fingerprintability
  of Tor Onion Services** 2021
  Rebekah Overdorf *(Drexel University)*, Mark Juarez, Gunes Acar *(imec-COSIC KU Leuven)*,
  Rachel Greenstadt *(Drexel University)*, Claudia Diaz *(imec-COSIC KU Leuven)*

- **The Waterfall of Liberty: Decoy Routing Circumvention that Resists Routing Attacks** 2037
  Milad Nasr, Hadi Zolfaghari, Amir Houmansadr *(University of Massachusetts, Amherst)*

- **Compressive Traffic Analysis: A New Paradigm for Scalable Traffic Analysis** 2053
  Milad Nasr, Amir Houmansadr, Arya Mazumdar *(University of Massachusetts, Amherst)*

Session J1: Outsourcing

- **Full Accounting for Verifiable Outsourcing** 2071
  Riad S. Wahby *(Stanford University)*, Ye Ji *(New York University)*,
  Andrew J. Blumberg *(University of Texas at Austin)*, Abhi Shelat *(Northeastern University)*,
  Justin Thaler *(Georgetown University)*, Michael Walfish, Thomas Wies *(New York University)*

- **Ligero: Lightweight Sublinear Arguments Without a Trusted Setup**... 2087
  Scott Ames *(University of Rochester)*, Carmit Hazay *(Bar-Ilan University)*,
  Yuval Ishai *(Technion and University of California, Los Angeles)*,
  Muthuramakrishnan Venkitasubramaniam *(University of Rochester)*

- **Homomorphic Secret Sharing: Optimizations and Applications** 2105
  Elette Boyle *(IDC)*, Geoffroy Couteau *(École Normale Supérieure, CNRS, PSL Research University, INRIA)*,
  Niv Gilboa *(Ben Gurion University)*, Yuval Ishai *(Technion and University of California, Los Angeles)*,
  Michele Orrù *(École Normale Supérieure, CNRS, PSL Research University, INRIA)*

Session J2: Fun with Fuzzing

- **DIFUZE: Interface Aware Fuzzing for Kernel Drivers** 2123
  Jake Corina, Aravind Machiry, Christopher Salls *(University of California, Santa Barbara)*,
  Yan Shoshitaishvili *(Arizona State University)*, Shuang Hao *(University of Texas at Dallas)*,
  Christopher Kruegel, Giovanni Vigna *(University of California, Santa Barbara)*

- **SemFuzz: Semantics-based Automatic Generation of Proof-of-Concept Exploits** 2139
  Wei You *(Indiana University, Bloomington)*,
  Peiyuan Zong, Kai Chen *(Institute of Information Engineering, Chinese Academy of Sciences
  & University of Chinese Academy of Sciences)*, XiaoFeng Wang *(Indiana University, Bloomington)*,
  Xiaojing Liao *(William and Mary)*, Pan Bian, Bin Liang *(Renmin University of China)*

- **SlowFuzz: Automated Domain-Independent Detection of Algorithmic
  Complexity Vulnerabilities** 2155
  Theofilos Petsios, Jason Zhao, Angelos D. Keromytis, Suman Jana *(Columbia University)*

Session J3: Problematic Patches

- **Identifying Open-Source License Violation and 1-day Security Risk at Large Scale** 2169
  Ruian Duan, Ashish Bijlani, Meng Xu, Taesoo Kim, Wenke Lee *(Georgia Institute of Technology)*

- **Keep me Updated: An Empirical Study of Third-Party Library Updatability on Android** 2187
  Erik Derr, Sven Bugiel *(Saarland University)*, Sascha Fahl, Yasemin Acar *(Leibniz University, Hannover)*,
  Michael Backes *(Saarland University)*

- **A Large-Scale Empirical Study of Security Patches** 2201
  Frank Li, Vern Paxson *(University of California, Berkeley)*

Session J4: Flash Security

- **DEFTL: Implementing Plausibly Deniable Encryption in Flash Translation Layer** 2217
  Shijie Jia, Luning Xia *(Chinese Academy of Sciences)*, Bo Chen *(Michigan Technological University)*,
  Peng Liu *(Pennsylvania State University)*

- **FlashGuard: Leveraging Intrinsic Flash Properties to Defend Against
  Encryption Ransomware** 2231
  Jian Huang *(Georgia Institute of Technology)*, Jun Xu, Xinyu Xing, Peng Liu *(Pennsylvania State University)*,
  Moinuddin K. Qureshi *(Georgia Institute of Technology)*

- **FirmUSB: Vetting USB Device Firmware using Domain Informed Symbolic Execution** 2245
  Grant Hernandez, Farhaan Fowze, Dave (Jing) Tian, Tuba Yavuz, Kevin R. B. Butler *(University of Florida)*

Session K1: Secure Computation

- **TinyOLE: Efficient Actively Secure Two-Party Computation from Oblivious
  Linear Function Evaluation** 2263
  Nico Döttling *(Friedrich-Alexander-University Erlangen-Nürnberg)*,
  Satrajit Ghosh, Jesper Buus Nielsen, Tobias Nilges, Roberto Trifiletti *(Aarhus University)*

- **Efficient Public Trace and Revoke from Standard Assumptions: Extended Abstract**............. 2277
  Shweta Agrawal *(IIT Madras)*, Sanjay Bhattacherjee *(Indian Statistical Institute)*,
  Duong Hieu Phan *(XLIM (U. Limoges, CNRS))*,
  Damien Stehlé *(ENS de Lyon, LIP (U. Lyon, CNRS, ENSL, INRIA, UCBL))*,
  Shota Yamada *(National Institute of Advanced Industrial Science and Technology (AIST))*

- **Distributed Measurement with Private Set-Union Cardinality** 2295
  Ellis Fenske *(Tulane University)*, Akshaya Mani *(Georgetown University)*,
  Aaron Johnson *(U.S. Naval Research Laboratory)*, Micah Sherr *(Georgetown University)*

Session K2: Fuzzing Finer and Faster

- **Designing New Operating Primitives to Improve Fuzzing Performance**.................................. 2313
  Wen Xu, Sanidhya Kashyap *(Georgia Institute of Technology)*, Changwoo Min *(Virginia Tech)*,
  Taesoo Kim *(Georgia Institute of Technology)*

- **Directed Greybox Fuzzing** 2329
  Marcel Böhme, Van-Thuan Pham, Manh-Dung Nguyen, Abhik Roychoudhury *(National University of Singapore)*

- **IMF: Inferred Model-based Fuzzer** 2345
  HyungSeok Han, Sang Kil Cha *(Korea Advanced Institute of Science and Technology)*

Session K3: Program Analysis

- **PtrSplit: Supporting General Pointers in Automatic Program Partitioning** 2359
  Shen Liu, Gang Tan, Trent Jaeger *(Pennsylvania State University)*

- **HexType: Efficient Detection of Type Confusion Errors for C++** 2373
  Yuseok Jeon, Priyam Biswas, Scott Carr, Byoungyoung Lee, Mathias Payer *(Purdue University)*

- **FreeGuard: A Faster Secure Heap Allocator** 2389
  Sam Silvestro, Hongyu Liu *(University of Texas at San Antonio)*, Corey Crosser *(US Military Academy)*,
  Zhiqiang Lin *(University of Texas at Dallas)*, Tongping Liu *(University of Texas at San Antonio)*

Session K4: Secure Enclaves

- **JITGuard: Hardening Just-in-time Compilers with SGX**.. 2405
  Tommaso Frassetto, David Gens, Christopher Liebchen, Ahmad-Reza Sadeghi
  (Technische Universität Darmstadt)

- **Leaky Cauldron on the Dark Land: Understanding Memory Side-Channel
  Hazards in SGX** 2421
  Wenhao Wang *(Institute of Information Engineering, Chinese Academy of Sciences
  & Indiana University, Bloomington)*, Guoxing Chen *(Ohio State University)*,
  Xiaorui Pan *(Indiana University, Bloomington)*,
  Yinqian Zhang *(Ohio State University)*, XiaoFeng Wang *(Indiana University, Bloomington)*,
  Vincent Bindschaedler *(University of Illinois at Urbana-Champaign)*,
  Haixu Tang *(Indiana University, Bloomington)*, Carl A. Gunter *(University of Illinois at Urbana-Champaign)*

- **A Formal Foundation for Secure Remote Execution of Enclaves** 2435
  Pramod Subramanyan, Rohit Sinha *(University of California, Berkeley)*,
  Ilia Lebedev, Srinivas Devadas *(Massachusetts Institute of Technology)*,
  Sanjit A. Seshia *(University of California, Berkeley)*

Demonstration

- **DEMO: Akatosh: Automated Cyber Incident Verification and Impact Analysis** 2463
  Jared M. Smith, Elliot Greenlee *(Oak Ridge National Laboratory & University of Tennessee)*,
  Aaron Ferber *(Oak Ridge National Laboratory)*

Posters

- **Poster: Adversarial Examples for Classifiers in High-Dimensional Network Data** 2467
  Muhammad Ejaz Ahmed, Hyoungshick Kim *(Sungkyunkwan University)*

- **POSTER: An Empirical Measurement Study on Multi-tenant Deployment Issues of CDNs** 2471
  Zixi Cai, Zigang Cao, Gang Xiong, Zhen Li, Wei Xia *(Institute of Information Engineering, Chinese Academy of Sciences & University of Chinese Academy of Sciences)*

- **POSTER: Actively Detecting Implicit Fraudulent Transactions** 2475
  Shaosheng Cao, XinXing Yang, Jun Zhou, Xiaolong Li, Yuan (Alan) Qi, Kai Xiao *(Ant Financial Services Group)*

- **POSTER: Semi-supervised Classification for Dynamic Android Malware Detection** 2479
  Li Chen, Mingwei Zhang, Chih-yuan Yang, Ravi Sahita *(Intel Labs)*

- **POSTER: Detection of CPS Program Anomalies by Enforcing Cyber-Physical Execution Semantics** 2483
  Long Cheng, Ke Tian, Danfeng (Daphne) Yao *(Virginia Tech)*

- **POSTER: A Comprehensive Study of Forged Certificates in the Wild** 2487
  Mingxin Cui, Zigang Cao, Gang Xiong, Junzheng Shi
  (Institute of Information Engineering, Chinese Academy of Sciences & University of Chinese Academy of Sciences)

- **POSTER: Rust SGX SDK: Towards Memory Safety in Intel SGX Enclave** 2491
  Yu Ding, Ran Duan, Long Li, Yueqiang Cheng, Yulong Zhang, Tanghui Chen *(Baidu X-Lab)*, Tao Wei *(Baidu X-Lab)*, Huibo Wang *(University of Texas -- Dallas)*

- **POSTER: Finding Vulnerabilities in P4 Programs with Assertion-based Verification** 2495
  Lucas Freire, Miguel Neves, Alberto Schaeffer-Filho, Marinho Barcellos *(UFRGS)*

- **POSTER: Covert Channel Based on the Sequential Analysis in Android Systems** 2499
  Jun-Won Ho, KyungRok Won, Jee Sun Kim *(Seoul Women's University)*

- **POSTER: Why Are You Going That Way? Measuring Unnecessary Exposure of Network Traffic to Nation States** 2503
  Jordan Holland, Max Schuchard *(University of Tennessee)*

- **POSTER: PriReMat: A Distributed Tool for Privacy Preserving Record Linking in Healthcare** 2507
  Diptendu Mohan Kar, Ibrahim Lazrig, Indrajit Ray, Indrakshi Ray *(Colorado State University)*

- **POSTER: AFL-based Fuzzing for Java with Kelinci** 2511
  Rody Kersten, Kasper Luckow *(Carnegie Mellon University Silicon Valley)*, Corina S. Păsăreanu *(Carnegie Mellon University Silicon Valley & NASA Ames Research Center)*

- **POSTER: Rethinking Fingerprint Identification on Smartphones** 2515
  Seungyeon Kim, Hoyeon Lee, Taekyoung Kwon *(Yonsei University)*

- **POSTER: X-Ray Your DNS** 2519
  Amit Klein *(Fraunhofer Institute for Secure Information Technology)*,
  Vladimir Kravtsov, Alon Perlmuter, Haya Shulman,
  Michael Waidner *(Fraunhofer Institute for Secure Information Technology & Hebrew University of Jerusalem)*

- **POSTER: Hidden in Plain Sight: A Filesystem for Data Integrity and Confidentiality** 2523
  Anne Kohlbrenner *(Carnegie Mellon University)*,
  Frederico Araujo, Teryl Taylor, Marc Ph. Stoecklin *(IBM T.J. Watson Research Center)*

- **POSTER: Watch Out Your Smart Watch When Paired** 2527
  Youngjoo Lee, WonSeok Yang, Taekyoung Kwon *(Yonsei University)*

- **POSTER: Intrusion Detection System for In-vehicle Networks using Sensor Correlation and Integration** 2531
  Huaxin Li, Li Zhao, Marcio Juliato, Shabbir Ahmed, Manoj R. Sastry, Lily L. Yang *(Intel Labs)*

- **POSTER: Practical Fraud Transaction Prediction** 2535
  Longfei Li, Jun Zhou, Xiaolong Li, Tao Chen *(Ant Financial Services Group)*

- **POSTER: Vulnerability Discovery with Function Representation Learning from Unlabeled Projects** 2539
  Guanjun Lin, Jun Zhang, Wei Luo, Lei Pan *(Deakin University)*,
  Yang Xiang *(Swinburne University of Technology)*

- **POSTER: Neural Network-based Graph Embedding for Malicious Accounts Detection** 2543
  Ziqi Liu, Chaochao Chen, Jun Zhou, Xiaolong Li, Feng Xu, Tao Chen *(Ant Financial Services Group)*,
  Le Song *(Ant Financial Services Group & Georgia Institute of Technology)*

- **POSTER: A Unified Framework of Differentially Private Synthetic Data Release with Generative Adversarial Network** 2547
  Pei-Hsuan Lu, Chia-Mu Yu *(National Chung Hsing University)*

- **POSTER: TOUCHFLOOD: A Novel Class of Attacks against Capacitive Touchscreens** 2551
  Seita Maruyama, Satohiro Wakabayashi, Tatsuya Mori *(Waseda University)*

- **POSTER: TouchTrack: How Unique are your Touch Gestures?** 2555
  Rahat Masood *(University of New South Wales (UNSW) & CSIRO Data61)*,
  Benjamin Zi Hao Zhao, Hassan Jameel Asghar, Moahmed Ali Kaafar *(CSIRO Data61)*

- **POSTER: PenJ1939: An Interactive Framework for Design and Dissemination of Exploits for Commercial Vehicles** 2559
  Subhojeet Mukherjee, Noah Cain, Jacob Walker, David White, Indrajit Ray,
  Indrakshi Ray *(Colorado State University)*

- **POSTER: Cyber Attack Prediction of Threats from Unconventional Resources (CAPTURE)** 2563
  Ahmet Okutan, Gordon Werner, Katie McConky, Shanchieh Jay Yang *(Rochester Institute of Technology)*

- **POSTER: Towards Precise and Automated Verification of Security Protocols in Coq** 2567
  Hernan M. Palombo, Hao Zheng, Jay Ligatti *(University of South Florida)*

- **POSTER: Probing Tor Hidden Service with Dockers** 2571
  Jonghyeon Park, Youngseok Lee *(Chungnam National University)*

- **POSTER: Evaluating Reflective Deception as a Malware Mitigation Strategy** 2575
  Thomas Shaw *(University of Tulsa)*, James Arrowood *(Haystack Security LLC)*,
  Michael Kvasnicka, Shay Taylor, Kyle Cook, John Hale *(University of Tulsa)*

- **POSTER: Improving Anonymity of Services Deployed Over Tor by Changing Guard Selection** 2579
  Abhishek Singh *(University of Oslo)*

- **POSTER: Inaudible Voice Commands** 2583
  Liwei Song, Prateek Mittal *(Princeton University)*

- **POSTER: Is Active Electromagnetic Side-channel Attack Practical?** 2587
  Satohiro Wakabayashi, Seita Maruyama, Tatsuya Mori, Shigeki Goto *(Waseda University)*,
  Masahiro Kinugawa *(National Institute of Technology, Sendai College)*,
  Yu-ichi Hayashi *(Nara Institute of Science and Technology)*

- **POSTER: BGPCoin: A Trustworthy Blockchain-based Resource Management Solution for BGP Security** 2591
  Qianqian Xing, Baosheng Wang, Xiaofeng Wang *(National University of Defense Technology)*

- **POSTER: Who was Behind the Camera? — Towards Some New Forensics** 2595
  Jeff Yan *(Linköping University)*, Aurélien Bourquard *(Massachusetts Institute of Technology)*

- **POSTER: A PU Learning based System for Potential Malicious URL Detection** 2599
  Ya-Lin Zhang *(Nanjing University & Ant Financial Services Group)*,
  Longfei Li, Jun Zhou, Xiaolong Li, Yujiang Liu, Yuanchao Zhang *(Ant Financial Services Group)*,
  Zhi-Hua Zhou *(Nanjing University)*

Tutorials

- **Identity Related Threats, Vulnerabilities and Risk Mitigation in Online Social Networks** 2603
  Leila Bahri *(Royal Institute of Technology - KTH)*

- **Web Tracking Technologies and Protection Mechanisms** 2607
  Nataliia Bielova *(Université Côte d'Azur, Inria)*

- **Tutorial: Private Information Retrieval** 2611
  Ryan Henry *(Indiana University)*

- **CCS'17 Tutorial Abstract / SGX Security and Privacy** 2613
  Taesoo Kim *(Georgia Institute of Technology)*, Zhiqiang Lin *(University of Texas at Dallas)*,
  Chia-che Tsai *(Stony Brook University & University of California, Berkeley)*

- **Cliptography: Post-Snowden Cryptography** 2615
  Qiang Tang *(New Jersey Institute of Technology)*, Moti Yung *(Snap Inc. & Columbia University)*

- **Cache Side Channels: State of the Art and Research Opportunities** 2617
  Yinqian Zhang *(Ohio Sate University)*

Workshop Summaries

- **10th International Workshop on Artificial Intelligence and Security (AISec 2017)** 2621
  Battista Biggio *(University of Cagliari)*, David Freeman *(Facebook, Inc.)*, Brad Miller *(Google Inc)*,
  Arunesh Sinha *(University of Michigan)*

- **ASHES 2017— Workshop on Attacks and Solutions in Hardware Security** 2623
  Chip Hong Chang *(Nanyang Technological University)*, Marten van Dijk *(University of Connecticut)*,
  Farinaz Koushanfar *(University of California, San Diego)*, Ulrich Rührmair *(Ruhr-University Bochum)*,
  Mark Tehranipoor *(University of Florida)*

- **CCSW'17 — 2017 ACM Cloud Computing Security** 2627
  Ghassan O. Karame *(NEC Laboratories Europe)*, Angelos Stavrou *(George Mason University)*

- **CPS-SPC 2017: Third Workshop on Cyber-Physical Systems Security and PrivaCy** 2629
  Rakesh B. Bobba *(Oregon State University)*, Awais Rashid *(Lancaster University)*

- **CCS'17 — Women in Cyber Security (CyberW) Workshop** 2631
  Danfeng (Daphne) Yao *(Virginia Tech)*, Elisa Bertino *(Purdue University)*

- **FEAST'17: The 2nd Workshop on Forming an Ecosystem Around Software Transformation** .. 2633
  Taesoo Kim *(Georgia Institute of Technology)*, Dinghao Wu *(Pennsylvania State University)*

- **MIST 2017: 9th International Workshop on Managing Insider Security Threats** 2635
  Ilsun You *(Soonchunhyang University)*, Elisa Bertino *(Purdue University)*

- **MTD 2017: Fourth ACM Workshop on Moving Target Defense (MTD)** 2637
  Hamed Okhravi *(MIT Lincoln Laboratory)*, Xinming Ou *(University of South Florida)*

- **PLAS 2017 – ACM SIGSAC Workshop on Programming Languages and Analysis
  for Security** 2639
  Nataliia Bielova *(INRIA)*, Marco Gaboardi *(University at Buffalo)*

- **SafeConfig'17: Applying the Scientific Method to Active Cyber Defense Research** 2641
  Nicholas J. Multari *(Pacific Northwest National Lab)*,
  Anoop Singhal *(National Institute of Standards and Technology)*, Erin Miller *(Pacific Northwest National Lab)*

- **16th Workshop on Privacy in the Electronic Society (WPES 2017)** 2643
  Adam J. Lee *(University of Pittsburgh)*

- **Workshop on Multimedia Privacy and Security** 2645
  Roger Hallman *(US Navy SPAWAR Systems Center Pacific)*, Kurt Rohloff *(New Jersey Institute of Technology)*,
  Victor Chang *(Xian Jiaotong Liverpool University)*

- **IoT S&P 2017: First Workshop on Internet of Things Security and Privacy** 2647
  Theophilus Benson *(Brown University)*, Peng Liu *(Penn State University)*,
  Srikanth Sundaresan *(Princeton University)*, Yuqing Zhang *(University of Chinese Academy of Sciences)*

Author Index 2649

CCS 2017 Conference Organization

General Chair: Bhavani Thuraisingham *(The University of Texas at Dallas)*

Program Chairs: David Evans *(University of Virginia)*
Tal Malkin *(Columbia University)*
Dongyan Xu *(Purdue University)*

Workshops Chairs: Taesoo Kim *(Georgia Tech)*
Cliff Wang *(Army Research Office)*

Tutorial Chairs: Guofei Gu *(Texas A&M)*
Maribel Fernandez *(Kings College, University of London)*

Poster/Demo Chairs: Kevin Hamlen *(The University of Texas at Dallas)*
Heng Yin *(University of California, Riverside)*

Treasurer: Alvaro Cardenas *(The University of Texas at Dallas)*

Web Chairs: JV Rajendran *(The University of Texas at Dallas)*
Gail-Joon Ahn *(Arizona State University)*

Panel Chairs: Ahmad-Reza Sadeghi *(TU Darmstadt, CYSEC)*
Yiorgos Makris *(The University of Texas at Dallas)*

Registration Chair: Murat Kantarcioglu *(The University of Texas at Dallas)*

Student Travel Grant Chairs: Hassan Takabi *(University of North Texas)*
Brent Kang *(KAIST)*
Zhi Wang *(Florida State University)*

Publicity Chair: Yvo Desmedt *(The University of Texas at Dallas)*
Giancarlo Pellegrino *(Saarland University)*
Daniel Xiapu Luo *(The Hong Kong Polytechnic University)*
Barbara Carminati *(University of Insubria)*

Social Media Chair: Siddharth Garg *(New York University)*

Proceedings Chairs: Matthew Wright *(Rochester Institute of Technology)*
Apu Kapadia *(Indiana University Bloomington)*

Sponsor/Industry Outreach Chairs: Janell Straach *(The University of Texas at Dallas)*
Peng Liu *(Penn State University)*
Gail-Joon Ahn *(Arizona State University)*

Program Committee *(continued)*: Tudor Dumitraş *(University of Maryland)*

Serge Egelman *(UC Berkeley / ICSI)*

Ittay Eyal *(Cornell University)*

Sascha Fahl *(Saarland University)*

Christopher Fletcher *(NVIDIA/UIUC)*

Aurélien Francillon *(EURECOM)*

Matt Fredrikson *(Carnegie Mellon University)*

Xinyang Ge *(Microsoft Research)*

Daniel Genkin *(University of Pennsylvania / University of Maryland)*

Rosario Gennaro *(City College of New York)*

Phillipa Gill *(University of Massachusetts Amherst)*

Dov Gordon *(George Mason University)*

Andreas Haeberlen *(University of Pennsylvania)*

J. Alex Halderman *(University of Michigan)*

Shai Halevi *(IBM Research)*

Matthew Hicks *(MIT Lincoln Laboratory)*

Michael Hicks *(University of Maryland)*

Thorsten Holz *(Ruhr-Universität Bochum)*

Amir Houmansadr *(University of Massachusetts Amherst)*

Yan Huang *(Indiana University)*

Kyu Hyung Lee *(University of Georgia)*

Trent Jaeger *(Penn State University)*

Suman Jana *(Columbia University)*

Limin Jia *(Carnegie Mellon University)*

Yier Jin *(University of Central Florida)*

Aaron Johnson *(U.S. Naval Research Laboratory)*

Philipp Jovanovic *(École Polytechnique Fédérale de Lausanne)*

Brent ByungHoon Kang *(KAIST)*

Aniket Kate *(Purdue University)*

Jonathan Katz *(University of Maryland)*

Stefan Katzenbeisser *(TU Darmstadt)*

Marcel Keller *(University of Bristol)*

Aggelos Kiayias *(University of Edinburgh)*

Taesoo Kim *(Georgia Tech)*

Yongdae Kim *(KAIST)*

Engin Kirda *(Northeastern University)*

David Kotz *(Dartmouth)*

Farinaz Koushanfar *(UC San Diego)*

Ralf Küsters *(University of Stuttgart)*

Andrea Lanzi *(University of Milan)*

Byoungyoung Lee *(Purdue University)*

Wenke Lee *(Georgia Tech)*

Brian N. Levine *(University of Massachusetts Amherst)*

Zhichun Li *(NEC Labs)*

Program Committee *(continued):* Zhou Li *(RSA)*

David Lie *(University of Toronto)*

Yao Liu *(University of South Florida)*

Matteo Maffei *(TU Vienna)*

Mohammad Mahmody *(University of Virginia)*

Z. Morley Mao *(University of Michigan)*

Ivan Martinovic *(University of Oxford)*

Michelle L. Mazurek *(University of Maryland)*

Jonathan McCune *(Google)*

Andrew Miller *(University of Illinois at Urbana-Champaign)*

Tal Moran *(IDC Herzliya)*

Muhammad Naveed *(University of Southern California)*

Nick Nikiforakis *(Stony Brook University)*

Hamed Okhravi *(MIT Lincoln Laboratory)*

Alina Oprea *(Northeastern University)*

Mathias Payer *(Purdue University)*

Adrian Perrig *(ETH Zurich)*

Michalis Polychronakis *(Stony Brook University)*

Georgios Portokalidis *(Stevens Institute of Technology)*

Bart Preneel *(KU Leuven)*

Zhiyun Qian *(University of California, Riverside)*

Kasper Rasmussen *(University of Oxford)*

Aseem Rastogi *(Microsoft Research India)*

Mariana Raykova *(Yale University)*

Kaveh Razavi *(Vrije Universiteit)*

William Robertson *(Northeastern University)*

Christian Rossow *(Saarland University)*

Mike Rosulek *(Oregon State University)*

Patrick Schaumont *(Virginia Tech)*

abhi shelat *(Northeastern)*

Micah Sherr *(Georgetown University)*

Timothy Sherwood *(UC Santa Barbara)*

Reza Shokri *(Cornell Tech)*

Stelios Sidiroglou-Douskos *(MIT)*

Chengyu Song *(UC Riverside)*

Douglas Stebila *(McMaster University)*

Deian Stefan *(UC San Diego)*

Gianluca Stringhini *(University College London)*

Kun Sun *(George Mason University)*

Ewa Syta *(Trinity College)*

Mohit Tiwari *(UT Austin)*

Patrick Traynor *(University of Florida)*

Carmela Troncoso *(IMDEA Software Institute)*

Blase Ur *(University of Chicago)*

Additional reviewers *(continued)*: Sergey Gorbunov

Paul Grubbs

Wenbo Guo

Johann Großschädl

Trinabh Gupta

Syed Kamran Haider

Ariel Hamlin

Wajih Ul Hassan

Ben Heidorn

Ethan Heilman

Nadia Heninger

Tamás Holczer

Sanghyun Hong

Hongxin Hu

Hong Hu

Heqing Huang

Zhen Huang

Jun Ho Huh

Siam Hussain

Yong Ho Hwang

Ahmad Ibrahim

Moshen Imani

Yuval Ishai

Saman Jafari

Stanislaw Jarecki

Roberto Jordaney

Yigitcan Kaya

Ryo Kikuchi

Donguk Kim Beom

Doowon Kim

Heyn Kim

Markulf Kohlweiss

Eleftherios Kokoris Kogias Vlad
    Kolesnikov

Maria Konte

Lucas Kowalczyk

Steve Kremer

Bogdan Kulynych

BumJun Kwon

Yu-Tsung (Eddy) Lee

Yue Li

Tongxin Li

Xiaojing Liao

Christopher Liechen

Yehuda Lindell

Xiao Liu

Andreas Lochbihler

Wouter Lueks

Alex Malozemoff

Andrea Mambretti

Piotr Mardziel

Christian Matt

Xianghang Mi

Reza Mirzazade

Varun Mishra

Esfandiar Mohammadi

Pedro Moreno Sanchez

Johannes Müller

Kartik Nayak

Kirill Nikitin

Ben Niu

Rebekah Overdorf

Simón Oya

Jun Pang

Dimitrios Papadopoulos

Charalampos Papamanthou

Bryan Parno

Marcus Peinado

Leo Perrin

Travis Peters

Giuseppe Petracca

Tim Pierson

Benny Pinkas

Yu Pu

Apostolos Pyrgelis

Rui Qiao

Samuel Ranellucci

Daniel Rausch

Bradley Reaves

M. Sadegh Riazi

Silas Richelson

Marc Roeschlin

Kurt Rohloff

Additional reviewers *(continued):*

Carlos Rubio Medrano
Ralf Sasse
Nolen Scaife
Guillaume Scerri
Guido Schmitz
Peter Scholl
Will Scott
Sovantharith Seng
Srinath Setty
Daniele Sgandurra
Junbum Shin
Victor Shoup
Payap Sirinam
Gary Soeller
Linhai Song
Ebrahim Songhori
Christoph Sprenger
Drew Springall
Rock Stevens
Octavian Suciu
Yuqiong Sun
Jianhua Sun
Pengfei Sun
Peter Yi
Ping Sun
Zhibo Sun
Stefano Tessaro
Aleksei Udovenko
Jonathan Ullman
Diego Valasquez
Ben VanderSloot
Luis Vargas
Daniel Votipka
Kyle Wallace

Shengye Wan
Boyang Wang
Pei Wang
Shuai Wang
Xiao Wang
Qinglong Wang
Weiren Wang
Li Wang
Xueqiang Wang
Wenhao Wang
Bogdan Warinschi
Daniel Wichs
Michelle Wong
David Wu
Xiaodi Wu
Eric Wustrow
Willem Wyndham
Weilin Xu
Zhang Xu
Dongpeng Xu
Carter Yagemann
Moosa Yahyazadeh
Yang Yang
Insu Yun
Santiago Zanella Béguelin
Danfeng Zhang
Ning Zhang
Tianwei Zhang
Xiaokuan Zhang
Kaixuan Zhang
Ziming Zhao
Yajin Zhou
Ruiyu Zhu
Ziyun Zhu

PLATINUM

Special Thanks To:

GOLD

SILVER

BRONZE

DEMO: Akatosh: Automated Cyber Incident Verification and Impact Analysis

Jared M. Smith
Oak Ridge National Laboratory
University of Tennessee, Knoxville
smithjm@ornl.gov

Elliot Greenlee
Oak Ridge National Laboratory
University of Tennessee, Knoxville
greenleeed@ornl.gov

Aaron Ferber
Oak Ridge National Laboratory
ferberae@ornl.gov

ABSTRACT

Akatosh, a U.S. Department of Homeland Security Transition to Practice Program (TTP) project developed by Oak Ridge National Laboratory with industry and academic partnership, enables automated, real-time forensic analysis of endpoints after malware-attacks and other cyber security incidents by automatically maintaining detailed snapshots of host-level activity on endpoints over time. It achieves this by integrating intrusion detection systems (IDS) with forensic tools. The combination allows Akatosh to collect vast amounts of endpoint data and assists in verifying, tracking, and analyzing endpoints in real time. This provides operations personnel and analysts as well as managers and executives with continuous feedback on the impact of malicious software and other security incidents on endpoints in their network.

CCS CONCEPTS

•Security and privacy →Malware and its mitigation; Intrusion detection systems; Operating systems security;

KEYWORDS

Incident Response; Forensic Analysis; Endpoint Security; Breach Remediation

1 INTRODUCTION

While Intrusion Detection Systems (IDS) can help prevent attacks on a system, they also incur a higher than desired false positive rate. When a cyber attack happens to break through an IDS or other defensive system, the effort of performing an analysis of the affected systems and the recovery from any potential infections is costly and time-consuming. Developed at Oak Ridge National Laboratory (ORNL), Akatosh is a highly configurable system based on the integration of the capabilities of one or more IDSfis and automated configuration and system verification.

With this integration, it is possible to analyze systems in near real-time and provide operations and forensic analyst personnel with continuous feedback on the impact of software, malware, and active users on deployed systems. By providing an interface between any number of IDSs and the Akatosh client, Akatosh is able to intelligently fisnapshotfi affected systems based on cues

CCS'17, October 30–November 3, 2017, Dallas, TX, USA
© 2016 Copyright held by the owner/author(s). ISBN 978-1-4503-4946-8/17/10.
DOI: http://dx.doi.org/10.1145/3133956.3138854

from the IDS. Before incidents, Akatosh takes regularly scheduled snapshots to account for states of the system over time. With these snapshots, it can automatically provide a succinct report on the Akatosh server by differentiating these previous known states and post-infection states based on the timing and metadata associated with IDS notifications to the client interface. With the differentiated states from any point in the history of the machine, Akatosh helps point out whether a true infection occurred, and if so, what was impacted, thus lowering the false positive rate of modern IDS products. With this data, it is also possible to analyze trends over time in attacks and come closer to conclusions on why a system was attacked.

Akatosh is a U.S. Department of Homeland Security (DHS) Transition to Practice program (TTP) project, and is one of eight technologies in the DHS TTP 2017 class being developed and led by industry and academic institutions such as MIT Lincoln Laboratory, MITRE, Worcester Polytechnic University, and Pacific Northwest National Laboratory. Through the DHS TTP program, we are working with industry partners to pilot the this technology, demonstrate it's capabilities at industry "demo days" in major international hubs, and ultimately license the research technology to partners with the goal of being integrated into production systems serving real users.

2 BACKGROUND

In practice, forensic analysts and other operations personnel face two distinct and important problems. In the realm of computer security defense mechanisms, IDSs consume information like network packets, endpoint statistics, and other metrics that the IDS uses to pick out anomalous behavior, which potentially represent cyber attacks. Unfortunately, IDSs have high false alert rates and the sheer number of alerts over time can overwhelm security operations personnel, which makes correctly identifying actual attacks difficult. Another problem faced by enterprises can be seen in a 2016 study by IBM and the Ponemon Institute [11], which found that among 383 companies, the cost of incident response and mitigation for a successful cyber attack accounted for 4 million USD on average per incident. over a quarter of the total cost was due to forensic activities associated with the breach. This cost largely comes from having to verify endpoint state and conduct forensic analysis after alerts from endpoints indicate that they were potentially impacted by an attack or related security incident.

3 SYSTEM DESIGN

System Architecture Akatosh starts by reducing the impact of false positives and the cost of incident response by enabling automated, real-time forensic analysis of endpoints when prompted

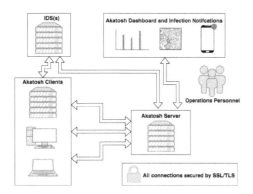

Figure 1: High-level architecture diagram for Akatosh.

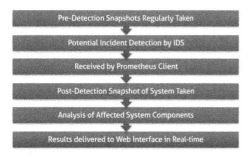

Figure 2: Step-by-step explanation of the Akatosh endpoint snapshot and real-time analysis process.

by IDS alerts. By doing these this, Akatosh helps operations personnel verify that an alert on an endpoint corresponds to a true cyber-attack. The system is comprised of small Akatosh client or agent, the Akatosh server, and the Akatosh dashboard, as depicted in Figure 1. The Akatosh clients live on network endpoints and take regularly scheduled baseline snapshots on configurable time intervals to record endpoint state over time.

These snapshots capture specific data about the endpoint, including processes, loaded drivers, registry entries, network connections, and other data. When an IDS detects anomalous behavior it alerts the Akatosh system. Depending on the nature of the alert (configured by the operators), the Akatosh client immediately takes a snapshot of the endpoint that generated the alert and sends the snapshot to the Akatosh server. The Akatosh server automatically produces a succinct incident report differentiating the post-alert snapshot from the most recent baseline snapshot. The Akatosh dashboard displays all endpoints being tracked, their status, the snapshot data being collected as the system receives IDS alerts, and the incident reports.

Figure 2 summarizes the underlying process described above. Akatosh automatically analyses the differences between pre-alert and post-alert snapshots in real-time and displays the results on the dashboard, showing the specific endpoint components affected by the anomalous behavior.

Time-Series State Differentiation Akatosh analyzes the parallel historical timeline of memory images for each client machine in order to provide insight into machine state differences. The majority of these images will reflect daily activity without a malicious presence, but this timeline also captures the critical period following an IDS alert. Consider the memory image taken before and just after such an alert; the apparent differences shed light on new files, processes, and a multitude of other system changes caused by possible malicious activity. In order to analyze the images, Akatosh integrates with existing memory forensics tools Volatility and Rekall [6, 8]. These two frameworks combine individual plugins for extracting various well-known operating system state data to provide a comprehensive view of machine memory. An example of a plugin would be the processes running on the machine, or the active and recently ended network connections. Akatosh then performs state differentiation across each plugin in order to pinpoint differences across images. By displaying these differences to forensic analysts, our system provides detailed context and a frame of reference which intends to speed up the process of recovery after an attack.

Classification of State Differences Using state differentiated images before and after a period of time, a classification can be made between detecting or not detecting malicious activity. Rather than examining the images themselves or other behavioral information, our system analyzes two kinds of state transitions: clean to clean and clean to infected. As forensic experts investigate alerts using the Akatosh system, a determination is made between real and false. This expert knowledge can be captured through classification algorithms. In order to produce a sample data set equivalent to this real knowledge, we capture machine state while infecting systems with malware. This process is performed programatically using Cuckoo Sandbox [3], an open source malware analysis system, to inject malware from online repositories and ORNL resources into virtual environments running software to approximate human behaviors like opening and closing software, navigating the internet, and sending emails [19]. This programmatic collection of machine images before and after software and malware has run on a system gives us a working dataset of images with which to feed through Akatosh.

Using this dataset we can perform feature extraction and a classification method survey. Hand-coded feature extraction per plugin is possible but knowledge and time intensive. This approach allows for pre-analysis using linear discriminant analysis to determine the plugins that contribute most to overall classification accuracy, guiding initial ordering of plugin results on the Akatosh system [12]. More generally, standard natural language pre-processing tools like bag of words and n-gram extraction can be co-opted to fit this type of document [20]. Our method survey covers standards in document classification such as naive bayes, expectation maximization, support vector machines, and decision trees [1] [18] [15]. The results of these are combined using classifier fusion to produce a binary recommendation with a specific confidence [16]. After the model crosses a pre-determined confidence threshold, Akatosh begins to make recommendations to analysts in two areas. Overall, the algorithm recommends high-confidence real alert predictions higher in the queue of new IDS alerts. For individual clients, the algorithm presents high-confidence real alert plugin results higher so that analysts can more quickly check these indicators. Through these recommendations, the overall time to recovery of an impacted machine is reduced.

Implementation Akatosh is implemented in Python [5], which allows the system to run on Windows, Linux, and Mac-based OSs. As stated earlier, Akatosh utilizes Volatility and Rekall [6, 8] for extracting machine state data from images. To capture images from machines, Akatosh uses the Rekall Memory Forensic Suite of imaging tools, which are used in other frameworks such as Google's GRR [7]. To store data on the server, Akatosh uses a combination of the battle-tested relational database, PostgreSQL, and a static file storage system, Minio, based on Amazon S3 [9, 13].

4 EVALUATION

Can We Scalably Collect Full State Captures from Hundreds of Endpoints? Akatosh can collect memory images of nearly any practical size (tested up to 64 GB) in less than 30 seconds for 16 GB images. Akatosh stores no data on client machines, as it transfers the images as they are captured. In the varying network conditions tested (between 10-1000 Mbps upload speeds), the transfer speed is bounded only by the speed at which memory can be captured. When images are stored on the server, images are encrypted with a 2048-bit key using the AES algorithm. Additionally, up to 60% on average of the original memory size can be compressed due to the nature of the image format, thus reducing 16 GB image captures to less than 8 GB when stored in Minio.

With respect to client performance overhead incurred due to imaging, no noticeable slowdowns can be seen from the client, and in our testing we saw no more than 10 to 30% CPU usage to image a machine. Finally, Akatosh currently scales up to 150+ machines and can load balance image capturing and state differentiation analysis effectively for a variety of clients, including Windows, Linux, and Mac.

Can We Surface Deeper Context to Existing Alerts with State Differences? The work described in the prior section on classification of memory diffs is still under active development; however, Akatosh has been tested against several pieces of historically significant malware, and has identified all of the components the tested malware was known to affect on client machines. The components known to be affected were pulled from a variety of published write-ups on the malware. The malware tested consisted of the Dark-Comet Trojan, the NJRat Trojan and Reverse Shell, and Stuxnet.

These results indicate that when Akatosh is alerted to an infection on a system where malware has infected the host in question, our system can identify the affected components and bring them to the attention of the incident response personnel. Future work remains to be done to test Akatosh against vast amounts of other malware and software, though early results are promising.

5 RELATED WORK

Akatosh is the first of its kind system to integrate automated forensic analysis with IDSs. Through this integration, Akatosh can perform a detailed analysis of the affected endpoints at the exact time of the incident, unlike current incident response systems, which are less reactive to immediate changes in endpoint state, at least at the level of detail that Akatosh provides.

Additionally, the Akatosh dashboard automatically provides reports showing a high-level overview of affected endpoint components that operations personnel and analysts as well as managers and upper-level executives can understand and dig into. Reports are generated in real-time without shutting down endpoints to perform the tedious task of imaging the machine and analyzing the image on a separate machine. Similar products in the space do not provide differentiated endpoints states to operations personnel [2, 10], and may also require manual analysis of endpoints causing analysts to shut down machines before examining their state [4].

While products exist to perform endpoint history analysis for non-security related domains, such as infrastructure monitoring [14, 17], these products do not transition well to verifying, tracking, and analyzing the impact of cyber attacks. By focusing on affected endpoint components, Akatosh assists in verifying incidents and automatically tracking and analyzing propagation over the components.

6 CONCLUSION AND FUTURE WORK

In this work we have presented a novel system developed to enhance context around existing alerts in modern security defense systems, while allowing the scalability to potentially thousands of machines and reducing the cost of mitigating breaches when they inevitably occur. In the coming months, Akatosh will be undergoing pilots at the U.S. Department of Energy HQ and MITRE, as well as undergoing active development to finish the full classification abilities of the system as well as continue to scale out to additional clients.

REFERENCES

[1] Sonal Salve Swati Vamney Bhawna Nigam, Poorvi Ahirwal. 2011. Document Classification Using Expectation Maximization with Semi Supervised Learning. (2011). https://arxiv.org/abs/1112.2028
[2] CarbonBlack. 1999. (1999). http://www.carbonblack.com
[3] Cuckoo. 2017. Cuckoo. (2017). https://cuckoosandbox.org/
[4] EndCase. 2017. EndCase. (2017). https://www.guidancesoftware.com/encase-forensic
[5] Python Software Foundation. 2017. Python. (2017). https://www.python.org/
[6] Volatility Foundation. 2017. Volatility. (2017). http://www.volatilityfoundation.org/
[7] Google. 2017. GRR. (2017). https://github.com/google/grr
[8] Google. 2017. Rekall. (2017). http://www.rekall-forensic.com/
[9] The PostgreSQL Global Development Group. 2017. PostgreSQL. (2017). https://www.postgresql.org/
[10] Tanium Inc. 1999. Endpoint Security and Systems. (1999). http://www.tanium.com
[11] Ponemon Institute and IBM. 2017. Cost of Data Breach Study. (2017). https://www.ibm.com/security/data-breach/
[12] et al. Mika, Sebastian. 1999. Fisher discriminant analysis with kernels. (1999). http://ieeexplore.ieee.org/abstract/document/788121/
[13] Minio. 2017. Minio. (2017). https://minio.io/
[14] PrometheusIO. 2017. PrometheusIO. (2017). https://prometheus.io/
[15] J.R. Quinlan. 1993. C4.5: Programs for Machine Learning. (1993). http://dl.acm.org/citation.cfm?id=152181
[16] D. Ruta and B. Gabrys. 2000. An Overview of Classifier Fusion Methods. (2000). http://eprints.bournemouth.ac.uk/9649/
[17] Splunk. 2017. Splunk. (2017). https://www.splunk.com/
[18] J.A.K. Suykens and J. Vandewalle. 1999. Least Squares Support Vector Machine Classifiers. (1999). https://link.springer.com/article/10.1023%2FA%3A1018628609742?LI=true
[19] TheZoo. 2017. TheZoo. (2017). https://github.com/ytisf/theZoo
[20] Hanna M. Wallach. 2006. Topic modeling: beyond bag-of-words. (2006). http://dl.acm.org/citation.cfm?id=1143967

Poster: Adversarial Examples for Classifiers in High-Dimensional Network Data

Muhammad Ejaz Ahmed
Sungkyunkwan University, Suwon
Republic of Korea
ejaz629@skku.edu

Hyoungshick Kim
Sungkyunkwan University, Suwon
Republic of Korea
hyoung@skku.edu

ABSTRACT

Many machine learning methods make assumptions about the data, such as, data stationarity and data independence, for an efficient learning process that requires less data. However, these assumptions may give rise to vulnerabilities if violated by smart adversaries. In this paper, we propose a novel algorithm to craft the input samples by modifying a certain fraction of input features as small as in order to bypass the decision boundary of widely used binary classifiers using Support Vector Machine (SVM). We show that our algorithm can reliably produce adversarial samples which are misclassified with 98% success rate while modifying 22% of the input features on average. Our goal is to evaluate the robustness of classification algorithms for high demensional network data by intentionally performing evasion attacks with carefully designed adversarial examples. The proposed algorithm is evaluated using real network traffic datasets (CAIDA 2007 and CAIDA 2016).

KEYWORDS

Network attacks; Adversarial Machine Learning; Network Intrusion; Evasion Attacks; High Dimensional Data.

1 INTRODUCTION

Machine learning is now entrenching in modern technology, allowing an overwhelming number of tasks to be performed automatically at lower costs. Giant tech companies like Google, Microsoft, and Amazon have already taken initiatives to provide their customers with APIs, allowing them to easily apply artificial intelligence techniques into their applications. For instance, machine learning (ML) applications includes image classification to scrutinize online contents, automatic caption generation for an image, spam email detection, and many more [4].

However, there have been some limitations of ML algorithms due to which an adversary able to craft inputs would profit from evading detection. An adversarial sample is an input crafted such that it causes an ML algorithm to misclassify it [5]. Note that adversarial samples are created at test time, i.e., the ML algorithm is already trained and deployed by the defender, and do not require any alteration of the training process. Many ML methods require the data `stationarity` assumption where training and testing data

CCS '17, October 30-November 3, 2017, Dallas, TX, USA
© 2017 Copyright held by the owner/author(s).
ACM ISBN 978-1-4503-4946-8/17/10.
https://doi.org/10.1145/3133956.3138853

are drawn from the same distribution (even when it is unknown). However, and attackers can often break this assumption by manipulating the input to the detector to get evasion because real-world data sources are not stationary. Moreover, another common assumption is that each datapoint is independent and identically distributed (i.i.d.); clearly this assumption can also be compromised by crafting the input with a little effort.

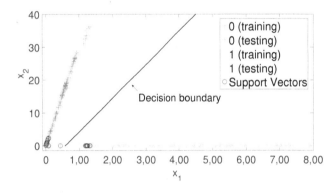

Figure 1: Network traffic features with classification (decision) boundary for a ML algorithm (SVM).

Since the real-world data sources do not follow the stationarity and i.i.d. assumptions, the ML models trained on such data sources could be vulnerable to be exploited by the attackers [1, 4, 6]. Fig. 1 shows real-world network traffic data (for two features x_1 and x_2) with the decision boundary of a binary classifier (SVM). Note that both features (x_1 and x_2) are linearly correlated for the class + (malicious traffic), where the correlation in the second feature (x_2) for class * (legitimate traffic) is extremely low (almost zero).

Under the uneven separation of both classes from the decision boundary of the classifier, an attacker can evade the detection system by slightly modifying a malicious datapoint (even a single feature) at the lower end of the decision boundary. For example, if a malicious datapoint is modified at the lower axis of x_2 by the attacker (by updating $x_1 \geq 100$), it can evade the decision boundary and will be labeled as `legitimate` by the classifier.

In this paper, we propose a novel algorithm for adversarial sample creation against a popular ML algorithm, i.e., SVM. Furthermore, our approach alters a small fraction of input features leading to significantly reduced distortion of the source inputs. Our algorithm relies on heuristic searches to find minimum distortions leading to the misclassification for target inputs. We show that the input samples can be perturbed such that it is misclassified as a legitimate class with 98% success while perturbing 22% of the input features on average. We performed extensive simulations on real-world network traffic with widely used 17 traffic features. In Section 2, we briefly describe the proposed approach for modifying the input features to bypass the classifier. Section 3 discusses the data used in our approach and the experiment results.

2 PROPOSED APPROACH

In this section we describe the proposed approach for identifying the features to be modified so that the classifier yields the adversarial output. We validate the proposed algorithm by using real traffic datasets.

2.1 Threat model

In our approach we assume that adversary can obtain query responses from the classifier. In case of intrusion detection system, the packets from malicious users are dropped by the intrusion detection system (IDS). Therefore, an adversary is aware of the dropped packets, thus features of these packets are recorded as training data. We further assume that adversary can observe legitimate packets by sniffing the network and therefore record the feature values of legitimate traffic [4]. In this way, dataset comprise of legitimate and malicious packets can be obtained by the adversary. Given a training set of m measurements consisting each of n features, our feature space becomes $\mathbf{X} \in \mathbb{R}^{m \times n}$. Note that our goal is to introduce minimum perturbation to a malicious datapoint so as to evade detection system.

2.2 Feature selection and modification

It has been shown that by using reduced set of features may require attackers to manipulate less features to evade the detection system [3]. The underlying idea of our approach is to select the features having most discriminative power for classification. Different methods in literature are proposed to obtain most distinguishing features such as information gains (IG), Chi Squared statistics, entropy, principal component analysis (PCA), mean and standard deviation of each dimension, skewness/kurtosis, cross correlation between dimensions, and ARIMA models, etc. In this paper, we restrict ourself to use IG to select the top K features having highest IG. After selecting-K top features, we take combination of the top K features to calculate two important metrics: distance and cross correlation.

In literature the distance between legitimate and malicious datapoints are used to quantify the differential between them [4]. However, in the proposed approach, in addition to calculate the distance (Euclidean) between each datapoint from legitimate and malicious traffic sources, we also compute the cross correlation $\gamma(x_1, x_2)$ between them. The Euclidean distance is the distance between two datapoints (one from each class, i.e., malicious and legitimate). Fig. 2 (left) show the Euclidean distance between each datapoint from legitimate and malicious datapoints for traffic features (total bytes received and total number of packets). Fig. 2 (right) show the the SVM classifier's decision boundary. Note that due to the non i.i.d. nature of real-world traffic sources, the adversary can craft (modify) datapoints (features) in the vulnerable area (shown in red-dashed circle) to misclassify the malicious datapoint as a legitimate. Also

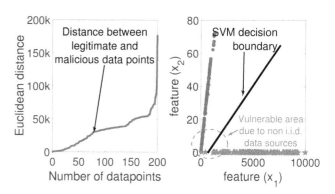

Figure 2: Euclidean distance between legitimate and malicious datapoints of Fig. 1, and classifier's uneven separation yields a vulnerable area which is exploited by the adversary.

note that if only one feature out of the two features is modified, the adversary can bypass the SVM's decision boundary.

Algorithm 1 Crafting adversarial sample.

$\{\mathbf{x}^i\}_{i=1}^{m}$ is the training data, each input feature vector has corresponding $\{y^i\}_{i=1}^{m}$ labels, y^* is the target network output (legitimate) class.

    Input: $\mathcal{D} = \{\mathbf{x}^i, y^i\}_{i=1}^{m}, \mathbf{Y}^*$.

    Result: $\mathbf{x}^*$ an adversarial datapoint.

1: K $\leftarrow$ select top-K feature based on the IG($\{\mathbf{x}^i, y^i\}_{i=1}^{m}$)

2: $\mathbf{X}_{\mathrm{mal}} = \{\mathbf{x}\}_{y=0}$ /* all malicious datapoints from the training data.*/

3: $\mathbf{X}_{\mathrm{leg}} = \{\mathbf{x}\}_{y=1}$ /* all legitimate datapoints from the training data.*/

4: **for all** $c \in$ Comb(K) **do**

5:     $(\mathbf{x}_{(c,1)}, \mathbf{x}_{(c,2)})$ is a feature-pair relative to cth combination.

6:     $E_d(\mathbf{x}_{(c,1)}, \mathbf{x}_{(c,2)}) \leftarrow \mathrm{Min}(\mathrm{EuclideanDistance}\{\mathbf{x}_{\mathrm{mal}}^i, \mathbf{x}_{\mathrm{leg}}^i\}_{i=1}^{n/2})$

7:     $R_{\mathrm{mal}}(\mathbf{x}_{(c,1)}, \mathbf{x}_{(c,2)}) = \mathrm{Avg}\left(xcorr\left(\mathbf{X}_{\mathrm{mal}}(\mathbf{x}_{(c,1)}, \mathbf{x}_{(c,2)})\right)\right)$.

8:     $R_{\mathrm{leg}}(\mathbf{x}_{(c,1)}, \mathbf{x}_{(c,2)}) = \mathrm{Avg}\left(xcorr\left(\mathbf{X}_{\mathrm{leg}}(\mathbf{x}_{(c,1)}, \mathbf{x}_{(c,2)})\right)\right)$.

9: $(\mathbf{x}_1, \mathbf{x}_2) \leftarrow$ select the combination having maximum $R_{\mathrm{mal}}(\mathbf{x}_{(c,1)}, \mathbf{x}_{(c,2)})$ and $R_{\mathrm{leg}}(\mathbf{x}_{(c,1)}, \mathbf{x}_{(c,2)})$, and minimum $E_d(\mathbf{x}_{(c,1)}, \mathbf{x}_{(c,2)})$.

10: **while** not successfully misclassified **do**

11:     $\mathbf{x} \leftarrow$ take a malicious datapoint having minimum $E_d(\mathbf{x}_1, \mathbf{x}_2)$ from $\mathbf{X}_{\mathrm{mal}}$.

12:     $\mathbf{x}^* \leftarrow$ replace the value of either feature ($\mathbf{x}_1$ or $\mathbf{x}_2$) with the $Avg(\mathbf{X}_{\mathrm{leg}})$.

Algorithm 1 enumerates the steps involved in modifying a malicious datapoint to bypass the detection system. In the first step, information gain (IG) for every feature is calculated and top-K features are selected. Malicious and legitimate traffic are represented by $\mathbf{X}_{\mathrm{mal}}$ and $\mathbf{X}_{\mathrm{leg}}$, respectively, (line 2-3). The combinations of the selected top-K features are computed, and for each feature-pair combination, the Euclidean distance between datapoints from malicious and legitimate traffic is computed, and a minimum of them

Table 1: Input features for a ML detector.

Feature	Description
#pkts	number of packets
#bytes	number of bytes
pkts (src -> dst)	packets from source to destination
bytes (src -> dst)	bytes from sources to destination
pkts (dst -> src)	packets from destination to source
bytes (dst -> src)	bytes from destination to source
Rel. Start	Relative start time of a connection
dur.	duration of a connection
bits (src -> dst)	bits from source to destination
bits (dst -> src)	bits from destination to source
IP-H-len	IP header length
pkt-len	packet length
ttl-avg	average time to live (TTL)
ttl-std	TTL standard deviation
inter-arr	interarrival time
proto-type	protocol type

is taken (line 6). We do so because we want to figure-out which features could minimally be perturbed to evade the detector. Then, cross-correlation is calculated between the selected features of malicious and legitimate traffic (line 7-8). The reason for this is to find features which could be exploited based on the i.i.d. assumption made by most ML classifiers. For example feature-pairs having higher cross-correlation will bias the decision boundary of SVM as shown in Fig. 2 (right), consequently an adversary can exploit lower regions of the feature-pairs to bypass the classifier's decision boundary. In the next step, from all the feature-pair combinations with respective minimum Euclidean distance and cross-correlations, we select feature-pairs having minimum Euclidean distance and maximum cross-correlations (line 9). It is to be noted that we used heuristics to obtain the maximum (cross-correlation) and minimum (Euclidean distance) since the problem under consideration is non-convex multi-variable optimization problem. The selected features (from line 9) are modified by our proposed approach so as to misclassify them. For that, a malicious datapoint having minimum E_d is selected for modification, and either feature (as obtained from line 9) is modified and replaced with the average of the same feature of legitimate data traffic. The modified feature is then tested if it is evades the detector.

3 DATA DESCRIPTION AND RESULTS

We evaluate the performance of the proposed approach by using real network traffic measurements from CAIDA2007 and CAIDA2016 traces. We extracted 16 features from those network traces. The features used are given in Table 1. CAIDA2007 dataset is five minutes, i.e., 300 s of anonymized traffic obtained during a DDoS attack in August 2007. These traffic traces recorded only attack traffic to the victim and response from the victim, whereas the legitimate traffic has been removed as much as possible. The CAIDA2016 dataset [2] consists of anonymized passive traffic measurements from passive monitors in 2016. It contains traffic traces from the 'equinix-chicago' high-speed monitor.

Table 2: Results of the proposed approach.

Dataset	Successfully misclassified	Features modified
Training	98.5%	20%
Validation	98.1%	25%
Test	97.3%	22%

In our experiments, we randomly extracted malicious and legitimate traffic from each dataset. The labels are provided for both the classes (legitimate and malicious). We trained the SVM classifier with providing 200 datapoints from each class. For the top-K, we set $K = 5$.

After the classifier (SVM) is trained, we carryout the evasion attack. Note that we do not consider the whole training data whereas we take a subset (50 datapoints from each class) of training and testing data from the whole dataset and craft them according to Algorithm 1. Then each modified datapoint is input to the trained SVM classifier to check if the datapoint is misclassified. The results are shown in Table 2. The success rate is defined as the percentage of adversarial datapoints that were successfully misclassified as legitimate where in actual they were malicious. The feature modification percentage is defined as the number of features that were modified out of the total number of input features. The proposed approach is aware of what features are needed to be modified at which location to evade the detection system.

4 CONCLUSIONS

We introduced an algorithm to modify a malicious input so that it cannot be undetected by a classifier using SVM. To achieve this goal, we exploited the non i.i.d. assumption of SVM classification which can lead to a biased decision boundary. By exploiting a certain region around the decision boundary and crafting the adversarial sample accordingly, we show that the adversary can successfully bypass the detector with the success rate of 98% by modifying 22% of input features on average. For future work, we will extend the proposed idea to study other machine learning algorithms employed in identifying malicious traffic.

ACKNOWLEDGMENTS

The work was supported in parts by National Research Foundation of Korea (No. 2017R1D1A1B03032966), IITP (No. B0717-16-0116), and ITRC (IITP-2017-2012-0-00646).

REFERENCES

[1] F. Giorgio B. Biggio and R. Fabio. 2013. Security evaluation of pattern classifiers under attack. *IEEE transactions on knowledge and data engineering* 26, 4 (2013), 984–996.
[2] CAIDA dataset. 2016. https://www.caida.org/data/. (2016).
[3] B. Biggio D. S. Yeung F. Zhang, P. P. Chan and F. Roli. 2016. Adversarial feature selection against evasion attacks. *IEEE Transactions on Cybernetics* 46, 3 (2016), 766–777.
[4] H. Zheng G. Wang, T. Wang and B. Y. Zhao. 2014. Man vs. Machine: Practical Adversarial Detection of Malicious Crowdsourcing Workers. *USENIX Security Symposium* (2014), 239–254.
[5] S. Jha M. Fredrikson Z. B. Celik N. Papernot, P. McDaniel and A. Swami. 2016. The limitations of deep learning in adversarial settings. *IEEE European Symposium on Security and Privacy (Euro S&P)* (2016), 372–387.
[6] Y. Qi W. Xu and D. Evans. 2016. Automatically evading classifiers. *In Proceedings of the Network and Distributed Systems Symposium (NDSS)* (2016), 1–15.

POSTER: An Empirical Measurement Study on Multi-tenant Deployment Issues of CDNs

Zixi Cai
Institute of Information Engineering, Chinese Academy of Sciences
School of Cyber Security, University of Chinese Academy of Sciences
caizixi@iie.ac.cn

Zigang Cao*
Institute of Information Engineering, Chinese Academy of Sciences;
School of Cyber Security, University of Chinese Academy of Sciences
caozigang@iie.ac.cn

Gang Xiong
Institute of Information Engineering, Chinese Academy of Sciences
School of Cyber Security, University of Chinese Academy of Sciences
xionggang@iie.ac.cn

Zhen Li
Institute of Information Engineering, Chinese Academy of Sciences
School of Cyber Security, University of Chinese Academy of Sciences
lizhen@iie.ac.cn

Wei Xia
Institute of Information Engineering, Chinese Academy of Sciences
School of Cyber Security, University of Chinese Academy of Sciences
xiawei@iie.ac.cn

ABSTRACT

Content delivery network (CDN) has been playing an important role in accelerating users' visit speed, bring good experience for popular web sites around the world. It has become a common security enhance service for CDN providers to offer HTTPS support to tenants. When several tenants are deployed to share a same IP address due to resource efficiency and cost, CDN providers should make comprehensive settings to ensure that all tenants' sites work correctly on users' requests. Otherwise, issues can take place such as denial of service (DOS) and privacy leakage, causing very bad user experience to users as well as potential economic loss for tenants, especially under the situation of hybrid deployment of HTTP and HTTPS. We examine the deployments of typical multi-tenant CDN providers by active measurement and find that CDN providers, namely Akaimai and ChinaCenter, have configuration problems which can result in DOS by certificate name mismatch error. Several advices are given to help to mitigate the issue. We believe that our study is meaningful for improving the security and the robustness of CDN.

KEYWORDS: CDN, HTTPS, certificate

1 INTRODUCTION

HTTPS is a widely used network protocol for secure web communications over public networks. More and more websites are deployed in the form of HTTPS. Until July 2017, according to Letsencrypt, the percentage of web pages loaded using HTTPS has exceeded half of the total, and the number of digital certificates has reached more than 40 million [1].

* corresponding author.

CDN or content distribution network is a geographically distributed network of proxy servers and their data centers to optimize security, performance and reliability. Web sites using HTTPS are deployed on CDNs in different ways, which can be divided into two modes according to whether the CDN node is shared, namely the dedicated IP and the shared IP. Many small and medium-sized sites will choose the latter due to economic reasons. For tenants, it is critical to understand how CDNs treat these websites deployed on CDNs which share a same IP. CDN acts as a proxy for those sites, therefore it assumes responsibility for providing secure access. For sites, it is important to understand the deployment of these multi-tenant CDNs, so they can select a more robust and secure CDN service provider, and try to avoid those CDN services with misconfigurations.

Although a lot of works have been carried out on HTTPS and CDN, we have not seen any systematical measurement and analysis that focus on the shared IP deployment mode in CDN and its impact on security, privacy and robustness of service yet. While the widely seen deployment approach may bring issues besides its convenience and higher exploitation of the machine resources.

In this paper, we measured the sites which were deployed on CDNs by different probing requests, summarized the typical characteristics among CDNs providers on the shared IP deployment mode, and discovered some misconfiguration problems with CDNs providers which may cause severe problems, especially when a node is deployed with HTTP and HTTPS sites, affecting users' experience on top popular sites. Some suggestions are offered to help CDN providers to mitigate the issues.

2 HOW MULTI-TENANT CDN PROCESS HTTPS

It is quite common that several web sites are deployed on one server in CDN for economic reasons. When a HTTPS ClientHello request arrives at the CDN server, a corresponding server certificate is required. If a mismatched certificate is returned to user, it will cause DOS or severe security warning. In practice, there are three common solutions exploited by CDN providers. The first solution is to assign a dedicated IP to each site to solve the conflict, which means one site monopolizes an IP. Wildcard SSL and Dedicated SSL are using this approach. The second is to add the Server Name Indication (SNI) support [2] , so the server can return the corresponding certificate according to the host name in SNI extension in ClientHello. Currently, SNI is supported in all popular browsers, so the solution is easy and economic. The third is to use a shared SSL certificate, which requires to put all sites' domains into the certificate's Subject Alternative Name (SAN) field [3]. However, security issues or privacy leakage may happen due to improper deployment in the real world. The general work mode of processing HTTPS request in CDN is shown in Fig. 1.

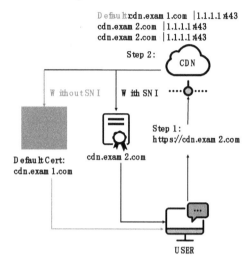

Figure 1: How CDN return certificate

3 OUR MESUREMENT

We try to identify the deployment problems of CDN through active probing techniques. Based on preliminary investigation, we choose the Alexa top 25,000 sites as our experiment objects since these sites are the most probably to exploit CDN to improve their users' experience.

To simulate the situation of accessing the site under different circumstances, we use different SSL/TLS protocol versions, different SNIs to establish SSL/TLS handshakes with the host of Alexa top 25,000 sites to obtain certificates [4]. The CDN node should select the appropriate certificate and return it to the client after it sends back the ServerHello message during the handshake. When multiple sites share one same IP, different certificates shall be return according to SNIs. In previous researches, configuration problems can be seen in the certificate properties [3-5], such as domain mismatches between certificates and websites [6].

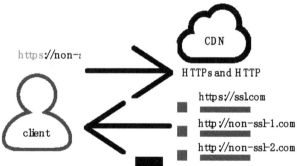

Figure 2: A user utilizes HTTPS to access websites

Fig. 2. shows a way for users to access the Internet through HTTPS. By entering "https" before a URL in the address bar of a

browser, they want to establish secure connections with sites that may not support HTTPS. We call it forcing HTTPS visiting. Generally, CDN must provide the appropriate response on this condition. However, different CDN service providers may have different responses in the real world. We analyze the certificates returned by CDNs, as well as the server's responses to reveal the typical issues in current CDN service.

4 RESULTS AND DISSCUSSIONS

4.1 Multi-tenant CDN deployment situation

We summarize the differences in the behavior of these CDN providers in Table 1. We tick the checkbox if we can obtain certificate in that case; otherwise we cannot. Results shown that SNI is widely deployed by multi-tenant CDNs. Most CDN service providers only offer a high version of the TLS protocol. Including Distilnetworks, Gannett, Fastly etc.

Table 1: **The inconsistent behavior of returning certificates by CDN providers**

CDN provider	TLS1.0	TLS1.2	SNI	NULL
cloudflaressl	√	√	√	√
akamai	√	√	√	
chinanetcenter	√	√	√	
edgecastcdn		√	√	
myqcloud		√	√	
incapsula		√	√	
azurewebsites		√	√	
wpengine		√	√	
alicdn		√	√	
baishancloud		√	√	
jiasule		√	√	
distilnetworks		√	√	√
fastly		√	√	√
yunjiasussl	√	√		√
insnw	√	√	√	√
sucuri	√	√	√	√
cloudfront	√	√	√	√

4.2 Cases of forcing HTTPS visiting

CDN providers should response reasonably to users visiting tenants' sites using HTTPS. If tenant's site supports HTTPS, the CDN should reply with the correct content. If tenant's site only supports HTTP, the CDN should make an automatic jump from HTTPS to HTTP and provide the web content. However, several CDN providers do not properly handle the subsequent steps, causing problems of providing the wrong certificate, DOS, even provide the HTTP web page using a mismatched certificate which belongs to another tenant. The responses of CDN are summarized as the three cases below.

4.2.1 Case of automatic jump

It is a common solution for CDN providers that website will automatically jump from HTTPS to HTTP to ensure the visibility of the content of the site. Many large CDN have adopted this approach, such as Cloudflaressl, and Cloudfront.

4.2.2 Case of privacy leakage

Figure 3: **Example of host name mismatch error. Using HTTPs to visit www.gmw.com and return certificate belong to 12306**

The process that CDN provides HTTPS services includes an SSL handshake, processing decrypted requests and returning content. Any of these steps can cause problems that lead to inconsistencies. Our experiment only focuses on the ClientHello and the certificate during TLS handshake. In our probing, a ClientHello of TLS version 1.2 carrying the correct SNI is sent to server, which imitates the normal behavior of visiting the site by modern mainstream browsers.

In Fig. 3, we illustrate this problem further by an example. When we force to visit one site by HTTPS that returns inconsistency through the Chrome browser, such as www.gmw.cn, we receive a certificate that belongs to kyfw.12306.cn (the official railway ticket selling site in China). After ignoring the wrong browser error message ERR_CERT_COMMON_NAME_INVALID and proceed to visit, web content of www.gmw.cn can still be provided through HTTPS. We think there are at least two configuration issues. First, after the correct SNI is provided, the server returns the wrong certificate. It is reasonable to suspect that CDN provider does not properly handle these SNIs in requests, especially considering that the client cannot obtain certificates from those servers when the SNI is not carried. Second, this is not just a problem with the SNI mechanism, because the server gets the corresponding host after decrypting the HTTPS request. This is the second chance that the CDN server can block the wrong service. However, we observe that the servers are still providing mismatched content.

3.2.2 Case of DOS

DOS can also be understood as a connection rejection on the page after ignoring browser certificate security alerts. Compared to

privacy leakage, DOS has made progress by interrupting web services after decrypting the HTTP request.

4 CONCLUSIONS

Many websites deliver content through CDN. When multiple sites share the same CDN node, especially when the HTTPS site and HTTP site are deployed together, the management of CDN becomes rather complex.

We investigate the deployment of multi-tenant CDN providers using different SSL/TLS versions and SNI hosts. By analyzing certificates, we find that CDN service providers have different strategies in dealing with SNI and TLS version, resulting in different compatibility and even practical problems.

Based on an in-depth analysis of the measurements results, we also find that sites preferring to use SNI SSL are more likely to have problems with inconsistency in certificates and domains. One main reason is that these CDN providers do not take all possible SNI scenarios into account and verify whether those sites on the CDN can provide HTTPS service and working properly. Especially when SSL certificate name mismatch error occurs, sites can still continue to provide access. We expect our work can raise the awareness of this problem in the community. We believe our study will be useful for improving transparency, privacy and security, as well as strengthening Robustness of CDN.

5 SUGGESTIONS AND FUTURE WORK

The short-term approach is to avoid hybrid deployment of HTTP and HTTPS which requires more complex processing mechanisms. The long-term strategies are to strengthen CDN's ability to deal with all kinds of situations and provide a wider range of HTTPS support.

We guess that some sites offering both HTTPS and HTTP are deployed on CDN nodes that only support HTTP speed up service, leading to problems. We will do further study to verify it.

ACKNOWLEDGMENTS

This work is supported by The National Natural Science Foundation of China (No. 61602472, No. U1636217) and The National Key Research and Development Program of China (NO. 2016YFB0801200).

REFERENCES

[1] Letsencrypt, HTTPS://letsencrypt.org/stats/. July 13, 2017.

[2] D. Eastlake 3rd and Huawei, Transport Layer Security (TLS) Extensions: Extension Definitions, IETF RFC 6066, January 2011; www.rfc-editor.org/rfc/rfc6066.txt.

[3] GB/T 7714 Housley R, Ford W, Polk W, et al. Rfc 5280: Internet x. 509 public key infrastructure certificate and crl profile[J]. 2008.

[4] Alexa Internet Inc., "Top 1,000,000 sites (updated daily)," HTTP://s3.amazonaws.com/alexa-static/top-1m.csv.zip, 2009–2011, [online; last retrieved inMay 2011].

[5] GB/T 7714 Durumeric Z, Kasten J, Bailey M, et al. Analysis of the HTTPS certificate ecosystem[C]//Proceedings of the 2013 conference on Internet measurement conference. ACM, 2013: 291-304.

[6] GB/T 7714 Amann B, Vallentin M, Hall S, et al. Revisiting SSL: A large-scale study of the internet's most trusted protocol[J]. ICSI, Tech. Rep., 2012.

[7] N. Vratonjic, J. Freudiger, V. Bindschaedler, and J.-P. Hubaux. The inconvenient truth about web certificates. In 10th Workshop on Economics in Information Security, 2011.

[8] R. Holz, L. Braun, N. Kammenhuber, and G. Carle. The SSL landscape: A thorough analysis of the x.509 PKI using active and passive measurements. In 11th ACM Internet Measurement Conference, Nov. 2011.

POSTER: Actively Detecting Implicit Fraudulent Transactions

Shaosheng Cao
AI Department (Hangzhou)
Ant Financial Services Group
shaosheng.css@antfin.com

XinXing Yang
AI Department (Beijing)
Ant Financial Services Group
xinxing.yangxx@antfin.com

Jun Zhou
AI Department (Beijing)
Ant Financial Services Group
jun.zhoujun@antfin.com

Xiaolong Li
AI Department (Seattle)
Ant Financial Services Group
xl.li@antfin.com

Yuan (Alan) Qi
AI Department (Hangzhou)
Ant Financial Services Group
yuan.qi@antfin.com

Kai Xiao
Security Department (Shanghai)
Ant Financial Services Group
xiaokai.xk@antfin.com

ABSTRACT

In this work, we propose to actively detect implicit fraudulent transactions. A novel machine learning method is introduced to distinguish anomalous electronic transactions based on the historical records. The transferor will be alerted during the on-going payment when the fraud probability is recognized as large enough. Compared with elaborative rule-based approaches, our model is much more effective in fraud detection.

CCS CONCEPTS

• **Security and privacy** → Intrusion/anomaly detection and malware mitigation; • **Computing methodologies** → Machine learning;

KEYWORDS

fraudulent transaction detection; transaction network; machine learning

ACM Reference Format:
Shaosheng Cao, XinXing Yang, Jun Zhou, Xiaolong Li, Yuan (Alan) Qi, and Kai Xiao. 2017. POSTER: Actively Detecting Implicit Fraudulent Transactions. In *Proceedings of CCS '17*. ACM, New York, NY, USA, 3 pages. https://doi.org/10.1145/3133956.3138822

1 INTRODUCTION

Alipay, currently known as Ant Financial Services Group, is the largest mobile and online platform and money-market fund all over the world. In terms of the statistics information at the middle of 2016, there are more than 100 million daily active users and about 450 million annual active users[1]. However, there exist more than ten thousands fraudulent transactions per day that cause great losses. It is therefore a core component for the payment security of monitoring suspicious transactions. In general, fraudulent transactions can be summarized into two different situations, i.e., judgement afterwards and active detection on the fly.

---

[1]https://en.wikipedia.org/wiki/Ant_Financial#cite_note-toknow-8

In the first scenario, if a user has been aware of being cheated and has accused to us, it is necessary to judge whether he (or she) is in a fraud or not, in terms of the supporting proofs, transaction details and the profile. The above is an **explicit** fraud judgement after the incident has happened. In a secondary and more important situation, we desire to actively detect such an **implicit** fraudulent transaction before a user finishes transfering money into suspicious persons.

We emphasize on active identification of the potentially implicit fraudulent fraud at risk control strategy, in order to alert the transferor as soon as the anomalous transaction is identified. Based on our observations, we found that 1) fraudulent manners are changed rapidly with new patterns and attacks, and 2) the number of fraudulent transactions is much less than normal ones. To address the problems, we propose a novel machine learning method, which is automatically adaptive with constantly changing means of frauds as time goes by.

2 RELATED WORK

Fraudulent transaction detection has been widely investigated in the literature, e.g., credit card fraud, telecommunication fraud, and etc. [3, 16]. Rule-based approaches are introduced to produce assertion statement of IF {conditions} and THEN {a consequent} by [9, 15]. Brause et al. propose to generalize association rules by comparing fraud and normal records [5], and [2] shows a way that generates decision variables to identify potentially fraudulent calls. Supervised learning methods are presented in many literature, which yield a fraud probability for the judgement of a new record. Linear discriminative models are employed in [11], and neural networks are utilized later [1, 10, 14].

As for extremely unbalanced data, several unsupervised methods have been applied. Nigrini shows the effectiveness of the Benford's law in accounting fraud [13], and Bolton et al. describe unsupervised profiling methods for the fraud detection of credit cards [4]. Aggregation strategies and clustering methods are used, instead of the analysis targeting on a single transaction record. Vadoodparast et al. combine three traditional clustering methods to achieve better performance [17], and Casas et al. leverage k-means to group network security data, whose centroids and labels are fed into a classifier [7]. Detailed aggregation strategies are shown for detecting credit card fraud in [12, 18].

3 OUR MODEL

In this section, we will give the details of the proposed model.

3.1 The Main components

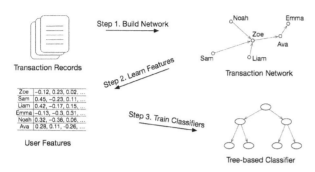

Figure 1: The trainer module of the proposed model.

Our model consists of two components, including trainer and predictor modules. As illustrated in Figure 1, we first build a transaction network from the historical records, and then learn user features using unsupervised learning. Finally, tree-based classifiers are trained by labeled transactions. Once user features and classifiers are ready, the predictor module of our model is able to yield a fraud probability score to alert the transferor if necessary, as described in Figure 2.

Figure 2: The predictor module of the proposed model.

The key of the task is to learn the topological feature information of each user node in the transaction network and train robust classifiers from unbalanced categories.

3.2 Learning User Features from Transaction Network

Since the fraud patterns vary over time, we aim to extract the useful features automatically. An electronic transaction involves two different roles of users, i.e, transferor and transferee, where a user is treated as a node and an edge exists if there is a transaction between them.

Let us define $G =< V, E >$ as the transaction network, where V is the collection of the nodes and E is the collection of the edges. Given the network G, our goal is to learn a representational matrix D ($D \in |V| \times d$), where the d-dimensional vector of the i-th row of learned matrix denotes the topological feature information of the i-th user node.

Intuitively, the most intimate nodes of a node are its (1 hop) neighbours, and next intimate ones are 2-hop neighbours, and so

on. Motivated by [6], we define the loss function by measuring the topological similarity between a node and its neighbours:

$$\mathcal{L}_1 = - \sum_{c \in \tau(w)} \left(\log \sigma(\vec{w} \cdot \vec{c}) + \sum_{i=1}^{\lambda} \mathbb{E}_{c' \sim U}[\log \sigma(-\vec{w} \cdot \vec{c'})] \right) \quad (1)$$

where $\mathcal{L}_1$ is the loss function, and $\tau(w)$ is the collection of neighbours of w within a fixed number of hops. $\mathbb{E}_{c' \sim U}[\cdot]$ denotes the expectation, where c' follows the node distribution U. c' is a negative sample that does not occur in the neighbours but is randomly selected from the whole node collection V, and λ represents the number of negative samples. $\vec{w}$ and $\vec{c}$ are the low dimensional representational vectors of the node w and its neighbour node c. Besides, σ is sigmoid function.

$\vec{w}$ is randomly initialized at first and updated by the term of partial derivative of the loss:

$$\vec{w}_{t+1} = \vec{w}_t - \alpha \cdot \frac{\partial \mathcal{L}_1}{\partial w} \quad (2)$$

where α is a hyper-parameter by means of learning rate. After enough iterations of updates, we get the final d-dimensional feature vector of node w. The procedure is not influenced by unbalanced labels at all, since only transaction records are needed.

3.3 Training Classifiers from Transaction Labels

We define $\mathcal{D} = \{(x_i, y_i)\}$ as the collection of labeled dataset, where x_i is the feature vector of the i-th instance and y_i is the label. The features of an instance are made up of the learned features of the involved transferor and transferee, as well as the basic information in the transaction situation. $y_i = 1$ when it is a fraudulent case; otherwise, $y_i = 0$. $\hat{y}_i$ denotes the predictive fraud score of the i-th instance by our model, and $l(y_i, \hat{y}_i)$ is a differentiable convex function of decision tree between y_i and $\hat{y}_i$. Besides, a regularization term $\Omega(\cdot)$ is also added. Inspired by [8], we show the loss as follows:

$$\mathcal{L}_2 = \sum_{i=1}^{|\mathcal{D}|} \left(g_i f(x_i) + \frac{1}{2} h_i f^2(x_i) \right) + \Omega(f) \quad (3)$$

where $\mathcal{L}_2$ is the loss function, g_i and h_i is the first order and second order partial derivative of $l(y_i, \hat{y}_i)$:

$$g_i = \frac{\partial l(y_i, \hat{y}_i)}{\partial \hat{y}_i} \qquad h_i = \frac{\partial^2 l(y_i, \hat{y}_i)}{\partial \hat{y}_i \partial \hat{y}_i} \quad (4)$$

Although linear classifiers like logistic regression are also widely applied in supervised learning, we choose the above gradient boosting based models instead as for its high accuracy in the case. When the training module is finished, the predictor module has the ability of active detection.

4 EXPERIMENTS

In this section, we will show the effectiveness of the proposed model versus rule-based approach in the real electronic transactions.

4.1 Benchmark, Baseline and Evaluation Metrics

We collect the transaction records from December 1, 2016 to February 20, 2017 in Alipay, from which about 57 million records are

Table 1: The performance comparison between baseline and our model.

Methods	F1	KS	AUC	REC@100	REC@500	REC@1000
Baseline	61.09%	86.18%	98.23%	73.04%	51.77%	41.93%
Our Model	**65.22%**	**88.75%**	**98.79%**	**78.00%**	**57.48%**	**48.26%**

sampled, so as to build the transaction network and learn user features. We also randomly select 2 million records from February 24, 2017 to April 9, 2017 for training the classifier, and adopt 0.8 million records from April 10, 2017 to April 20, 2017 as the test dataset.

In order to test the performance of our model, we compare the experimental results with the rule-based baseline. Inspired by several guidelines[2], dozens of the rules are summarized from the current transfer environments. For example, if the IP address or telephone are from a same city, if the transferees has been complained in the past and so on.

To make a fair comparison, we evaluate using different evaluation metrics. Receiver Operating Characteristic (ROC) curve reflects the diagnostic capacity of a binary classifier, which is decided by drawing true positive rate against the false positive rate, while Area Under a Curve (AUC), as described by its name, is the value of the area under (the ROC) curve[3]. Another important metric is Precision-Recall (PR) plotting curve as the discrimination threshold varies, and the F1 Score is interpreted as harmonic mean of precision and recall[4]. Besides, Kolmogorov-Smirnov (KS) test is a nonparametric test of probability distribution between predictive results and golden standard[5].

4.2 Empirical Results

As described in Table 1, our proposed method can consistently outperform baseline over different testing metrics. In practice, we pay more attention on recall at k predictive samples. Specifically, the value of "REC@100" equals 73.04% means recall value is 73.04% if we alert only 1 time in 100 transaction records. So the higher value of "REC@k" is, the more accurate it is. In addition, both AUC values are close to 100%, as for extremely few fraudulent transactions in statistics.

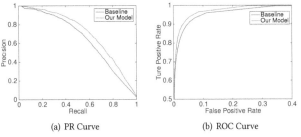

(a) PR Curve   (b) ROC Curve

Figure 3: PR Curve and ROC Curve

Figure 3 shows the PR curve and the ROC curve of our model against baseline. Obviously, in the PR curve, the performance of our model outperforms baseline consistently. For the other comparison of the ROC curve, it is easy to observe that the true positive rate is 93.56% of our model when false positive rate is 5%. By contrast, the value of baseline is only 90.58% with same false positive rate.

5 CONCLUSION

We propose a novel method for actively detecting implicit fraudulent transactions. From the empirical results, the proposed model significantly outperforms rule-based baseline. In our future work, we will investigate more possible solutions to reduce the fraud cases further.

ACKNOWLEDGEMENT

The authors thank the anonymous reviewers for their valuable suggestions.

REFERENCES

[1] Emin Aleskerov, Bernd Freisleben, and Bharat Rao. 1997. Cardwatch: A neural network based database mining system for credit card fraud detection. In *CIFEr*. IEEE, 220–226.
[2] Gerald Donald Baulier, Michael H Cahill, Virginia Kay Ferrara, and Diane Lambert. 2000. Automated fraud management in transaction-based networks. (Dec. 19 2000). US Patent 6,163,604.
[3] Richard J Bolton and David J Hand. 2002. Statistical fraud detection: A review. *Statistical science* (2002), 235–249.
[4] Richard J Bolton, David J Hand, et al. 2001. Unsupervised profiling methods for fraud detection. *Credit Scoring and Credit Control VII* (2001), 235–255.
[5] R Brause, T Langsdorf, and Michael Hepp. 1999. Neural data mining for credit card fraud detection. In *ICTAI*. IEEE, 103–106.
[6] Shaosheng Cao, Wei Lu, and Qiongkai Xu. 2015. Grarep: Learning graph representations with global structural information. In *CIKM*. ACM, 891–900.
[7] Pedro Casas, Alessandro D'Alconzo, Giuseppe Settanni, Pierdomenico Fiadino, and Florian Skopik. 2016. POSTER:(Semi)-Supervised Machine Learning Approaches for Network Security in High-Dimensional Network Data. In *CCS*. ACM, 1805–1807.
[8] Tianqi Chen and Carlos Guestrin. 2016. Xgboost: A scalable tree boosting system. In *SIGKDD*. ACM, 785–794.
[9] William W Cohen. 1995. Fast effective rule induction. In *ICML*. 115–123.
[10] Sushmito Ghosh and Douglas L Reilly. 1994. Credit card fraud detection with a neural-network. In *System Sciences*, Vol. 3. IEEE, 621–630.
[11] David J Hand. 1981. Discrimination and classification. *Wiley Series in Probability and Mathematical Statistics, Chichester: Wiley, 1981* (1981).
[12] Sanjeev Jha, Montserrat Guillen, and J Christopher Westland. 2012. Employing transaction aggregation strategy to detect credit card fraud. *Expert systems with applications* 39, 16 (2012), 12650–12657.
[13] Mark J Nigrini. 1999. I've got your number. *Journal of accountancy* 187, 5 (1999), 79.
[14] Raghavendra Patidar, Lokesh Sharma, et al. 2011. Credit card fraud detection using neural network. *IJSCE* 1, 32-38 (2011).
[15] J Ross Quinlan. 1990. Learning logical definitions from relations. *Machine learning* 5, 3 (1990), 239–266.
[16] Donald Tetro, Edward Lipton, and Andrew Sackheim. 2000. System and method for enhanced fraud detection in automated electronic credit card processing. (Aug. 1 2000). US Patent 6,095,413.
[17] Massoud Vadoodparast, Abdul Razak Hamdan, et al. 2015. Fraudulent Electronic Transaction Detection Using Dynamic KDA Model. *IJCSIS* 13, 3 (2015), 90.
[18] Christopher Whitrow, David J Hand, Piotr Juszczak, D Weston, and Niall M Adams. 2009. Transaction aggregation as a strategy for credit card fraud detection. *Data Mining and Knowledge Discovery* 18, 1 (2009), 30–55.

---

[2] https://www.bluefin.com/merchant-support/identifying-fraudulent-transactions
[3] https://en.wikipedia.org/wiki/Receiver_operating_characteristic#Area_under_the_curve
[4] https://en.wikipedia.org/wiki/F1_score
[5] https://en.wikipedia.org/wiki/Kolmogorov-Smirnov_test

POSTER: Semi-supervised Classification for Dynamic Android Malware Detection

Li Chen, Mingwei Zhang, Chih-yuan Yang, Ravi Sahita

Security and Privacy Lab, Intel Labs, Hillsboro, OR

ABSTRACT

Manually labeling the large number of samples of Android APKs into benign or different malicious families requires tremendous human effort, while it is comparably easy and cheap to obtain a large amount of unlabeled APKs from various sources. Moreover, the fast-paced evolution of Android malware continuously generates derivative and new malware families. These families often contain new signatures, which can escape detection that uses static analysis. These practical challenges can also cause classical supervised machine learning algorithms to degrade in performance.

We propose a framework that uses model-based semi-supervised (MBSS) classification scheme built using dynamic Android API call logs. The semi-supervised approach efficiently uses the labeled and unlabeled APKs to estimate a finite mixture model of Gaussian distributions via conditional expectation-maximization and efficiently detects malware during out-of-sample testing. We compare MBSS with the popular malware detection classifiers such as support vector machine (SVM), k-nearest neighbor (kNN) and linear discriminant analysis (LDA). Under the ideal classification setting, MBSS has competitive performance with 98% accuracy and very low false positive rate for in-sample classification. For out-of-sample testing, the out-of-sample test data exhibit similar behavior of retrieving phone information and sending to the network, compared with in-sample training set. When this similarity is strong, MBSS and SVM with linear kernel maintain 90% detection rate while kNN and LDA suffer great performance degradation. When this similarity is slightly weaker, all classifiers degrade in performance, but MBSS still performs significantly better than other classifiers.

KEYWORDS

Android dynamic malware analysis, semi-supervised machine learning, robust machine learning

1 MOTIVATION

The rampant evolution of Android malware makes it more sophisticated to avoid detection and more difficult to classify using commonly-used machine learning algorithms. Human effort of labeling the malware as malicious or benign cannot keep up with the pace of the voluminous generation of Android malware, resulting in an imbalance of much more unlabeled data than labeled data. Even VirusTotal could take a long time to finalize the prediction of

CCS '17, October 30-November 3, 2017, Dallas, TX, USA

© 2017 Copyright held by the owner/author(s).

ACM ISBN 978-1-4503-4946-8/17/10.

https://doi.org/10.1145/3133956.3138838

large amount of unlabeled data. Further, this can cause supervised learning algorithms to degrade in performance.

Furthermore, due to this imbalance of unlabeled and labeled data, the distribution observed from the labeled data can be different from the actual data distribution. This is seen in malware detection, as study suggests that malware family exhibit polymorphic behaviors. Translated into machine learning, it implies that at testing phase, the test data can be similarly distributed as the training data, but is not identically distributed as the training data. Classical supervised machine learning algorithms can suffer performance degradation when tested on samples that do not distribute identically as the training data.

2 PROPOSED FRAMEWORK

To address the above challenges, we propose a framework of utilizing model-based semi-supervised (MBSS) classification on the dynamic behavior data for Android malware detection. We focus on detecting malicious behavior at runtime by using dynamic behavior data. The main advantage of semi-supervised classification is the strong robustness in performance for out-of-sample testing. The model-based semi-supervised classification uses both labeled and unlabeled data to estimate the parameters, since unlabeled data usually carries valuable information on the model fitting procedure.

Specifically, we use mixture modeling to achieve the classification task. Mixture modeling is a type of machine learning technique, which assumes that every component of the mixture represents a given set of observations in the entire collection of data. Gaussian mixture modeling is the most popularly used applied and studied technique.

We run the Android applications in our emulator infrastructure and harvest the API calls at runtime. Our framework efficiently uses the labeled and unlabeled behavior data to estimate a set of finite mixture models of Gaussian distributions via conditional expectation-maximization, and uses the Bayesian information criterion for model selection. We compare MBSS with the popular malware detection classifiers such as SVM, kNN and LDA. We demonstrate that MBSS has competitive performance for in-sample classification, and maintains strong robustness when applied for out-of-sample testing. We consider semi-supervised learning on dynamic Android behavior data a practical and valuable addition to Android malware detection.

3 DATA GENERATION AND PREPARATION

Malicious and benign APKs were downloaded from VirusTotal and Google Play respectively. Both samples were uploaded to our emulator infrastructure for execution. Our Android emulator (AE) runs in a emulator machine. Each machine may contain multiple emulators. The downloaded APKs were dispatched by the scheduler and installed to new emulator instances for execution. Since most of

Android applications are UI-based, merely launching the application may be insufficient to expose its behaviors. An automation tool is developed to provide simulated human interactions, such as clicks, and sensor events, such as GPS location. In addition, this tool navigates the UI automatically without human intervention. We harvest applications behavior logs through Android Debug Bridge (ADB) [1] and aggregate them into the disk.

We capture dynamic behavior of each android application by executing it in our emulator. The instrumentation of Android runtime was implemented by Xposed [6] in a similar environment like CuckooDroid[5]. The dynamic log consists of a time sequence of API calls made by an application to the Android runtime. Since current Android runtime export more than 50K APIs, for efficiency, we carefully select 160 API calls that are critical to change Android system state such as sending short messages, accessing website, reading contact information, etc. Our selection of Android API function comes from the union of function set selected by three well-known open source projects: AndroidEagleEye [3], Droidmon [4], and Droidbox [2].

As a result, our data consists of the dynamic traces of the APKs as samples, and the feature space of our data set is the collection of n-gram of APIs. That is, suppose the unique number of n-concatenated API calls is d, then a sample APK is represented by $x = (0, 0, .., 1, .., 1, .., 0) \in \{0, 1\}^d$, where 1 denotes the existence of an n-API call sequence and 0 otherwise.

4 MODEL-BASED SEMI-SUPERVISED CLASSIFICATION

In the model-based semi-supervised approach, the data x is assumed to be distributed from a mixture density $f(x) = \sum_{k=1}^{K} \pi_k f_k(x)$, where $f_k(\cdot)$ is the density from the k-th group and π_k is the probability that an observation belongs to group k. Each component is Gaussian, which is characterized by its mean μ_k and covariance matrix Σ_k. The probability density function for the k-th component is thus

$$f_k = f_k(x, \mu_k, \sigma_k) = \frac{\exp(-\frac{1}{2}(x - \mu_k)^T \Sigma_k^{-1}(x - \mu_k))}{\sqrt{\det(2\pi\Sigma_k)}}. \quad (1)$$

The mean $\mu = (\mu_1, ..., \mu_K)$, covariance matrix $\Sigma = (\Sigma_1, ..., \Sigma_K)$ and the population distribution $\pi = (\pi_1, ..., \pi_K)$ are the parameters to be estimated from the mixture models.

Denote $\theta := (\mu, \Sigma)$ as all the parameters in the Gaussian components. Hence we want to estimate π and θ. Denote $\mathcal{X}_n = \{X_1, ..., X_n\}$ as the training data and $\mathcal{Y}_n = \{Y_1, ..., Y_n\}$ as the training labels, where for the i-th observation, denote $Y_{ik} = 1$ if the observation comes from group k and 0 otherwise. Denote the unknown labels of the unlabeled data as $\mathcal{Y}_M = \{Y_{n+1}, ..., Y_{n+m}\}$.

In our framework, we apply model-based semi-supervised classification using both labeled and unlabeled Android behavioral data to develop the classification decision for the unlabeled data. The likelihood of the complete-data consisting of labeled and unlabeled data is

$$L_C(\pi, \theta | \mathcal{X}_n, \mathcal{Y}_n, \mathcal{X}_m, \mathcal{Y}_m)$$
$$= \Pi_{i=1}^{n} \Pi_{k=1}^{K} [\pi_k f(x_i | \theta_k)^{Y_{ik}}] \Pi_{j=n+1}^{n+m} \Pi_{k=1}^{K} [\pi_k f(X_j | \theta_k)]^{Y_{jk}}. \quad (2)$$

Essentially we treat the data with unknown labels as missing data to include them in the complete likelihood.

To estimate the unknown parameters and maximize the log-likelihood of the complete data, we use the conditional expectation-maximization (CEM) algorithm [8]. It is used to solve the likelihood maximization on the complete data, and consists of four main steps:

- **Initialization**;
- **Calculate expectation**;
- **Maximize the expectation**;
- **Stop until convergence**.

Parameter estimation via CEM results in multiple models depending on the Gaussian shapes. We proceed with model selection using the Bayesian information criterion, given by

$$\text{BIC}(M_i) = 2 \log L_C - \ln(n + m)l, \quad (3)$$

where $\log L_C$ is the maximum likelihood of the complete data, $n + m$ is the number of obeservations, and l is the number of parameters.

5 RESULTS

We experiment using the dynamic logs obtained from our Android emulator. We compare MBSS with some of the most popular malware classifiers: SVM, kNN and LDA. We conduct two categories of experiments: in-sample validation and out-of-sample validation. In-sample validation is the typical classification setting where a dataset is split into training and test set. A classifier is trained on the training set and expected to perform well when tested on the test set. Cross validation is usually employed to assess the performance of a classifier. In-sample classification provides the ideal classification scenario, where test data distribution is the same as the training data distribution.

Our next set of experiments focuses on out-of-sample testing. An out-of-sample experiment uses the classifier trained and validated on the in-sample data, and predicts the labels of incoming unlabeled data. The vast majority of the unlabeled data are not guaranteed to follow the same distribution as the in-sample training data. This is a challenge for machine learning algorithms used for practical applications. We consider a classifier robust and practical when it can still achieve reasonably well performance for out-of-sample classification. All the APKs for our experiments are retrieved from VirusTotal, and the experiments are conducted in R [9], [10], [7].

5.1 In-sample validation

We first demonstrate that for in-sample classification, MBSS has competitive performance when compared with SVM with radial kernel, SVM with linear kernel, 3NN and LDA.

As in-sample dataset, we obtain 55994 Android APK dynamic logs from our emulator with 24217 benign Android APKs and 31777 malicious APKs. The in-sample malicious behaviors include stealing location, device ID, MAC information, dynamic code loading behavior, and sending the information to outside network. The label distribution is (43%, 57%) and the chance accuracy (classification accuracy when randomly guessing) is 0.57.

We conduct 10-fold cross validation, report the accuracy mean by averaging the accuracies and calculate the standard deviation of the accuracies across all the 10 folds, and report the similar metrics for false positive rates. As indicated in Table 1, all the classifiers have

Table 1: Classification performance comparison for all five classifiers. All classifiers have competitive classification performance for in-sample testing. For OOS1, MBSS and SVM with linear kernel achieve the highest detection rate. For OOS2, MBSS performs significantly better than all other classifiers. Due to too many ties for 3NN, we do not report its result here.

Classifier	Mean ACC	Sd ACC	Mean FP	Sd FP	DR for OOS1	DR for OOS2
MBSS	97.6%	0.002	3%	0.004	90.0%	55.3%
SVM (radial)	98.8%	0.002	1.8%	0.003	0	0.06%
SVM (linear)	98.6%	0.001	2%	0.003	90.8%	35.4%
3NN	97.9%	0.001	3%	0.004	68.4%	NA
LDA	90.0%	0.003	6%	0.003	9.4%	33.8%

competitive performance. Under this ideal classification scenario, SVM with radial and linear kernels demonstrate the best performance with accuracies at 98.8% and 98.6% respectively and false positive rates both at 2%, 3NN and MBSS have similar performance of accuracy at 97.6% and 97.9% respectively and false positive rate at 3%, while LDA shows lesser performance with accuracy at 90% and false positive at 6%. The receiver operating curve (ROC) of MBSS in the 10-th fold classification and the area under the curve is 0.99.

5.2 Out-of-sample classification

Here we report the detection rate (DR), which is defined by the number of correctly classified malware APKs divided by the total number of out-of-sample test data. After validating that these classifiers have high accuracy and low false positive in Section 5.1, we use them to test on incoming samples. Under this practical and realistic scenario, the test samples do not follow very similar distribution as the training samples. In this case, the classifiers with high accuracy degrade, sometimes even significantly, for out-of-sample testing.

5.2.1 OOS1: Out-of-sample with malicious similarity to in-sample data. We first apply the five classifiers on a dataset of 12185 malicious APKs and report the detection rate. These out-of-sample APKs exhibit similar malicious behaviors of intercepting and sending messages without the user's consent as in the training set.

To visualize this similarity, we conduct principal component analysis (PCA) and inspect the scatter plots of the first four principal components (PC). (See poster for details)

The sixth column in Table 1 demonstrates the detection rates of the five classifiers. Both SVM with linear kernel and MBSS have detection rate of 0.9, while the performance of 3NN is 0.68 and LDA has the lowest detection rate of 0.1. A dramatic performance degradation is seen for SVM with radial kernel, which went from the best in-sample performing classifier to the worst classifier with detection rate near 0. The significant degradation of LDA is due to its highly parametric nature. In this case, SVM with linear kernel and MBSS maintain relatively stable detection rate.

Next, we examine the detection rate as we vary the test size. We apply the classifiers on the randomly selected $\{0.1\%, 1\%, 20\%, 50\%, 90\%\}$ of the test data with independent Monte Carlo replications at $\{50, 30, 20, 10, 5, 1\}$ respectively. We also observe the superior performance of MBSS at 0.9, compared with other classifiers.

5.2.2 OOS2: Out-of-sample with dissimilar distribution to in-sample data. Our next out-of-sample experiment applies the five classifiers onto a dataset of 11986 malicious APKs, whose malicious behaviors primary include stealing private information, sending it

to the Internet through commodity command and control (C&C) server, but do not include dynamic code loading behavior. This slight similarity in malicious behavior can been seen in the data distribution as reflected by the principal components achieved from principal component analysis.

The last right column in Table 1 demonstrates the detection performance of the five classifiers. All classifiers degrade in performance. However SVM with linear kernel degrades in performance significantly. The result of 3NN is omitted, because it fails due to too many ties. MBSS performs significantly better than the other classifiers.

We vary the test size to examine the out-of-sample classification performance. As we vary the test size, we apply the classifiers on the randomly selected $\{0.1\%, 1\%, 20\%, 50\%, 90\%\}$ of the test data with independent Monte Carlo replications at $\{50, 30, 20, 10, 5, 1\}$ respectively. We also observe the robust performance of MBSS compared to the great degradation by other classifiers.

6 CONCLUSION

In this poster, we demonstrate the effectiveness of using model-based semi-supervised learning (MBSS) approach on dynamic Android behavior data for Android malware detection. We show that for in-sample testing, MBSS has competitive accuracy and false positive rate compared with the most popular malware classifiers. For out-of-sample testing, MBSS produces significantly higher detection rate compared with the other classifiers in consideration. We are optimistic that the framework of semi-supervised learning for dynamic analysis is valuable and practical for anti-malware research.

REFERENCES

[1] 2008. Android Debug Bridge. https://developer.android.com/studio/command-line/adb.html. (2008).
[2] 2012. Droidbox. https://github.com/pjlantz/droidbox. (2012).
[3] 2014. MindMac/AndroidEagleEye. https://github.com/MindMac/AndroidEagleEye. (2014).
[4] 2015. Droidmon. https://github.com/idanr1986/droidmon. (2015).
[5] 2016. CuckooDroid - Automated Android Malware Analysis. https://github.com/idanr1986/cuckoo-droid. (2016).
[6] 2016. rovo89/Xposed. https://github.com/rovo89/xposed. (2016).
[7] Chris Fraley, Adrian E. Raftery, Thomas Brendan Murphy, and Luca Scrucca. 2012. *mclust Version 4 for R: Normal Mixture Modeling for Model-Based Clustering, Classification, and Density Estimation.*
[8] Tony Jebara and Alex Pentland. 1998. Maximum conditional likelihood via bound maximization and the CEM algorithm. In *Proceedings of the 11th International Conference on Neural Information Processing Systems.* MIT Press, 494–500.
[9] R Core Team. 2016. *R: A Language and Environment for Statistical Computing.* R Foundation for Statistical Computing, Vienna, Austria.
[10] Niamh Russell, Laura Cribbin, and Thomas Brendan Murphy. 2014. *upclass: Updated Classification Methods using Unlabeled Data.* R package version 2.0.

POSTER: Detection of CPS Program Anomalies by Enforcing Cyber-Physical Execution Semantics*

Long Cheng
Department of Computer Science
Virginia Tech, USA
chengl@vt.edu

Ke Tian
Department of Computer Science
Virginia Tech, USA
ketian@vt.edu

Danfeng (Daphne) Yao
Department of Computer Science
Virginia Tech, USA
danfeng@vt.edu

ABSTRACT

In this work, we present a new program behavior model, *i.e.*, the event-aware finite-state automaton (*e*FSA), which takes advantage of the event-driven nature of control programs in cyber-physical systems (CPS) and incorporates event checking in anomaly detection. *e*FSA provides *new detection capabilities to detect data-oriented attacks* in CPS control programs, including *attacks on control intensity* (*i.e.*, hijacked for/while-loops) and *attacks on control branch* (*i.e.*, conditional branches). We implement a prototype of our approach on Raspberry Pi and evaluate *e*FSA's performance by conducting CPS case studies. Results show that it is able to effectively detect different CPS attacks in our experiments.

KEYWORDS

Anomaly detection; Cyber-physical systems; Data-oriented attacks

1 INTRODUCTION

Control programs are critical to the proper operations of cyber-physical systems (CPS), as anomalous program behaviors can have serious consequence, or even cause devastating damages to physical systems [1]. Recent studies [1, 3] have shown that control programs suffer from a variety of runtime software exploits. These attacks can be broadly classified into two categories: control-oriented attacks and data-oriented attacks. The former exploits memory corruption vulnerabilities to divert a program's control flows. The latter manipulates data variables without violating the program's control flow integrity (CFI). Because existing CFI-based solutions are rendered defenseless under data-oriented attacks, such threats are particularly alarming in CPS.

We focus on two types of runtime data-oriented attacks against control programs. *i) Attacks on control branch*, which corrupt critical decision making variables at runtime to execute a *valid-yet-unexpected* control-flow path (*e.g.*, allowing liquid to flow into a tank despite it is full or preventing a blast furnace from being shut down properly). *ii) Attacks on control intensity*, which corrupt

sensor data variables to manipulate the amount of control operations, *e.g.*, affecting the number of loop iterations to dispense too much drug [1]). These data-oriented attacks result in inconsistencies between the physical context and program execution, where executed control-flow paths do not correspond to the observations in the physical environment. Unfortunately, there exist very few defences [1, 6] and they are ineffective to prevent both attack types due to the lack of runtime execution semantics checking.

In many instances, CPS can be modeled as event-driven control systems. We refer to events as occurrences of interest that come through the cyber-physical observation process or emitted by other entities, and trigger the execution of corresponding control actions. We present an event-aware finite-state automaton (*e*FSA) model to detect anomalous control program behaviors particularly caused by data-oriented attacks. By enforcing runtime cyber-physical execution semantics (*i.e.*, the physical context that triggers corresponding CPS program behaviors), *e*FSA detects subtle data-oriented exploits when a specific physical event is missing (*i.e.*, not observed) along with the corresponding event dependent state transition.

We implement a proof-of-concept prototype on Raspberry Pi platform. Our prototype features: i) A gray-box FSA model that examines the return addresses on the stack when system calls are made. ii) An LLVM-based event dependence analysis tool to extract event properties from programs and correlate the physical context with runtime program behaviors, which we refer to as cyber-physical execution semantics. iii) A near-real-time anomaly detector, with both local and distributed event verifiers to assess the physical context. We evaluate *e*FSA's performance by conducting CPS case studies. Our results show that *e*FSA is able to successfully detect different data-oriented attacks. The runtime anomaly detector takes ~0.0001s to check each state transition in *e*FSA model, ~0.063s for the local event verification, and ~0.211s for the distributed event verification.

2 THE PROPOSED APPROACH

2.1 Attack Model

We assume that the adversary is able to launch runtime software exploits which may be unknown or known but unpatched at the time of intrusion. We are not concerned how attackers gained entry into the devices and launch different attacks, but focus on uncovering abnormal program execution behaviors after that. We mainly focus on runtime software exploits, and thus sensor data spoofing attacks in the physical domain are out of the scope of this work. We assume the initial state (*i.e.*, the training stage) of the application is trustworthy, which is a general requirement of most behavior-based intrusion detection systems. We also assume the runtime

*This work has been supported in part by Security and Software Engineering Research Center (S2ERC), a NSF sponsored multi-university Industry/University Cooperative Research Center (I/UCRC). The full version of this work can be found in [2].

monitoring module is trusted and cannot be disabled or modified. This assumption is reasonable because it can be achieved by isolating the monitoring module from the untrusted target program with hardware security support such as ARM's TrustZone [1].

2.2 Design Overview

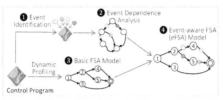

Fig. 1: *e*FSA model construction in the training phase. This workflow can be generalized to non-FSA anomaly detection frameworks (*i.e.*, augmenting an existing program behavior model with contextual integrity).

Fig. 1 shows the workflow of constructing the *e*FSA program behavior model in our design. There are four main steps in the training phase. We first identify CPS events involved in the control program (❶). After that, we perform the event dependence analysis to generate an event-annotated control flow graph (❷), which identifies event triggered instructions/statements of the program. Then, we construct the basic finite-state automaton (FSA) model based on dynamic profiling (❸). Given an event-annotated CFG, we are able to identify the event-driven system call sequences. By augmenting the event-driven information on top of the basic FSA, we generate our event-aware FSA (*i.e.*, *e*FSA) for CPS control program behavior modeling (❹).

The basic FSA model aims at detecting control-oriented attacks. Our main contribution lies in the event awareness enhancement based on the FSA model, which checks the consistency between runtime behavior and program execution semantics. In the testing phase, an anomaly is marked if there exists a state transition deviated from the automaton, or a mismatch between the physical context and program control-flow path.

2.3 Construction of *e*FSA Model

Event Identification and Dependence Analysis: In order to discover the triggering relationship between external events and internal program control flows, we first identify what events are involved in a CPS program. Without loss of generality, we define two types of events in control programs: i) binary events and ii) non-binary events. Binary events return either `True` or `False`, which are defined in terms of pre-specified status changes of physical environments and provide notifications to the control program. Non-binary events correspond to the sensor-driven control actions within a for/while loop, *e.g.*, sensor values affect the amount of control operations. We present an LLVM-based method for reasoning triggering relationship between external events and internal program control flows. Our key idea is to search for an LLVM branch instruction that is data-dependent on any sensor-reading API, and at least an actuation API is control-dependent on this branch instruction. The search is performed through backward data dependence analysis and forward control dependence analysis.

Event Awareness Enhancement: Our *e*FSA model extends the FSA [5] model with external context constraints, where event dependent state transitions in FSA are labeled with event constraints. The FSA construction is based on tracing the system calls and program counters (PC) made by a control program under normal execution. Each distinct PC (*i.e.*, the return address of a system call) value indicates a different state of the FSA, and each system call corresponds to a state transition. Then, we apply the event dependence analysis results to augment the event-driven information over the underlying FSA, and finally construct the *e*FSA model. Fig. 2(a) shows a pictorial example program. The learnt *e*FSA model is shown in Fig. 2(b), where an event dependent transition is labeled by "$[\frac{System\ Call}{PC}]$||Events". In this example, there are two binary events and one non-binary event. We identify binary-event dependent state transitions $[\frac{S_1}{3}\frac{S_2}{6}]|E_1$, $[\frac{S_1}{3}\frac{S_4}{9}]|E_2$, and a non-binary-event dependent control intensity loop $[\frac{S_2}{6}\frac{S_3}{7}]$. It also contains an implicit event dependent transition $[\frac{S_1}{3}\frac{S_5}{10}]|(\overline{E_1} \wedge \overline{E_2})$. *e*FSA expresses causal dependencies between physical events and program control flows. By checking execution semantics at runtime, *e*FSA improves the robustness against data-oriented attacks by increasing the difficulties that an attack could bypass the anomaly detection.

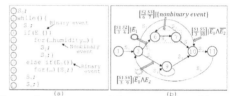

Fig. 2: Example of *e*FSA model construction: (a) an example program; (b) the corresponding *e*FSA model.

3 CPS CASE STUDY

We conduct a CPS case study, and evaluate *e*FSA's detection capability against runtime data-oriented attacks.

SyringePump[1]. The control program originally takes remote user commands via serial connection, and translates the input values into control signals to the actuator. SyringePump is vulnerable since it accepts and buffers external inputs that might result in buffer overflows [1]. We modify the syringe pump application, where external inputs are sent from the control center for remote control, and environmental events drive the pump's movement. Specifically, in the event that the relative humidity value is higher than a specified threshold, the syringe pump movement is triggered. In addition, the amount of liquid to be dispensed is dependent on the humidity value subtracted by the threshold value.

3.1 Detecting Attacks on Control Branch

In this experiment, we evaluate *e*FSA's security guarantees against control branch attacks. We set the threshold to $40rH$, *i.e.*, when the relative humidity value is higher than $40rH$, it drives the movement of syringe pump by sending control signals to dispense liquid. The buffer overflow attack manipulates the humidity sensor values to purposely trigger `event-push` control actions without receiving an external event or environmental trigger. Such an attack leads to unintended but valid control flows. Fig. 3 illustrates an example

---

[1] https://github.com/control-flow-attestation/c-flat

of the experiment. The remote user command corrupts the humidity sensor value to be 48.56rH, which falsifies the return value of event-push to be True. For each intercepted system call, we check if there exists an outgoing edge labelled with the system call name from the current state in FSA. In case of any event-driven state transition according to eFSA, the event verifier checks consistency between the runtime execution semantics (e.g., the instantaneous humidity value) and program internal state. As shown in Fig. 3, eFSA raises an alarm when it finds a mismatch between the execution semantics and program behavior.

Fig. 3: An instance of detecting attacks on control branch

3.2 Detecting Attacks on Control Intensity

In this experiment, we set the threshold to 30rH, and demonstrate that eFSA is able to detect control intensity attacks with only system call traces. In SyringePump, the corrupted humidity value determines the amount of liquid to be dispensed, which equals to the humidity value subtracted by 30rH in this test. In the training stage, we obtain the number of system calls invoked in each loop iteration. Then, we model the relationship between sensor measurements and the amount of system calls in a control intensity loop. Through control intensity analysis, we know the number of system calls with no event occurrence is 40 per scan cycle, and each loop iteration (i.e., dispensing a unit of liquid) in the control intensity loop corresponds to 3 system calls.

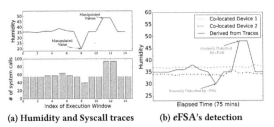

(a) Humidity and Syscall traces   (b) eFSA's detection

Fig. 4: An instance of detecting attacks on control intensity

Fig. 4(a) shows the value changes of the humidity variable and system call amount per scan cycle of SyringePump. The normal humidity value fluctuates between 34 rH and 38rH. As a result, the amount of liquid to be dispensed is subsequently changed, which is reflected by the number of system calls in each control loop. We manipulate the humidity values to be 20rH and 48rH, respectively. In the monitoring phase, by observing the number of system calls in each control loop, we can reversely derive the changes of physical environment based on our control intensity regression model as

shown in Fig. 4(b). In this test, if the difference between the derived value and the sampled average value from event verifier is larger than 3rH, we consider it an anomaly. By checking the humidity measurements from two co-located devices (i.e., denoted as devices 1 and 2), our distributed event verifier detects that the program's runtime behaviors are incompatible with physical contexts. Thus, eFSA successfully detects the control intensity attacks.

3.3 Runtime Overhead

We measure the performance overhead incurred by eFSA's anomaly detector on Raspberry Pi. We employ the user-space strace software to collect system calls in our prototype. The system call tracing overhead has no difference between FSA and eFSA, incurring 1.5x~2x overhead in our experiments. For performance consideration, alternative tracing techniques may be adopted in replacing the strace to improve the tracing performance. For example, authors in [4] show that the overhead of hardware-assisted system call tracing on ARM platform is sufficiently small to ignore.

The average delay out of more than 1000 runs for each state transition (i.e., each intercepted system call) checking is around 0.0001s. It takes 0.063s on average to perform the local event checking. The end-to-end latency for the distributed event checking from each co-located device can be broken down into two main parts: i) network communication around 0.042s, and ii) sensor reading delay around 0.0582s. In our experiment, we deploy two co-located devices, and thus the total distributed event checking delay is around 0.212s. It is expected that the overhead of distributed event checking is linearly proportional to the number of event verification sources.

4 CONCLUSION

In this work, we present a CPS-specific program behavior model eFSA, which advances the state-of-the-art program behavior modelling by augmenting an existing program behavior model with physical context awareness. eFSA detects subtle data-oriented exploits in CPS if a specific physical event is missing along with the corresponding event dependent state transition. We implement a proof-of-concept prototype to demonstrate the feasibility of our approach. Real-world CPS case study demonstrates eFSA's efficacy against different data-oriented attacks. As for our future work, we plan to integrate physics-based models into our approach, design robust event verification mechanisms, and extend our design paradigm to support actuation integrity for fine-grained anomaly detection at the instruction level.

REFERENCES
[1] T. Abera, N. Asokan, L. Davi, J. Ekberg, T. Nyman, A. Paverd, A. Sadeghi, and G. Tsudik. C-FLAT: control-flow attestation for embedded systems software. In *CCS*, 2016.
[2] L. Cheng, K. Tain, and D. D. Yao. Enforcing cyber-physical execution semantics to defend against data-oriented attacks. In *ACSAC*, 2017.
[3] L. Garcia, F. Brasser, M. H. Cintuglu, A.-R. Sadeghi, O. Mohammed, and S. A. Zonouz. Hey, my malware knows physics! attacking plcs with physical model aware rootkit. In *NDSS*, 2017.
[4] Z. Ning and F. Zhang. Ninja: Towards transparent tracing and debugging on arm. In *USENIX-Security*, 2017.
[5] R. Sekar, M. Bendre, D. Dhurjati, and P. Bollineni. A fast automaton-based method for detecting anomalous program behaviors. In *IEEE Security and Privacy*, 2001.
[6] M.-K. Yoon, S. Mohan, J. Choi, M. Christodorescu, and L. Sha. Learning execution contexts from system call distribution for anomaly detection in smart embedded system. In *IoTDI*, 2017.

POSTER: A Comprehensive Study of Forged Certificates in the Wild

Mingxin Cui
Institute of Information Engineering, CAS
School of Cyber Security, University of Chinese
Academy of Sciences
cuimingxin@iie.ac.cn

Zigang Cao
Institute of Information Engineering, CAS
School of Cyber Security, University of Chinese
Academy of Sciences
caozigang@iie.ac.cn

Gang Xiong*
Institute of Information Engineering, CAS
School of Cyber Security, University of Chinese
Academy of Sciences
xionggang@iie.ac.cn

Junzheng Shi
Institute of Information Engineering, CAS
School of Cyber Security, University of Chinese
Academy of Sciences
shijunzheng@iie.ac.cn

ABSTRACT

With the widespread use of SSL, many issues have been exposed as well. Forged certificates used for MITM attacks or proxies can make SSL encryption useless easily, leading to privacy disclosure and property loss of careless victims. In this paper, we implement a large scale of passive measurement of SSL/TLS and analyze the forged certificates in the wild comprehensively. We measured SSL/TLS connection for 16 months on two large research networks, which provided a total of 100 Gbps bandwidth. We gathered nearly 135 million leaf certificates and studied the forged ones. Our findings reveal main reasons of signing forged certificates, and show the preference of them. Finally, we find out several suspicious servers that might be used for MITM.

CCS CONCEPTS

• **Networks** → *Network measurement*; • **Security and privacy** → *Network security*;

KEYWORDS

Forged Certificate, SSL MITM, Passive Measurement

1 INTRODUCTION

SSL/TLS (we refer to SSL/TLS as SSL for brevity in this paper) is the most widely used encryption protocol to ensure the security of network communication. X.509 certificate plays an important role in SSL PKI (Public Key Infrastructure), which is the basis of SSL encryption framework. With the widespread use of SSL, many issues have been exposed

*Corresponding author.

as well. In this paper, we focus on the status quo of forged certificates.

A certificate is used to identify the peer server or client in SSL handshake period. An SSL MITM attack usually uses a forged certificate to deceive careless users, leading to the privacy disclosure and property loss of the victims. The number of forged certificates is increasing as the widespread use of HTTPS, so it is necessary to conduct a comprehensive study of the status quo of forged certificates.

Though many researchers have published their works on the certificate ecosystem [2] [3] [4] and MITM of SSL [1] [5], there are few papers focusing on the forged certificates in the wild. Huang et al [6] implemented a method to detect the occurrence of SSL MITM attack on Facebook and analyzed forged SSL certificates of Facebook in 2014, but they only studied the forged certificates of Facebook.

In this paper, we conduct a comprehensive study of forged certificates in the wild. We implemented a 16-month passive measurement from November 2015 to February 2017 to collect the real-world SSL certificates on two large research networks. These two networks can totally provide over 100Gbps bandwidth, covering more than 17 million IPv4 addresses and nearly 30 million actual users. During the measurement, we collected nearly 135 million leaf certificates totally, including more than 64 million forged ones. After an in-depth analysis and traceability, we find that though many forged certificates can be attributed to antivirus software, security gateways, content filters, and proxies, which has been mentioned in [6]. Besides, we find a considerable number of forged certificates are issued by a serial of similar self-signed CAs. The analysis result shows that certificates related to finance prefer to be forged.

Our contributions can be summarized as follows. Firstly, we conducted a large scale of passive measurement to draw an overall scene of forged certificates in the wild. Secondly, we analyze the forged certificates from three aspects: CA, certificate, and server. Our analysis reveals the main causes and the preference of forged certificates. Thirdly, we find out several suspected SSL MITM attacks and trace out the suspicious servers.

Table 1: Certificates Dataset Size

Certificate Types	#(Unique Certificates)	Percentage
CAs	879,707	0.65%
Leaf Certs(Not Forged)	70,459,293	51.86%
Leaf Certs(Forged)	64,528,037	47.49%
Totally	135,867,037	100%

Table 2: Top 20 Issuers of Forged Certificates

Cert Issuer CN	
Cisco Umbrella Secondary SubCA *	FortiGate CA
Zscaler Intermediate Root CA (*.net)	Websense
Sophos Web Appliance	mitmproxy
OpenDNS Intermediate nrt-SG	Web Gateway
Avella School District Proxy CA	Essentra
Sophos SSL CA_C01001BKK84Y2F1	*.securly.com
Bureau Veritas	Self-signed
Lightspeed Rocket	Egedian
DO_NOT_TRUST_FiddlerRoot	Gadang Proxy CA
McAfee Web Gateway	SSL-SG1-HK1

The remainder of this paper is structured as follows. Section 2 elaborates our measurement framework and the details of collected data. We show the real-world forged certificate situation and try to trace and identify SSL MITM attacks in Section 3. Section 4 concludes this paper and list the future work we intend to do.

2 MEASUREMENT AND DATASET

2.1 Passive Measurement Framework

In order to study the malware and Trojan viruses spreading in the SSL encrypted networks, we implemented passive measurement on two large research networks, namely *China Education and Research Network* and *China Science and Technology Network* from May 2016 to May 2017. These networks could provide 61,440 Mbps and 47,104 Mbps bandwidth respectively, covering more than 17 million IPv4 addresses and nearly 30 million users. Our program collected the certificates and connection information (mainly the servers and connection counts) after an anonymous processing. Useful data would be added into the corresponding dataset. The framework of our passive measurement is shown in Figure 1.

2.2 Dataset

During the measurement, we collected nearly 136 million unique certificates, including nearly 135 million end-entity ones and 879,707 CAs. We then gathered more than 64 million forged certificates by validating certificate chains, as shown in Table 1. We parsed the forged certificates and extracted basic information to compose our dataset. And for each SSL connection, we stored the server ip, server port, and the basic statistics as well.

Table 3: Top 10 Forged Certificates

Cert Subject CN	#(Forged Certs)
*.tmall.com	131,091
*.taobao.com	119,496
*.aliexpress.com	13,211
img.alicdn.com	10,290
yy.com	6,961
www.amazon.com	6,137
api.paypal.com	5,440
*.tanx.com	4,803
mobile.paypal.com	4,745
ru.aliexpress.com	4,684

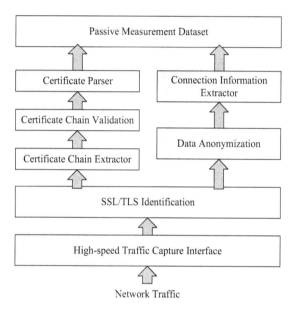

Figure 1: Passive Measurement Framework

2.3 Ethical Considerations

Considering the privacy and ethical issues in the passive measurement, we implement an anonymous process while dealing with the data. The client ip of each connection has been encrypted before collected by the measurement system. Thus, we do not know, and actually do not care about, the real client ip address of each SSL connection. We focus on the certificates and corresponding servers, not the user privacy.

3 FORGED CERTIFICATE IN THE WILD

3.1 Issuers of Forged Certificates

We analyzed the forged certificates and tried to find out the main causes. Table 2 lists the top 20 issuers that issued most forged certificates. These issuers could be divided into several classes. Some issuers are related to security products or antivirus softwares, such as *Cisco Umbrella Secondary*

Table 4: Suspicious Malicious MITM Servers

Suspicious Server	#port	#(port,cert)	#connection	Location	Organization	Domain
62.210.69.21	500(2876-3375)	9,067	61,932	France	ONLINE SAS	poneytelecom.eu
62.210.169.111	25 (4772-4796)	268	93,931	France	ONLINE SAS	poneytelecom.eu
195.154.161.44	441(2604-3100)	1,521	2,142	France	liad-Entreprises	poneytelecom.eu
195.154.161.209	500(3336-3835)	9,118	66,125	France	liad-Entreprises	poneytelecom.eu

SubCA *, and *Zscaler Intermediate Root CA (*.net)*, and *Sophos Web Appliance*. Some issuers are used for content filters, such as *.securly.com* and *Egedian*. Some issuers refer to SSL proxies. And there is no doubt that lots of forged certificates are issued for MITM attacks.

3.2 Preference of Forged Certificates

We analyze the forged certificates in two aspects: subject and issuer. From the subject point of view, we reveal the preference of forged certificates. Table 3 shows the top 10 forged certificates. Most of these certificates are related to finance. The reason is obvious: MITM attackers are more interested in the wallets of the victims. This law also applies to the whole dataset. Taking the usage of SSL proxies into account, it's not surprising that many unknown certificates have been forged.

We also find a considerable number of forged certificates are issued by a serial of similar self-signed CAs. The issuer CN of these forged certificates follows the regular expression "[0-9a-z]{16}", such as *000b3ae6c82f4368* and *ffec5faf668ae0d6*. More than 400,000 forged certificates are issued by this kind of CAs. And they account for more than 75% of forged certificates in Table 3, involving all items.

3.3 Suspicious MITM Servers

Forged certificates with similar issuer CNs mentioned above caused our attention. We suspected that these forged certificates were issued by the same series of MITM attacks. Thus we analyzed the connection information of the corresponding certificates to verify our suspicion. We randomly selected 3 days connection data on 05/31/2016, 07/31/2016, and 02/28/2017, and extracted the corresponding server information. We obtained totally 796 servers, 2,458 server (*ip,port*) tuples and 21,361 (*ip,port,certificate*) triples from 229,817 connections. We suspected four ip addresses shown in Table 4 should be attributed to MITM attacks for the reasons below:

(1) These ips belong to a same Organization and locate in the same country.

(2) These ips covered more than 93% triples and more than 97% connections.

(3) The corresponding port number of each ip is incremented continuously, and the number of connections for each (*ip,port,certificate*) triple is less than 10.

(4) The forged certificates used by these servers are mainly related to less than 15 domains, most of which provided financial services.

We would focus on these servers and try to verify our suspicion.

4 CONCLUSION AND FUTURE WORK

In this paper, we implemented a large scale of passive measurement to study the status quo of forged certificates. We collected more than 64 million forged certificates and conducted an in-depth study. Our analysis revealed the causes and preference of forged certificates. We also detected several suspected SSL MITM attacks due to the analysis and traced out the suspicious servers.

Future Work. Up to now our focus was on the analysis of forged certificates based on the passive measurement. A passive HTTPS scan of Alexa Top 1 million domains would be implemented next. Combined with the results of passive and active measurement, we could get a more accurate and real scene of forged certificates in the wild. What's more, we would train a machine learning model to detect SSL MITM attacks using the dataset we've collected.

ACKNOWLEDGMENTS

This work is supported by The National Key Research and Development Program of China (No. 2016YFB0801200) and The National Natural Science Foundation of China (No. 61602472, No. U1636217).

REFERENCES

[1] Italo Dacosta, Mustaque Ahamad, and Patrick Traynor. 2012. Trust no one else: Detecting MITM attacks against SSL/TLS without third-parties. In *European Symposium on Research in Computer Security*. Springer, 199–216.

[2] Zakir Durumeric, David Adrian, Ariana Mirian, Michael Bailey, and J Alex Halderman. 2015. A search engine backed by Internet-wide scanning. In *Proceedings of the 22nd ACM SIGSAC Conference on Computer and Communications Security*. ACM, 542–553.

[3] Zakir Durumeric, James Kasten, Michael Bailey, and J Alex Halderman. 2013. Analysis of the HTTPS certificate ecosystem. In *Proceedings of the 2013 conference on Internet measurement conference*. ACM, 291–304.

[4] Ralph Holz, Lothar Braun, Nils Kammenhuber, and Georg Carle. 2011. The SSL landscape: a thorough analysis of the x. 509 PKI using active and passive measurements. In *Proceedings of the 2011 ACM SIGCOMM conference on Internet measurement conference*. ACM, 427–444.

[5] Ralph Holz, Thomas Riedmaier, Nils Kammenhuber, and Georg Carle. 2012. X. 509 forensics: Detecting and localising the SSL/TLS men-in-the-middle. *Computer security–esorics 2012* (2012), 217–234.

[6] Lin Shung Huang, Alex Rice, Erling Ellingsen, and Collin Jackson. 2014. Analyzing forged SSL certificates in the wild. In *Security and privacy (sp), 2014 ieee symposium on*. IEEE, 83–97.

POSTER: Rust SGX SDK: Towards Memory Safety in Intel SGX Enclave

Yu Ding, Ran Duan, Long Li, Yueqiang Cheng,
Yulong Zhang, Tanghui Chen, Tao Wei
Baidu X-Lab
Sunnyvale, CA
{dingyu02,duanran01,lilong09,chengyueqiang,ylzhang,
chentanghui,lenx}@baidu.com

Huibo Wang*
UT Dallas
Richardson, Texas
hxw142830@utd.edu

ABSTRACT

Intel SGX is the next-generation trusted computing infrastructure. It can effectively protect data inside enclaves from being stolen. Similar to traditional programs, SGX enclaves are likely to have security vulnerabilities and can be exploited as well. This gives an adversary a great opportunity to steal secret data or perform other malicious operations.

Rust is one of the system programming languages with promising security properties. It has powerful checkers and guarantees memory-safety and thread-safety. In this paper, we show Rust SGX SDK, which combines Intel SGX and Rust programming language together. By using Rust SGX SDK, developers could write memory-safe secure enclaves easily, eliminating the most possibility of being pwned through memory vulnerabilities. What's more, the Rust enclaves are able to run as fast as the ones written in C/C++.

CCS CONCEPTS

• **Security and privacy** → **Trusted computing**; **Software security engineering**;

KEYWORDS

Intel SGX; Rust programming language; SDK

1 INTRODUCTION

Intel SGX provides a hardware based Trusted Execution Environment (TEE) called 'SGX enclave', along with Intel Active Management Technology (AMT) module and Internet remote attestation infrastructure for the whole Intel SGX ecosystem. The core of Intel SGX technique is the memory encryption engine [7] in CPU and the CPU is the key component inside the trusted boundary. It limits memory access by enforcing checks on TLB access and memory address translation. Also, the memory encryption engine automatically encrypts data when evicting pages to the untrusted memory region. However, SGX enclaves could have memory corruption vulnerabilities and could be exploited and hi-jacked [9, 12] and thus

---

*Huibo Wang contributed to this work during her internship at Baidu X-Lab.

secrets would be leaked in such attacks. Researchers have proposed several techniques for hardening Intel SGX [8, 11], but these solutions are only exploit mitigations. We still need an ultimate solution with memory safety guarantee for Intel SGX enclaves.

Rust programming language [10] is becoming more and more popular in system programming. It intrinsically guarantees memory safety and thread safety. The performance of Rust program is almost the same to C++ program [1]. Servo [5] and Redox [3] are browser and operating system written in Rust, indicating that Rust can do almost everything on popular architectures. We believe that Rust best fits for developing basic system components.

In this paper, we show Rust SGX SDK a framework that connects Intel SGX and Rust programming language, making it easy for developers to write safe and memory-bug-free SGX enclaves. By building enclaves in Rust on top of our Rust SGX SDK, there is no need for adapting any advanced exploit mitigation techniques such as ASLR, ROP gadget mitigation or CFI enforcement.

Rust SGX SDK has been open-sourced on Github [4]. Intel recommends this SDK on its official SGX homepage.

In summary, our contributions are:

(1) We first introduce Rust ecosystem to the Intel SGX community, bringing both security and functionality to Intel SGX programming.
(2) We propose the rules-of-thumb in memory safe/unsafe hybrid SDK designing to achieve good balance between security and functionality.
(3) We identify the main challenges in connecting Intel SGX and Rust, and then we design and build Rust SGX SDK that addresses all identified challenges efficiently and effectively.

2 RATIONALE AND CHALLENGES

2.1 Memory safety rules-of-thumb

Based on whether using Intel SGX SDK or not, there are two reasonable directions to build Rust SGX SDK. The first one is to build it from scratch, without relying on the Intel's SGX SDK. The pure Rust version could achieve better safety, but it weakens the functionality. It would become even worse with many new features added into the Intel SGX SDK periodically. sgx-utils [6] is such an open-source project and but it is outdated now. The second direction is to build it upon the Intel SGX SDK. It is not a pure Rust version, but it could significantly benefit from Intel's efforts, and is able to achieve good balance between safety and functionality with carefully designed architecture. In our Rust SGX SDK project, we choose the second one. To get better functionality along with strong security guarantees, we come up with the following rules-of-thumb for hybrid memory-safe architecture designing:

(1) Unsafe components should be appropriately isolated and modularized, and the size should be small (or minimized).
(2) Unsafe components should not weaken the safe, especially, public APIs and data structures.
(3) Unsafe components should be clearly identified and easily upgraded.

Here the unsafe components include both the modules written in memory-unsafe languages (such as C/C++), and the unsafe codes which reside in the modules written in memory-safe languages (such as Rust). Memory-safety oriented SGX SDK would benefit a lot from following these rules. Enclaves built on top of our Rust SGX SDK would benefit from the strong safety guarantees, as well as new features and performance optimizations brought by Intel.

2.2 Main Challenges

The first real challenge is threading. Thread of Intel SGX enclave does not have its own life cycle, no matter the enclave's TCSPolicy is BOUND or UNBOUND [2]. In an enclave with BOUND TCSpolicy, an enclave 'thread' consumes one fixed 'TCS' slot, and binds its life to a POSIX thread. When the POSIX thread exits, the corresponding enclave 'thread' releases the occupied 'TCS' thread slot . In an enclave with UNBOUND TCSpolicy, an enclave 'thread' comsumes an available 'TCS' slot from the pool and releases it on EEXIT. As a result, raw SGX thread has neither constructor nor destructor, and TLS data even remains after EEXIT. All these characterstics conflict with Rust thread model.

The second challenge is the initiation of static data. For example, C++0x allows initializer lists for standard containers. In normal user space applications, the global data structures are initiated before main begins. However, in SGX, there is no such initiation procedure. After the enclave is loaded, nothing would be executed until the first ECALL instruction. How to implement the static data initiation in Rust is a challenge.

The third challenge is to implement Rust style mutex using SGX style mutex. The SGX style mutex is very similar to pthread mutex. But Rust mutex is vastly different from it. Rust mutex directly binds to the protected data and needs to be constructed together with the data it binds to. We need to properly implement Rust style mutex using SGX style mutex.

3 SDK OVERVIEW

Fig. 1 shows the architecture of our Rust SGX SDK. In the trusted environment, a.k.a. SGX enclave, the SGX enclave is loaded into the protected memory along with the enclave's metadata. The SGX enclave binary is linked to Intel SDK libraries, such as libsgx_tstdc.a. Intel SGX SDK exposes standard C/C++ interface to the upper level. Rust SGX SDK is built on top of these Intel SGX SDK libraries, providing Rust style data structures and APIs to developers. For example, Rust has its own vector data structure collections::vec::Vec and Rust SGX SDK includes the implementation and exports it. In addition, Intel SGX SDK has APIs such as sgx_rijndael128GCM_encrypt and Rust SGX SDK re-exports them in Rust calling convention, e.g., using name rsgx_rijndael128GCM_encrypt for the above API. In

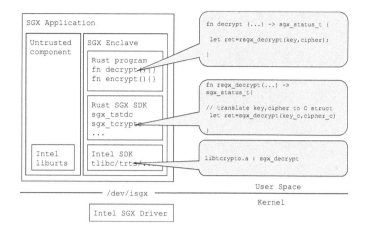

Figure 1: Overview of Rust SGX SDK

this way, Rust SGX SDK allows developers to write Rust codes in Intel SGX enclaves.

Rust SGX SDK is written in Rust using 19K SLoC. We ship it along with code samples and documents and has 44K SLoC in total.

4 SOLUTION

For the threading problem, we limit the ability of Intel SGX threading.

(1) For the enclave with BOUND TCSpolicy, our Rust SGX SDK supports TLS. Developers could write constructor function for the TLS data in Rust SGX enclave. But in the current version of Rust SGX SDK, these constructors would not be executed automatically , which means that developers need to initiate TLS data explicitly. Destructors of TLS data are unsupported in the current version. Supporting destructors and automatically destructing TLS data require re-writing the code in the untrusted part, which will be our next step.
(2) For the enclave with UNBOUND TCSpolicy, our Rust SGX SDK does not support TLS. The reason is that in such programs, every ECALL would trap into the enclave with an undetermined TCS slot. So it is impossible to support TLS in this scenario. The only way to support TLS data in UNBOUND TCSpolicy is software simulation, instead of using native TCS slot.

We also implemented Rust style park and unpark for threading control.

To support global data initiation, we have done the following:

(1) We utilize the undocumented function init_global_object provided in libsgx_trts from Intel SGX SDK. This function would retrieve the .init_array section of the enclave and initialize them during the first ECALL. It gives us the ability to initiate global data.
(2) We implemented a Rust macro init_global_object! to put data in a special section: .init_array. By using this macro, developers could put data directly into the global data section, which will be initiated during the first ECALL.

```
#[no_mangle]
pub extern "C" fn say_something(some_string: *const u8, some_len: u32) -> sgx_status_t {
    unsafe {
        ocall_print_string(some_string as *const c_uchar, some_len as size_t);
    }
    let hello_string = "This is a Rust String!";
    unsafe {
        ocall_print_string(hello_string.as_ptr() as *const c_uchar,
                           hello_string.len() as size_t);
    }
    sgx_status_t::SGX_SUCCESS
}
```

Figure 2: A helloworld enclave code sample in Rust

(3) We implemented Rust style `Once` in Rust SGX SDK by utilizing native `std::sync::atomic::AtomicPtr`. `Once` is useful in such one-time initialization.

(4) We ported a Rust crate `lazy_static` with the support of `Once`. `lazy_static` is the most easy-to-use and well adopted crate to initiate global data.

With the above supports, Rust SGX SDK offers the global data initiation elegantly.

To provide Rust style mutex, we looked into Rust's source code. We found that Rust's implementation of mutex is based on `sys::Mutex`. The primitives provided by `sys::Mutex` can be re-implemented using Intel SGX's mutex. Based on this observation, we implemented a wrapper layer to convert Intel SGX's raw mutex to Rust style raw mutex. Thus we can smoothly port Rust mutex over the wrapper layer.

To support Rust style exception handling, we redefined Rust 'panicking' and 'panic' mechanism. In Rust, throwing an exception is triggering the `panic!` macro and catching an exception requires `panic::unwind` function. Rust's `std` provides this mechanism. But in SGX, we do not have `std`, same as many embedded systems. To solve this, we provided panic handling setter `set_panic_handler` to customize panic handler, and we implemented the whole unwind mechanism to support `panic::unwind`. Developers need to customize the exception handler at first, and use `panic::unwind {..}` to handle all exceptions.

5 A RUNNING EXAMPLE

Fig. 2 shows an example of Rust code to print "Hello World" from a Rust enclave. This example is self-explained and easy to understand with basic knowledge of Rust and SGX. For more code examples, please refer to our Github repository [4].

6 FUTURE WORK

The current latest release of Rust SGX SDK is v0.2.0. In our v1.0.0 version, we plan to provide a full-fledged `sgx_tstd` library which could be used as `std` inside enclave. By leveraging this library, it is easier for developers to port third-party crates into Intel SGX. Meanwhile, we are also working on an untrusted runtime library `sgx_urts`, which enables the development of Rust code in the SGX untrusted environment as well.

REFERENCES

[1] BENCHMARKING DYNAMIC ARRAY IMPLEMENTATIONS. https://lonewolfer.wordpress.com/2014/09/24/benchmarking-dynamic-array-implementations/.
[2] Intel Software Guard Extensions SDK for Linux OS Developer Reference. https://download.01.org/intel-sgx/linux-1.9/docs/Intel_SGX_SDK_Developer_Reference_Linux_1.9_Open_Source.pdf.
[3] Redox OS. https://www.redox-os.org/.
[4] Rust SGX SDK. https://github.com/baidu/rust-sgx-sdk.
[5] Servo, the Parallel Browser Engine Project. https://servo.org/.
[6] sgx-utils. https://github.com/jethrogb/sgx-utils.
[7] S. Gueron. 2016. Memory Encryption for General-Purpose Processors. *IEEE Security Privacy* 14, 6 (Nov 2016), 54–62. https://doi.org/10.1109/MSP.2016.124
[8] Dmitrii Kuvaiskii, Oleksii Oleksenko, Sergei Arnautov, Bohdan Trach, Pramod Bhatotia, Pascal Felber, and Christof Fetzer. 2017. SGXBOUNDS: Memory Safety for Shielded Execution. In *Proceedings of the Twelfth European Conference on Computer Systems (EuroSys '17)*. ACM, New York, NY, USA, 205–221. https://doi.org/10.1145/3064176.3064192
[9] Jaehyuk Lee, Jinsoo Jang, Yeongjin Jang, Nohyun Kwak, Yeseul Choi, Changho Choi, Taesoo Kim, Marcus Peinado, and Brent ByungHoon Kang. 2017. Hacking in Darkness: Return-oriented Programming against Secure Enclaves. In *26th USENIX Security Symposium (USENIX Security 17)*. USENIX Association, Vancouver, BC, 523–539. https://www.usenix.org/conference/usenixsecurity17/technical-sessions/presentation/lee-jaehyuk
[10] Nicholas D. Matsakis and Felix S. Klock, II. 2014. The Rust Language. *Ada Lett.* 34, 3 (Oct. 2014), 103–104. https://doi.org/10.1145/2692956.2663188
[11] Jaebaek Seo, Byounyoung Lee, Seongmin Kim, Ming-Wei Shih, Insik Shin, Han, and Taesoo Kim. 2017. SGX-Shield: Enabling Address Space Layout Randomization for SGX Programs. In *Proceedings of the 2017 Annual Network and Distributed System Security Symposium (NDSS)*.
[12] Nico Weichbrodt, Anil Kurmus, Peter Pietzuch, and Rüdiger Kapitza. 2016. AsyncShock: Exploiting Synchronisation Bugs in Intel SGX Enclaves. In *European Symposium on Research in Computer Security*. Springer International Publishing, 440–457.

POSTER: Finding Vulnerabilities in P4 Programs with Assertion-based Verification

Lucas Freire, Miguel Neves, Alberto Schaeffer-Filho, Marinho Barcellos

UFRGS

{lmfreire,mcneves,alberto,marinho}@inf.ufrgs.br

ABSTRACT

Current trends in SDN extend network programmability to the data plane through the use of programming languages such as P4. In this context, the chance of introducing errors and consequently software vulnerabilities in the network increases significantly. Existing data plane verification mechanisms are unable to model P4 programs or present severe restrictions in the set of modeled properties. To overcome these limitations and make programmable data planes more secure, we present a P4 program verification technique based on assertion checking and symbolic execution. First, P4 programs are annotated with assertions expressing general correctness and security properties. Then, the annotated programs are transformed into C code and all their possible paths are symbolically executed. Results show that it is possible to prove properties in just a few seconds using the proposed technique. Moreover, we were able to uncover two potential vulnerabilities in a large scale P4 production application.

KEYWORDS

P4; Verification; Programmable Data Planes

1 INTRODUCTION

Data plane programmability allows operators to deploy new communication protocols and develop network services with agility. Through the use of programming languages such as P4, it is possible to specify in a few instructions which and how packet headers are manipulated by the different forwarding devices in the infrastructure. Despite the flexibility provided by this paradigm, the security of data plane programs is a challenge that needs to be addressed before it can be widely adopted.

If, on the one hand, P4 adds a new programming axis (the network data plane), on the other hand, it also increases the chance of introducing bugs due to incorrect protocol implementations. Such bugs can be easily transformed into vulnerabilities if exploited towards the violation of network security policies. The traditional way to overcome this problem is by checking if the network satisfies the intended properties using formal verification techniques (e.g., model checking or symbolic execution). Several mechanisms have been developed in this direction [3, 5, 6], but none of them is capable of efficiently verifying security properties of (P4) data plane programs.

With the goal of enabling the verification of general correctness and security properties in P4 programs, we propose a mechanism based on assertions and symbolic execution. First, a P4 program is annotated with assertions expressing the intended properties. The annotated program is then automatically translated into a C-based model, which is symbolically executed by an engine that traverses all its possible paths. Our mechanism can prove if a property is satisfied by verifying if any execution path in the model violates the assertions specified.

We prototyped the proposed mechanism using the KLEE symbolic engine and the reference P4 compiler provided by the *P4 Language Consortium*[1]. Results show that the proposed mechanism is capable of verifying security properties in the order of seconds for programs expressing packet processing pipelines with up to 15 tables.

2 VERIFYING P4 PROGRAMS

The P4 programming language aims at enabling the data plane programming of network devices in a simple and architecture-independent manner. A P4 program describes how incoming packet bits are parsed into headers and manipulated by actions specified in tables, which in turn are organized in pipelines described by control blocks. Figure 1 shows an example of what would be a vulnerability in a P4 program. This code snippet specifies a packet processing pipeline containing two tables (*tcp_table* and *acl_table*), invoked inside an *ingress* control block. While one would reasonably expect *acl_table* to be applied to both TCP and UDP traffic, UDP packets bypass the filtering.

```
1 control ingress() {
2   apply {
3     ...
4     if (headers.ip.nextHeader == TCP) {
5       tcp_table.apply();
6       // ACL applied over TCP traffic only
7       acl_table.apply();
8     }
9     ...
10  }
11}
```

Figure 1: An example of vulnerability in a P4 program

Assuming that the network security policy disallows this kind of practice, the program in question could be used as the starting point of many attacks. Since current verification approaches do not enable expressing and automatically verifying security properties

---

[1]p4.org

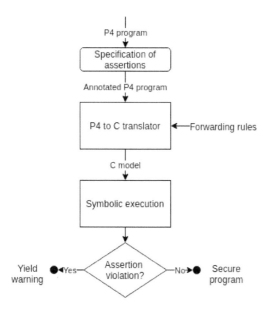

Figure 2: Control flow of the verification process.

of P4 programs, we propose a novel mechanism to identify this type of vulnerability.

Overview. The key idea consists of verifying models of the original programs annotated with assertions. Figure 2 shows the verification workflow. First, the P4 program developer or network operator annotates the code with assertions to guarantee general properties of interest. These properties can reflect a network security policy or simply represent the expected program behavior. Once annotated, a translation process takes place to automatically generate an equivalent program model using the C language. Optionally, forwarding rules can also be used as input to the translator to restrict verification to a given network configuration. The generated model is then verified by a symbolic engine, which either proves that the assertions are true for all the program execution paths, or reports assertion violations as soon as they are found. If no assertion is violated, the P4 program is considered secure regarding the analyzed properties. Otherwise, the respective violation is reported, allowing the developer or operator to correct the program.

Specifying assertions. To include assertions in a P4 program, we defined a specification language that allows the expression of properties of interest. Our language uses the code annotation mechanism available in P4 through an *assert* annotation. Each assertion a is composed of an expression e or method $m \in$ {*forward, traverse_path, constant, if, extract_header, emit_header*}. The set of methods was designed to facilitate the specification of security properties commonly required (e.g., network isolation, header integrity, information flow). Semantically, each assertion represents a boolean that should evaluate to a true or false logical value. In this sense, expressions have the same semantics as their equivalent in the P4 language, while methods have their own semantics. For example, *traverse_path* indicates if a given program section was executed, while *constant(f)* is true if the header field f is not changed during program execution.

Constructing C models. Once a P4 program is annotated, our mechanism generates an equivalent C model through a translation process. The process as a whole comprises two steps: (i) transforming the P4 program into a directed acyclic graph (DAG); and (ii) transforming the generated DAG into C code using the nodes of interest. We use C structs to model P4 headers and translate the remaining P4 structures (i.e., tables, actions, control blocks, and parsers) to multiple C functions. Each assertion type is modeled in C using a particular approach. In general, we use global boolean values initially set to false. They are assigned to true in different locations of the model depending on the semantics of the assertion used. P4 externs (i.e., device specific functionalities) can be integrated into the translator through libraries.

Symbolically executing program models. The generated C model is verified by a symbolic engine, which will traverse all possible paths in the program while treating the incoming packet headers as symbolic values. The number of execution paths is essentially given by the number of tables and actions used. Whenever a table can only be accessed under some condition (e.g., depending on some specific protocol), a new execution path is created. The same happens whenever multiple actions can be invoked by a given table.

3 EVALUATION

The main goals of our experiments are: (i) to answer if it is possible in fact to find vulnerabilities in P4 programs using the proposed mechanism, and (ii) to assess how long it takes to verify properties of interest according to different program characteristics. We have prototyped the proposed mechanism using KLEE (version 1.3.0) as the symbolic engine. To build C models, we first convert a P4 program to its JSON representation using the reference compiler provided by the *P4 Language Consortium*, then we translate the JSON model (represented as a DAG) to C code using a translator implemented specifically for this purpose. The translator source code, as well as the scripts and workloads used were made publicly available online[2]. All the experiments were performed using a linux virtual machine (kernel version 4.8.0) with one 3 GHz core and 16 GB of RAM.

3.1 Security analysis

To demonstrate the potential of the proposed verification mechanism as a defense tool against network attacks originated from vulnerabilities in P4 programs, we have selected the DC.p4 program as a case study. DC.p4 was proposed by [4], and captures the behavior of a data center switch. We have chosen this program due to its complexity (more than 2500 lines of P4 code) and representativeness of real scenarios. We have verified it with the goal of finding vulnerabilities that can be exploited by potential attacks.

Code circumvention. The first set of performed experiments is related to the verification of vulnerabilities in security functionalities implemented by the program (e.g., VLAN and ACL to provide network isolation). We verify if it is possible to circumvent any of

[2]https://github.com/ufrgs-networks-group/assert-p4

these functionalities in such a manner as to bypass the enforcement of the corresponding security policies. We used assertions using the format *if(bypass == 0, traverse_path)* to express this type of property, where *bypass == 0* indicates that the security functionality is active (i.e., it was configured by the administrator), and *traverse_path* verifies if the functionality is being executed for every possible input.

Given the program complexity, the coverage of all feasible paths takes in the order of days to finish. However, it was not necessary to traverse all paths to find assertion violations. Our verifier was capable of finding paths containing violations of the tested properties in less than 10 seconds. We have found that even though the program supports multiple options of access control lists (e.g., level 2 and 3 lists), IPv4 packets do not go through a level 2 list, which can be transformed in a vulnerability depending on the configuration adopted by the network administrator (e.g., if the administrator decides to only configure a level 2 ACL).

Traffic amplification. Some functionalities of the DC.p4 program (e.g., packet mirroring) involve replication of traffic among the device ports, being usually part of a network monitoring task. If wrongly executed, such procedures can become the source of attacks based on packet replication or traffic amplification [2]. In this regard, we verify if the replication procedures in the DC.p4 program are correctly executed. We have used assertions in the format *! (outport == original_port && constant(outport))* inside actions that replicate the traffic to express these properties. The first part of the assertion above tests if the outgoing port of the replicated packet is the same as of the original packet, whereas the second part tests if such port is changed during the replicated packet processing.

As in the previous case, our mechanism was able to find property violations quickly (less than 13 minutes). Overall, the program is general enough to allow the control plane to configure the outgoing port of both the original packet and its replica, while not applying any modification to the replica headers. Thus, it is the control plane responsibility to ensure that the device table configuration does not cause a single packet to be forwarded multiple times to the same destination, which is difficult to guarantee.

3.2 Performance

In this section, we assess how our proposed verification mechanism scales according to P4 program characteristics. To this end, we used the Whippersnapper [1] programmable data plane benchmark to synthetically generate P4 programs with different pipeline sizes (i.e., number of tables). Additionally, we tested the impact of varying the quantity of actions associated with each table. In this case, we consider a program with only two tables (with the goal of minimizing this factor in the verification time), using scripts to insert new actions.

As expected, the verification time grows exponentially to variations applied to the number of tables. Pragmatically, however, it takes around a minute to check programs containing pipelines with up to 15 tables (Figure 3(a)), which includes various existing P4 programs. We can also observe that the execution time grows polynomially with relation to varying the number of actions (Figure 3(b)). In this case, the degree of the polynomial depends on the

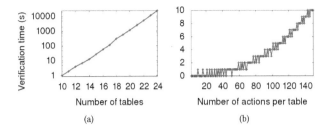

Figure 3: Performance analysis of the proposed mechanism.

quantity of tables of the P4 program (e.g., two for the tested program). In practice, given a program containing p sequential tables, where each table can invoke one among q different actions, a total of q^p distinct paths should be symbolically executed. Pragmatically, P4 programs do not usually have more than a dozen actions in each table, which makes the proposed mechanism feasible for the majority of the existing instances.

4 CONCLUSION

We presented an assertion language that can be used by P4 programmers to express correctness and security properties of a specific implementation. Our solution is more expressive than other data plane verification approaches, being the first work to allow proving properties specific to P4 source code and optionally the forwarding rules used by its tables. We evaluated our approach by proving properties of traffic replication and circumvention of security functionalities in the DC.p4 program. Its performance analysis revealed that despite the efficiency in verifying small programs, the execution time grows rapidly with relation to the number of tables and actions. Therefore, we are working to extend SymNet, a high-performance network-oriented symbolic execution engine [6], to enable the scalable modeling of P4 programs.

REFERENCES

[1] Huynh Tu Dang, Han Wang, Theo Jepsen, Gordon Brebner, Changhoon Kim, Jennifer Rexford, Robert Soulé, and Hakim Weatherspoon. 2017. Whippersnapper: A P4 Language Benchmark Suite. In *Proceedings of the Symposium on SDN Research (SOSR '17)*. ACM, New York, NY, USA, 95–101. https://doi.org/10.1145/3050220.3050231
[2] Johannes Krupp, Michael Backes, and Christian Rossow. 2016. Identifying the Scan and Attack Infrastructures Behind Amplification DDoS Attacks. In *Proceedings of the 2016 ACM SIGSAC Conference on Computer and Communications Security (CCS '16)*. ACM, New York, NY, USA, 1426–1437. https://doi.org/10.1145/2976749.2978293
[3] Nuno Lopes, Nikolaj Bjørner, Nick McKeown, Andrey Rybalchenko, Dan Talayco, and George Varghese. 2016. *Automatically verifying reachability and well-formedness in P4 Networks*. Technical Report.
[4] Anirudh Sivaraman, Changhoon Kim, Ramkumar Krishnamoorthy, Advait Dixit, and Mihai Budiu. 2015. DC.P4: Programming the Forwarding Plane of a Data-center Switch. In *Proceedings of the 1st ACM SIGCOMM Symposium on Software Defined Networking Research (SOSR '15)*. ACM, New York, NY, USA, Article 2, 8 pages. https://doi.org/10.1145/2774993.2775007
[5] Sooel Son, Seungwon Shin, Vinod Yegneswaran, Phillip Porras, and Guofei Gu. 2013. Model checking invariant security properties in OpenFlow. In *2013 IEEE International Conference on Communications (ICC)*. IEEE, 1974–1979.
[6] Radu Stoenescu, Matei Popovici, Lorina Negreanu, and Costin Raiciu. 2016. SymNet: Scalable Symbolic Execution for Modern Networks. In *Proceedings of the 2016 ACM SIGCOMM Conference (SIGCOMM '16)*. ACM, New York, NY, USA, 314–327. https://doi.org/10.1145/2934872.2934881

POSTER: Covert Channel Based on the Sequential Analysis in Android Systems*

Jun-Won Ho
Dept. of Information Security
Seoul Women's University
Seoul, South Korea
jwho@swu.ac.kr

KyungRok Won, Jee Sun Kim
Dept. of Information Security
Seoul Women's University
Seoul, South Korea
rafaelawon@swu.ac.kr,kjsrlawltjs@swu.ac.kr

ABSTRACT

Due to the wide spread of android smartphones, different types of attacks have emerged against android systems and accordingly many researches have been accomplished in the android security. In particular, a variety of covert channels have been recently developed in android systems. They are usually built up by utilizing physical media and distinct characteristics of systems in the literature. To the best of our information, however, we do not find out any research work establishing covert channels in android systems on basis of the sequential analysis, which is a kind of statistical decision theory. This is mainly because the sequential analysis has been conventionally treated as defense technique in terms of security. In contrast to this common application of the sequential analysis, we discover a new covert channel based on the sequential analysis in android systems. The key idea of newly devised covert channel is to harness the sequential analysis in order to encode (resp. decode) private information bits to (resp. from) multiple sequences of randomly selected data. Through simulation, we demonstrate that our developed covert channel works efficiently and thus it could be substantial threat to android systems.

KEYWORDS

covert channel, sequential analysis, android

1 INTRODUCTION

Covert channels are considered to be stealthy passages through which private information can be leaked from systems in concealed manner. Moreover, attacker can exploit covert channel to propagate attack control messages to malicious entities. In this sense, covert channels are substantial threat against the normal functions of systems and thus the considerable number of researches on them have been achieved in variety of systems. In particular, covert channels are harmful in android systems from the perspective that they could be used to leak private information from android smartphones and thus could menace the security of android ecosystem. In order to defend against covert channels in android systems, it is thus very

*This work was supported by the National Research Foundation of Korea (NRF) grant funded by the Korea government (MSIP) (No. 2016R1C1B1014126).

imperative to discover as many kinds of covert channels as possible that could operate in android systems. In order to fulfill this need, a diversity of covert channels have been proposed in the literature. Lalande et al. [3] proposed several android covert channels based on the task list, process priority, and screen state. Novak et al. [4] designed various android covert channels with using physical media such as ultrasound, flash, vibration, camera, speaker, and accelerometer. Qi et al. [5] exploited user behavior for covert channel establishment.

Although these related work cover covert channels based on various features of systems, user behavior, and physical media in android smartphones, they do not consider covert channels rooted on the sequential analysis. This is because the sequential analysis [7] has been prevalently used as statistical decision process and attack detection mechanism such as mobile sensor replica detection [1], port scan detection [2], and even covert channel detection [6], leading to exclusion from the stepping stones for covert channel establishment. In contrast to these conventional applications of the sequential analysis, we discover a new covert channel that harnesses the Sequential Probability Ratio Test (SPRT) in the sequential analysis [7]. For the SPRT-based covert channel, we make use of the fact that many android applications generally utilize that diverse types of variable sensory and GPS data provided by android systems. More specifically, the SPRT-based covert channel makes the SPRT encode (resp. decode) private information bits to (resp. from) multiple sequences of randomly chosen data. We believe that the SPRT-based covert channel expands the extent of possible covert channels in android systems, contributing to the research of covert channel detection. We describe the details of our newly devised covert channel and present the simulation results of it in the following sections.

2 SPRT-BASED COVERT CHANNEL ESTABLISHMENT

Most android smartphones are equipped with diverse sensors such as accelerometer, ambient light and proximity sensors, gyroscope, compass, and GPS systems. Hence, substantial number of android applications use a variety of variable sensory and GPS data from these sensors and GPS systems. For covert channel establishment, although we can use any types of variable sensory and GPS data provided by android systems, we focus on the location data consisting of latitude and longitude in this paper. This is mainly because many users make use of android applications sending location information to server in order to obtain location-related services.

Indeed, if we use a series of location data for covert channel development, it will seem to be straightforward to design covert channel in such a way that each location information is used to encode and decode a single private information bit. However, this method has the weakness that it is relatively easier to reveal the private information bits from location values than using multiple location information. To pacify this limitation, we propose the SPRT-based covert channel in which the SPRT encodes (resp. decodes) a single private information bit to (resp. from) a sequence of randomly chosen location values and thus the number of location values used for encoding and decoding processes are randomly determined, leading to being difficult to unveil private information bits from location information. Furthermore, the SPRT makes a decision with a small amount of location information and hence it will require little time to perform encoding and decoding processes. This will be considerable benefit for the attacker in the sense that the likelihood of being detected will be diminished.

How the SPRT is adapted to establish covert channel for private information transmission from a trojan android application to a trojan server is described as follows. Let us consider a trojan android application that transmits its location information to the trojan server in order to get the location-related services. We first assume that trojan app owns private information leaked from android systems. We also assume that the attacker can obfuscate this trojan app to avoid the static analysis detection and can install the obfuscated version of trojan app in android smartphone. This assumption is achievable because the attacker can develop his own obfuscation mechanism for the evasion from static analysis detection. Moreover, we assume that trojan app employs random selection process of location information periodically obtained from android systems. In this process, trojan app sends its location information to the trojan server with a certain probability. This assumption is reasonable in the sense that trojan app users will not likely have difficulty in acquiring seamless location-related services as long as the time period for location information collection is maintained as reasonably small. Additionally, this random selection strategy has advantage of reducing communication costs incurred by location information transmission to the trojan server.

2.1 Encoding Private Information Bits

Let us first consider the encoding process for a private information bit. When obtaining the first pair of latitude and longitude (A_1, O_1), trojan app accepts (A_1, O_1). Each time obtaining a pair of latitude and longitude (A_i, O_i) $(i \geq 2)$, trojan app performs *random location selection process* in the following manner. If trojan app wishes to encode private information bit 1 and both $|A_i - A_{i-1}| \geq \delta_a$ and $|O_i - O_{i-1}| \geq \delta_o$ hold, it selects (A_i, O_i) with probability p_s $(p_s > 0.5)$, where δ_a and δ_o are pre-configured thresholds. If trojan app wishes to encode a private information bit 0 and both $|A_i - A_{i-1}| \geq \delta_a$ and $|O_i - O_{i-1}| \geq \delta_o$ do not hold, it selects (A_i, O_i) with probability p_s. If all of the above two conditions do not hold, it selects (A_i, O_i) with probability p_u $(p_u < 0.5)$.

Trojan app performs the SPRT with only pairs (A_k, O_k) and (A_{k+1}, O_{k+1}) that are chosen by random location selection process $(k \geq 1)$. We first define the kth sample D_k as a Bernoulli random variable such that $D_k = 1$ if $|A_{k+1} - A_k| \geq \delta_a$ and $|O_{k+1} - O_k| \geq \delta_o$ hold. Otherwise, $D_k = 0$. Given the success probability c of the Bernoulli distribution, $c = \Pr(D_k = 1) = 1 - \Pr(D_k = 0)$ holds. In

the SPRT, null hypothesis (H_0) indicates that the value of private information bit is 0 and alternate hypothesis (H_1) indicates that the value of private information bit is 1. Under these definitions of H_0 and H_1, we preconfigure c_0 and c_1 ($c_0 < c_1$) such that the likelihood of H_0 (resp. H_1) acceptance increases if $c \leq c_0$ (resp. $c \geq c_1$) holds.

By the definition of the SPRT [7], given a sequence of $D_1, \ldots, D_j$ ($j \geq 1$), the log-probability ratio Q_j on j samples is given by

$$Q_j = \ln \frac{\Pr(D_1, \ldots, D_j | H_1)}{\Pr(D_1, \ldots, D_j | H_0)}$$

In the sense that location information provided by android systems is usually independent of each other, it is reasonable that D_k is assumed to be independent and identically distributed. Under the i.i.d. assumption, we define E_j as the number of times that $D_k = 1$ in the j samples. We also denote α' (resp. β') as a false positive rate (resp. a false negative rate) that is configured by user. If trojan app wants to encode private information bit 1 and $E_j \geq \frac{\ln \frac{1-\beta'}{\alpha'} + j \ln \frac{1-c_0}{1-c_1}}{\ln \frac{c_1}{c_0} - \ln \frac{1-c_1}{1-c_0}}$ holds, the SPRT accepts H_1 and thus encoding private information bit 1 is completed. If trojan app wants to encode private information bit 0 and $E_j \leq \frac{\ln \frac{\beta'}{1-\alpha'} + j \ln \frac{1-c_0}{1-c_1}}{\ln \frac{c_1}{c_0} - \ln \frac{1-c_1}{1-c_0}}$ holds, the SPRT accepts H_0 and thus encoding private information bit 0 is completed.

If trojan app wants to encode private information bit 1 (resp. 0) and $E_j \leq \frac{\ln \frac{\beta'}{1-\alpha'} + j \ln \frac{1-c_0}{1-c_1}}{\ln \frac{c_1}{c_0} - \ln \frac{1-c_1}{1-c_0}}$ (resp. $E_j \geq \frac{\ln \frac{1-\beta'}{\alpha'} + j \ln \frac{1-c_0}{1-c_1}}{\ln \frac{c_1}{c_0} - \ln \frac{1-c_1}{1-c_0}}$) holds, the j th sample is revoked from the SPRT and the SPRT proceeds with new samples. Additionally, the pair of latitude and longitude (A_{j+1}, O_{j+1}) contributing to the jth sample is removed from the random location selection process. The rational behind the exclusion of the jth sample in this case is to prevent private information bit from being incorrectly encoded. If all of the above three conditions do not hold, the SPRT goes on with new samples. The above encoding process is repeatedly applied to a series of private information bits.

During the encoding process, trojan app sends the pairs of latitude and longitude, which are chosen from random location selection process and are fed into the SPRT, to trojan server.

2.2 Decoding Private Information Bits

Each time receiving the pairs of latitude and longitude from trojan app, trojan server decodes private information bits by performing the SPRT on these pairs of latitude and longitude in accordance with the same configuration parameter values, sampling method, and i.i.d assumption as used in the encoding process. If $E_j \geq \frac{\ln \frac{1-\beta'}{\alpha'} + j \ln \frac{1-c_0}{1-c_1}}{\ln \frac{c_1}{c_0} - \ln \frac{1-c_1}{1-c_0}}$ holds, the SPRT accepts H_1 and thus decoding private information bit 1 is completed. If $E_j \leq \frac{\ln \frac{\beta'}{1-\alpha'} + j \ln \frac{1-c_0}{1-c_1}}{\ln \frac{c_1}{c_0} - \ln \frac{1-c_1}{1-c_0}}$ holds, the SPRT accepts H_0 and thus decoding private information bit 0 is completed. If all of the above two conditions do not hold, the SPRT goes on with new samples.

3 SIMULATION STUDY

For the evaluation of our newly proposed covert channel, we write a simple simulation program to emulate the SPRT-based covert

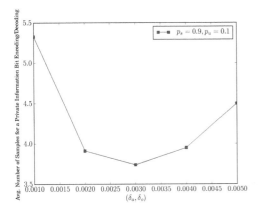

Figure 1: Average number of samples required to encode/decode a private information bit while (δ_a, δ_o) is changed from 0.001 to 0.005.

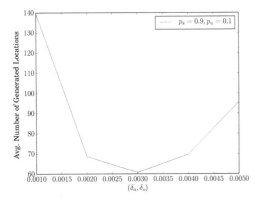

Figure 2: Average number of locations generated per simulation run while (δ_a, δ_o) is changed from 0.001 to 0.005.

channel establishment between trojan app and trojan server. Specifically, the latitude and longitude of trojan app are initially set to 35.0 degree north and 127.0 degree east, respectively. These initial settings represent the latitude and longitude of some area in South Korea. We select a range value uniformly at random in [0, 0.01]. The next pair of latitude and longitude is computed by adding the range value to the current pair of latitude and longitude or subtracting it from the current pair of latitude and longitude. Decision on whether to add or subtract is randomly done. We repeat this process to generate a series of pairs of latitude and longitude. We perform random location selection process and the SPRT with each pair of latitude and longitude.

In simulation program, we set $p_s = 0.9$ and $p_u = 0.1$. We also configure $\alpha' = \beta' = 0.01$ and $c_0 = 0.1$ and $c_1 = 0.9$. The number of private information bits to encode is set to 8 and the value of each private information bit is randomly determined. In addition, we have five distinct configurations of $\delta_a = \delta_o$ ranging from 0.001 to 0.005 in an increase of 0.001. We report the average results of 1000 simulation runs.

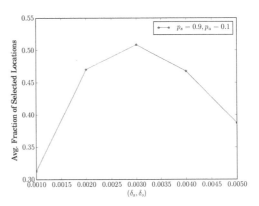

Figure 3: Average fraction of locations selected for the SPRT while (δ_a, δ_o) is changed from 0.001 to 0.005.

As displayed in Figure 1, we perceive that the number of samples required for a private information bit encoding/decoding is below 5.33 on an average in all five configurations of (δ_a, δ_o). This means that a few number of location values are sufficient to encode/decode a private information bit, leading to fast private information bit transmission to trojan server and fast private information bit interpretation in trojan server. As shown in Figures 2 and 3, when $\delta_a = \delta_o = 0.003$, an average number of generated locations and an average fraction of selected locations reaches its minimum and maximum in all five configurations of (δ_a, δ_o), respectively. We infer from this observation that the higher fraction of selected locations contributes to the lower number of generated locations. Moreover, we also see that an average number of samples for a private information bit encoding/decoding reaches its minimum when $\delta_a = \delta_o = 0.003$. This observation signifies that an increase in average fraction of selected locations likely leads to a decrease in average number of samples for a private information bit encoding/decoding.

REFERENCES

[1] Jun-Won Ho, Matthew K. Wright, and Sajal K. Das. 2011. Fast Detection of Mobile Replica Node Attacks in Wireless Sensor Networks Using Sequential Hypothesis Testing. *IEEE Trans. Mob. Comput.* 10, 6 (2011), 767–782.
[2] J. Jung, V. Paxon, A.W. Berger, and H. Balakrishnan. 2004. Fast Portscan Detection Using Sequential Hypothesis Testing. In *IEEE Symp. Security and Privacy.* 211–225.
[3] Jean-François Lalande and Steffen Wendzel. 2013. Hiding Privacy Leaks in Android Applications Using Low-Attention Raising Covert Channels. In *2013 International Conference on Availability, Reliability and Security, ARES 2013, Regensburg, Germany, September 2-6, 2013.* 701–710. https://doi.org/10.1109/ARES.2013.92
[4] Edmund Novak, Yutao Tang, Zijiang Hao, Qun Li, and Yifan Zhang. 2015. Physical media covert channels on smart mobile devices. In *Proceedings of the 2015 ACM International Joint Conference on Pervasive and Ubiquitous Computing, UbiComp 2015, Osaka, Japan, September 7-11, 2015.* 367–378. https://doi.org/10.1145/2750858.2804253
[5] Wen Qi, Yichen Xu, Wanfu Ding, Yonghang Jiang, Jianping Wang, and Kejie Lu. 2015. Privacy Leaks When You Play Games: A Novel User-Behavior-Based Covert Channel on Smartphones. In *23rd IEEE International Conference on Network Protocols, ICNP 2015, San Francisco, CA, USA, November 10-13, 2015.* 201–211. https://doi.org/10.1109/ICNP.2015.40
[6] K. P. Subbalakshmi, Rajarathnam Chandramouli, and Nagarajan Ranganathan. 2007. A Sequential Distinguisher for Covert Channel Identification. *International Journal of Network Security* 5, 3 (November 2007), 274–282.
[7] A. Wald. 2004. *Sequential Analysis.* Dover Publications.

POSTER: Why Are You Going That Way? Measuring Unnecessary Exposure of Network Traffic to Nation States

Jordan Holland

University of Tennessee
jholla19@vols.utk.edu

Max Schuchard

University of Tennessee
mschucha@utk.edu

ABSTRACT

In this work, we examine to what extent the Internet's routing infrastructure needlessly exposes network traffic to nations *geographically* irrelevant to packet transmission. We quantify what countries are *geographically logical* to see on a network path traveling between two nations through the use of convex hulls circumscribing major population centers, and then compare that to the nation states observed in utilized paths. Our preliminary results show that the majority of paths, 52%, unnecessarily expose traffic to at least one nation. We also explore which nation states are disproportionately allowed to observe and manipulate a larger fraction of Internet traffic than they otherwise should.

1 INTRODUCTION

The Internet is comprised of independent networks called Autonomous Systems (ASes), which depend on each other for inter-network connectivity. Network traffic must often traverse multiple ASes in order to reach its final destination. Any adversarial transit AS situated between sender and receiver can degrade network availability, violate data integrity, and undermine confidentiality and anonymity properties. We term such an adversary a *path based adversary*. However, a more powerful class of adversary also exists, **the nation states where the utilized network infrastructure is physically located**. Revelations in recent years about the extent to which countries such as the United States, Great Britain, and other members of the so called Five Eyes intelligence alliance have integrated dragnet surveillance into core Internet transit links that reside within their borders [4] only underscores the importance of understanding such nation state level path based adversaries.

Inter-domain routing decisions, which are made at the AS level, typically result in paths that generally expose traffic to as few ASes as possible, and reduces the capability of any one AS level path based adversary. However, a path that *appears* low risk, spanning only a single transit AS, might actually involve a large number of nation states in the process of traversing that lone AS. This means that network traffic is exposed to potentially a much broader collection of actors than the AS level path suggests. Additionally, since inter-AS routing focuses on the *logical* topology rather than the *geographic* topology, routing decisions can result in exposing traffic to nations which do not lie between the geographic locations of the sender and receiver. This additional exposure to nations not necessary for transmission of data needlessly increases the power of nation state level path based adversaries.

In this work, we examine to what extent the Internet's routing infrastructure exposes network traffic to nations that do not lie along the *geographically logical* path between sender and receiver. In order to do this, we must first quantify what countries we *geographically expect* to see on a network path traveling between two nations. We accomplish this by establishing which nations reside inside of the population biased convex hull between two countries. When then compare the set of nation states data actually traverses by examining traceroutes conducted on the RIPE Atlas [5] measurement infrastructure. We present preliminary results of what fraction of paths contain nations unnecessary to the transmission of data between source and destination, finding that more than 52% of tested paths involved at least one extraneous nation. We also explore which nation states are the benefactors of these "bad" (in the geographic sense) paths, allowing them to observe and manipulate a larger fraction of Internet traffic than they otherwise should.

2 APPROACH

Our goal is to accurately measure the fraction of paths which do not expose their traffic to nations not required for the actual transmission of data. To do this we first must establish a set of expected countries traffic could be exposed to during transit between a particular source/destination pair, what we term *geographically normal* or simply *normal*. After establishing this, we can then compare the normal set to the observed set of countries traffic is *actually* exposed to.

Defining the normal path from one country to another was done using the *convex hull* between a set of points that define the country containing the source and a set of points that define the country containing the destination. The *convex hull* of a set of points S in n dimensions is the intersection of all convex sets containing S. For N points $p1, ..., pN$, the convex hull C is then given by the expression:

$$C = \sum_{j=1}^{N} \lambda_j \rho_j : \lambda_j \geq 0 \ \forall j \ and \ \sum_{j=1}^{N} \lambda_j = 1 \qquad (1)$$

CCS '17, October 30-November 3, 2017, Dallas, TX, USA
© 2017 Copyright held by the owner/author(s).
ACM ISBN 978-1-4503-4946-8/17/10.
https://doi.org/10.1145/3133956.3138842

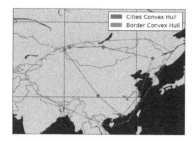

Figure 1: A comparison of the border based convex hull and population biased convex hull between China and Mongolia. Note that over 83% of China's population lives on its eastern coast.

Using the definition of a convex hull allowed us to mathematically define and generate a "normal" path between two countries given two sets of points that define the countries. A more intuitive way to think about the definition of a convex hull is: given a set of points, what is the shape a stretched rubber band takes when encompassing all of them.

One option for defining the set of points that make up a country is to utilize the nation's political borders. In order to accomplish this, we utilized shapefiles which contain points that define polygons of the actual borders of each country. However, the political borders of a country does not necessarily reflect where bulk the Internet infrastructure of the country is located; as this generally lies in the more populated areas. To address, this we built a separate definition of each country using the latitude and longitude of the top 15 most populous cities in each country [3].

Figure 1 shows an example of the two construction techniques for the path between China and Mongolia. The population based convex hull results in a stricter version of a normal path between two countries and accurately reflects the fact that 83% of China's population, including all of its major cities, reside in the eastern portion of the country. The border based convex hull includes countries in the wrong cardinal direction, such as India and Vietnam, a result of China's concave shape. We chose to use the city based construction of a convex hull for the measurements contained inside this work. For each pair of countries, we build the set of expected nations on paths between the two countries by building the convex hull between them, taking into account the spherical nature of the Earth, and enumerating all nations that either partially or completely reside inside the convex hull.

Establishing the utilized path from one IP address to another was achieved using Ripe Atlas traceroutes data [5] from March 2016 to April 2017. In order to expand the number of source/destination pairs, we inferred the path from each hop contained in the traceroute to the destination, rather than simply that of the originating node. The result was a data set of over 26 million different paths to test against our definitions of normal. Each IP address in the path was mapped back to the country and AS it was located. The correct country was done using the geolite IP geolocation database [2], while the accuracy of geolocation is at times limited in its precision, it has been show to be accurate at a country level [6]. To build

the mapping between IP address and owning AS, we consulted routing tables from the CAIDA infrastructure [1]. Using this information we parsed our IP level paths into AS/Nation State tuples and compressed repeated instances of the same tuple down to a single instance. Establishing if a path was considered **normal** was achieved with simple set comparison between the expected set of nations and the set of observed nations.

3 RESULTS

All together, we examined over 26,000,000 traceroute paths involving 77,187 different ASes and 249 different countries. As a metric of normalcy, we have defined **degree of normality (DoN)** as:

$$DoN = \frac{total\ "normal\ paths"\ seen}{total\ paths\ seen} \tag{2}$$

Over the entirety of the paths we examined, the total DoN was .473. Additionally, figure 2a shows that as the length of a path grows, the DoN immediately drops below .5, and continues to degrade as the path length grows.

We split the overall summary of DoN into three levels: AS, country, and regional. Additionally, we split scenarios for AS and country levels into the following based on if the entity is: the data source, the destination, neither the source or destination (a transit entity), and all three. At the AS level, figure 2b shows that in general, the DoN for paths transiting most ASes and starting in most ASes follow the same curve. However, the curve for paths to ASes demonstrates a trend of higher DoN, suggesting that a minority of the destinations, by AS, contribute to poor DoN. When examining the paths at a country level, we see the same trends as at the AS level. The curves for seeing a country in a path, a country transiting data, and beginning from a country all almost mirror each other. Following the AS level data, the curve for paths to countries is shifted right, suggesting that many countries are more difficult to get to while staying inside our defined normal path. Further examination needs to be done to determine if many of the ASes that have a low DoN coincide with the countries that have a low DoN.

We see in Table 1 that certain regions have better Degree of Normality when the path is to them than from them. For instance, the Americas have a higher than average DoN when the path ends or starts there, but a much lower DoN when they are found transiting a traceroutes message. Part of this could be explained by the smaller number of countries in the Americas, particularly North America. When having more adjacent countries, such as in Europe, there are more choices of countries to route through, and could naturally bring down the DoN for the region.

Table 1: Regional Degree of Normality

	Africa	Americas	Asia	Europe	Oceania
DoN From	.2003	.6214	.2933	.4853	.2817
DoN To	.2057	.6348	.2399	.4756	.2035
DoN Transit	.1799	.2849	.1666	.3806	.1507
DoN In	.1937	.3565	.2319	.4484	.2062

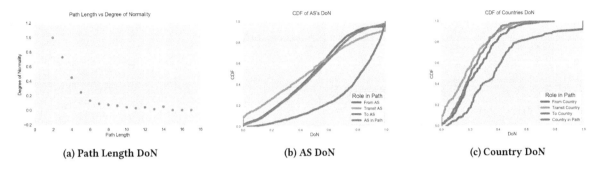

(a) Path Length DoN   (b) AS DoN   (c) Country DoN

Figure 2: Examining DoN at different levels

Table 2: Region to Region Degree of Normality

To \ From	Africa	Americas	Asia	Europe	Oceania
Africa	.4491	.3536	.0821	.1861	.0337
Americas	.2354	.7756	.4383	.6411	.4666
Asia	.0834	.3733	.3159	.2065	.1476
Europe	.1970	.6042	.2547	.5061	.1417
Oceania	.0420	.2265	.1554	.0550	.8477

Table 2 examines DoN on a region to region basis. When staying inside a region, all but Africa and Asia have above the overall average DoN. Interestingly, a traceroute traveling from Europe to the Americas has a better chance of following a normal path than a path staying inside Europe. Table 2 also shows that the DoN from one region to another is highly symmetrical; the DoN traversing *from* region 1 to region 2 is typically close to the DoN when traversing from region 2 *to* region 1.

Finally, we present a case study of one of the most interesting countries in our measurements: the United States. Of the over 26,000,000 examined paths, the United States showed up in roughly 52% of them, with a DoN of .345, well below the overall average of .473. However, paths *to* the United States have an average DoN of .725. This discrepancy in the degree of normality between the paths it is found *in* and the paths *ending there* can be found when examining who benefits from "bad" paths the most, shown in figure 3. The United states is the largest benefactor in seeing data it should not, showing up 6,796,688 paths that it should not have been in. Further examining this trend, we see in Table 3 that the US shows up in many European countries paths that it should not, but encompasses all regions when looking at the top 9 countries it benefits from the most. This is made more confusing given that paths contributing to this will transit across the Atlantic, to the United States, and then return back across the Atlantic to Europe.

Future Work In the future, we plan to expand our measurements to look at countries that see temporary, but marked, changes in their DoN, and attempt to establish the root cause of such changes. We are interested in examining if adversarial actions could result in a temporarily reduced DoN for nations, or if particular nations could inordinately benefit from adversarial reductions in DoN. Lastly, we wish to examine if nations can adjust their routing policies in an

Table 3: Countries the United States Benefits from Most

Country	Number of Paths Ruined
Great Britain	695,534
Denmark	513,468
France	457,116
Australia	272,705
Netherlands	271,090
Russia	266,742
Japan	235,016
Italy	219,951
Spain	208,898

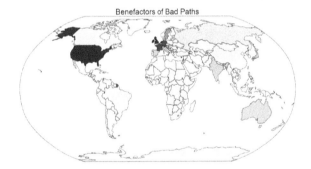

Figure 3: A visual representation of who benefits the most from "bad" paths

effort to increase their DoN, effectively reducing their exposure to nation state level path adversaries.

REFERENCES

[1] CAIDA AS relationship dataset.   http://www.caida.org/data/active/as-relationships/index.xml.
[2] Geolite database. https://dev.maxmind.com/geoip/legacy/geolite/.
[3] The geonames database. http://download.geonames.org/export/dump/.
[4] The NSA uses powerful toolbox in effort to spy on global networks.   http://www.spiegel.de/international/world/the-nsa-uses-powerful-toolbox-in-effort-to-spy-on-global-networks-a-940969.html.
[5] The ripe atlas dataset. https://atlas.ripe.net/.
[6] Y. Shavitt and N. Zilberman. A geolocation databases study. *IEEE Journal on Selected Areas in Communications*, 29(10):2044–2056, 2011.

POSTER: PriReMat: A Distributed Tool for Privacy Preserving Record Linking in Healthcare

Diptendu Mohan Kar
Colorado State University
Diptendu.Kar@colostate.edu

Ibrahim Lazrig
Colorado State University
Ibrahim.Lazrig@colostate.edu

Indrajit Ray
Colorado State University
Indrajit.Ray@colostate.edu

Indrakshi Ray
Colorado State University
Indrakshi.Ray@colostate.edu

ABSTRACT

Medical institutions must comply with various federal and state policies when they share sensitive medical data with others. Traditionally, such sharing is performed by sanitizing the identifying information from individual records. However, such sanitization removes the ability to later link the records belonging to the same patient across multiple institutions which is essential for medical cohort discovery. Currently, human honest brokers assume stewardship of non sanitized data and manually facilitate such cohort discovery. However, this is slow and prone to error, not to mention that any compromise of the honest broker breaks the system. In this work, we describe PriReMat, a toolset that we have developed for privacy preserving record linkage. The underlying protocol is based on strong security primitives that we had presented earlier. This work describes the distributed implementation over untrusted machines and networks.

1 INTRODUCTION

PriReMat is a distributed application to perform privacy preserving record linkage in the healthcare area. The distributed application is executed by a group of healthcare providers who are ready to share (or publish) patient related data and a group of healthcare researchers (subscribers) that have the need for the data minus the personally identifying information in the data but need the ability to link records belonging to the same patient. PriReMat uses a semi-trusted third party to facilitate the record linkage. The role of the third party is to automatically and blindly perform record matching on encrypted data. The third party is honest in the sense that it follows the protocol correctly but is not trusted to keep a secret, secret. It is curious about the sensitive information contained in individual records. However, PriReMat ensures that it is prevented from getting any useful information without colluding with publishers. PriReMat is based on our earlier work that is described in [6]. We also identified a security weakness in our earlier work, which we fix in PriReMat.

CCS '17, October 30-November 3, 2017, Dallas, TX, USA
© 2017 Copyright held by the owner/author(s).
ACM ISBN 978-1-4503-4946-8/17/10.
https://doi.org/10.1145/3133956.3138845

PriReMat is implemented using Oracle's Java^{TM} technology. We used the following packages from the Java Development Kit (JDK) 1.8.0131: *java.io, java.math, java.net, java.sql, java.util.* The MySQL database management system acts as the data source. The three major components of PriReMat namely, the *Broker, Publisher, and Subscriber* are independent of each other and coordinate via passing messages. When distributed over a network, any host on the network can function as any one of the three components. The databases for the broker and publisher needs to be configured during installation. The publishers and the subscribers need to execute some protocol to know the IP address of the broker.

In this implementation, we use the El-Gamal cryptosystem along with its multiplicative homomorphic property. Although there are several APIs available for the El-Gamal cryptosystem, none of them that we could identify implement the homomorphic property. As a result, the entire cryptosystem had to be designed from scratch to include this property. We plan to release this new API to the public domain via Github so that others may benefit from our implementation.

2 RELATED WORK

Privacy preserving data sharing has been a well-studied problem, particularly in the context of sharing information from databases controlled by multiple parties. In our setting, the challenge is that competing publishers who are not ready to reveal any information about their data to each other but nonetheless would like to anonymously and securely share some information with the subscriber. In addition, the subscriber is not only interested in querying their data separately, but across jointly in order to find connected records across the databases. Furthermore, the subscriber wants to be able to retrieve updates about some previously queried entities – a requirement that we call retrospective queries.

Searchable encryption schemes where the data to be joined must be encrypted under same key (such as [2, 7, 8], cannot directly be applied to our scenario. On the other hand, private set intersection [4, 5] and multi-party computation are potential solutions but are not very efficient for large settings. Yin and Yau [9] propose a privacy preserving repository for data integration across data sharing services that allow owners to specify integration requirements and data sharing services to safeguard their privacy. However, the scheme requires a mandatory secret sharing between competing parties and is not acceptable under our setup. A similar problem occurs with the scheme proposed by Carbunar and Sion [1]. Chow et al.'s proposed protocol [3], called Two-Party Query computation, has limited applicability to our scenario since it does not support retrospective queries.

3 PRIREMAT SCHEME CONSTRUCTION

Our scheme works in three phases: the *setup* phase, the *encryption of query results* phase, and the *secure record matching* phase. We briefly describe the phases here. The interested reader is referred to [6] for further details.

Setup: The setup phase generates the publishers' key converters that allow the broker to transform an encrypted data into another encrypted data with a different key without first decrypting it. A publisher collaborates with other publisher's to generate its key converter. When a publisher joins a group for the first time, it goes through the setup phase. An existing publisher also needs to participate in the setup phase, if a refreshing of keys is required when new publishers join the system. These key converters are delegated to the third party (broker) and are used to convert records encrypted under different keys of different publishers, to records encrypted under a common key. This common key is such that it cannot be reconstructed by any of the parties, namely, individual publishers, broker and subscribers without collusion.

We use the ElGamal homomorphic cryptosystem that supports product operations over the encrypted keys. At the end of this phase, every publisher is associated with a special key converter that allows the broker to perform the matching process.

Encryption of query results: This phase is triggered by a query sent by a subscriber requesting information from publishers. This represents a *data pull* model; however, our scheme can be also used in a *data push* mode where publishers send data directly to the broker, which then redirects the data to the corresponding subscribers. After executing the query, each publisher encrypts the identifying parts of the query results using a cryptosystem that relies on the DDH (Decisional Diffie-Hellman) or DL (Discrete Logarithm) hardness assumptions, such as the ElGamal cryptosystem.

Finally, each record is composed of the encrypted identification part, plus, the other client's information. The data in plaintext in each record will be sanitized if necessary, according to the publisher's policy, before being sent to the broker. Sanitizing techniques details are out of the scope of this work.

Secured Record Matching: The broker receives the encrypted identifiers with different keys from different publishers. The broker's job is to merge similar clients' records from different publishers such that they will map to the same newly generated identifier. The broker will use the key converters form each publisher to change the encryption key in such a way that similar data will be deterministically encrypted with the same key without requiring any decryption to be performed along the way.

In order to maintain the linkages between publishers' data records and the randomly generated identifiers for subscribers, the broker keeps track of the processed identifiers for both flows, i.e., from publishers to subscribers and vice versa. The aim of this mapping is two folds: first, we do not want to give the ability to the subscribers to know whether they share the same client and second give the ability to the broker to map back these random values to the same client.

4 ADDRESSING SECURITY WEAKNESS OF EARLIER WORK

Our previous work [6] had a security weakness: After the completion of the setup phase, each publisher has their individual "key-converter" and "encryption key". This "key-converter" and "encryption key" does not change for each of the associated publishers unless the setup phase is executed again. This implies that if the same records are requested by the subscriber, again and again, the broker can infer this by studying the incoming encrypted records from the publisher. We eliminate this PriReMat by utilizing an additional step in the encryption of query results phase. After the completion of setup phase, when any publisher receives a query via the broker, it chooses a new random number r_{new}, encrypts it with the broker's public key and homomorphically multiplies with its existing "key-converter". Also, the publisher computes the modulo inverse of r_{new}, r_{new}^{-1} and homomorphically multiplies with the existing "encryption key". This additional step ensures that even the same record when fetched more than once will result in a different cipher text but still the common records can be determined.

5 IMPLEMENTATION

PriReMat is implemented as three independently executing components. *Broker, Publisher, and Subscriber*. In a given setup, we assume that there can be only one instance of the Broker application running. However, there can be multiple instances of the Publisher and Subscriber components. Each instance of a component executes as a multi-threaded process. Also, we assume that the databases used by the publishers and the subscribers have the same schema. PriReMat uses MySQL for these databases. Any one or all of the three components can be distributed over a network. All communications between these components are of the form of "events" and are comprised of different message types. The broker is provided a port number on which it listens for all incoming requests. A listener thread runs on that port and upon receiving a request it is passed on to another thread which processes the request depending on its type. The publisher and the subscriber need to provide the IP address and the port number of the broker to connect and register with it.

When a publisher or subscriber connects using the broker's IP address and port, a registration request is sent to the broker and upon successful registration, the broker sends a registration response with a success message and the next ID from a list of sequentially increasing ID numbers for the publishers and subscribers. The broker keeps a list of all publishers and subscribers that it is presently connected to by maintaining a database with their IP address and listening port number and ID numbers. The publisher and the subscriber when connecting chooses a randomly available port and runs a listener thread on that port. This port information is shared with the broker during registration so that the broker is able to send messages to this port. When any message is received by the publisher or subscriber on its listening port, it passes the request to another thread which then processes it depending on its type.

As soon as there are two registered publishers, the broker generates a list ("PublisherNeighborOverlay") which contains information about a publisher and its downstream publisher (next higher ID). This information is sent to each publisher at the initiation of the setup phase. Whenever a new publisher joins the system or an existing publisher leaves the system this "PublisherNeighborOverlay" list is updated. In our implementation, the setup phase is triggered by the broker as soon as there are two registered publishers. Whenever any new publisher joins or any existing publisher leaves, the setup phase is re-invoked.

During the setup phase, the broker sends a setup initiate request to each of the active publishers and shares its cryptographic primitives - *prime, generator, and public key* and also the neighbor information. Each publisher after its designated task creates a setup forward request and forwards the result to its neighbor. The setup forward message contains an origin field and a traversed nodes field. When the setup forward message returns to the originating publisher, it compares the origin and the traversed nodes information to infer that its key-converter has been created. It then sends a setup completed message to the broker and stores the key-converter. A sequence diagram of the setup phase is described below.

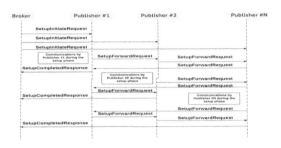

Figure 1: Setup phase sequence diagram

When the subscriber sends a query to the broker to fetch records, the broker computes the list of the publishers ("QueriedPublishersList") from which the records needs to be fetched and forwards the query to the respective publishers. The publishers after encrypting the records with their own encryption key send the result back to the broker along with their key-converter. The publishers also send an acknowledgment message to the broker notifying that it has completed sending all the records. The broker upon receiving the encrypted records from each publisher, re-encrypts them with their provided key-converter. When the broker receives all the acknowledgment messages, it compares the source with the list of all the publishers it had sent the request to. When all of the publishers have finished sending their records, the broker compares the re-encrypted records for any common record and sends the result to the subscriber. The broker keeps a mapping between the encrypted records received from each publisher and the re-encrypted record. The publishers also keep a mapping between the original record and the encrypted record. A sequence diagram of phase 2 and 3 together is described below.

When the subscriber needs to look-up more information about any record (retrospective query), it provides the re-encrypted ID to the broker. The broker from its mapping table finds the received record ID and the publisher associated with it and sends a request to those publishers. The publishers also contain their mapping table and from there each publisher finds the exact record requested and sends the requested information back to the broker which it then forwards to the subscriber.

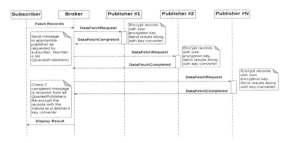

Figure 2: Phase 2 and 3 sequence diagram

6 ACKNOWLEDGEMENT

This work was partially supported by the U.S. NSF CNS under Grant No. 1650573, by the NIST under Grant No. 60NANB16D250, University of Colorado Anschutz Medical Center, CableLabs, Furuno Electric Company and SecureNok.

7 CONCLUSIONS

This work describes PriReMat, a software that we have developed for performing privacy preserving record linkage in the healthcare sector without using manually participating honest brokers. The work is based on our earlier work [6] and addresses a certain weakness in that work. PriReMat is a completely distributed application that can be ported easily to any architecture and OS supporting the Java technology. Different components of the application have been implemented as multithreaded processes. A secondary contribution of this work is the development of an API for the El-Gamal cryptosystem that enables the use of the multiplicative homomorphic property of this cryptosystem. We have tested this system on synthetic datasets and are currently working with the Anschutz Medical Center of the University of Colorado, Denver to field test it on live data.

REFERENCES

[1] B. Carbunar and R. Sion. 2012. Toward private joins on outsourced data. *Knowledge and Data Engineering, IEEE Transactions on* 24 (2012), 1699–1710.
[2] M. Chase and S Kamara. 2010. Structured encryption and controlled disclosure. In *Proceedings of the 16th International Conference on the Theory and Application of Cryptology and Information Security.* Singapore, 577–594.
[3] S. S. Chow, J. H. Lee, and L. Subramanian. 2009. Two-party computation model for privacy- preserving queries over distributed databases. In *Proceedings of the 2009 Network and Distributed System Security Symposium.* San Diego, CA, USA.
[4] D. Dachman-Soled, T. Malkin, M. Raykova, and M. Yung. 2012. Effcient robust private set intersection. *International Journal of Applied Cryptography* 2 (2012), 289–303.
[5] S. Kamara, P. Mohassel, M. Raykova, and S. Sadeghian. 2013. *Scaling private set inter- section to billion-element sets.* Technical Report. MSR-TR-2013-63.
[6] Ibrahim Lazrig, Tarik Moataz, Indrajit Ray, Indrakshi Ray, Toan Ong, Michael G. Kahn, Frédéric Cuppens, and Nora Cuppens-Boulahia. 2015. Privacy Preserving Record Matching Using Automated Semi-trusted Broker., In Proceedings of the 29th IFIP TC 11, WG 11.3 Conference on Data and Applications Security and Privacy. *DBSec* 9149 (2015), 103–118.
[7] E. Stefanov, M. van Dijk, E. Shi, C. W. Fletcher, L. Ren, X. Yu, and S. Devadas. 2013. Path ORAM: an extremely simple oblivious RAM protocol. In *ACM Conference on Computer and Communications Security.* 299–310.
[8] M. Strizhov and I. Ray. 2014. Multi-keyword similarity search over encrypted cloud data. In *Proceedings of 29th IFIP TC 11 International Conference, Marrakech, Morocco.* 52–65.
[9] S. Yau and Y. Yin. 2008. A privacy preserving repository for data integration across data sharing services. *Services Computing, IEEE Transactions on* 1 (2008), 130–140.

POSTER: AFL-based Fuzzing for Java with Kelinci*

Rody Kersten
Carnegie Mellon University Silicon
Valley
Moffett Field, California
rody.kersten@sv.cmu.edu

Kasper Luckow
Carnegie Mellon University Silicon
Valley
Moffett Field, California
kasper.luckow@sv.cmu.edu

Corina S. Păsăreanu
Carnegie Mellon University Silicon
Valley
NASA Ames Research Center
Moffett Field, California
corina.pasareanu@sv.cmu.edu

ABSTRACT

Grey-box fuzzing is a random testing technique that has been shown to be effective at finding security vulnerabilities in software. The technique leverages program instrumentation to gather information about the program with the goal of increasing the code coverage during fuzzing, which makes gray-box fuzzers extremely efficient vulnerability detection tools. One such tool is AFL, a grey-box fuzzer for C programs that has been used successfully to find security vulnerabilities and other critical defects in countless software products. We present KELINCI, a tool that interfaces AFL with instrumented Java programs. The tool does not require modifications to AFL and is easily parallelizable. Applying AFL-type fuzzing to Java programs opens up the possibility of testing Java based applications using this powerful technique. We show the effectiveness of KELINCI by applying it on the image processing library APACHE COMMONS IMAGING, in which it identified a bug within one hour.

CCS CONCEPTS

• **Software and its engineering** → **Software testing and debugging**; *Dynamic analysis*; • **Security and privacy** → **Software and application security**;

KEYWORDS

AFL, Fuzzing, Random Testing, Java

ACM Reference Format:
Rody Kersten, Kasper Luckow, and Corina S. Păsăreanu. 2017. POSTER: AFL-based Fuzzing for Java with Kelinci. In *Proceedings of CCS '17, Dallas, TX, USA, October 30-November 3, 2017*, 3 pages.
https://doi.org/10.1145/3133956.3138820

1 INTRODUCTION

Fuzz testing [6, 10] is an automated testing technique that is used to discover security vulnerabilities and other bugs in software.

*This material is based on research sponsored by DARPA under agreement number FA8750-15-2-0087. The U.S. Government is authorized to reproduce and distribute reprints for Governmental purposes notwithstanding any copyright notation thereon. The views and conclusions contained herein are those of the authors and should not be interpreted as necessarily representing the official policies or endorsements, either expressed or implied, of DARPA or the U.S. Government.

In its simplest, black-box, form, a program is run on randomly generated or mutated inputs, in search of cases where the program crashes or hangs. More advanced, white-box, fuzzing techniques leverage program analysis to systematically increase code coverage during fuzzing [2, 5, 9]. Grey-box fuzzers leverage program instrumentation rather than program analysis to gather information about the program paths exercised by the inputs to increase coverage. An extensive list of tools can be found here: https://github.com/secfigo/Awesome-Fuzzing#tools. Popular tools available for Java include EvoSuite [3] and Randoop [7].

1.1 AFL

American Fuzzy Lop (AFL) is a security-oriented grey-box fuzzer that employs compile-time instrumentation and genetic algorithms to automatically discover test cases that trigger new internal states in C programs, improving the functional coverage for the fuzzed code [11]. AFL has been used to find notable vulnerabilities and other interesting bugs in many applications and has helped make countless non-security improvements to core tools. For example, AFL was instrumental in finding several of the Stagefright vulnerabilities in Android, the Shellshock related vulnerabilities CVE-2014-6277 and CVE-2014-6278, Denial-of-Service vulnerabilities in BIND (CVE-2015-5722 and CVE-2015-5477), as well as numerous bugs in (security-critical) applications and libraries such as OPENSSL, OPENSSH, GNUTLS, GNUPG, PHP, APACHE, IJG JPEG, LIBJPEG-TURBO and many more.

It supports programs written in C, C++, or Objective C, compiled with either GCC or CLANG. On Linux, the optional QEMU mode allows black-box binaries to be fuzzed, too. There are variants and derivatives of AFL that allow fuzzing of Python, Go, Rust, OCaml, etc.—yet there is no support for Java programs. The only effort that we are aware of uses the GNU Compiler for Java (GCJ), a free compiler for the Java programming language, that was meant to compile Java source code to machine code for a number of CPU architectures. However, it is no longer maintained [4]. In this paper, we present KELINCI[1], which addresses this gap. We demonstrate the effectiveness of the tool by applying it to the image processing library, APACHE COMMONS IMAGING, where it found a bug within one hour of analysis.

2 KELINCI

Inspired by the success of AFL we developed KELINCI, with the goal of applying AFL-style fuzzing to Java based applications. KELINCI provides an interface to execute AFL on Java programs. It adds AFL-style instrumentation to Java programs and communicates results

___

[1]Kelinci means rabbit in Indonesian, the language spoken on the Java island.

Kelinci overview

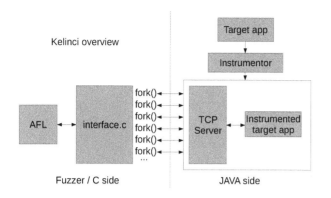

Figure 1: Overview of the design of KELINCI.

back to a simple C program that interfaces with the AFL fuzzer. It does not require any modifications to AFL, but instead behaves exactly as a C program that was instrumented by one of AFL's compilers. The tool is available at https://github.com/isstac/kelinci.

The overall design of KELINCI is depicted in Fig. 1. The first step when applying the tool is to add AFL-style instrumentation to a Java program. AFL uses a 64 kB region of shared memory for communication with the target application. Each basic block is instrumented with code that increments a location in the shared memory bitmap corresponding to the branch made into this basic block.

The Java version of this instrumentation is the following:

```
Mem.mem[id^Mem.prev_location]++;
Mem.prev_location = id >> 1;
```

In this example, the Mem class is the Java representation of the shared memory and also holds the (shifted) id of the last program location. The id of a basic block is a compile-time random integer, where $0 \leq id < 65536$ (the size of the shared memory bitmap). The idea is that each jump from a block $id1$ to a block $id2$ is represented by a location in the bitmap $id1 \oplus id2$. While obviously there may be multiple jumps mapping to the same bitmap location, or even multiple basic blocks which have the same id, such loss of precision is considered rare enough to be an acceptable trade-off for efficiency. The reason that the id of the previous location is shifted is that, otherwise, it would be impossible to distinguish a jump $id1 \rightarrow id2$ from a jump $id2 \rightarrow id1$. Also, tight loops would all map to the location 0, as $id \oplus id = 0$ for any id.

Instrumentation is added to the program using the ASM byte-code manipulation framework [1]. Basic blocks are instrumented as described, the Mem class is added, as well as a TCP server component, which handles communication with the C side and execution of the target application on incoming files.

AFL expects two pieces of information from an instrumented application. First, the application should be running a fork server, which responds to requests from the fuzzer to fork the process and run the forked process on the provided input file. Second, the application is expected to connect to the shared memory and write to locations corresponding to branches in the program. The interface.c component implements a fork server that is identical to the one in programs instrumented by an AFL compiler. When a request to fork comes in, it creates a fork of itself that sends

the provided file over to the Java side, receives the result (shared memory plus error status) once the run is done, writes results to shared memory and crashes if the Java program resulted in an exception escaping the main method.

For a given input file generated by the fuzzer, the interaction between the C and Java sides is as follows:

(1) interface.c receives a fork request from AFL.
(2) One of the forked interface.c processes loads the provided input file, the other keeps running the fork server.
(3) The former interface.c process sends the provided input file over a TCP connection to the KELINCI server.
(4) The KELINCI server receives the incoming request and enqueues it.
(5) The KELINCI server processes the request by writing the incoming input file to disk, starting a new thread in which the main method of the target application is called on the provided input and monitoring it. If the thread throws an exception that escapes main, it is considered a bug. If the thread does not terminate within a given time-out, it is considered a hang.
(6) The KELINCI server communicates the results back to the C side. The shared memory bitmap is sent over the TCP connection, as well as the status (OK, ERROR or TIMEOUT).
(7) On the C side, the received bitmap is written to shared memory. Depending on the received status, the program exits normally, aborts or keeps looping until AFL hits its time-out.

To use the tool, the user first runs the Instrumentor on the target application. Next, the user starts the KELINCI server in the instrumented program. Finally, the user executes AFL on interface.c. The fuzzer is unaware that it is actually analyzing a Java program.

3 EVALUATION

To evaluate KELINCI we ran it on a JPEG parser. We chose APACHE COMMONS IMAGING because it is written completely in Java and the APACHE COMMONS libraries are well-known. The version we analyzed is release candidate 7 ("commons-imaging-1.0-RC7"). We compare this against a run of AFL on the DJPEG utility that comes with the IJG JPEG library[12].

The first notable observation is that the behavior of KELINCI on APACHE COMMONS IMAGING is similar to the behavior of AFL on DJPEG: it quickly finds that if the first byte is 0xFF, new behavior is triggered. Using this second-generation test-case, KELINCI finds after approximately 20 minutes that if the next byte is 0xD8, many new behaviors are triggered. In fact, as AFL on DJPEG also showed, the two bytes 0xFF 0xD8 that KELINCI finds are the correct markers for the start of a JPEG image. As inputs that cause previously unexplored program behaviors are prioritized by AFL, the fuzzer will get incrementally closer to valid JPEG inputs.

After running KELINCI on our case study for 32 minutes, it found a bug: the value of segment length bytes is not properly validated. Each JPEG segment starts with a two-byte unsigned integer specifying the segment size. As the specified size includes these two bytes, the program subtracts 2 from the size before it is used. It then attempts to allocate a buffer for the segment, which fails (with a NegativeArraySizeException) if the specified size is 0 or 1. If this exception is not properly caught by a (server) application using

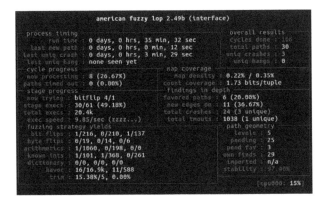

Figure 2: Snapshot of the AFL interface while fuzzing APACHE COMMONS IMAGING. The fuzzer has been running for 35 minutes, in which the target application was executed on 20400 different inputs. A total of 30 program behaviors have been explored, of which 3 result in a crash. While the paths leading to these 3 crashes are different, the cause is the same (NegativeArraySizeException in the readBytes() method in org.apache.commons.imaging.common.BinaryFunctions).

the library, a malicious user could cause a crash by sending a faulty JPEG[2].

A snapshot of the AFL interface after running KELINCI on APACHE COMMONS IMAGING for 35 minutes, presenting the results obtained so far, is shown in Fig. 2.

4 DISCUSSION

The design of the tool with a TCP connection and file IO adds overhead; furthermore running Java programs is much slower that running native programs. For example, on APACHE COMMONS IMAGING, KELINCI is approximately a factor 500 slower than AFL on C. Despite this, KELINCI is still useful in practice as evidenced by our findings which were obtained on a single machine. In addition, the autonomy of the tool—separating the fuzzer from the application being fuzzed—enables KELINCI to leverage a distributed infrastructure that would make it possible to perform scalable, parallel fuzzing; a powerful advantage of KELINCI. We intend to extend interface.c to connect to an array of servers, to enable this distributed approach.

Another limitation of KELINCI is that different runs are executed within the same Java Virtual Machine (JVM) in new threads. This assumes that the different runs are independent, i.e. they cannot influence each other. This is not true in general, as, for instance, different threads could access the same static locations. Even with only a single executor thread, static locations might not be properly reset. A more precise implementation would be to create a new JVM for each run, or to fork the entire JVM before starting the host program. Analogous to many design decisions in AFL, we take a *best effort* approach, where precision is traded against efficiency or, in this case, simplicity.

---

[2]See https://issues.apache.org/jira/browse/IMAGING-203 for the bug report.

5 CONCLUSIONS

We have presented KELINCI, which, to the best of our knowledge, is the only currently viable option to apply AFL-style fuzzing to Java programs. It does not require modifications to the fuzzer, is highly parallelizable and has discovered a real bug in the popular image processing library, APACHE COMMONS IMAGING.

AFL has proved to be exceptionally successful at discovering security vulnerabilities. Compared to available tools for Java fuzzing, such as EvoSuite and Randoop, AFL operates at the system level while the other tools generate unit tests and is specifically targeted to security vulnerabilities. KELINCI opens up the possibility of testing Java based applications using this powerful technique.

Future Work. We intend to enable connecting the fuzzer side to an array of servers running KELINCI instrumented applications. This would enable running as many instances as desired in parallel in the cloud (the Java side can already accept requests from multiple fuzzer clients). It is expected that such parallelization creates a near-linear increase in performance.

We intend to use KELINCI as a platform for finding time/time vulnerabilities (notably Denial-of-Service). This research direction would comprise adding a *cost* dimension to AFL's logic for prioritizing inputs to fuzz, e.g., inputs that yield long computation times are more likely to be fuzzed.

Analogous to the work on MAYHEM [2] and DRILLER [9], we also intend to combine KELINCI with symbolic execution, using Symbolic PathFinder [8].

REFERENCES

[1] ASM. 2017. http://asm.ow2.org/. (2017). Accessed August 11, 2017.
[2] S. K. Cha, T. Avgerinos, A. Rebert, and D. Brumley. 2012. Unleashing Mayhem on Binary Code. In *2012 IEEE Symposium on Security and Privacy*. 380–394. https://doi.org/10.1109/SP.2012.31
[3] Gordon Fraser and Andrea Arcuri. 2011. Evosuite: automatic test suite generation for object-oriented software. In *Proceedings of the 19th ACM SIGSOFT symposium and the 13th European conference on Foundations of software engineering*. ACM, 416–419.
[4] GCJ – GCC Wiki. 2017. https://gcc.gnu.org/wiki/GCJ. (2017). Accessed August 11, 2017.
[5] Patrice Godefroid, Michael Y. Levin, and David Molnar. 2012. SAGE: Whitebox Fuzzing for Security Testing. *Queue* 10, 1, Article 20 (Jan. 2012), 8 pages. https://doi.org/10.1145/2090147.2094081
[6] Barton P. Miller, Louis Fredriksen, and Bryan So. 1990. An Empirical Study of the Reliability of UNIX Utilities. *Commun. ACM* 33, 12 (Dec. 1990), 32–44. https://doi.org/10.1145/96267.96279
[7] C. Pacheco, S.K. Lahiri, M.D. Ernst, and T. Ball. 2007. Feedback-directed Random Test Generation. In *Proceedings of the International Conference on Software Engineering (ICSE)*. 75–84. https://doi.org/10.1109/ICSE.2007.37
[8] Corina S. Pasareanu, Willem Visser, David H. Bushnell, Jaco Geldenhuys, Peter C. Mehlitz, and Neha Rungta. 2013. Symbolic PathFinder: integrating symbolic execution with model checking for Java bytecode analysis. *Autom. Softw. Eng.* 20 (2013), 391–425.
[9] Nick Stephens, John Grosen, Christopher Salls, Andrew Dutcher, Ruoyu Wang, Jacopo Corbetta, Yan Shoshitaishvili, Christopher Kruegel, and Giovanni Vigna. 2016. Driller: Augmenting Fuzzing Through Selective Symbolic Execution.. In *NDSS*, Vol. 16. 1–16.
[10] Michael Sutton, Adam Greene, and Pedram Amini. 2007. *Fuzzing: brute force vulnerability discovery*. Pearson Education.
[11] Michal Zalewski. 2017. American Fuzzy Lop (AFL). http://lcamtuf.coredump.cx/afl/. (2017). Accessed August 11, 2017.
[12] Michal Zalewski. 2017. Pulling JPEGs out of thin air. https://lcamtuf.blogspot.com/2014/11/pulling-jpegs-out-of-thin-air.html. (2017). Accessed August 11, 2017.

POSTER: Rethinking Fingerprint Identification on Smartphones

Seungyeon Kim
Yonsei University
Seoul, Korea
tribunus000@yonsei.ac.kr

Hoyeon Lee
Yonsei University
Seoul, Korea
yeoni_2@yonsei.ac.kr

Taekyoung Kwon*
Yonsei University
Seoul, Korea
taekyoung@yonsei.ac.kr

ABSTRACT

Modern smartphones popularly adopt a small touch sensor for fingerprint identification of a user, but it captures only a partial limited portion of a fingerprint. Recently we have studied a gap between actual risk and user perception of latent fingerprints remaining on a smartphone, and developed a fake fingerprint attack that exploits the latent fingerprints as actual risk. We successfully reconstructed a fake fingerprint image in good quality for small touch sensors. In this paper, we subsequently conduct post hoc experimental studies on the facts that we have missed or have since learned. First of all, we examine that the presented attack is not conceptual but realistic. We employ the reconstructed image and make its fake fingerprint, using a conductive printing or a silicon-like glue, to pass directly the touch sensor of real smartphones. Our target smartphones are Samsung Galaxy S6, S7 and iPhone 5s, 6, 7. Indeed we have succeeded in passing Galaxy S6, S7, and now work on the remaining smartphones. We also conduct an experimental study for one of our mitigation methods to see how it can reduce actual risk. Finally, we perform a user survey study to understand user perception on the fake fingerprint attacks and the mitigation methods.

KEYWORDS

smartphone; smudge; fingerprint spoofing; user perception

1 INTRODUCTION

Fingerprint identification is widely adopted in today's smartphones because of its convenience and believed-safety for device unlocking, and this trend is expected to continue in the future. One of the problems in fingerprint identification on smartphones is that the touch sensor used here is very small — it is capable of capturing only a partial limited portion of a fingerprint. Accordingly, various methods of manufacturing counterfeit fingerprints and passing the small touch sensors have been disclosed [2, 4, 7], but they commonly required a firm impression of a target user's fingerprint or its clear image in a good condition — unrealistic in a sense of attacks.

Lately, aiming at realistic attacks, we studied a fake fingerprint attack called SCRAP, which exploits only smudges and latent fingerprints remaining on a smartphone, i.e., without requiring the firm impression of a user, and successfully showed to reconstruct a fake fingerprint image in good quality for small touch sensors [5].

*Corresponding author.

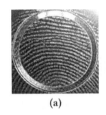  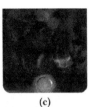

(a)   (b)   (c)

Figure 1: Touch ID and smudges. (a) Full submission (passed with a partial portion of a fingerprint) (b) Half submission (surprisingly also passed with only a half of the partial portion) (c) Daily smudges remaining on a smartphone.

However, the question still remains: Is it possible for the SCRAP attack to pass small touch sensors of real smartphones?

In this paper, to explore the answers, we subsequently conduct post hoc experimental studies on the facts that we have missed or have since learned. As pictured in Figure 1, we found that only a half submission of a partial fingerprint successfully passed Touch ID as in Figure 1-(b), while latent fingerprints were easily detected from daily smudges as in Figure 1-(c). After reviewing the SCRAP attack, we proceed with real attack experiments against real smartphones, such as Galaxy (Samsung Galaxy) S6, S7 and iPhone 5s, 6, 7, and examine our mitigation methods as well experimentally. Finally, we perform a user survey study to understand user perception on the fake fingerprint attacks and the mitigation methods.

2 SCRAP ATTACK (ACSAC'17)

We briefly review our recent work [5] about the fake fingerprint attack that directly exploits latent fingerprints remaining on a smartphone. We call our attack SCRAP. The basic idea of SCRAP was to exploit fingerprint smudges left on a home button (as a key index of an authentic fingerprint) and more smudges [1] left on a touch screen (as a richer source of the authentic fingerprint) of a smartphone exposed to a daily use. There were several challenges to implement this idea. One was to examine the user's behavior whether the same finger is used for activities on both home button and touch screen. Another was to technically reconstruct an image of an authentic fingerprint in good quality, only from the messy smudges found as above. The other was to measure the quality of the reconstructed image for verification of the success in our attack.

To investigate user's touch behavior and perception gap, we conducted in-person surveys involving 82 participants. The survey results showed that the fingers most frequently used on the touch screen and the home button are the same, and the user's risk perception is very low. To reconstruct an authentic fingerprint image from messy smudges, we used domain knowledge of image processing and succeeded in reconstruction experiments that involve seven users in six conditions. The procedure of SCRAP includes (1) photographic smudge collection, (2) fingerprint smudge matching that

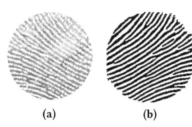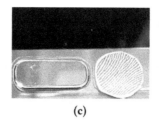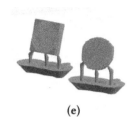

(a)   (b)   (c)   (d)   (e)

Figure 2: Attack experiments. (a) Fingerprint image produced by the SCRAP attack [5]. (b) Submission image: (a) was flipped and reversed, and then SourceAFIS was applied for enhancement. (c) Printed image of (b) with an AgIC conductive ink on the conductive paper (width 9.5mm). (d) Fake submission to Galaxy S7 with the printed image: The printed image was turned over and put on the touch sensor. As a result, the smartphone was successfully unlocked. (e) 3D modeling of the SCRAP images.

involves image preprocessing and SIFT-based matching, (3) image quality assessment that involves damage identification and correction decision, and (4) fingerprint image construction that involves image postprocessing for quality improvement. We measured the quality of the reconstructed image with regard to minutiae quality, match scores, and fingerprint image quality (NFIQ) under the domain of NIST Biometric Image Software (NBIS).

3 EXPERIMENTAL STUDY

We conduct the post hoc experimental study of the SCRAP attack using various materials and strategies on commodity smartphones. Our target devices include Galaxy S6, S7 and iPhone 5s, 6, 7 in our experiments. We asked a target user to enroll the fingerprint. To perform real attack experiments, we examined the well-known fingerprint spoofing techniques that actually required a firm impression of a fingerprint, and employed such experimental settings. They include forgery techniques using wood glue [6], conductive printing [2], and mold combining of hot glue and wood glue [7]. We apply the fingerprint image reconstructed by SCRAP to such settings. Figure 2 and Table 1, respectively, show the results in progress of our experiments. To form fake fingerprints, we use polyvinyl acetate emulsion and EPSON L361 printer (AgIC conductive ink and AgIC special paper) in each experiment scenario.

3.1 Conductive Printing

In 2016, Cao et al. [2] showed that a conductive printing is a potential forgery method for attacking smartphone touch sensors. They used AgIC conductive ink and AgIC special paper to print out a firm impression of a fingerprint, and used the print as a fake fingerprint for their attack. They claimed that this method is much faster and more consistent than conventional forgery methods using wood glue. They conducted experiments with Galaxy S6 and Huawei Honor 7 to prove the effectiveness of the proposed method. However, Cao et al. required that a firm impression of a fingerprint must be provided or scanned from the target user, for their attack.

In our experiment, we adopted the Cao et al.'s conductive printing method for the SCRAP image reconstructed by our attack. The forgery procedure is as follows. First of all, we follow the procedure of the SCRAP attack, as summarized in Section 2, and prepare a reconstructed SCRAP image, e.g., as shown in Figure 2-(a). For conductive printing, we flip horizontally the SCRAP image and reverse its black/white color, so as to directly submit the print-out to a touch sensor. Before printing, we reform the reverse image

Table 1: Summary of attack experiments.

Material	Source	Success
Conductive printing	Firm impression	Galaxy S6, S7
	SCRAP image	Galaxy S6, S7
Silicon-like glue	Firm impression	iPhone 5s, 6, 7 / Galaxy S6, S7
	SCRAP image	in progress

with SourceAFIS library [9] for improvement. Finally, we print out the image using AgIC conductive ink and AgIC special paper.

Figures 2-(a) to (c) show a forgery example of the SCRAP image. We then turn over the printed image and put it on the touch sensor of Galaxy S6 and S7, as shown in Figure 2-(d). We successfully unlocked the target smartphones with the conductive print-out of the SCRAP image. Figure 3-(a) shows that three participants unlocked Galaxy S7 using the print-out of the SCRAP attack without difficulties, i.e., in one or two attempts.

We additionally conducted a half submission experiment, as we described in Figure 1, for the same target devices with participant P1. We asked P1 to submit only a half of the print-out for unlocking, and as shown in Figure 3-(b), P1 unlocked Galaxy S7 in two or four attempts. Since Galaxy S6 and S7 allow up to 14 times in the first hour (37 times in the first 24 hours) along the failed attempts, our attack is definitely actual risk to Samsung Galaxy series.

Unfortunately, we found that the conductive printing methods failed against iPhone series even with a firm impression. Thus, we move on to the wood glue method for iPhones.

3.2 Wood Glue and 3D Printing

Wood glue is a widely-used forgery material for fingerprint spoofing attacks. We also verified that wood glue can be used with a firm impression of a fingerprint to bypass Touch ID of iPhones, as summarized in Table 1. We asked a participant to firmly press a candle-based mold, so that the fingerprint is taken in good quality, and put wood glue onto the mold. We then obtained the forged fingerprint in silicon-like form, and successfully passed the touch sensors of both iPhone 5s, 6, 7 and Galaxy S6, S7 by exploiting it. Thus, to adopt the SCRAP image in this attack setting, we need to build a mold based on the SCRAP image. For the purpose, we are working on 3D modeling and printing of a fake 3D fingerprint and we will use the 3D printout to make a candle-based mold. Figure

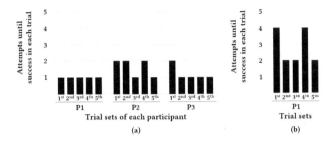

(a)

(b)

Figure 3: Attack experiment results: Conductive printing of the SCRAP image was exploited against Galaxy S7. (a) Unconstrained full submission of the conductive printing was asked to three participants. (b) Half submission was asked to P1.

2-(e) shows a modeling example of the SCRAP image. Finally, we plan to put wood glue onto the mold again.

4 MITIGATION

To mitigate the forgery problems we raised above, a touch sensor must be able to obtain a larger area of user's fingerprint. Interestingly, Apple, Samsung, and many other manufacturers have a plan to introduce the under-screen touch sensor, which enables a larger sensor under the touch screen. For instance, Apple recently patented under-screen fingerprint recognition systems that use acoustic imaging [3] or conductive scanning [8], expected to be an alternative to the futuristic Face ID of iPhone X.

With this trend, we proposed a mitigation method assuming the under-screen touch sensor as shown in Figure 4, and its appearance is a slight modification of the slide bar which was used in the previous iPhone models [5]. We may expect many users are already familiar with such an interface. The user is asked to unlock iPhone by sliding the circle to left or right. When a user touches the circle, the under-screen touch sensor will read the fingerprint. The swiping action required to slide the bar will then remove the fingerprint smudge on the touch sensor as shown in Figure 4-(d). We also proposed to read the remaining smudges, as shown in Figure 5-(c) and (f), to distinguish a real fingerprint from a fake fingerprint.

5 CONCLUSION

We performed post hoc experimental studies regarding the SCRAP attack [5], which has been introduced recently as a practical attack to circumvent fingerprint identification on smartphones, and the following mitigation method. We have validated prior fingerprint spoofing techniques to evaluate the practical effectiveness of the SCRAP attack. Based on the previous work, we attempted to construct a methodology for deceiving smartphone fingerprint biometrics by combining proven methods and new methods with SCRAP techniques. Our mitigation method assumed an adoption of under-screen touch sensors, of which the adaptation is expected in the near future [3, 8]. So, we also performed a small experiment to see its effect on a touch screen.

We plan to conduct a survey study to understand user perception of the fake fingerprint attacks and the mitigation methods. The procedure of this survey is as follows. First, we ask users if latent fingerprints remaining on a smartphone is perceived as actual risk.

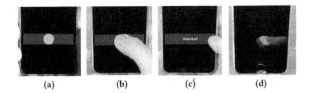

(a)　　(b)　　(c)　　(d)

Figure 4: Mitigation concept assuming under-screen sensors. (a) Slide bar (b) Pressing (c) Sliding (d) Smudge.

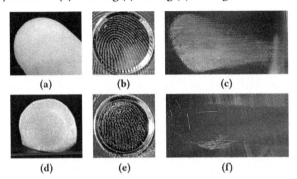

(a)　　(b)　　(c)

(d)　　(e)　　(f)

Figure 5: Comparison of actual and fake fingerprint smudges. (a) Actual finger (b) Smudge after Touch ID unlock action with actual finger. (c) Smudge after Slide Touch ID unlock action with actual finger. (d) Wood glue fake finger. (e) Smudge after Touch ID unlock action with fake finger. (f) Smudge after Slide Touch ID unlock action with fake finger.

We then show the SCRAP attack is possible and ask users again about possible changes in their perception. Finally, we introduce our mitigation method and let participants try our prototype, and ask them about acceptance of the mitigation method.

ACKNOWLEDGMENTS

This work was partly supported by the Institute for Information & communications Technology Promotion (IITP) grant funded by the Korea government (MSIT) (No.2017-0-00380), and also by the MSIT under the ITRC (Information Technology Research Center) support program (IITP-2017-2016-0-00304) supervised by the IITP.

REFERENCES

[1] Adam J. Aviv, Katherine Gibson, Evan Mossop, Matt Blaze, and Jonathan M. Smith. 2010. Smudge attacks on smartphone touch screens. In *Proceedings of WOOT '10*, Vol. 10. 1–7.
[2] Kai Cao and Anil K. Jain. 2016. *Hacking mobile phones using 2D printed fingerprints*. Technical Report. Department of Computer Science and Engineering, Michigan State University.
[3] Eric Decoux and Patrick Bovey. 2017. Marking comprising two patterns on a surface. (Aug. 2017). US Patent 9,747,473.
[4] JLaservideo. 2016. *How To Copy a Fingerprint Like a Spy - iPhone Touch ID Hack!!!* https://www.youtube.com/watch?v=bp-MrrAmprA.
[5] Hoyeon Lee, Seungyeon Kim, and Taekyoung Kwon. 2017. Here is your fingerprint! actual risk versus user perception of latent fingerprints and smudges remaining on smartphones. In *Proceedings of ACSAC '17*.
[6] Marc Rogers. 2014. *Hacking Apple TouchID on the iPhone 6*. https://www.youtube.com/watch?v=GPLiEC_tG1k.
[7] Oki Rosgani. 2013. *faking the Apple trackID fingerprint sensor*. https://www.youtube.com/watch?v=qjRD8_ZoGuE.
[8] Dale R Setlak. 2017. Electronic device including finger biometric sensor carried by a touch display and related methods. (Feb. 2017). US Patent 9,582,102.
[9] Robert Važan. 2017. *SourceAFIS*. https://sourceafis.angeloflogic.com/.

Poster: X-Ray Your DNS

Amit Klein[§], Vladimir Kravtsov[§‡], Alon Perlmuter[§‡], Haya Shulman[§‡] and Michael Waidner[§‡]

§Fraunhofer Institute for Secure Information Technology SIT

‡The Hebrew University of Jerusalem

ABSTRACT

We design and develop DNS X-Ray which performs analyses of DNS platforms on the networks where it is invoked. The analysis identifies the caches and the IP addresses used by the DNS platform, fingerprints the DNS software on the caches, and evaluates vulnerabilities allowing injection of spoofed records into the caches. DNS X-Ray is the first tool to perform an extensive analysis of the caching component on the DNS platforms.

In addition, DNS X-Ray also provides statistics from previous invocations, enabling networks to check which for popular DNS software on the caches, the number of caches typically used on DNS platforms and more.

We set up DNS X-Ray online, it can be accessed via a website dns.xray.sit.fraunhofer.de.

1 INTRODUCTION

Domain Name System (DNS), [RFC1034, RFC1035], was conceived in the 80s as a basic lookup functionality. Since then DNS evolved into a complex ecosystem. It is increasingly utilised to facilitate a wide range of applications and constitutes an important building block in the design of scalable network architectures. Nowadays DNS resolution platforms are typically composed of multiple IP addresses and caches, which may be hosted on different networks and operated by different entities. The configuration, software and location of these components has direct impact on the security and performance of networks. In practice, network operators often have only a vague knowledge of the configuration of their DNS platforms, on the devices that are connected, the number of caches used, the operating systems (OSes) and DNS software (SW) that they are running, in which networks and Internet Service Providers (ISPs) the resolving machines are hosted, and more. Understanding the inner workings of DNS is important also for design of defences for DNS and mechanisms that utilise DNS, e.g., client subnet in DNS queries [RFC7871].

Measuring DNS Platforms. Due to the significance of DNS and its increasing complexity, the research and operational communities invest considerable efforts to study the DNS infrastructure; see Related Work, Section 2. [9] measured the client side of the DNS infrastructure of *open* resolvers, in order to identify the hosts that communicate with the clients and nameservers in DNS lookups.

Recently [6] studied vulnerabilities in caches to injection of spoofed records. [5] devised approaches for measuring the internal components of DNS infrastructure. We build upon the methodologies for studying the DNS platforms presented in [5] to design and implement a tool we call DNS X-Ray for evaluation of DNS resolution platforms. We create a webpage through which DNS X-Ray can be accessed and invoked dns.xray.sit.fraunhofer.de, and upon invocation it analyses the DNS platform on the network on which it is run. During the analysis, DNS X-Ray identifies different components on the platform and discovers and characterises the DNS caches, including the DNS software on the caches, and the vulnerabilities in the caches that allow injection of DNS records.

DNS X-Ray also provides statistics of all the DNS platforms on which it was evaluated. Therefore, clients obtain information not only about the DNS platforms on their networks but can also compare the results to the other platforms in the Internet.

The challenge with studying the caches is that the caches cannot be directly accessed neither by the clients nor by the nameservers, and all the communication with the caches is performed via the ingress and egress resolvers on DNS platforms (see Figure 1). In addition, there are also intermediate caches, such as those in the operating systems or in browsers, we also explain how DNS X-Ray bypasses the intermediate caches.

DNS X-Ray also identifies all the IP addresses used by the tested DNS platform, which networks and ISPs host the DNS platform, and also checks for adoption of best security practices, see [RFC5452], such as whether the ports' and transaction identifiers (TXIDs) are securely selected, and if the caches are vulnerable to injection of spoofed records. This enables security experts as well as non experts to learn about the misconfigurations or vulnerabilities on their networks and allows network and security researchers to obtain insights into DNS resolution platforms in different networks and countries. We make the DNS X-Ray tool as well as the statistics available at use dns.xray.sit.fraunhofer.de. Furthermore, DNS X-Ray tool is the first to enable an in depth study of the caching component on DNS platforms. It improves the current understanding of the DNS resolution platforms and serves as a building block for further research on DNS performance and security.

DNS Resolution Platforms. DNS X-Ray studies complex as well as simple DNS platforms; a general model for DNS resolution platforms is illustrated in Figure 1. The platform consists of a set (2^{32-x}) of ingress IP addresses which handle DNS queries from the clients, a set of n caches, and a set (2^{32-y}) of egress IP addresses, which communicate with the nameservers if the queries from the clients cannot be satisfied from (one of) the caches.

This infrastructure corresponds to complex platforms such as Google Public DNS, and it can also be abstracted to incorporate a very simple version for a DNS resolution platforms with a single IP

CCS '17, October 30-November 3, 2017, Dallas, TX, USA

© 2017 Copyright held by the owner/author(s).

ACM ISBN 978-1-4503-4946-8/17/10.

https://doi.org/10.1145/3133956.3138821

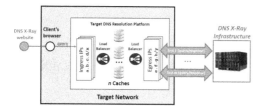

Figure 1: DNS X-Ray and DNS platforms.

address which performs both the ingress and egress functionalities and uses a single cache.

2 RELATED WORK

Recently, Schomp et al [9], measured the client side of the DNS infrastructure of *open recursive resolvers*, in order to identify the different hosts that participate in DNS lookups. Their study focused only on IP addresses that communicate either with the name servers or the clients and does not go deeper into the caching components and the mapping between the IP addresses and the caches. DNS X-Ray provides insights into the caching component and its interaction with the other components in DNS platforms.

A number of other studies were conducted on open resolvers, e.g., [7, 10], where the IPv4 address block is scanned for hosts responding to requests on port 53. However, recently it was shown by [2, 15] that most such open resolvers are either (misconfigured) home routers and mismanaged (security oblivious) networks or malicious networks operated by attackers (where the open DNS resolver is set up for malware communication to the command and control servers). Our study focuses on studying the internal structures of DNS platform, fingerprinting the software of DNS caches, evaluating vulnerabilities to cache injection (by overwriting cached records with new values), and other properties of DNS resolvers.

To optimise content distribution networks (CDNs) [11] ran a study associating DNS resolvers with their clients, and also designed approaches to fingerprint the DNS software passively (on DNS traces). Their study was performed on a limited set of DNS software (Bind9, Mac OS X and Microsoft) using `nslookup` and tracing the queries' pattern issued by the resolver in the lab. This work was extended by [1], which fingerprinted a limited set of DNS software (Bind, Unbound and Microsoft) but also without using active fingerprinting methods in the wild. Both works [1, 11] use flags and fields in DNS header (incl. `CD`, `DO`, to EDNS and CNAME chains), and patterns in DNS queries to fingerprint DNS software; example patterns include the maximal queried length of CNAME chains, presence of requests for AAAA (following requests for A records). Turning DNSSEC (DO bit in EDNS) and IPv6 off would prevent them from distinguishing between different resolvers' software.

Prior work, [14], also used server selection mechanism to perform an in lab fingerprint of resolver software of DNS software, Bind, PowerDNS, Unbound, DNSCache, MicrosoftDNS. The nameserver selection allows to characterise the software used by the egress DNS resolver. Server selection behaviour can be modified in the configuration file by adjusting the `target-fetch-policy` to 0 0 0

0 0 in Unbound. This will cause the resolver not to fetch additional nameservers and to use only one.

In contrast to previously proposed approaches DNS X-Ray allows repetitive and evaluation of networks, identifies a wide range of DNS software, and can detect vulnerabilities in caches it has not modelled before.

A study by [8] suggested to remove the DNS resolution platforms, and to leave the resolution to end hosts, arguing that the overhead on the existing end hosts would not be significant. Our study can be used for analysis of the complexity of the caching component and the impact on the networks if it were removed.

DNS cache poisoning attacks exploit vulnerabilities in caches to inject spoofed records [3, 4, 12].

Also relevant to our research are online tools for measuring the zone configuration in the nameservers and tools for measuring resolvers. AFNIC operates the Zonemaster[1], which crawls domains and provides information about the connectivity and configuration of the zonefile and the nameservers. There are also commercial services, such as[2] which monitor latency and availability of nameservers. Tools for measuring resolvers focus on checking whether the ports are randomly selected. Such service is offered by the DNS OARC via a `porttest` tool. These tools do not provide an insight into the internals of the DNS resolution platforms.

3 DNS X-RAY

System Design. DNS X-Ray is composed of a client side script running in browsers, nameservers hosting our zone files to which we trigger DNS requests and a website, which displays the analysis of DNS platforms and statistics in form of graphs and charts of all the collected data. DNS X-Ray components are illustrated in blue in Figure 1. Using our own nameservers allows us to receive requests from the tested DNS platforms and based on requests/responses to learn information about the components in a tested DNS platform. We use two hierarchies in DNS for our study each is configured in a separate zonefile. DNS X-Ray is running on four Ubuntu servers and uses MongoDB to store the collected raw data. Our implementation of the DNS resolution functionality is based on the Stanford DNS server. The analysis of the statistics is performed by Perl scripts on the webserver.

Methodology. DNS X-Ray uses the standard DNS request/response behaviour. Client side script triggers specially crafted DNS requests for records in our domains. The DNS requests (including the requested records and their type), that arrive from the DNS platforms at our nameservers, are used to infer information about the caches hidden behind the IP addresses of the tested DNS platform. DNS X-Ray 'decouples' the caches from the IP addresses and counts the number of caches and the IP addresses. Based on the caching behaviour, specifically *eviction of cached records* and *overwriting of the cached records with new values*, we learn the DNS software on the caches. DNS X-Ray also infers the operating system on the caches based on ports' allocation by egress IP addresses in DNS platform.

Data Collection and Statistics Generation. After each evaluation of DNS X-Ray on a new network the data is added to the

---

[1]http://zonemaster.net/
[2]http://dnscheck.pingdom.com/

database and the statistics are recalculated to incorporate the new results.

We analyse the collected data and generate the following output: the number of caches used by the tested DNS resolution platform, DNS software on the caches, number of egress IP addresses, networks and countries where the egress IP addresses are hosted, whether the egress resolvers use random source ports and TXIDs.

The focus of DNS X-Ray is to collect the basic information about the components on the DNS platforms, and in particular to characterise the caching component, e.g., its software. Nevertheless, we implemented DNS X-Ray in a modular way so that we can easily extend it with new graphs and charts. Specifically, we store *all* the collected data during the evaluation of a given DNS platform in a database, hence we can define new graphs that would be calculated over all the previously collected data. For instance, we can extend DNS X-Ray to present statistics about the latency to each DNS platform, nameserver selection, IP identifier assignment or even support of cryptography, such as DNSSEC validation [RFC4033-RFC4035].

Non-Exposure to Attacks. DNS X-Ray does not expose to attacks neither the network on which it is evaluated nor other networks. A user can only evaluate the security of DNS platform on a network to which it has access. This does not introduce an additional threat to the network on which a user evaluates DNS X-Ray. Since the user anyway has access to its network - it can itself trigger queries to DNS platform to evaluate its security. We do not allow evaluating networks to which a user does not have access to. Finally, the traffic volume that is generated to measure the DNS platform is moderate (14 tests each repeated 30 times) and lasts for 5-10 minutes.

Bypassing Local Caches. Upon invocation on a given network, a script running in client's browser causes the stub resolver on client's machine to send DNS requests to the resolution platform (Figure 1). However, since DNS X-Ray does not have a direct access to the DNS resolution platform, the requests will go through intermediate caches; see [5] for more details. To cope with intermediate caches DNS X-Ray maps the same hostname to multiple aliases using CNAME records. We setup q DNS records in our `cache.example` zone mapping them to CNAME DNS record as follows:

```
x-1.cache.example   IN CNAME name.cache.example
x-2.cache.example   IN CNAME name.cache.example
...
x-q.cache.example   IN CNAME name.cache.example
name.cache.example  IN A      a.b.c.d
```

Then the script running in client's browser triggers q DNS requests for names `x-1.cache.example`,...,`x-q.cache.example`. The local caches are not involved in the resolution process (specifically in resolving the CNAME redirection) and only receive the final answer.

4   CONCLUSIONS

Our current view of basic Internet components is based on standardisation documents and initial designs. However, most systems significantly evolved since their conception. Furthermore, typically the networks or Internet operators make different choices when setting up their infrastructure. In order to evaluate or improve security of the basic Internet components a clear understanding thereof is important. We design and implement DNS X-Ray - which enables users to evaluate DNS platforms and security of their components, as well as to obtain collective information about DNS platforms in other networks in the Internet. DNS X-Ray is important to allow clients to identify vulnerabilities in their DNS platforms even if DNSSEC validation [RFC4033-RFC4045] is applied. This ensures security even when DNSSEC is incorrectly adopted [13].

ACKNOWLEDGEMENT

The research reported in this paper has been supported in part by the German Federal Ministry of Education and Research (BMBF), by the Hessian Ministry of Science and the Arts within CRISP (www.crisp-da.de/) and co-funded by the DFG as part of project S3 within the CRC 1119 CROSSING. This work was also partially supported by the HUJI Cyber Security Research Center in conjunction with the Israel National Cyber Bureau in the Prime Minister's Office.

REFERENCES

[1] Ruetee Chitpranee and Kensuke Fukuda. 2013. Towards passive DNS software fingerprinting. In *Proceedings of the 9th Asian Internet Engineering Conference.* ACM, 9–16.

[2] David Dagon, Niels Provos, Christopher P Lee, and Wenke Lee. 2008. Corrupted DNS Resolution Paths: The Rise of a Malicious Resolution Authority.. In *NDSS.*

[3] Amir Herzberg and Haya Shulman. 2013. Fragmentation considered poisonous, or: One-domain-to-rule-them-all. org. In *Communications and Network Security (CNS), 2013 IEEE Conference on.* IEEE, 224–232.

[4] Amir Herzberg and Haya Shulman. 2013. Socket overloading for fun and cache-poisoning. In *Proceedings of the 29th Annual Computer Security Applications Conference.* ACM, 189–198.

[5] Amit Klein, Haya Shulman, and Michael Waidner. 2017. Counting in the Dark: Caches Discovery and Enumeration in the Internet. In *The 47th IEEE/IFIP International Conference on Dependable Systems and Networks (DSN).*

[6] Amit Klein, Haya Shulman, and Michael Waidner. 2017. Internet-Wide Study of DNS Cache Injections. In *INFOCOM.*

[7] Marc Kührer, Thomas Hupperich, Jonas Bushart, Christian Rossow, and Thorsten Holz. 2015. Going wild: Large-scale classification of open DNS resolvers. In *Proceedings of the 2015 ACM Conference on Internet Measurement Conference.* ACM, 355–368.

[8] Kyle Schomp, Mark Allman, and Michael Rabinovich. 2014. DNS resolvers considered harmful. In *Proceedings of the 13th ACM Workshop on Hot Topics in Networks.* ACM, 16.

[9] Kyle Schomp, Tom Callahan, Michael Rabinovich, and Mark Allman. 2013. On measuring the client-side DNS infrastructure. In *Proceedings of the 2013 conference on Internet measurement conference.* ACM, 77–90.

[10] Kyle Schomp, Tom Callahan, Michael Rabinovich, and Mark Allman. 2014. Assessing dns vulnerability to record injection. In *Passive and Active Measurement.* Springer, 214–223.

[11] Craig A Shue and Andrew J Kalafut. 2013. Resolvers revealed: Characterizing DNS resolvers and their clients. *ACM Transactions on Internet Technology (TOIT)* 12, 4 (2013), 14.

[12] Haya Shulman and Michael Waidner. 2014. Fragmentation considered leaking: port inference for DNS poisoning. In *International Conference on Applied Cryptography and Network Security.* Springer, 531–548.

[13] Haya Shulman and Michael Waidner. 2017. One Key to Sign Them All Considered Vulnerable: Evaluation of DNSSEC in Signed Domains. In *The 14th USENIX Symposium on Networked Systems Design and Implementation (NSDI).* USENIX.

[14] Yingdi Yu, Duane Wessels, Matt Larson, and Lixia Zhang. 2012. Authority Server Selection of DNS Caching Resolvers. *ACM SIGCOMM Computer Communication Reviews* (April 2012).

[15] Jing Zhang, Zakir Durumeric, Michael Bailey, Mingyan Liu, and Manish Karir. 2014. On the Mismanagement and Maliciousness of Networks. In *to appear) Proceedings of the 21st Annual Network & Distributed System Security Symposium (NDSS'14), San Diego, California, USA.*

POSTER: Hidden in Plain Sight: A Filesystem for Data Integrity and Confidentiality

Anne Kohlbrenner*
Carnegie Mellon University
akohlbre@andrew.cmu.edu

Frederico Araujo   Teryl Taylor   Marc Ph. Stoecklin
IBM T.J. Watson Research Center
{frederico.araujo, terylt}@ibm.com, mpstoeck@us.ibm.com

ABSTRACT

A filesystem capable of curtailing data theft and ensuring file integrity protection through deception is introduced and evaluated. The deceptive filesystem transparently creates multiple levels of stacking to protect the base filesystem and monitor file accesses, hide and redact sensitive files with baits, and inject decoys onto fake system views purveyed to untrusted subjects, all while maintaining a pristine state to legitimate processes. Our prototype implementation leverages a kernel hot-patch to seamlessly integrate the new filesystem module into live and existing environments.

We demonstrate the utility of our approach with a use case on the nefarious Erebus ransomware. We also show that the filesystem adds no I/O overhead for legitimate users.

KEYWORDS

Intrusion Detection and Prevention; Cyber Deception; Filesystems

1 INTRODUCTION

In today's modern digital age, the compromise or theft of data can have severe consequences on individuals, governments, enterprises, and cloud environments. Capitalizing on data as the new digital currency, cybercrime has become a big money business, with criminals stealing millions of credit card numbers [9] and holding data ransom, costing businesses millions of dollars to regain access to their data [5]. Given the alarming rate and scope of recent attacks, new approaches are needed to effectively identify and dissuade attackers trying to steal or destroy their targets' crown jewels.

Existing approaches to prevent data theft only work under special circumstances. For example, current ransomware protections focus on preventing malware from running, maintaining backups, or trying to reverse engineer custom cryptography schemes. Unfortunately, such reactive approaches have been proven inadequate, as 71% of companies attacked by ransomware still have their files successfully encrypted [7], with less than half being able to recover from backups [8].

Other protective measures, such as deceptive files [2, 4] and canaries [1], alert defenders of an attacker's presence by leaving deceptive breadcrumbs among the legitimate files on the filesystem, which trigger a beacon when accessed. However, to avoid confusing legitimate users, the users must either be aware of the decoys, which

*Work completed while the author was at IBM T.J. Watson Research Center.

is difficult to maintain in shared systems, or the decoys must be identifiable by users while being indiscernible to attackers—a nontrivial property to achieve in practice. Unfortunately, such deceptive files do not prevent the attacker from stealing sensitive data.

To overcome these disadvantages, our work introduces a new filesystem, DcyFS, which protects files at their place of rest. DcyFS seeks three main objectives: (1) stop the theft, modification, and destruction of important data by untrusted subjects (e.g., applications, users), (2) deceive, misdirect, and disinform adversaries, and (3) construct a new sensor able to detect the presence of attackers on production systems.

Contributions. DcyFS takes a fundamentally different approach to the data theft and integrity problem with a new filesystem that can monitor file accesses transparently, hide sensitive data, create decoy files, and modify existing files to provide a fake system view to untrusted subjects (e.g., processes and users). DcyFS actively captures filesystem events and correlates them with other system features (e.g., user, process name, time) to create targeted filesystem *views* that hide high-value assets and expose enticing breadcrumbs to detect deliberate tampering with filesystem data. Such *context-awareness* minimizes false alarms by curtailing inadvertent, legitimate access to breadcrumbs—by exposing more "truthful" views of the filesystem to trustworthy processes—while maximizing chances of attack detection by strategically overlaying deceptive objects atop the base filesystem.

Specifically, our contributions can be summarized as follows:

- The design of a new *stacking* filesystem to augment standard filesystems with denial and deception capabilities, such as hiding resources from untrusted processes, redacting or replacing assets to protect sensitive data, and injecting breadcrumbs to disinform and misdirect attackers.

- The creation of a Virtual File System (VFS) module to enable transparent integration with legacy environments. A tiny kernel hot-patch interposing `exec` allows DcyFS to be installed without system restart.

- An evaluation showing that our approach can detect and resist real ransomware attacks, and preliminary benchmarks demonstrate that DcyFS can defend against data theft and filesystem tampering without incurring significant overhead.

- An approach that enforces file integrity protection without requiring file access mediation. It also supports the implementation of access control policies, and enables the automation of decoy injection in commodity filesystems.

2 SYSTEM OVERVIEW

Figure 1 presents an architectural overview of DcyFS. The core components of the system are a set of filesystem overlays that are deployed on a per-process basis, providing each process with a different *view* of the filesystem—computed as the *union* of the

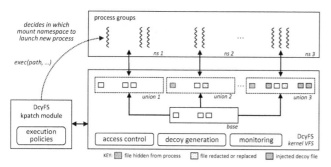

Figure 1: Architectural Overview of DcyFS

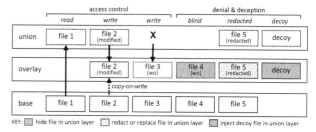

Figure 2: DcyFS's access control, denial, and deception

base filesystem and the *overlay*. To alter the resulting union, each overlay has the ability to (1) hide base files, (2) modify their content by overlaying a different file with the same name, and (3) inject new files that are not present in the host system. File writes are stored in the overlay protecting base files from being overwritten. This forms the basis of a stackable filesystem that can be mounted atop different base filesystem types (e.g., block, network) to offer data integrity protection and enhanced detection against data-stealing attacks.

To effectively and securely construct filesystem overlays, DcyFS leverages the kernel's mount namespace capability to swap the root filesystem to a specially-crafted union mount. The mount namespace is an operating system construct that provides an isolated mount point list for every process residing in a particular namespace—a process inside the namespace observes a different filesystem than the base system. Processes are moved, upon creation, into a mount namespace based on some notion of trust.

For our initial prototype, we built a simple trust model based on white/black listing. The model maps a user name, binary hash, or process name to a set of configurations describing an overlay. The configuration can specify which files and directories to show in the overlay, which ones to hide, and which ones to replace with another file. Trusted processes are presented with a *pristine* (unaltered) view of the filesystem.

2.1 Design & Implementation

To achieve transparency and minimize performance overhead, our DcyFS requires a small modification to the kernel—deployed as a kernel hot patch (patching the kernel while it is running)—and the installation of a kernel module implementing monitoring, access control, and decoy creation and injection capabilities. The hot patch modifies the kernel's exec family of functions to drop newly created processes into a new mount namespace protected by the union filesystem. The particular overlay is chosen based on a pre-defined trust model. Note that child processes automatically inherit their parent namespace, unless otherwise specified by the trust model.

We implemented DcyFS using Linux's OverlayFS union filesystem, which creates an upper mount and a lower mount, where the lower mount is the base file system, and the upper mount is the overlay. Figure 2 illustrates this concept, showing the base and overlay mounts, and the resulting union of the two mounts that serves as the namespace's pivot. To hide a base file or directory, DcyFS simply marks it as deleted in the overlay. Decoy files are similarly placed in carefully-chosen locations inside the upper mount, and existing files can be replaced or redacted for attacker deception [3].

Our initial prototype was developed for Ubuntu 16.04 LTS, leveraging VFS and its mature mount namespace implementation. Recently, Windows Server 2016 was released with native namespace support and an overlay filesystem driver, mirroring its open-source counterpart. We plan to port DcyFS to Windows as future work.

2.2 Filesystem Denial & Deception

Changes made by untrusted processes do not affect the base filesystem, protecting legitimate users from seeing malicious changes as well as effectively keeping a uncorrupted copy of the filesystem immediately before the malicious process started. DcyFS can hide particular files and directories from the process, thus curtailing sensitive data leaks. Additionally, the filesystem module is capable of generating encrypted files and implanting decoys in the overlay to replace sensitive files in the base filesystem. DcyFS transparently monitors and logs access to such files. Moreover, only the untrusted process is affected by the hidden and decoy files, leaving legitimate users free of confusion.

3 EVALUATION

3.1 Experimental Setup

Since processes are moved to an overlay upon startup, DcyFS can potentially affect process startup time, specially for untrusted processes, where a crafted overlay is purveyed in lieu of the unaltered (empty) version presented to trusted processes. To test the overhead of the overlay creation, we built a program whose entry point simply exited, and timed its execution three different scenarios: a baseline evaluation without DcyFS, a whitelisted execution and a blacklisted execution, both with DcyFS. For the untrusted execution, an empty overlay was created. We used perf stat -r 100000 to measure the execution time, running on a virtual machine with Ubuntu 16.04 LTS.

Table 1 shows the results, which demonstrate that DcyFS does not affect the startup time of trusted processes, and incurs an overhead of 1.66 ms for trusted processes. Figure 3 shows that untrusted processes startup time is quickly dominated by overlay creation and injection of decoys. However, both sources of startup overhead can be significantly reduced by simply creating overlays with decoy files ahead of time, reducing startup costs to moving the new program into an overlay. This is left as future work.

To assess the impact of the union filesystem on file I/O throughput, we used the Flexible Filesystem Benchmark and measured R/W throughput on the same machine, with and without DcyFS. For programs running in an overlay, the R/W throughput dropped from 634/641 MB/s to 456 MB/s for both read and write. This is due to the copy-on-write strategy implemented by the union filesystem. We plan to investigate techniques to reduce this overhead.

Table 1: Process startup time benchmark.

Benchmark	Startup time
Without DcyFS (baseline)	0.380 ms
Trusted process	0.378 ms
Untrusted process	2.046 ms

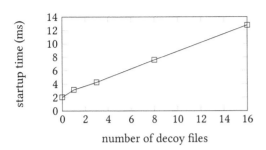

Figure 3: Process startup time vs. number of decoy files.

3.2 Use Cases

Data Theft Protection and Deception. A typical social engineering attack usually starts with a spear phishing email containing a malicious attachment. When the recipient (e.g., a government official whose machine is protected with DcyFS) clicks on the attachment, a remote access terminal (RAT) is transparently installed. Since the RAT is untrusted, it is immediately given its own view of the filesystem, where sensitive files are hidden, or masked by fake versions. For example, the attacker gets to see a fake or redacted spreadsheet, while the original is safe from the attacker's view.

Ransomware Detection. Since DcyFS prevents processes from making changes to the host filesystem (integrity protection), it is an effective defense against ransomware. To evaluate DcyFS's ability to prevent damage from ransomware, we used the Erebus family of ransomware. Erebus has Windows and Linux variants that hit companies in South Korea. At least one company has paid $1.62 million in ransom [5]. To test the effectiveness of DcyFS against Erebus, we ran the ransomware under two conditions: (1) in a situation where the parent process was untrusted, such as a file browser or instance of a shell, and (2) when Erebus was run from a trusted parent, but Erebus itself was untrusted. In the first case, the files that Erebus encrypted were visible from the parent process only. The rest of the system was unaffected. In the second case, the damage from Erebus was not seen at all on the system, although Erebus could be seen to run by monitoring the internals of DcyFS.

While this test was a success in preventing Erebus from damaging the system, it could also be used to detect that a program was malware. Ransomware often tries to hide its presence until it has finished its encryption. For example, Erebus initially sleeps for five minutes before starting to encrypt files, presumably to reduce the chance that the user will suspect which executable caused the problem. Once the user notices that their files have been encrypted, it is difficult to trace back and find out which program was malicious; however, since DcyFS runs each untrusted program in a separate overlay, we can examine which overlay has encrypted files in it to know which executable is to blame.

4 RELATED WORK

In recent years, there has been a few filesystem solutions specifically targeted towards defense against ransomware. Paybreak allows ransomware to encrypt the files on a system, but stores the crypto keys by hooking Windows Crypto API, so that it can reverse the encryption. While working well against ransomware, it cannot defend against malware that deletes or corrupts data. ShieldFS [6] is a copy-on-write filesystem, which enforces that all processes must write to an overlay as protection, until a detector determines that a process is not ransomware based on file I/O stats. Redemption [10] is similar to ShieldFS except that it uses more features to detect ransomware behavior, including the entropy of data blocks, number of file writes, number of directory traversals, and number of file conversions. While these approaches also provide integrity guarantees against ransomware, they are unable to deal with other types of malware, nor do they deal with data confidentially and deception, which is handled seamlessly by DcyFS.

5 DISCUSSION AND FUTURE WORK

DcyFS enables the construction of realistic, but completely false, views of the filesystem to untrusted processes. To a process running in an overlay, it appears that it is able to view, extract, and modify real data. However, it may be viewing decoy files or missing sensitive files, and its file modifications will not be seen outside its overlay. This is done transparently, without advertising itself to the untrusted process, and without affecting other legitimate processes. Next, to make decoy files both less visible to trusted users and more visible to attackers, DcyFS actively moves decoys into place for untrusted programs. This means that decoys can be stored out of the way of trusted users (e.g., in a hidden directory), as well as being visible in normal locations for untrusted programs.

Currently, our trust model is rule-based using basic white/black listing. In the future, we plan to expand this model to take into account which user is executing the program, how that user is authenticated, and past behaviors of the user and the process to determine its trustworthiness.

The changes made by untrusted processes are currently only visible to that process and disappear on reboot. In situations where an untrusted process should become trusted, such as being vouched for by a more trusted subject, those changes could be copied from the overlay and merged into the real filesystem. The prototype supports decoy files that are created manually; however, this is unnecessary. DcyFS could automatically create decoy files based on different formats, such as data that appears to be encrypted, or files containing fake keys or passwords. The system should also learn the content of overlays based on past process behaviors to streamline overlay generation.

REFERENCES

[1] Thinkst Canary . 2017. Canarytokens. (2017).
[2] Jim Yuill annd Mike Zappe, Dorothy Denning, and Fred Feer. 2004. Honeyfiles: deceptive files for intrusion detection. In *Proc. Annual IEEE SMC Info. Ass. Work.*
[3] Frederico Araujo and Kevin W Hamlen. 2015. Compiler-instrumented, Dynamic Secret-Redaction of Legacy Processes for Attacker Deception. In *Usenix Sec. Sym.*
[4] Brian M. Bowen, Shlomo Hershkop, Angelos D. Keromytis, and Salvatore J. Stolfo. 2009. Baiting Inside Attackers Using Decoy Documents. In *Proc. Int. ICST Conf. Security and Privacy in Communication Networks.*
[5] Ziv Chang, Gilbert Sison, and Jeanne Jocson. 2017. Erebus Resurfaces as Linux Ransomware. (2017).
[6] Andrea Continella, Alessandro Guagnelli, Giovanni Zingaro, Giulio De Pasquale, Alessandro Barenghi, Stefano Zanero, and Federico Maggi. 2016. ShieldFS: A Self-healing, Ransomware-aware Filesystem. In *Proc. Annual Computer Security Applications Conf.*
[7] Jonathan Crowe. 2017. 2017 Ransomware Trends and Forecasts. (2017).
[8] Brianna Gammons. 2017. 4 Surprising Backup Failure Statistics that Justify Additional Protection. (2017).
[9] Kevin Granville. 2015. 9 Recent Cyberattacks Against Big Businesses. (2015).
[10] Amin Kharraz and Engin Kirda. 2017. Redemption: Real-time Protection Against Ransomware at End-Hosts. In *Proc. Sym. Res. in Attacks, Intrusions and Defenses.*

POSTER: Watch Out Your Smart Watch When Paired

Youngjoo Lee
Yonsei University
Seoul, Korea
yj.lee91@yonsei.ac.kr

WonSeok Yang
Yonsei University
Seoul, Korea
zmsenqn@yonsei.ac.kr

Taekyoung Kwon*
Yonsei University
Seoul, Korea
taekyoung@yonsei.ac.kr

ABSTRACT

We coin a new term called *data transfusion* as a phenomenon that a user experiences when pairing a wearable device with the host device. A large amount of data stored in the host device (e.g., a smartphone) is forcibly copied to the wearable device (e.g., a smart watch) due to pairing while the wearable device is usually less attended. To the best of knowledge, there is no previous work that manipulates how sensitive data is transfused even without user's consent and how users perceive and behave regarding such a phenomenon for smart watches. We tackle this problem by conducting an experimental study of data extraction from commodity devices, such as in Android Wear, watchOS, and Tizen platforms, and a following survey study with 205 smart watch users, in two folds. The experimental studies have shown that a large amount of sensitive data was transfused, but there was not enough user notification. The survey results have shown that users have lower perception on smart watches for security and privacy than smartphones, but they tend to set the same passcode on both devices when needed. Based on the results, we perform risk assessment and discuss possible mitigation that involves volatile transfusion.

KEYWORDS

wearable device; data extraction; data transfusion; risk assessment

1 INTRODUCTION

Wearable computing devices are "miniature" electronic products worn by users and so in general they are lack of a conventional user interface and a wide network connectivity. For example, Apple Watch provides a "38 or 42mm" force touch display and a tiny crown along with haptic engines, sensors, Bluetooth, and Wi-Fi in ad-hoc mode for interactions only in near range. Therefore, wearable computing devices require a host device, such as a smartphone, for their connectivity, functionality, and usability to be enriched.

First of all, a personal wearable device must be initially paired to the host device for new device initialization and personalization — this process is called a pairing. For instance, a user initially needs to pair a maiden smart watch to his smartphone through a Bluetooth or NFC channel before use. The smart watch is then allowed to communicate with the paired smartphone for further data updates and backups while in use, e.g., SMS notification, weather forecast

update, and health record backup, even without requiring user consciousness on the paired connections. Now both devices may need to be attended at the same level.

In this paper, we deal with data security problems that can occur in device pairing of smart watches, and coin a new term called *data transfusion*. We approach the problems in two-fold study design. First we perform an experimental study to extract data from smart watches paired with a smartphone in different phases. We consider three popular platforms such as Android Wear, watchOS, and Tizen in our experiments. Second we conduct a survey study to understand user perception and behavior with regard to the so-called data transfusion. Based on these studies, we perform risk assessment on smart watches and discuss how to reduce the risk.

There have been several previous works that manipulated data extraction of smart watches from forensic perspectives. They include Do et al.'s work, respectively, on Samsung Galaxy Gear [2], and Baggili et al.'s work on Samsung Galaxy Gear2 Neo and LG G Watch [1]. Compared to the elegant previous works, our study is more uniquely focused on exploring the phenomenon called data transfusion (saying, not only extracted data) by concrete experiments accompanying user surveys and risk assessment. To the best of our knowledge, this is the first work to arise such implication.

2 THREAT MODEL - DATA TRANSFUSION

Our main focus is on what happens in a wearable device due to pairing. For initialization and personalization, the devices need to exchange necessary data and particularly the data stored in the host device that belongs to a user. As for such data transferred from the host device, we set the following definitions.

Definition 2.1. Device pairing is a process that sets up an initial linkage between a wearable computing device and a host device to allow further reciprocal interactions, and it necessarily accompanies a data exchange between those devices.

Definition 2.2. Data transfusion is a phenomenon that is caused by a device pairing — the host device infuses a copy of its (locally stored) secret and/or private user data into the paired wearable device to serve further paired actions.

The following threat model then raises research questions under data transfusion. *An adversary who acquired a user's wearable device, e.g., a smart watch, could have a chance from it to obtain user's secret and/or private data that might also be stored in a host device, i.e., a smartphone.* What kind of data could be found on the fly and how secret and/or private are they? Do those devices provide an unlock mechanism in the same degree of security? If they aren't, it may intrinsically be a great problem. But if they are, we may tackle another threat. *An adversary who also acquired a user's host device, could have a chance from the wearable device to find user's behavioral characteristics originally observed in the host device. For*

*Corresponding author.

Table 1: Experimental setup: types of pairing devices

Wearable Devices	Host Devices
Sony SmartWatch3 (Android Wear 1.3) LG G Watch (Android Wear 1.4)	LG Nexus 5X (Android 7.0)
Samsung Galaxy Gear (Tizen 2.2.1.1) Samsung Galaxy Gear2 Neo (Tizen 2.2.1.2)	Samsung Galaxy S3 (Android 4.3)
Apple Watch (WatchOS 3.1)	Apple iPhone 6S Plus (iOS 10.1.1)

Table 2: Experimental results of data transfusion

Platform / Data	Android Wear	Tizen	watchOS
Encrypted Lock Pattern	□ □ ■	⊠ ⊠ ⊠	⊠ ⊠ ⊠
Contact	■ ■ ■	■ ■ ■	■ ■ ■
SMS/MMS/Messenger	■ ■ ■	□ ■ ■	■ ■ ■
E-mail	□ ■ ■	□ ■ ■	□ ■ ■
Memo	□ ■ ■	⊠ ⊠ ⊠	⊠ ⊠ ⊠
Wi-Fi SSID/Password	■ ■ ■	⊠ ⊠ ⊠	⊠ ⊠ ⊠
Photo	■ ■ ■	■ ■ ■	□ □ □
Fitness Data	■ ■ ■	□ ■ ■	□ □ □
Location	□ □ ■	⊠ ⊠ ⊠	⊠ ⊠ ⊠
Calendar	□ ■ ■	□ ■ ■	□ □ ■
Host Device Info.	⊠ ⊠ ⊠	■ ■ ■	⊠ ⊠ ⊠
Host Installed Apps	■ ■ ■	⊠ ⊠ ⊠	□ ■ ■

□: Not transfused, ■: Transfused, ⊠: Unavailable
Three squares represent phase t_1, t_2 and t_3 for each platform

instance, does a user set the same passcode to unlock both devices? If the user does, a resource-limited wearable device could be a good medium target to attack the host device. An adversary could have at least double the chance of guessing a passcode. Finally we are also wondering if users are properly notified and aware of such phenomena and threats.

3 EXPERIMENTAL STUDY

Experiment Setup and Design. We conduct an experimental study of data extraction considering data transfusion in actual user environments. As summarized in Table 1, we attempt to extract stored data from five smart watch models, respectively, operated in three different platforms (Android Wear, watchOS, Tizen). In more concrete, we extract data in three subsequent phases of device connections: t_1, t_2, and t_3. At phase t_1, we disable network interfaces and isolate the smart watch to see data transfusion right after the initial pairing process. At t_2, we let the smart watch connected to the host smartphone to see data transfusion in the basic user mode. At t_3, we install additional apps to the smartphone and smart watch to see data transfusion in more complex use cases.

Experimental Results. In the experiment, we were able to extract various kinds of transfused data from smart watches at different phases. Table 2 illustrates the results of data transfusion at each phase according to the types of platforms. We also tried to observe whether enough notification was given for data transfusion.

To extract data from SmartWatch3 in Android Wear, it was possible to boot into recovery or bootloader mode without submitting a lock pattern although SmartWatch3 was locked by the lock pattern. We were able to observe transfused data even from t_1 without solid notifications or warnings. None of the retrieved files except for the pattern lock file were encrypted, and it was possible to analyze them with text and hexadecimal editors only. In watchOS, we externally observed the data transfusion phenomenon as a user because it was unable to bypass the locked state. In Tizen which was default in unlocked state, interestingly, the same transfusion results were observed at t_2 and t_3, respectively. This was because Tizen did not store the data from additionally installed apps.

To be specific, we extracted user's own Contact information and SMS/MMS messages which have a high risk score according to the risk assessment in Section 5. Also, we extracted Wi-Fi connection information such as Wi-Fi SSID, Wi-Fi password and encryption type (WPA-PSK). Some sensitive data that were never used by the smart watch but rather used by the paired smartphone was leaked from the smart watch. Especially, we retrieved encrypted lock pattern from SmartWatch3 which was cryptographically hashed by SHA-1. We were able to disable the pattern lock authentication simply by deleting the file in custom recovery mode. Once deleted, SmartWatch3 did not request users to unlock the lock pattern any more. Furthermore, we were able to crack the hashed lock pattern by generating a rainbow table with a simple Python script [4]. This implicates that the host smartphone paired to this smart watch could also be unlocked if users set the same lock pattern on both devices.

Moreover, we observed data transfusion from additionally installed fitness app called Strava. We observed fitness logs such as time, speeds, distance, accuracy data in clear text.

4 SURVEY STUDY

Survey Design and Study Method. The aim of our survey is to empirically understand how users think about data transfusion phenomenon. For survey, we point out research questions that satisfy our purpose.

(1) Is there any difference in users' security and privacy related perception on smart watch compared with smartphone?

(2) Have users seen the notification message that indicates transferring of the information? And does it affect users awareness of data transferring, effectively?

(3) Do users set the same passcode for both smartphone and smart watch?

We strive to recruit 205 participants (189 self-identified as male and 16 as female) who use both smartphone and smart watch. We validate actual smart watch users by requiring users to take a picture of the message that we sent. The model of the smart watches consists as follows: 49% of Samsung gear users, 43% of Apple Watch users and 8% of others. We present what we observed and analyzed in the following subsections.

Lower Risk Perception on Smart Watch. To obtain quantitative and qualitative understandings of how users' risk perception vary across smartphone and smart watch, we compare participants' risk perception of smart watch to that of smartphone in three perspectives: awareness of data storing, awareness of data leakage and awareness of security threat when lost. All three results show lower percentage on a smart watch than that of smartphone which indicate that users have lower risk perception on a smart watch.

Moderate Perception on Data Transfusion. It is necessary to have notification messages that indicate some sensitive data such as contact list, call records and GPS data in a smartphone can be transferred to a smart watch when paired. Apple, Sony and LG watch inform users with notification message but Samsung Gear does not. We separated participants into this two groups and asked *if they have seen the notification message.* Among the users who use smart watch with notification message, only 50% answered that they have seen it. And, 57% of the users whose smart watch lacks the notification message answered that they have seen the notification message. This results can be implied that whether the smart watches have notification or not, it does not affect the users. Furthermore, 85.2% of people who are aware of data transfusion initially were also aware of it when in use. Initial awareness plays significant role in continuous awareness, putting more weight on a high necessity of well-defined notification on a smart watch from the initial pairing process.

User's Behavioral Practice Different from User Perception. Based on the results showing that users tend to have lower risk perception on smart watches than smartphones, we expect that users set the different passcode for respective devices. However, users tend to set the same passcode on both devices and do not behave as they perceive. When we asked participants to answer *if they actually use or will use the same passcode on both a smartphone and a smartwatch*, 78% of participants who are using the same locking method on smartphone and smart watch actually use the same passcode on both devices. User's actual behavior seems to be far below their awareness and there is a gap between perceived risk and the actual risk.

5 RISK ASSESSMENT

From the experimental results, we observed that sensitive data are transfused from a smartphone to a smart watch. Subsequently, we perform risk assessment of smart watch data by considering the transfused user-specific data as an asset [3]. Firstly, we classify data into four categories according to the context of data: controls of device, communications, sensor data and user written data. Secondly, we define data and assign the impact score in terms of security and privacy. Lastly, we calculate the risk score by multiplying the impact score and the likelihood score of transfused data as follows.

$$Risk_{platform}(data) = Impact(data) * Likelihood_{phase}(data)$$
(1)

As the data to be transfused are different according to the transfusion phase, to reflect this, we scored the points that are likely to be transfused for each data as likelihood score. The likelihood, since we experimented independently on different platforms, must be a value that is different according to the platform. The sum of the risk score at t_3 is as follows on each platform: Android Wear - 78, Tizen - 65 and watchOS - 49. Figure 1 shows the risk score of transfused data on each platform at t_3.

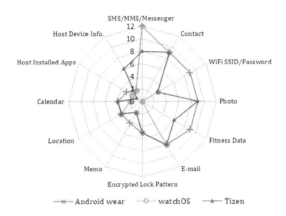

Figure 1: Risk scores of transfused data in each platform

6 DISCUSSION AND MITIGATION

We conducted both experimental and survey studies with regard to data extracted from smart watches by focusing on the data transfusion phenomenon, and performed risk assessment. We observed that rare notification lowered user perception on data transfusion and could be a trigger of security or privacy related incidents. For mitigation, if a smart watch is isolated, we propose transfused data to be removed from the smart watch after a certain amount of time according to *the descending order of the priority*, that is, from the highest priority based on our risk assessment levels shown in Figure 1. When the original user returns and wears the smart watch again, the removed data is re-transfused. We call this strategy *volatile transfusion* that enables safe data elimination when the device is separated from its user or the host device. We also propose to provide an explicit notification message to the user regarding data transfusion of the high priority data. It would also be considerable to request a user's active response, e.g., by swiping the items to be transfused. Future work may include a longitudinal user study adopting suggested mitigations with simulation experiments. We expect to observe how users react and compromise between usability and security when using smart watches.

ACKNOWLEDGMENTS

This work was partly supported by the National Research Foundation of Korea (NRF) grant funded by the Korea government (MSIT) (No. NRF-2 015R1A2A2A01004792), and also by the MSIT under the ITRC (Information Technology Research Center) support program (IITP-2017-2012-0-00646) supervised by the the IITP (Institute for Information & communications Technology Promotion).

REFERENCES

[1] Ibrahim Baggili, Jeff Oduro, Kyle Anthony, Frank Breitinger, and Glenn McGee. 2015. Watch what you wear: preliminary forensic analysis of smart watches. In *ARES Conference Proceedings.* IEEE, 303–311.
[2] Quang Do, Ben Martini, and Kim-Kwang Raymond Choo. 2017. Is the data on your wearable device secure? An Android Wear smartwatch case study. *Software: Practice and Experience* 47, 3 (2017), 391–403.
[3] I ISO and I Std. 2011. Iso 27005: 2011. *Information technology–Security techniques–Information security risk management. ISO* (2011).
[4] Michael Spreitzenbarth. 2012. Cracking the Pattern Lock on Android. (2012). https://forensics.spreitzenbarth.de/2012/02/28/cracking-the-pattern-lock-on-android/

POSTER: Intrusion Detection System for In-vehicle Networks using Sensor Correlation and Integration

Huaxin Li
Intel Labs
huaxin.li@intel.com

Li Zhao
Intel Labs
li.zhao@intel.com

Marcio Juliato
Intel Labs
marcio.juliato@intel.com

Shabbir Ahmed
Intel Labs
shabbir.ahmed@intel.com

Manoj R. Sastry
Intel Labs
manoj.r.sastry@intel.com

Lily L. Yang
Intel Labs
lily.l.yang@intel.com

ABSTRACT

The increasing utilization of Electronic Control Units (ECUs) and wireless connectivity in modern vehicles has favored the emergence of security issues. Recently, several attacks have been demonstrated against in-vehicle networks therefore drawing significant attention. This paper presents an Intrusion Detection System (IDS) based on a regression learning approach which estimates certain parameters by using correlated/redundant data. The estimated values are compared to observed ones to identify abnormal contexts that would indicate intrusion. Experiments performed with real-world vehicular data have shown that more than 90% of vehicle speed data can be precisely estimated within the error bound of 3 kph. The proposed IDS is capable of detecting and localizing attacks in real-time, which is fundamental to achieve automotive security.

CCS CONCEPTS

•Security and privacy → Intrusion detection systems;

KEYWORDS

vehicular security; in-vehicle intrusion detection system; cyber-physical security

1 INTRODUCTION

The increasing adoption of electronics in vehicles (e.g., electronic control unit, infotainment, V2X) has led to an expanding attack surface and even making them vulnerable to physical and remote attacks [5, 9]. The commonality among these attacks is that attackers were able to inject messages and tamper with the data in the CAN bus. Therefore, they were able to impersonate as valid electronic control units (ECUs) to subsequently perform malicious actions (e.g. braking) and deviate the system from a safe operational regime. The underlying problem that enabled the aforementioned attacks is the lack of proper message integrity in the CAN bus, which allows illegitimate messages can be consumed by the system as authentic ones. Cryptographic mechanisms for data origin authentication may not fully resolve the problem as ECUs, since attackers who

CCS'17, Oct. 30–Nov. 3, 2017, Dallas, TX, USA.
© 2017 Copyright held by the owner/author(s). ISBN 978-1-4503-4946-8/17/10.
DOI: http://dx.doi.org/10.1145/3133956.313884

Figure 1: The intrusion detection system is deployed on gateway and monitors CAN bus messages

have gained software execution on ECUs can still send their own authentic messages but with the attacker's malicious payload.

To ensure security and safety, it is crucial to employ intrusion detection systems (IDS) capable of deeply inspecting the bus and detecting anomalies. Meta-data based IDS focuses on each message by examining its message ID [6], frequency [7, 10], clock-skew [1], etc. Data content based IDS examines data content of messages by building machine learning models [3] and information theory models [8] for each kind of message data payload. There are limitations on what kind of attack each of the aforementioned methods can detect. For example, frequency-based IDS [7, 10] is able to detect message injection attacks by analyzing message frequencies. IDS based on physical properties [1] can identify impersonation attacks by fingerprinting each ECU. However both of them are unable to detect data alteration/falsification attacks. [3] and [8] can detect simple data spoofing attacks by examining the message content, but requires attack samples in its training phase. These limitations not only reduce the feasibility of intrusion detection in practice, but also fall short in detecting some more sophisticated types of attacks, for instance, when sensor readings are spoofed.

In this paper, we propose a machine learning based in-vehicle intrusion detection system based on correlations and redundancy among multiple sensors for detecting data spoofing attacks. Pairwise correlations between vehicular sensors have been analyzed in [2]. In our approach, a regression model is trained to integrate correlations from multiple sensors and estimate a targeted sensor value using other correlated parameters in real time. The difference between the estimated value and observed value of this sensor data is used as a signal for detecting anomalies. The integration of multiple heterogeneous sensors increases the attacker's difficulty of bypassing the IDS, while making the IDS more stable under different scenarios. As shown in Fig. 1, the IDS can be used in the vehicle's gateway to simultaneously monitor CAN messages containing real-time sensor signals. Experimental results on a real car show that our intrusion detection system is capable of effectively detecting sensor spoofing attacks.

2 METHODOLOGY

2.1 Problem Formulation

In order to detect anomalies, it is first necessary to estimate a targeted sensor value using other correlated parameters . It can be formulated as a prediction problem and modeled using regression models in machine learning. Regression models aim at describing statistical process for estimating the relationships among variables. So in the training phase, a set of correlated signals values are used to train a regression model M.

Given a trained regression model M and a set of parameters $S = \{s_1, s_2, ..., s_n\}$ (e.g., s_1=speed, s_2=acceleration, s_3=engine speed) extracted from CAN bus messages. Inputs of M are parameters values except one targeted value s_i that is being estimated (e.g., speed), i.e., $S-s_i$, and the output is the estimated value of s_i, denoted as s_i'. Then anomalies can be flagged by comparing s_i' with observed s_i.

2.2 Features and Model

In order to estimate the targeted sensor's values, correlated sensor values should be chosen as features of the regression model. The choice of features can be either 1) based on domain knowledge, which means people know which parameters are correlated to the targeted one based on common sense. For example, it should be expected that engine speed and longitudinal acceleration are highly correlated to the vehicle speed. 2) based on correlations, which means pairwise correlations of sensor values during some time are computed (e.g., using Pearson correlation coefficient), and high-correlation sensors are chose as the features.

Table 1 contains features we used to estimate vehicle speed as an example. They are collected from heterogeneous sensors and sent to CAN bus through multiple ECUs. For ease of presentation, we use vehicle speed and related sensor as an example throughout this paper. Without loss of generality, this model can be applied to other sensors by selecting correlated features.

Table 1: Features used for estimating vehicle speed

Features	Unit	Source ECU
Engine speed	rpm	PCM
Longitudinal acceleration	m/sec2	RCM
Lateral acceleration	m/sec2	RCM
Brake pedal	%	ABS
Yaw rate	m/sec2	ABS
Steering angle	degree	SASM
Gear	-	TCM

We choose Random Forest Regressor as the regression model in this paper. It is an ensemble of different regression trees and is used for nonlinear multiple regression [4]. A continuous estimated value will be given as the output of the model at each prediction.

2.3 Detection

At each time instance, an observed parameter's value can be interpreted from a corresponding CAN message. Meanwhile, we can estimate a value using other sensors' values extracted from other CAN messages, which is denoted as the estimated value. A simple strategy is to set a threshold for the difference between estimated values and observed values. For the examples shown in this paper, a speed threshold of 5 kilometer per hour (kph) is considered. Thus, a speed reading is considered normal if the difference between an observed value and its corresponding estimated value is less than 5 kph. Additional strategies can be applied to strengthen the confidence in the anomaly recognition. For example, if there are multiple consecutive estimations exceed the threshold, or majority of estimation exceeds the threshold over a period of time.

3 EVALUATION

To evaluate the performance of our IDS, we collected CAN data from a real car and simulated sensor spoofing attacks. The experimental settings is based on a Ubuntu 16.04 laptop connected to the car's CAN bus through ODB-II socket. Then the car was driven for collecting data. We collected three segments of driving in the city traffic (denoted as City1, City2, City3, respectively), and one segment of driving one a highway (denoted as HighWay). In the average, each segment contains more than 20 minutes of driving data.

We first evaluated the accuracy of the estimation to reflect the feasibility of our approach. For city driving data, each time we use two of the driving segments to train the regression model, and then estimate the speed in the remaining driving segment using features in Table 1. For highway driving data, we use the first half of data as training data, and the second half of data as testing data.

Table 2: Performance of estimating vehicle speed

Scenario	Error Mean (kph)	Error Median (kph)	Error ≤ 3 kph (%)
City1	0.996	0.147	91.25
City2	1.146	0.132	94.92
City3	0.670	0.222	91.38
HighWay	1.605	0.388	93.61

Table 2 shows the experiments results, where the (estimation) error is defined as $abs(estimated\ values - observed\ values)$. Table 2 shows that mean and median values of estimation error are closed to real observed values, and more than 90% of estimations can be done with errors smaller than 3 kph. This means that most of the estimation are accurate, and if we observe a sequence of estimated values exceed the threshold, we have high confidence to identify an attack. False positive will be caused by inaccurate estimations, and it can be reduced by: 1) increasing the training data, 2) leveraging sensor redundancy to improve estimation accuracy

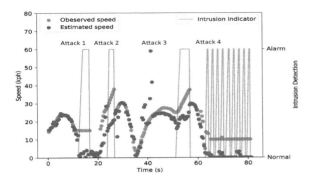

Figure 2: Illustration of intrusion detection

by taking homogeneous parameters into account (e.g., GPS speed, wheel speed v.s. vehicle speed). This will be discussed in Section 4.1.

The feasibility of detecting attacks are demonstrated by considering four types of sensor spoofing attacks:

Attack 1: spoofing sensor readings to a fixed value. For example, spoofing vehicle speed to 15 kph.

Attack 2: spoofing sensor readings to values that are deviated from real values. For example, adding an extra 15 kph to current speed readings.

Attack 3: gradually changing sensor readings. For example, adding 0.01 kph to the deviation of the current speed until reaching the attacker's goal.

Attack 4: alternately and repeatedly sending malicious and normal sensor readings. For example, the attacker can send several modified messages and then send several unaltered messages to mislead the IDS.

Fig. 2 demonstrates these four kinds of sensor spoofing attacks and the corresponding detection results respectively. Attack 1 and Attack 2 are immediately detected because the spoofed values exceed the threshold. Attack 3 is detected once the deviation exceeds the threshold of 5 kph. It means that the spoofing cannot exceed the threshold, which limits attackers' capability of spoofing sensor values and ensures safety to some extent. Attack 4 can also be detected because normal estimation should be dominated during a time period. This limits the number of messages that can spoofed by the attackers. Several wrong estimations occur at around 40th second, but they don't trigger alarms (false positives) based on our design (because they are not dominant during that time). False positives can be further minimized by increasing estimation accuracy and adopting different strategies in future work. Besides, our experiments show that these detection can be accomplished in real time, which means computations of the model will not cause delay.

4 DISCUSSION AND ANALYSIS

4.1 Sensor Redundancy

To optimize the estimation, we can further leverage redundancy among sensors. The redundancy can be found in 1) different CAN bus networks sent by different ECUs. For example, we can find vehicle speed values in both Powertrain (PT) and Chassis (CH) networks. 2) homogeneous sensors. For example, the speed computed at four wheels (i.e., wheel speed) and speed computed by GPS signals (i.e., GPS speed) are good references for vehicle speed.

These redundant data/sensors can be taken as features of the model to improve accuracy. For example, after adding wheel speed as a feature, the average errors for estimating vehicle speed became only 0.101 kph.

4.2 Incremental learning

Another factor that affects estimation accuracy is under different contexts (e.g., road condition, topology, weather), the correlations among sensors would change therefore causing false positives. A solution to mitigate the influence of contexts is incrementally train the model using new data in real time, so that the model can be adjusted to learn the correlations under new contexts.

4.3 Attack Localization

The IDS introduced in this paper is capable of not only detecting intrusion/anomalies, but also localizing the parameter that was compromised. For example, when longitudinal acceleration is modified by increasing 2 m/s^2, the model targeting at longitudinal acceleration triggers an alarm immediately, while the model targeting at vehicle speed will not be sharply affected.

5 CONCLUSIONS

In this paper, we propose an approach to integrate multiple correlated/redundant parameters to detect sensor data spoofing attacks for in-vehicle networks. The proposed approach uses a Random Forest Regression as a predictor of our model. As studied in this paper, more than 90% vehicle speed parameters can be estimated by our model within the error bound of 3 kph, which provides a safety boundary. Experiments on vehicle data show that the proposed approach can effectively detect intrusion attacks and anomalies in real time, but also determine the compromised parameter during the attack.

REFERENCES

[1] Kyong-Tak Cho and Kang G Shin. 2016. Fingerprinting Electronic Control Units for Vehicle Intrusion Detection.. In *USENIX Security Symposium*. 911–927.
[2] Arun Ganesan, Jayanthi Rao, and Kang Shin. 2017. *Exploiting Consistency Among Heterogeneous Sensors for Vehicle Anomaly Detection*. Technical Report. SAE Technical Paper.
[3] Min-Joo Kang and Je-Won Kang. 2016. Intrusion detection system using deep neural network for in-vehicle network security. *PloS one* 11, 6 (2016), e0155781.
[4] Andy Liaw, Matthew Wiener, et al. 2002. Classification and regression by randomForest. *R news* 2, 3 (2002), 18–22.
[5] Charlie Miller and Chris Valasek. 2015. Remote exploitation of an unaltered passenger vehicle. *Black Hat USA* 2015 (2015).
[6] MarchettiiiijŇ Mirco and Dario Stabili. 2017. Anomaly detection of CAN bus messages through analysis of ID sequences.. In *Intelligent Vehicles Symposium (IV)*.
[7] Michael R Moore, Robert A Bridges, Frank L Combs, Michael S Starr, and Stacy J Prowell. 2017. Modeling inter-signal arrival times for accurate detection of CAN bus signal injection attacks: a data-driven approach to in-vehicle intrusion detection. In *Proceedings of the 12th Annual Conference on Cyber and Information Security Research*. ACM, 11.
[8] Michael Müter and Naim Asaj. 2011. Entropy-based anomaly detection for in-vehicle networks. In *Intelligent Vehicles Symposium (IV), 2011 IEEE*. IEEE, 1110–1115.
[9] Keen Security Lab of Tencent. 2016. Car Hacking Research: Remote Attack Tesla Motors. (sep 2016). http://keenlab.tencent.com/en/2016/09/19/Keen-Security-Lab-of-Tencent-Car-Hacking-Research-Remote-Attack-to-Tesla-Cars/
[10] Hyun Min Song, Ha Rang Kim, and Huy Kang Kim. 2016. Intrusion detection system based on the analysis of time intervals of CAN messages for in-vehicle network. In *Information Networking (ICOIN), 2016 International Conference on*. IEEE, 63–68.

POSTER: Practical Fraud Transaction Prediction

Longfei Li, Jun Zhou, Xiaolong Li, Tao Chen
Ant Financial Services Group, China
{longyao.llf, jun.zhoujun, xl.li, boshan.ct}@antfin.com

ABSTRACT

Nowadays, online payment systems play more and more important roles in people's daily lives. A key component of these systems is to detect and prevent fraud transactions. In industrial practice, such a task is separated into two phases: 1) mining evidential features to describe users, 2) building an effective model based on these features. Generally speaking, the most popular fraud transaction detection systems use elaborately designed features to build tree based models, sometimes a subsequent linear model is added to improve the behaviour. However, the designed features usually contains only static features, while dynamic features are not considered. In addition, the subsequent model can only learn a linear combination, which may always be unsatisfactory. To address these issues, we present a systematic method, which extracts not only users' static features but also dynamic features based on their recent behaviors. Moreover, N-GRAM model is employed to handle the dynamic features so that time series information is addressed. Based on the extracted features, a tree based model is applied and the outputs of it are regarded as new generated feature representations, which will be further inputted into a Deep Neural Network (DNN) to learn the complex relationships and form the final classification model. Extensive experiments show that our proposed model (with both static and dynamic features) significantly outperforms the existing methods.

KEYWORDS

Fraud Transaction Detection; GBDT; DNN

1 INTRODUCTION

Online payment is becoming more and more important in people's daily lives. A giant online payment system, such as PayPal, WeChat pay, and Alipay, can have hundreds of millions of users and generates millions of online transactions per day. Although online payment brings more convenience to people, it also faces more and more challenges as the network environment becoming more and more complex. One of the critical challenges is fraud transactions which will harm both the account holders and platform. The ability to detect and prevent fraud transactions is thus very crucial for online payment systems.

Fraud transaction detection is very challenging. First, it is not a simple binary classification problem, as we need to build a regression or scoring model and choose a threshold to differentiate fraud and normal transactions. Furthermore, the suspicious transaction will be suspended with a notification sending to the involved users.

A false alarm of fraud transaction will lower down transaction success rate and even harm the user experience. Last but not least, in an online payment platform, in order to protect the user accounts, usually we use multiple authentication methods such as face recognition, SMS etc, which will cost a lot of money. An accurate data-driven method can help to reduce such cost. In this paper, we will present a practical data-driven method for fraud transaction detection in our production system, for which we shall share our experience in feature engineering and model design.

Feature Engineering. Traditionally, we build a model based on users' static features, such as trade amounts and trade frequencies, for fraud detection. However, static features only contain the historical profiles of a user, which do not include dynamic user behaviors. In this work, we propose to not only extract static user features from their profiles, but also dynamic features from their recent behaviors. Specifically, we find that the dynamic features from user behaviors help to significantly improve model performance compared with only using the static features in our task.

Model Design. Usually we can build a linear model such as Logistic Regression(LR), or a nonlinear model such as Deep Neural Network(DNN), or tree based model, such as RF and GBDT for the task. For linear or nonlinear model, usually some feature transformation such as feature discretization need to be conducted before feeding the raw features into the model. For tree-based model, the raw features can be directly fed in, as the model is able to split the numerical values accordingly. This property and the strong representation power of tree based models make them widely adopted in the industries. Despite this, an RF or GBDT model is a linear combination of separate trees, which can be observed from Eq. (1),

$$F(x) = \sum_{i=1}^{n} \gamma_i h_i(x) + const, \tag{1}$$

where γ_i is the weight of the i-th trees, and $h_i(x)$ is the output of i-th tree. In practice, these linear weights may not be optimal, since the old weights $\gamma_1, \ldots, \gamma_i$ are never updated when a new tree h_{i+1} is introduced. To solve this issue, some researchers use LR to re-learn the weights and treat the tree-based model as feature transform method [3], which archives better results. However, LR cannot catch the connections among the features, which may limit the performance of the transaction risk estimation. So, we propose to use DNN for learning the new weights of different trees, denoted as GBDT-DNN for convenience. Extensive experiments show that our GBDT-DNN hybrid model with dynamic feature significantly outperforms all the other baselines.

In summary, our main contributions are:

- We propose to extract dynamic user behaviors for the task of fraud transaction detection;
- We propose a GBDT-DNN model for the task;

CCS '17, October 30-November 3, 2017, Dallas, TX, USA
© 2017 Copyright held by the owner/author(s).
ACM ISBN 978-1-4503-4946-8/17/10.
https://doi.org/10.1145/3133956.3138826

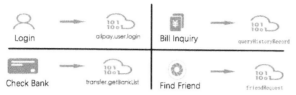

Remote procedure call(RPC) from Alipay APP

Figure 1: Remote Procedure Call Protocol

- Extensive experiments show our methods significantly outperform other baselines. We deployed our method in a real application and shared our experience.

2 ARCHITECTURE

In this section, we will introduce the details of both feature engineering and model design.

2.1 Feature Engineering

We have mainly used two types of features, one is user profile features which are static, the other is user behavior features which are dynamic.

User profile features: According to a person's transaction and shopping records in the platform, we can get some profiles of the person, such as working place, living place, credit score (similar with FICO score), trading amount, etc, which demonstrates a person's consuming ability and consumption habits. The rationale of using such features is that an unusual transaction amount or location may be with fraud.

Dynamic features: When a user is using the platform's services, we can record which services this user have used. As shown in Fig 1, behaviors like login, check bill, check bank card will be recorded in our database. From these operation behaviors, we can learn the user's common behavior patterns.

The operation behaviors can be treated as a time series data. Common methods for handling such data are discussed as follows.

First, simply using a statistic of the appearance of user behaviors. Specifically, we use a binary vector representation of user behaviors, where the total length of the vector is the dimension of behaviors and the value at each dimension indicate the presence or absence of the corresponding behavior. Second, the behavior sequence matters as the same click behaviors but with difference sequences reveal different transaction status. To make use of such sequential information, we can use N-gram features (capture at most length N sequences). In our study, we found that a binary vector representation of all behavior features has shown to have competitive performance and could be easily deployed in an industrial scale application.

2.2 model design

In this section we present our proposed hybrid model structure: the concatenation of boosted decision trees and deep neural network classifier, as illustrated in Figure 2.

The boosted decision trees are shown to be a powerful model to transform the original features of an instance [3], which can then

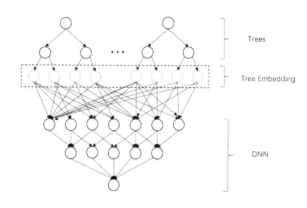

Figure 2: Hybrid model structure. Input features are transformed by boosted decision trees. The output of each individual tree is treated as a categorical input feature feeding to a fully connected DNN.

be utilized by other models to further get even higher accuracy. Specifically, we use each learned individual tree as a categorical feature, where the value is set as the index of the leaf node the instance falls in. As a result, if there are n trees in the GBDT model, the transformed feature of an instance is given in terms of a structured vector $x = (e_{i_1}, ..., e_{i_n})$, where e_{i_k} is the i_k-th unit vector with the dimension of d_k, where d_k is the number of leaf nodes at k-th tree, and i_k is the index of the leaf node where the current instance falls into at k-th tree. Such feature extraction method will not bring too much pressure for online systems. In the training phase, we also assume that a binary label $y \in \{1, 0\}$ is given for each transaction, to indicate whether it is risky or not. Finally, we can use the transformed feature to train a DNN model, which can further outperform GBDT.

The DNN model used in our study is a five-layer fully connected network. It has three hidden layers each coupled with a Rectifier function as the activation function. The output layer uses the sigmoid function. Empirical studies show a deeper network structure does not provide significant improvements.

3 EXPERIMENT

In this section, we will represent our experiment.

3.1 Experimental Setup

In our experiments, we used a real historical transaction dataset from a giant online payment platform. The features of each instance consists of transactional information, user information and user behavior records as is mentioned in section 2.1, besides, for dynamic features, user's interactions with the the APP during the recent two days are selected as feature, if the number of interaction is bigger than 200, we will drop the old interactions, at the same time, low-frequency interaction behaviors are filtered out to focus on high-frequency behaviors.

The dimensions of the static features dimension is 273 and dynamic features dimension is 2790.

To perform rigorous and controlled experiments, we prepared a sufficiently large dataset which consists of transactions records from 5 months in 2016. To simulate the online environment, we divide the whole dataset into a training set, a validation set, and a testing set according to the time stamps. Specifically, the data from the first three months is treated as the training set, the next month as the validation set, and the last month as the testing set. As we notice that the risky samples are too rare while non-risk samples are too many, we downsample the non-risky samples to balance the proportion between them. The details of the data sizes are summarized in Table 1.

Table 1: Statistics of Datasets in Millions

Data set	train set	validation set	test set
Size(M)	7.3	2.4	2.3

To validate the effectiveness of the proposed GBDT-DNN and dynamic feature, we compare a number of state-of-the-art techniques on our transaction dataset, which includes:

- LR: the Logistic Regression algorithm [1];
- DNN: Deep Neural Networks with plain feature;
- GBDT: Gradient Boosting Decision Tree;
- GBDT-LR: LR with GBDT transformed feature;

Since our dataset is large and security, we use KunPeng algorithm platform which is quite similar with Pettum which contain all the algorithm we used in our experiments except LSTM.

For GBDT, we use 400 trees and restrict the max depth of each tree as 3, to cover more features (and their correlations) and prevent over-fitting. For DNN and GBDT-DNN, they have the same network structure: three fully connected hidden layers with 256,128,128 hidden units, respectively. The Rectifier function is adopted as active function. The output of DNN is compressed by the sigmoid function, and the optimization solver adopted is Adagrad [2].

3.2 Comparison with Baseline Models

Firstly we compare all the methods only based on the static features, where **Recall At Top Percent (RATP)** is used to evaluate their performance. RATP@r is the recall of the subset which consists of the instances with the top r percentage of prediction scores. The results are summarized in the Table 2.

Table 2: RATP Result with static feature

Model Structure	RATP@0.02	RATP@0.05	RATP@0.1
LR	0.402	0.534	0.602
DNN	0.425	0.634	0.683
GBDT	0.524	0.718	0.792
GBDT-LR	0.525	0.723	0.796
GBDT-DNN	**0.546**	**0.734**	**0.803**

From the test RATP in Table 2, we observe GBDT-DNN significantly outperforms all the baselines. Since transaction amount is so huge, a little improvement can significantly decrease the number

of people to be disturbed. We can find that GBDT-DNN always outperforms all the other baselines when we use different percentages (0.02%, 0.05%, 0.1%). For example, GBDT-DNN is 2.1%, 1.6% better than GBDT under RATP@0.02 and RATP@0.05, respectively. These observations show that the proposed GBDT-DNN can significantly improve RATP.

3.3 Importance of Behavioral Features

In this subsection, we shall examine the importance of behavior features.

Table 3: AUC Results on adding behavior features (Beh) to the original model (Orig).

Model	LR	DNN	GBDT	GBDT-LR	GBDT-DNN
Orig.	0.9546	0.9675	0.9922	0.9923	0.9934
+Beh.	0.9612	0.9721	0.9935	0.9936	**0.9944**

Firstly, we use Area-Under-ROC (AUC) to evaluate the methods, which is shown in Table 3. Since the majority of the transaction is non-fraud, the baseline AUC score is pretty high. Our GBDT-DNN helps increase AUC by more than 0.08% relative to that of GBDT. However, a small improvement on the AUC helps to prevent a large number of fraud transactions. To validate this, again, we evaluate the methods in terms of RATP as shown in Table 4.

Table 4: RATP Results with behavioral features. The relative improvements over static features are shown in brackets.

Model Structure	RATP@0.02	RATP@0.05	RATP@0.1
LR	0.411(+2.2%)	0.551(+3.2%)	0.632(+5.0%)
DNN	0.429(+0.9%)	0.644(+1.6%)	0.714(+4.5%)
GBDT	0.538(+2.7%)	0.732(+1.9%)	0.812(+2.5%)
GBDT-LR	0.541(+3.0%)	0.732(+1.2%)	0.814(+2.3%)
GBDT-DNN	**0.568**(+4.0%)	**0.751**(+2.3%)	**0.832**(+3.6%)

From RATP results in Table 4, we find that after using behavior features, almost every algorithm makes an impressive improvement from at 0.9% to 5.0%. And our proposed GBDT-DNN model still outperforms all the other algorithms.

4 CONCLUSIONS

In this work, we demonstrate a systematic way to extract user features regarding their profiles and recent behaviors for fraud transaction detection task. We further present a hybrid model to tackle this task, which uses DNN to boost GBDT results. Experiments have been conducted on a real large-scale dataset to show the effectiveness of our proposed model. Our model has also been deployed in a giant online payment platform and outperformed the previous production system significantly. As future work, we seek to use a unified model to automatically learn high-level features from raw data for fraud transaction detection.

REFERENCES

[1] Galen Andrew and Jianfeng Gao. 2007. Scalable training of L 1-regularized log-linear models. In *ICML*.
[2] John Duchi, Elad Hazan, and Yoram Singer. 2011. Adaptive subgradient methods for online learning and stochastic optimization. *JMLR* (2011).
[3] Xinran He and et al. 2014. Practical lessons from predicting clicks on ads at facebook. In *Proceedings of the Eighth International Workshop on Data Mining for Online Advertising*.

POSTER: Vulnerability Discovery with Function Representation Learning from Unlabeled Projects

Guanjun Lin, Jun Zhang, Wei Luo, Lei Pan
School of Information Technology, Deakin University,
Australia
Geelong, VIC
{lingu,jun.zhang,wei.luo,l.pan}@deakin.edu.au

Yang Xiang
Digital Research & Innovation Capability Platform,
Swinburne University of Technology, Australia
Melbourne, VIC
yxiang@swin.edu.au

ABSTRACT

In cybersecurity, vulnerability discovery in source code is a fundamental problem. To automate vulnerability discovery, Machine learning (ML) based techniques has attracted tremendous attention. However, existing ML-based techniques focus on the component or file level detection, and thus considerable human effort is still required to pinpoint the vulnerable code fragments. Using source code files also limit the generalisability of the ML models across projects. To address such challenges, this paper targets at the function-level vulnerability discovery in the cross-project scenario. A function representation learning method is proposed to obtain the high-level and generalizable function representations from the abstract syntax tree (AST). First, the serialized ASTs are used to learn project independence features. Then, a customized bi-directional LSTM neural network is devised to learn the sequential AST representations from the large number of raw features. The new function-level representation demonstrated promising performance gain, using a unique dataset where we manually labeled 6000+ functions from three open-source projects. The results confirm that the huge potential of the new AST-based function representation learning.

KEYWORDS

vulnerability detection; cross-project; AST; representation learning

1 INTRODUCTION

Vulnerability detection is an important problem for mitigating security risks in software. Early and accurate detection is the key that makes machine learning (ML) based automatic vulnerability detection techniques a preferred approach, as manual inspection has been infeasible with program source codes growing exponentially. Scandariato et al. [5] applied ML techniques for detecting vulnerable components on Android applications. Shin et al. [6] used models trained on early versions of Firefox and Linux kernel for vulnerable files detection on subsequent versions. These approaches mainly focus on component- or file-level vulnerability detection. A finer-grained approach was presented by Yamaguchi et al. [7] for extrapolating vulnerable functions. Nevertheless, their method works on the within-project domain.

In this paper, we propose an approach for function-level vulnerability detection on cross-project scenario. We overcome the difficulty of obtaining manual labels by leveraging well-understood complexity metrics (used as a *proxy*), which can be automatically generated at large scales. Such complexity metrics data are subsequently used to bootstrap the generation of rich representations of the abstract syntax trees (ASTs) of functions. Our approach builds on the assumption that vulnerable programming patterns are associated with many potential vulnerabilities, and these patterns can be discovered by analyzing the program's ASTs. To capture local and relational features in a function, we use bi-directional Long Short-Term Memory (LSTM) [3] networks for learning high-level representations of ASTs. Our empirical studies illustrate that the obtained representations reveals important signals which can distinguish between neutral and vulnerable functions.

Our contributions can be summarized as follows:

- We propose a learning framework for functions-level vulnerability detection on cross-project domains.
- We develop an approach to extract the sequential features of ASTs which represent the structural information of functions for vulnerability detection.
- We implement a stacked LSTM network and use a proxy as the substitute of data labels for acquiring high-level representations of ASTs which can be used as indicators for vulnerability detection.

2 FUNCTION REPRESENTATION LEARNING

Figure 1 illustrates the work flow of our proposed framework which contains 4 stages. The first stage is data collection. Our experiments include three open-source projects: LibTIFF, LibPNG and FFmpeg whose source code can be downloaded from Github. We extract raw features from the ASTs of functions in the second stage. In stage three, we design a stacked LSTM network and introduce a proxy for learning AST representations of functions. The last stage is to examine prediction capability of the learned representations in detecting vulnerable functions on real-world cases.

2.1 AST Sequential Processing

We used "*CodeSensor*[1]", which is a robust parser implemented by [8] based on the concept of *island grammars* [4], so we could extract ASTs from source code without a working build environment.

An AST represents programming patterns by depicting the structural information of the code (i.e. a function). It reveals the relationships of components of a function in a tree view and contains

CCS'17, , Oct. 30–Nov. 3, 2017, Dallas, TX, USA.
© 2017 Copyright held by the owner/author(s).
ACM ISBN ISBN 978-1-4503-4946-8/17/10.
https://doi.org/http://dx.doi.org/10.1145/3133956.3138840

---

[1] http://codeexploration.blogspot.com.au/

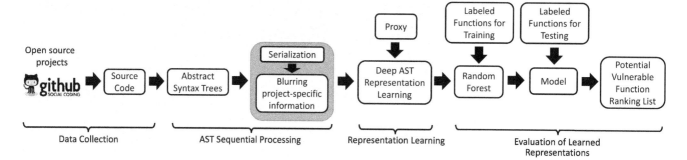

Figure 1: The work flow of our proposed framework

control flow at function level. To preserve the structural information, we use depth-first traversal to map the nodes of ASTs to elements of vectors so that each node will become an element of a vector. The sequence of elements in a vector partially reflects the hierarchical position of the nodes in an AST. After mapping the AST of a function to a vector, it will be in a form like: [*foo, int, params, int, x, stmnts, decl, int, y, op, =, call, bar,...*]. The first element *foo* is the name of the function, and the second element *int* denotes the return type of function *foo*. The third and fourth elements *params* and *int* specify that function *foo* takes a parameter which is an *int* type, and so on. For this textual vector, we treat it as a "sentence" with semantic meanings. The semantic meaning is formed by the elements of the vector and their sequence.

Due to our data being collected from three different software projects which follow distinct naming conventions, a universal naming criterion is required to normalize the project-specific names. For instance, it is very unlikely for project LibPNG to have a function named exactly the same in FFmpeg. What we do is to blur the names that are project-specific and replace them with "proj-specific" terms.

With function-level vulnerability detection, a sufficient amount of labeled data are required to train a statistical model. However, such labels are usually obtained through manual process. Instead of using actual labels, we use a proxy to approximate the functionality of the label. In this paper, we choose the proxy from code metrics as these metrics are quality measures for quantifying programs' complexity in software tests [2], therefore they were important indicators of faults and vulnerabilities in software [1] and [6]. Thanks to *Understand*[2], a commercial code enhancement tool, we are able to collect function-level code metrics from source code.

2.2 Deep AST Representation

There is a strong resemblance between ASTs and "sentences" in natural languages, which motivates us to apply LSTM for learning high-level representations. The vectors mapped from an AST containing components in a sequence reflect the tree structural information. Namely, the structure of an AST is partially preserved by elements assembled in a sequence through depth-first traversal. In this sense, the converted vectors contain semantic meanings which are formed by the sequential context of elements like [*main, int, decl, int, op,..., return*]. Altering the sequence of any element changes the semantic meanings. More importantly, there are connections among elements, which forms the context information.

For instance, the first element of a vector is the name of a function, followed closely by its return type. The element immediately after function name "*main*" should be its return type such as "*int*" or "*void*", and should not be other C/C++ keywords such as "*decl*" or "*return*". LSTM' architecture is built for handling such data. So, we assume that a function with vulnerability will display certain "linguistic" oddities discoverable by LSTM.

Another reason which justifies the application of LSTM is that the vulnerable programming patterns in a function can usually be associated with more than one lines of code. When we map functions to vectors, patterns linked to vulnerabilities are related to multiple elements of the vector. The standard RNNs are able to handle short-term dependencies such as the element "*main*" which should be followed by type name "*int*" or "*void*", but they have problem of dealing with long-term dependencies such as capturing the vulnerable programming patterns that are related to many continuous or intermittent elements. Therefore, we use RNN with LSTM cells to capture long-term dependencies for learning high-level representations of potential vulnerabilities.

The architecture of our LSTM-based network contains 5 layers. The first layer is for embedding which maps each element of the sequence to a vector of fixed dimensionality. The second and third layers are stacked LSTM layers each of which contains 64 LSTM units in a bi-directional form (altogether 128 LSTM units per layer). The stacked LSTM layers are capable of learning higher-level abstractions. The last two layers are dense layers with "ReLU" and "Linear" activation functions for converging a 128-dimensionality output to a single dimensionality. The choice of loss function in our experiments is "MSE". We feed the network with extracted ASTs of the three open-source projects. Instead of using labels of the input ASTs, we used a code metric as a proxy for obtaining the representations which are the output of the third layer.

3 EMPIRICAL STUDY

We apply the random forest algorithm to evaluate the effectiveness of the learned AST representations.

Among the functions that we used for obtaining AST representations, we manually label them as vulnerable or neutral so we can examine how effective the learned representations are when using them as features for vulnerability detection. For acquiring

---

[2]https://scitools.com/

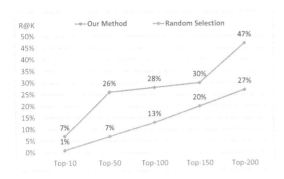

Figure 2: The R@K comparison between our method and random selection on cross-project scenario

vulnerable functions, we refer to the National Vulnerability Database (NVD)[3] and the Common Vulnerability and Exposures (CVE)[4], which are publicly available vulnerability data repositories. Our labels are according to the records until 20th July 2017. Then, excluding the identified vulnerable functions, we select the remaining functions as neutral ones. Before mapping ASTs to vectors, we truncate the trees that are more than 14 layers. When converting ASTs to vectors, we truncate the vectors containing more than 620 elements and pad them with 0s for vectors having fewer elements.

Due to the vulnerability inspection mainly being a manual process, it is not cost-effective for a practitioner to check on every function on the code base. It is practical to examine a small portion of code that is most likely to be vulnerable. For the evaluation, we retrieve a list of functions ranked by their probabilities of being vulnerable. The performance of our method is measured by the proportion of vulnerable functions returned in a function list. Hence, the metrics that we apply for evaluation is top-k recall ($R@K$). In our context, the R@K refers to the proportion of vulnerable functions which are in the retrieved top-k function list.

To evaluate the effectiveness of the learned representations on cross-project scenario, firstly, we combine the ASTs of the functions from three projects and feed them to the LSTM network. In this paper, we choose the "*essential complexity*" as the proxy for acquiring the representations. Secondly, we group the learned representations according to projects and use the FFmpeg and LibTIFF for training a random forest algorithm to test on the LibPNG. Totally, our training set contains 5736 functions among which there are 274 vulnerable functions. There are 750 functions in the testing set containing 43 vulnerable ones. Figure 2 illustrates that with our method, 20 vulnerable functions can be identified by checking the returned 200 functions. With random selection, one can only cover 27% of vulnerable functions by chance when examining 200 randomly selected functions.

To test that the LSTM networks truly pick up the vulnerable patterns hidden in the ASTs, we train a random forest classifier using essential complexity alone and compared whether its predicting power is stronger than the learned representations. The outcome shows that within top 50 retrieved functions, the learned representations exhibit more predicting power than the random selection scheme.

[3] https://nvd.nist.gov/
[4] https://cve.mitre.org/

4 DISCUSSION

This work, although in its early stage, has already demonstrated the feasibility and potential of learning deep representation from AST and proxy metrics. In particular, the project-independent AST representations provide new angles for vulnerable function discovery. We see several lines of research to extend the current work.

Alternative proxies. The proxy selected will affect the representation learned. We will evaluate other proxies, such as the line-of-code or cyclomatic complexity. Other metrics or information of programs can also serve as proxies. Moreover, to avoid overfitting, we can consider multiple proxies for guiding the new representation learning. This can be achieved using the multi-task deep-learning approach with shared modeling component.

The generalisability of representation can be further improved with a more flexible architecture such as the sequence-to-sequence network. This will eliminate the dependence on proxies. The current work benefits from the evaluation on a small set of labels manually curated. We are continuing the data labeling process. More labeled data will no doubt allow us to gain more insights into how deep learning can help reveal program vulnerabilities.

5 CONCLUSIONS

We propose an approach for automatic learning high-level representations of functions based on their ASTs. With an AST parser, we are able to extract functions' ASTs and convert them to vectors. To handle cross-project detection, we blur the project-specific contents while preserving the structural information by leveraging a stacked LSTM network for capturing representations that depict the intrinsic patterns of the vulnerable functions. Our experiment demonstrated that the learned representations were effective for cross-project vulnerability detection at function level.

ACKNOWLEDGEMENT

Guanjun Lin is supported by the Australian Government Research Training Program Scholarship. And this work was supported by the National Natural Science Foundation of China (No. 61401371).

REFERENCES

[1] Istehad Chowdhury and Mohammad Zulkernine. 2011. Using complexity, coupling, and cohesion metrics as early indicators of vulnerabilities. *Journal of Systems Architecture* 57, 3 (2011), 294–313.
[2] Emanuel Giger, Marco D'Ambros, Martin Pinzger, and Harald C Gall. 2012. Method-level bug prediction. In *Proceedings of the ACM-IEEE international symposium on Empirical software engineering and measurement*. ACM, 171–180.
[3] Sepp Hochreiter and Jürgen Schmidhuber. 1997. Long short-term memory. *Neural computation* 9, 8 (1997), 1735–1780.
[4] Leon Moonen. 2001. Generating robust parsers using island grammars. In *Reverse Engineering, 2001. Proceedings. Eighth Working Conference on*. IEEE, 13–22.
[5] Riccardo Scandariato, James Walden, Aram Hovsepyan, and Wouter Joosen. 2014. Predicting vulnerable software components via text mining. *IEEE Transactions on Software Engineering* 40, 10 (2014), 993–1006.
[6] Yonghee Shin, Andrew Meneely, Laurie Williams, and Jason A Osborne. 2011. Evaluating complexity, code churn, and developer activity metrics as indicators of software vulnerabilities. *IEEE Transactions on Software Engineering* 37, 6 (2011), 772–787.
[7] Fabian Yamaguchi, Felix Lindner, and Konrad Rieck. 2011. Vulnerability extrapolation: assisted discovery of vulnerabilities using machine learning. In *Proceedings of the 5th USENIX conference on Offensive technologies*. USENIX Association, 13–13.
[8] Fabian Yamaguchi, Markus Lottmann, and Konrad Rieck. 2012. Generalized vulnerability extrapolation using abstract syntax trees. In *Proceedings of the 28th Annual Computer Security Applications Conference*. ACM, 359–368.

POSTER: Neural Network-based Graph Embedding for Malicious Accounts Detection

Ziqi Liu[†★], ChaoChao Chen[†★], Jun Zhou[†], Xiaolong Li[†], Feng Xu[†], Tao Chen[†], Le Song[†‡]

[†]Ant Financial Services Group, Hangzhou, China
[‡]Georgia Institute of Technology, Atlanta, USA
{ziqiliu,chaochao.ccc,jun.zhoujun,xl.li,fuyu.xf,boshan.ct,le.song}@antfin.com

ABSTRACT

We present a neural network based graph embedding method for detecting malicious accounts at Alipay, one of the world's leading mobile payment platform. Our method adaptively learns discriminative embeddings from an account-device graph based on two fundamental weaknesses of attackers, i.e. device aggregation and activity aggregation. Experiments show that our method achieves outstanding precision-recall curve compared with existing methods.

KEYWORDS

Malicious account detection; Graph embedding

1 INTRODUCTION

Large scale online services such as Gmail[1], Facebook[2] and Alipay[3] have becoming popular targets for cyber attacks. By creating malicious accounts, attackers can propagate spam messages, seek excessive profits, which are essentially harmful to the eco-systems.

Many existing security mechanisms to deal with malicious accounts have extensively studied the attack characteristics [1, 3–6] which hopefully can discern the normal and malicious accounts. To exploit such characteristics, existing research mainly spreads in three directions. First, *Rule-based methods* directly generate sophisticated rules for identification. For example Xie et al. [5] proposed "spam payload" and "spam server traffic" properties for generating high quality regular expression signatures. Second, *Graph-based methods* reformulate the problem by considering the connectivities among accounts. This is based on the intuition that attackers can only evade individually but cannot control the interactions with normal accounts. For example, Zhao et al. [6] analyzed connected subgraph components by constructing account-account graphs to identify large abnormal groups. Third, *Machine learning-based*

methods learn statistic models by exploiting large amount of historical data. For examples, Huang et al. [3] extracted features based on graph properties and built supervised classifiers for identifying malicious account. Cao et al. [1] advanced the usages of aggregating behavioral patterns to uncover malicious accounts in an unsupervised machine learning framework.

As attacking strategies from potential adversaries change, it is crucial that a good system could adapt to the evolving strategies [1, 6]. We summarize the following two major observations from attackers as the fundamental basis of our work. (1) *Device aggregation*. Attackers are subjected to cost on computing resources. That is, due to economic constraints, it is costly if attackers can control a large amount of computing resources. As a result, most accounts owned by one attacker or a group of attackers will signup or sigin frequently on only a small number of resources. (2) *Activity aggregation*. Attackers are subject to the limited time of campaigns. Basically, attackers are required to fulfil specific goals in a short term. That means the behaviors of malicious accounts controlled by single attacker could burst in limited time. We illustrate such two patterns from the dataset of Alipay in Figure 1.

The weaknesses of attackers have been extensively analyzed, however, it's still challenging to identify attackers with both high precision and recall[4]. Existing methods usually achieve very low false positive by setting strict constraints but potentially missing out the opportunities on identifying much more suspicious accounts, i.e. with a high false negative rate. The reason is that the huge amount of benign accounts interwined with only a small number of suspicious accounts, and this results into a low signal-to-noise-ratio. It is quite common that normal accounts share the same IP address with malicious accounts due to the noisy data, or the IP address comes from a proxy. Thus make it important to jointly consider the "Device aggregation" and "Activity aggregation" altogether.

In this work, we propose Graph Embeddings for Malicious accounts, (GEM), a novel nueral network-based graph technique, which *jointly* considers "Device aggregation" and "Activity aggregation" in a unified model. Our proposed method essentially models the topology of account-device graph, and simultaneously considers the characteristics of activities of the accounts in the local structure of this graph. The basic idea of our model is that whether a single account is normal or malicious is a function of how the other accounts "congregate" with this account in the topology, and how those other accounts shared the same device with this account "behave" in timeseries. Unlike existing methods that one first studies the graph properties [3] or pairwise comparisons of account

---

[1]https://mail.google.com
[2]https://www.facebook.com
[3]http://render.alipay.com/p/s/download

---

*Equal contribution.

CCS'17, October 30-November 3, 2017, Dallas, TX, USA,
© 2017 Copyright held by the owner/author(s).
ACM ISBN 978-1-4503-4946-8/17/10.
https://doi.org/10.1145/3133956.3138827

---

[4]https://en.wikipedia.org/wiki/Precision_and_recall

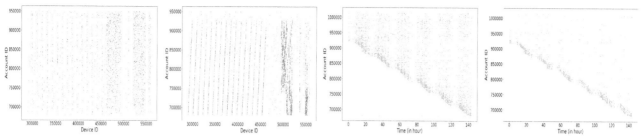

Figure 1: Device aggregation patterns: normal accounts (*first*) v.s. malicious accounts (*second*), malicious accounts tend to aggregate; Activity aggregation patterns: normal accounts (*third*) v.s. malicious accounts (*fourth*), new registered malicious accounts tend to be active only in a short term.

activities [1] then feeds into a machine learning framework, our proposed method directly learns a function for each account given the context of the local topology and other account activities nearby thanks to the representation power of neural networks.

We deploy the proposed work as the real system at Alipay. It can detect hundreds of thousands malicious accounts daily. We empirically show that the experimental results significantly outperform the results from a "Graph-based" system in terms of both precision and recall.

We summarize the contributions of this work as follows:

- We propose a novel neural network based graph embedding method for identifying malicious accounts by jointly capturing two of attackers' weaknesses, summarized as "Device aggregation" and "Activity aggregation".
- Our method is applied at Alipay, one of the largest third-party mobile and online payment platform serving hundreds of million users.

2 THE PROPOSED METHODS

2.1 Problem Definition

Assuming a set of N_c accounts $\{1, ..., i, ...N_c\}$ and associated N_d devices $\{1, ..., j, ...N_d\}$ in our dataset. We observe a set of M edges $\{(i, j)\}$ between accounts and devices over a time period $[0, T]$. Each edge denotes that the account i has activities, e.g. signup, login and so on, on device j. As such, we have a graph $G \in \{0, 1\}^{N_c, N_d}$ consists of accounts and devices as vertices , with edges connecting them. Note that the "device" here could be a much more broad concept. For example, the device could be an IP address, an IMEI ID of a cell phone, or even a like page in facebook. Furthermore, we do not limit the bipartite graph with only one type of devices. Instead, we support more than two types of devices

Associated with this graph, we can further observe the activities of each account. Assuming a N_c by p matrix $X \in \mathbb{R}^{N_c, p}$, with each row x_i denotes activities of account i. In practice, the activities of account i over a time period $[0, T)$ can be discretized into p time slots, where the value of each time slot denotes the count of the activities in this time slot.

Our goal is to discriminate between malicous and normal accounts. That is, we want to learn a function f, such that given any account i, the graph G and activities X, the learned function f can correctly identify whether the account i is malicious or not, i.e. $f(i, G, X) = y_i \in \{-1, 1\}$, where y_i denotes the true label of account i.

2.2 A Motivating Example

We demonstrate how we can identify malicious accounts intuitively based on the ideas of "Device aggregation" and "Activity aggregation" in this section.

Device aggregation. The basic idea of device aggregation is that if an account connects with a large number of other accounts by sharing the same device or a set of devices, then such accounts would be suspicious. One can simply calculate the size of the connnected subgraph components as a measure for each account as in [6].

Activity aggregation. The basic idea of activity aggregation is that if accounts sharing the common devices behave in batches, then those accounts are suspicious. One can simply define the inner product of activities of two accounts sharing the same device as a measure of affinity, i.e. $S_{i,i'}^a = \langle x_i, x_{i'} \rangle$. Apparently the consistent behaviors over time between account i and i' mean high degrees of affinity. Such measures of affinity between two accounts can be further used to split a giant connected subgraph to improve the false positive rate [6].

The measures in this section are intuitive, however, they are sensitive to noisy data as discussed in section 1.

2.3 Our Methods

As discussed in above sections, to judge whether an account i is malicious or not, it depends on how the other accounts "congregate" around the same device together with account i, i.e. local topology, and also depends on the behaviors of those accounts in time series.

Inspired by a recent work from Dai et al. [2] that it builds connections between neural networks and graphical models [2] for the modeling of relational data. They show that one can effectively learn the sufficient statistics (embeddings) of each structured data (itself a graph) by considering the attributes of each node and their relations in the graph.

In our problem, we treat each vertex (i.e. account or device) in graph G as a data point, with edges in G denote the relations among those data points. We hope to learn effective embeddings μ_i for each vertex i based on "Device aggregation" and "Activity aggregation" by propagating transformed activities X in local topology of graph G:

$$\mu_i^0 \leftarrow 0 \quad \text{for all } i \tag{1}$$

$$\text{for} \quad t = 1, ..., C$$

$$\mu_i^t \leftarrow \mathcal{T}(W x_i + V \sum_{j \in \mathcal{N}(i)} \mu_j^{t-1})$$

where $\mathcal{T}$ denotes a nonlinear transformation, e.g. a rectifier linear unit activation function, $\mathcal{N}(i)$ means the set of i's neighbors, $W \in \mathbb{R}^{k,p}$ and $V \in \mathbb{R}^{k,k}$ are parameters to control the "shape" of the desired function given the connectivities and related activities of accounts, with the hope that they can automatically capture more effective patterns compared with the intuitive patterns discussed in section 2.2. We let k denote the embedding size, and empirically set $k = 16$ and $C = 5$.

To effectively learn W and V, we link those embeddings to a standard logistic loss function:

$$\min_{W,V,u} \mathcal{L}(W, V, u) = -\sum_{i=1}^{N_c} \log \sigma\left(y_i \cdot (u^\top \mu_i)\right) \quad (2)$$

where σ denotes logistic function $\sigma(x) = \frac{1}{1+\exp{-x}}$, and $u \in \mathbb{R}^k$.

Our algorithm works interatively in an Expectation Maximization style. In e-step, we compute the embeddings based on current parameters W, V as in Eq (1). In m-step, we optimize those parameters in Eq (2) while fixing embeddings.

3 EXPERIMENTS

3.1 Datasets

We depoly our method at Alipay[5], the world's leading mobile payment platform served more than 450 millions of users since 2013. Our system targets on millions of new registered accounts daily. We will not reveal some detailed numbers due to information sensitivity.

In our system, to predict new registered accounts daily, we train our model using data from past 7 days. This leads to several millions of accounts, tens of million associated devices, and billions of edges between those accounts and devices having activities like "signin" and "signup".

To get the activities x_i, we discretize the activities in hours, i.e. $p = 7 \times 24 = 168$ slots, with the value of each slot as the counts of i having activities in the time slot.

As a result, we get the million by tens of million sparse matrix G with billions of non-zero entries. After we discretize the activities of each account, we get the million by 168 matrix X.

3.2 Experimental Settings

We describe our experimental settings as follows.

Evaluation. Alipay first identifies suspicious accounts and observes those accounts in a long term. Afterwards, Alipay is able to give labels to those accounts with the benefit of hindsight. In the following sections, we will evaluate the precision and recall curve on such "ground truth" labels.

Comparison Methods. We compare our methods with a baseline method, connected subgraph components, which is similar to the methods in [6]. The method first builds an account-account graph, and we define the weight of each edge as the inner product of two accounts x_i and $x_{i'}$ described in section 2.2. The measure of such affinity can help us split out normal accounts in a giant connected subgraph, to further balance the trade-off between precision and recall.

[5]https://en.wikipedia.org/wiki/Ant_Financial

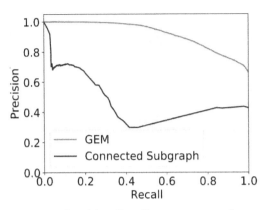

Figure 2: Precision-Recall curves on test data.

3.3 Results

We report the comparison results of all the methods in Figure 2. As we can see, our proposed method GEM significantly outperforms the connected subgraph methods in terms of both precision and recall. One of the largest connected subgraph consists of a total of 800 accounts aggregating together in our experimental dataset, that leads to high precision at low recall from the results of the connected subgraph method. However, it is extremely hard for such methods to retain consistent high precision/recall curves when the size of identified connected subgraphs tends to be small. On the other hand, GEM can automatically learn topological and activity patterns from data and results into a consistent high precision/recall curve.

4 CONCLUSION

In this paper, we present a real system deployed at Alipay, for detecting malicious accounts. We summarize two fundamental weaknesses of attackers, namely "Device aggregation" and "Activity aggregation", and naturally propose a neural network method based on account-device graphs. Our methods achieve promising precision-recall curves compared with existing methods. In future, we are interested in building a real-time malicious account detection system based on dynamic graphs instead of the proposed daily detection system.

REFERENCES

[1] Qiang Cao, Xiaowei Yang, Jieqi Yu, and Christopher Palow. 2014. Uncovering large groups of active malicious accounts in online social networks. In *Proceedings of the 2014 ACM SIGSAC Conference on Computer and Communications Security*. ACM, 477–488.
[2] Hanjun Dai, Bo Dai, and Le Song. 2016. Discriminative embeddings of latent variable models for structured data. In *International Conference on Machine Learning*. 2702–2711.
[3] Junxian Huang, Yinglian Xie, Fang Yu, Qifa Ke, Martin Abadi, Eliot Gillum, and Z Morley Mao. 2013. Socialwatch: detection of online service abuse via large-scale social graphs. In *Proceedings of the 8th ACM SIGSAC symposium on Information, computer and communications security*. ACM, 143–148.
[4] Gianluca Stringhini, Pierre Mourlanne, Gregoire Jacob, Manuel Egele, Christopher Kruegel, and Giovanni Vigna. 2015. Evilcohort: detecting communities of malicious accounts on online services. USENIX.
[5] Yinglian Xie, Fang Yu, Kannan Achan, Rina Panigrahy, Geoff Hulten, and Ivan Osipkov. 2008. Spamming botnets: signatures and characteristics. *ACM SIGCOMM Computer Communication Review* 38, 4 (2008), 171–182.
[6] Yao Zhao, Yinglian Xie, Fang Yu, Qifa Ke, Yuan Yu, Yan Chen, and Eliot Gillum. 2009. BotGraph: Large Scale Spamming Botnet Detection.. In *NSDI*, Vol. 9. 321–334.

POSTER: A Unified Framework of Differentially Private Synthetic Data Release with Generative Adversarial Network

Pei-Hsuan Lu and Chia-Mu Yu

National Chung Hsing University, Taiwan

ABSTRACT

Many differentially private data release solutions have been proposed for different types of data with the sacrifice of inherent correlation structure. Here, we propose a unified framework of releasing differentially private data. In particular, our proposed generative adversarial network (GAN)-based framework learns the input distribution, irrespective of tabular data and graphs, and generates synthetic data in a differentially private manner. Our preliminary results show the acceptable utility of the synthetic dataset.

1 INTRODUCTION

Privacy is of paramount importance particularly for machine learning and data analysis tasks on datasets with individual information. For example, the Netflix challenge releases the anonymized data, seeking for the performance improvement. Despite a success for crowdsourcing, Netflix challenge is also a classic example of how the wrongly anonymized data expose the individual information.

The above scenario motivates the problem of *private data release*, where sensitive dataset needs to be sanitized before released. A straightforward idea is to release the anonymized data (e.g., k-anonymity). Unfortunately, these *ad hoc* anonymization techniques are designed without the consideration of attacker's knowledge, and are subject to linkage attack and homogeneity attack etc.

1.1 Differential Privacy

Differential privacy (DP) is a provable privacy notion. With the sensitive dataset D to be released, (non-interactive) DP requires that only the sanitized dataset $A(D)$ can be released, where A is a randomized algorithm such that the output of A reveals limited information about any particular record in D. Formally, a randomized algorithm A satisfies (ϵ, δ)-differential privacy (ϵ, δ)-DP, if for any two datasets D_1 and D_2 differing only in one record, and for any possible output O of A, we have $\Pr[A(D_1) = O] \leq e^\epsilon \Pr[A(D_2) = O] + \delta$, where two datasets are neighboring if they differ in only one record.

The Laplace and Gaussian mechanisms achieve certain form of (ϵ, δ)-DP. In particular, the former aims to release the output of a numeric function F by adding i.i.d. noise η into each output value of F. The noise η is sampled from a Laplace distribution $\text{Lap}(\lambda)$ with $\Pr[\eta = x] = \frac{1}{2\lambda} e^{-|x|/\lambda}$. The latter provides (ϵ, δ)-DP if the Gaussian noise $\mathcal{N}(0, \Delta_F^2 \cdot \sigma^2)$ is applied, where $\mathcal{N}(0, \Delta_F^2 \cdot \sigma^2)$ is the Gaussian distribution with mean 0 and standard deviation $\Delta_F \cdot \sigma$, $\delta \geq \exp(-\sigma^2 \epsilon^2/2)/1.25$, and $\epsilon < 1$.

Given a differentially private algorithm, the composition of the algorithm and post-processing steps is still differentially private. The most useful is the sequential composition theorem, In essence, given a (ϵ_1, δ_1)-DP algorithm A_1 and (ϵ_2, δ_2)-DP algorithm A_2, the $A_2(A_1(D), D)$ satisfies $(\epsilon_1 + \epsilon_2, \delta_1 + \delta_2)$-DP. A special case is that given a (ϵ_1, δ_1)-DP algorithm A_1 and the post-processing A_2, the $A_2(A_1(D))$ is still (ϵ_1, δ_1)-DP. Namely, the post-processing without accessing D does not consume privacy budget ϵ.

1.2 Recent Work on Private Data Release

Many efforts have been devoted to developing techniques for private data release. A useful technique in publishing tabular data is to first learn the inherent data distribution from original dataset D. Then, the data owner generates and releases synthetic dataset D' via random sampling from the data distribution. Since D' and D share the same data distribution, the analysis results are supposed to be similar. PrivBayes [6] constructs a Bayesian network (BN) to learn the data distribution. After adding noises to BN, data owner performs random sampling from the noisy data distribution. A subsequent work, JTree [3], follows the similar strategy.

On the other hand, different techniques are used in releasing graph statistics. Consider the case of publishing node degree distribution. A common approach is to construct a projective graph $\hat{G}$ from the original graph G. After that, a differentially private histogram for node degree distribution is then released [4, 5].

Unfortunately, we face two research challenges. **(C1)** First, for high-dimensional dataset with the large domain size of each attribute and with complex correlation among attributes, modeling the data distribution consumes considerable time and even computationally infeasible. Very often, the design choice is to keep the pairwise correlation among attributes in the learned data distribution. However, by doing so, the data user may gain inaccurate result when issuing multidimensional query to synthetic data. **(C2)** Second, while currently different DP techniques need to be used on different types of data, the lack of a unified framework for generating differentially private synthetic data leads to the increased complexity in managing the risk of information disclosure. In this paper, we propose to use generative adversarial network as a foundation of such a unified framework.

1.3 DNN and GAN

Deep neural networks (DNN) composed of multiple interconnected layers, each of which contains a number of neurons, have proved the remarkable capability on various machine learning tasks. In essence, DNN, as a parameterized function, extracts the hidden structure behind the data. The DNN with varying parameters can be trained to fit any given finite set of input/output examples. To train a DNN, we define a loss function $\mathcal{L}$ that represents the mismatch between the data and DNN output. A common setting of the loss is $\mathcal{L}(\theta) = \frac{1}{n} \sum_i \mathcal{L}(\theta, x_i)$ with the training examples $\{x_1, \ldots, x_n\}$.

CCS '17, October 30-November 3, 2017, Dallas, TX, USA
© 2017 Copyright held by the owner/author(s).
ACM ISBN 978-1-4503-4946-8/17/10.
https://doi.org/10.1145/3133956.3138823

Training aims to find θ such that the $\mathcal{L}(\theta)$ is minimized. However, due to the complex structure of DNN, $\mathcal{L}$ is usually non-convex and difficult to minimize. In practice, one usually resorts to stochastic gradient decent (SGD) algorithm to minimize $\mathcal{L}$.

Generative models, as opposed to discrimitive models (e.g., DNN), allow one to generate samples from the data distribution. Generative adversarial network (GAN) is composed of two networks, generator and discriminator. The former seeks to create synthetic data satisfying the data distribution, while the latter determines whether the data from generator is a synthetic or true data sample. Recently, GAN gains a huge success in synthesizing meaningful images.

2 PROPOSED METHOD

In this section, we present a series of differentially private synthetic data generation algorithms for tabular data and graphs[1].

2.1 Basic Idea

Here, we still follow the similar strategy in [3, 6], learning the input distribution for private data release. However, since training an optimal BN is NP-Hard, one explicitly removes correlation among attributes for efficiency [6]. We make an observation that a well-trained machine learning (ML) model also aims to approximate the input distribution without removal of explicit structures. Thus, we deal with the challenge (**C1**) by learning the input distribution with ML model. Note that we particularly consider deep learning (DL) family, because DL can easily gain speedup with the GPUs whereas whether BN and JT algorithms can be parallelized remain unclear. On the other hand, in fact, if the input data are well-represented, DL is able to learn the input distribution, irrespective of the form of input data. Hence, one can develop a differential private DL model to approximate the input distribution, from which one generates and publishes the synthetic data, resolving the challenge (**C2**).

2.2 DP-DNN for Tabular Data

We first present a differential private data release scheme, DP-DNN, by taking advantage of DNN, as a strawman solution. The idea behind our design is the observation that a well-trained DNN inherently models the original dataset $D \in \mathbb{R}^{n \times m}$. Thus, a DNN model trained from D can be used by the sampling procedure for data synthesis.

However, we need to deal with two obstacles when implementing the above idea. First, recent research results show that DNN model itself may expose the privacy of training data. Thus, we instead train a DNN in a differentially private manner. In particular, by using the recent moment accountant approach in manipulating the privacy parameters ϵ and δ in differential privacy [1], we construct a DNN with fully connected layers via differentially private SGD. In essence, due to the use of differentially private SGD, DP-DNN reveals no individual information in D. Second, DNN is supposed to take as input the labelled dataset but D might be unlabelled (i.e., no clear distinction between quasi-identifiers and sensitive attributes). Here, we propose to randomly pick an attribute as a label for records in D, turning an unlabelled dataset to labelled one. In essence, this design choice does not change the structure of D; only the way for DP-DNN to perceive the data is changed.

After DP-DNN construction, data owner generates a uniformly random sample $a \in \mathbb{R}^{1 \times (m-1)}$. Data owner sets $D' = D' \cup \{[a\ \mathrm{DP\text{-}DNN}(a)]$

$\mathbb{R}^{1 \times m}\}$, where D' denotes the synthetic dataset and DP-DNN(a) denotes the prediction made by DP-DNN on a. The above procedures are repeated until the number of records of D' reaches n. The above sampling procedures can be thought of as a post-processing and do not consume privacy budget ϵ. The above sampling procedures can also be optimized. First, with the knowledge of the value ranges of attributes, one can guarantee that the random samples will not be significantly deviated from the population, if samples are randomly drawn from a limited value range. Second, with the knowledge of proportions of each label, when the inclusion of [a DP-DNN(a)] results in a significant deviation from the proportion of DP-DNN(a) in D, [a DP-DNN(a)] is dropped. Figures 1 and 2b show the experiment results of DP-DNN.

The dataset for all the experiment results in Secs. 2.2~2.3 are Wine Data Set[2], and each result in Figures 1~5 is the average of ten independent experiments. *Classification accuracy* quantifies the similarity between how classification work on D and D', *Bhattacharyya distance* measures the dissimilarity between D and D', and *correlation matrix* in Figure 2 visualizes whether D' preserves the correlation structure in D.

Though Figure 1 shows promising results, the correlation matrix, as shown in Figure 2, shows the weakness of DP-DNN. More precisely, due to the independent sampling, by comparing Figure 2a and Figure 2b, one can easily find that the synthetic dataset does not preserve the correlation among attributes in D.

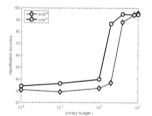 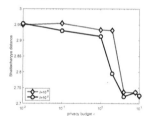

(a) classification accuracy.   (b) Bhattacharyya distance.

Figure 1: DP-DNN results with varying ϵ's and δ's.

2.3 DP-GAN for Tabular Data

With the observation that GAN can approximate the input distribution, we construct a differentially private GAN, DP-GAN, for private data synthesis. More specifically, we train a DP-GAN, perform random sampling from DP-GAN, and release the dataset composed of random samples. The only obstacle is how to make GAN differentially private. We make an observation that though GAN consists of two parts, generator and discriminator, only the latter has the access to D, when learning the input distribution. Therefore, since the discriminator of GAN in our consideration is a DNN, we construct DP-GAN by simply using DP-DNN in Sec. 2.2 in place of the ordinary DNN.

We note that at the time of writing, we also found that Beaulieu-Jones et al. [2] also propose similar idea on differentially private data synthesis. However, they craft a DP-GAN based on AC-GAN, a variant of GAN, while our design of DP-GAN is based on the DC-GAN (ordinary GAN) with DNN as discriminator. Moreover, our further discussion on the novel use of DP-GAN (see Sec. 2.4 and Sec. 2.5 is also not included in [2].

---

[1]The source code of all the proposed algorithms can be downloaded from https://goo.gl/94qyQz.

[2]Wine Data Set: https://archive.ics.uci.edu/ml/datasets/wine

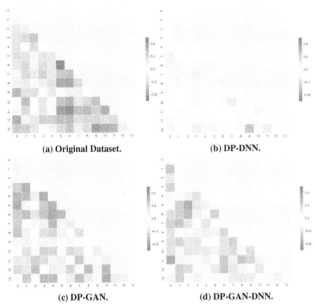

(a) Original Dataset.   (b) DP-DNN.

(c) DP-GAN.   (d) DP-GAN-DNN.

Figure 2: Correlation matrices from different solutions.

The experiment results are shown in Figures 2c and 3. One can easily see that, compared to DP-DNN, though more correlations among attributes in D are preserved in DP-GAN, both classification accuracy and Bhattacharyya distance are even worse, rendering the impracticality of such a design of DP-GAN.

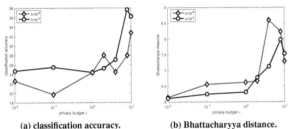

(a) classification accuracy.   (b) Bhattacharyya distance.

Figure 3: DP-GAN results with varying ϵ's and δ's.

2.4 DP-GAN-DNN for Tabular Data

The failure of DP-DNN in preserving the correlation structure in D stems from the independently random sampling. In essence, if random samples to be sent to DP-DNN naturally satisfy the input distribution, D' generated from DP-DNN could better preserve the correlation structure in D. Thus, a straightforward idea is to combine the use of DP-DNN and DP-GAN such that random samples to be sent to DP-DNN are first generated by DP-GAN. All the remaining procedure are exactly the same as those in Sec. 2.2.

The experiment results are shown in Figures 2d and 4, where the classification accuracy reaches the acceptable level and Bhattacharyya distance is also reduced, compared to DP-GAN. One can also see from Figures 2a and 2d that more correlations among attributes in D are now preserved.

2.5 DP-GAN for Graph

We also consider publishing node degree distribution of a given grpah in the sense of node-DP [4, 5], instead of the tabular data. The similar approach is conducted; data owner learns the input distribution, and publishes the synthetic node degree distribution. Nonetheless, the obstacle is that, in contrast to the tabular data case

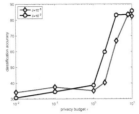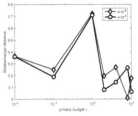

(a) classification accuracy.   (b) Bhattacharyya distance.

Figure 4: DP-GAN-DNN results with varying ϵ's and δ's.

where one see each record as a sample from an inherent data distribution, now we have a single instance of graph and therefore cannot train a DP-GAN. To solve this issue, we first generate graph isomorphisms of the original graph G. Then, we vectorize the adjacency matrix of each graph isomorphism as a row vector (record). All the vectorized adjacency matrices can be stacked together and regarded as a tabular data, each record from which is sampled from an inherent edge distribution. All the remaining procedures are the same as ones in Sec. 2.3.

The dataset for all the experiment results in Sec. 5 is Zachary's Karate Club[3], and each result in Figure 5 is the average of ten independent experiments. *L1 Error* measures the dissimilarity between the released and true node degree distribution. $|E'|/|E|$ is a ratio of the number $|E'|$ of edges in the synthetic graph G' and the number $|E|$ of edges in G. The experiment results in Figure 5 show that DP-GAN achieves less information loss than the state-of-the-art solution [4].

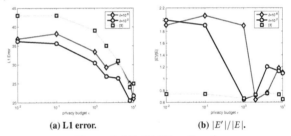

(a) L1 error.   (b) $|E'|/|E|$.

Figure 5: DP-GAN for Graph.

3 CONCLUSION

The GAN-based framework of differentially private data release shows a great potential in preserving the data utility and unifying the DP approaches for different types of data.

REFERENCES

[1] M. Abadi, A. Chu, I. Goodfellow, H. B. McMahan, I. Mironov, K. Talwar, and L. Zhang. Deep learning with differential privacy. *ACM CCS*, 2016.
[2] B. K. Beaulieu-Jones, Z. Wu, C. Williams, and C. S. Greene. Privacy-preserving generative deep neural networks support clinical data sharing. *bioRxiv*, July 5, 2017.
[3] R. Chen, Q. Xiao, Y. Zheng, and J. Xu. Differentially private high-dimensional data publication via sampling-based inference. *ACM KDD*, 2015.
[4] W.-Y. Day, N. Li, and M. Lyu. Publishing graph degree distribution with node differential privacy. *ACM SIGMOD*, 2016.
[5] S. Raskhodnikova and A. Smith. Lipschitz extensions for node-private graph statistics and the generalized exponential mechanism. *IEEE FOCS*, 2016.
[6] J. Zhang, G. Cormode, C. M. Procopiuc, D. Srivastava, and X. Xiao. Privbayes: private data release via bayesian networks. *ACM SIGMOD*, 2014.

---

[3] https://networkdata.ics.uci.edu/data.php?id=105

POSTER: TOUCHFLOOD: A Novel Class of Attacks against Capacitive Touchscreens

Seita Maruyama
Waseda University, Japan
maruyama@nsl.cs.waseda.ac.jp,

Satohiro Wakabayashi
Waseda University, Japan
wakabayashi@goto.info.waseda.ac.jp

Tatsuya Mori
Waseda University, Japan
mori@nsl.cs.waseda.ac.jp

ABSTRACT

We present a novel class of attacks against capacitive touchscreens, which are common in devices such as smartphones and tablet computers. The attack we named TOUCHFLOOD aims to scatter touch events, alternating the selection of buttons on a screen. The key idea of TOUCHFLOOD is to intentionally cause a malfunction by injecting intentional noise signals from an external source. This paper describes the attack as well as the experimental results that clarify the conditions for successful attacks. The demo videos of the experiments using a smartphone are available at https://goo.gl/56G79e.

CCS CONCEPTS

• **Security and privacy** → **Hardware attacks and countermeasures**; **Mobile platform security**;

KEYWORDS

Touchscreen, Attack, Smartphone

1 INTRODUCTION

The majority of the current mobile devices, such as smartphones and tablets, are equipped with touchscreens. While there are various technologies for sensing touch, mutual capacitive sensors are widely used in smartphones as they have high resolution and multi-touch support [1]. This work introduces a novel class of attacks against capacitive touchscreens, named *TOUCHFLOOD*. The attack aims to alter the selection of a button on a screen; that is, when a victim thinks that she/he touches the cancel button, the attack can scatter the recognized touched position and make the operating system recognize another button, such as OK, as having been touched, which may lead to security threats, such as installing malware. There have been many studies on the side-channel attacks that target touchscreens (LCD's) [2, 4]. To the best of our knowledge, while these attacks passively steal data from the touchscreens, our TOUCHFLOOD is the first attack that *actively* irradiates signals toward touchscreens to cause targeted malfunctions. In the paper, we present the basic mechanism of TOUCHFLOOD and reveal the conditions that are needed to establish the attack.

CCS '17, October 30-November 3, 2017, Dallas, TX, USA
© 2017 Copyright held by the owner/author(s).
ACM ISBN 978-1-4503-4946-8/17/10.
https://doi.org/10.1145/3133956.3138829

2 DESCRIPTIONS OF THE TOUCHFLOOD ATTACK

A mutual capacitive touchscreen controller consists of the grid of the transmitter (TX) electrodes and receiver (RX) electrodes, which are mutually coupled. These TX/RX electrodes are used for sensing touch events. As the human body has a capacitance, it can act as a capacitor. When a finger approaches the screen's surface, it extracts an electric charge from the touchscreen through mutual capacitance. Thus, the touchscreen controller can detect touches by measuring the changes in electric current that flows into the RX electrodes; the current changes are caused by the changes in capacitance between the TX and RX electrodes. The pair of TX and RX electrodes for which the changes are detected is used to locate the area of touch.

It is known that a touchscreen controller in a smartphone can malfunction due to noise signals leaked from the smartphone's battery charger or screen [3]. touchscreen controller manufacturing companies have developed countermeasures against the electromagnetic interference (EMI) caused by noise signals, which are relatively weak. However, when a stronger noise signal is intentionally applied to a touchscreen controller, false touch events can be generated. As some hobbyists have reported [7], it is known that false touch events occur when a smartphone is brought close to a toy plasma ball, which is powered by an oscillator and a high voltage transformer circuit, producing a large alternating voltage, typically around 2–5 kV and around 30 kHz [6].

The key idea of TOUCHFLOOD is to cause an intentional malfunction by injecting intentional noise signals externally. We found that producing large alternating voltages at a specific frequency near a touchscreen can cause a malfunction through capacitive coupling with the RX electrodes. Injecting the intentional noise forces to change the current flow of the RX electrodes, and the touchscreen controller incorrectly recognizes the changes of current flow as the changes of capacitance, which will be detected as pseudo touch events.

Threat model As our prototype uses a thin copper sheet, it can be hidden inside a common object such as a table. By installing a maliciously programmed NFC tag under the tabletop, an attacker can take control of the particular UI components on a smartphone [5]. Given these setups, a victim will encounter an unexpected dialogue box that asks whether s/he permits the request, e.g., installing a malicious application. Although the victim aims to cancel the request, TOUCHFLOOD will alter the selection, letting the smartphone install the malware.

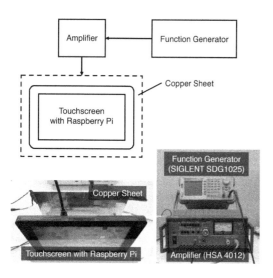

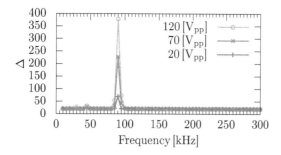

Figure 1: Experimental setup.

Figure 2: The effect of different frequencies on touchscreen.

3 EXPERIMENTS

To study the conditions that can cause the "false touches," we conduct several experiments using the touchscreen controller that provides raw data collected from the capacitive sensors.

3.1 Experimental setup

Figure 1 shows our experimental setup. Our objective is to measure the effect of noise signals on the behavior of touchscreens. For this experiment, we use the Raspberry Pi 7-inch Touchscreen Display. As an intentional noise signal, we use the sine-wave signal generated by a function generator. We set a copper sheet parallel to the touchscreen controller. This copper sheet is used to create a capacitive coupling with the capacitive sensors. The distance between the sheet and controller was set to 7 cm. We note that the attack can be applied from the rear side of a touchscreen controller, i.e., the rear side of a smartphone.

3.2 Effect of the frequencies and voltage values

We generate sine-wave noise signals with different frequencies and voltage values. We record raw capacitance values and touch events using the software we developed. Since the touchscreen has 264 capacitance sensors, which consists of a 12 × 22 matrix, we can

obtain 264-dimensional time-series data. This setup enables us to analyze the spatial patterns of the generated touch events.

To measure the interference intensity on the touchscreen, we introduce a metric, Δ, defined as follows.

$$\delta_i = x_i - \bar{x}_i$$
$$\Delta = \max_i(\delta_i) - \min_i(\delta_i),$$

where x_i ($i \in \{1, \ldots, 264\}$) is a measured value for each sensor and $\bar{x}_i$ ($i \in \{1, \ldots, 264\}$) is a measured value for each sensor when noise is not injected, respectively. We note that x_i is a variable of time; our capacitance logger sampled the raw values at the rate of 7 times per second. In contrast, $\bar{x}_i$ was set as a static value, which was collected when no signal was injected. If no noise signal is applied, Δ becomes roughly 20 when there are no touch events on the screen and Δ becomes greater than 250 when a finger touches the screen. Thus, the metric Δ can measure the impact of noise interference.

We measured Δ, applying noise signal to the copper sheet with three different voltages (20 Vpp, 70Vpp, and 120Vpp) and frequencies, ranging from 5 kHz to 300 kHz. Figure 2 shows the results. We first notice that there are clear peaks at the frequency of 90 kHz. This result indicates that there is a characteristic frequency of noise that can affect the touch controller. This frequency differs for different models of touchscreen controllers. So, specifying the model of the target is crucial to the success of the attack. To this end, a device fingerprinting technique can be used. We also notice that the effect of noise becomes larger with higher voltages in the signals. As we shall show in the next section, we need to apply a higher voltage to cause false touch events.

3.3 Spatial distribution of the false touch events

We now study the positions of the touch events caused by the noise signals. In this experiment, nothing touches the screen. Using our monitoring software, we record touch positions for 30 seconds with the sampling rate of two samples per second. The touchscreen has an 800×480 resolution and supports a 10-point multi-touch. The touchscreen controller is capable of reporting up to 10 positions per sample. Note that the touch events are collected from the outputs of the touchscreen controller, not from an operating system.

We used three different voltages (20 Vpp, 70 Vpp, and 120 Vpp) and the following two representative frequencies: 60 kHz as a frequency not affecting Δ and 90 kHz as a frequency affecting Δ the most. As expected, the touchscreen did not report any touch events with the 60 kHz frequency. In the following, we omit the results for the 60 kHz frequency. Figure 3 shows the results for the 90 kHz frequency. First, we notice that the touchscreen controller does not recognize touch events when the voltage is set to 20 Vpp. We also see that higher voltage signals cause false touch events more frequently. Second, we see intrinsic spatial patterns of touch events, which spread out on the screen linearly. We also see that many touch events are focused on the top or bottom edges of the screen panel. These observations indicate that even if an attacker waits for a long time, it seems unlikely that a false touch can be fired at

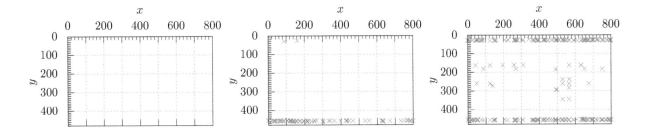

Figure 3: Coordinates of the touch points reported by the touchscreen controller. The injected signals had three different voltage values. The frequency was set to 90 kHz. Left: 20 Vpp, Center: 70 Vpp, Right: 120 Vpp

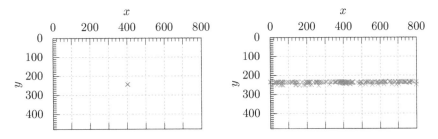

Figure 4: Coordinates of the touch points reported by the touchscreen controller. While the experiment a finger keeps touching the point centered on the screen. Left: no signal is applied. Right: a signal with 20 Vpp and 90 kHz is applied.

target coordinates with a high probability, given the skewed spatial distribution.

3.4 Limiting the dispersion with a real touch event

After several trials, we found that touching a screen can fix the skewed spatial distribution of false touches. Although not conclusive due to the "black box" nature of the touchscreen controllers, we conjecture that touching the screen with a finger stabilizes the area of capacitive coupling. The positive feature of this phenomenon is that while touching the screen makes the distribution focus on a certain area, it still keeps scattering the touch events; thus, false touch events can be created in a more predictable way.

We repeated the similar experiments, but added a finger touch this time. Figure 4 shows the experiment results. Under the low voltage signal of 20 Vpp, the false touch events occur only if a finger touches the screen. More importantly, we can see that the positions of the false touches are centered on the line where the true touch point is located. These are desirable characteristics because usually, GUI buttons are aligned in a row, e.g., CONNECT/CANCEL, YES/NO, or OK/CANCEL. Assuming that the touch events are uniformly scattered along a line, an attacker can expect that a touch event will be scattered on a wrong button with a probability of 1/2. We note that screen orientation also matters. If a screen is in portrait mode, scattered touch events along the vertical line may not produce a touch event on the targeted button. By making use of the device's fingerprinting techniques, an attacker can obtain

the information about the model, as well as the current screen orientation; this information will be used to check whether or not TOUCHFLOOD attack is effective.

4 CONCLUSION

We introduced a novel class of attacks against capacitive touchscreens. Using an off-the-shelf touchscreen display, we presented the actual conditions needed for the successful attacks. Future works include an in-depth understanding of the mechanism of the attack, evaluation of the attack using smartphones and tablet computers, and the end-to-end attack combined with techniques that trigger a malicious touch event. We also need to develop effective countermeasures against the attack.

REFERENCES

[1] Li Du. 2016. An Overview of Mobile Capacitive Touch Technologies Trends. *arXiv preprint arXiv:1612.08227* (2016).
[2] Y. Hayashi, N. Homma, M. Miura, T. Aoki, and H. Sone. 2014. A Threat for Tablet PCs in Public Space: Remote Visualization of Screen Images Using EM Emanation. In *Proceedings of the 2014 ACM SIGSAC Conference on Computer and Communications Security (CCS '14)*. 954–965.
[3] Hans W. Klein. 2013. Noise Immunity of Touchscreen Devices. http://www.cypress.com/file/120641/download. (2013).
[4] Federico Maggi, Simone Gasparini, and Giacomo Boracchi. 2011. A fast eavesdropping attack against touchscreens. In *Information Assurance and Security (IAS), 2011 7th International Conference on*. IEEE, 320–325.
[5] Seita Maruyama, Satohiro Wakabayashi, and Tatsuya Mori. 2017. Trojan of Things: Embedding Malicious NFC Tags into Common Objects. *CoRR* abs/1702.07124 (2017). http://arxiv.org/abs/1702.07124
[6] University of Oxford Department of Physics. 2012. Plasma ball. http://www2.physics.ox.ac.uk/accelerate/resources/demonstrations/plasma-ball. (2012).
[7] soomiq. 2014. Iphone goes Crazy Out of Control near Plasma ball. https://www.youtube.com/watch?v=bD_lv22T6Xo. (2014).

POSTER: TouchTrack: How Unique are your Touch Gestures?

Rahat Masood
University of New South Wales (UNSW), CSIRO Data61
Sydney, Australia
rahat.masood@student.unsw.edu.au

Hassan Jameel Asghar
CSIRO Data61
Sydney, Australia
hassan.asghar@data61.csiro.au

Benjamin Zi Hao Zhao
CSIRO Data61
Sydney, Australia
ben.zhao@data61.csiro.au

Mohamed Ali Kaafar
CSIRO Data61
Sydney, Australia
dali.kaafar@data61.csiro.au

ABSTRACT

This paper studies a privacy threat induced by the collection and monitoring of a user's touch gestures on touchscreen devices. The threat is a new form of persistent tracking which we refer to as "touch-based tracking". It goes beyond tracking of virtual identities and has the potential for cross-device tracking as well as identifying multiple users using the same device. To demonstrate the likelihood of touch-based tracking, we propose an information theoretic method that quantifies the amount of information revealed by individual features of gestures, samples of gestures as well as samples of gesture combinations, when modelled as feature vectors. We have also developed a purpose-built app, named "TouchTrack" that collects data from users and informs them on how unique they are when interacting with their touch devices. Our results from 89 different users indicate that writing samples and left swipes can reveal 73.7% and 68.6% of user information, respectively. Combining different combinations of gestures results in higher uniqueness, with the combination of keystrokes, swipes and writing revealing up to 98.5% of information about users. We correctly re-identify returning users with a success rate of more than 90%.

KEYWORDS

Touch-based Tracking, Mobile Privacy, Behavioural Biometrics, Touch Gestures

1 INTRODUCTION

In this paper, we postulate that the very distinguishability of touch-based gestures constitutes a major privacy threat as it enables a new form of tracking of individuals. We call this notion "touch-based tracking," which is the ability to continuously and surreptitiously observe, track and distinguish users via their touch gestures while they are interacting with touchscreen devices.

As opposed to "regular" tracking mechanisms (e.g., based on cookies, browser fingerprints) which track virtual identities [1–3], touch-based tracking is subtle and riskier as it allows the tracking and identification of the actual (physical) person operating the

device. Touch-based tracking also leads to cross-device tracking where same user can potentially be traced on multiple mobile devices. Additionally, we also envision the risk of distinguishing and tracking multiple users accessing the same device. Not all use cases of touch-based tracking are negative. It can also be beneficial to users and service providers alike. For instance, the identification of multiple users using the same device may help in providing content more suitable for each of them. Nevertheless, touch-based tracking performed in any of the above cases can provide a more complete view of a user's behavior and can be used for a range of purposes including targeted ads, profiling, and spamming. Our main contributions are as follows:

Contributions: We investigate the potential of using touch-based gestures for tracking, which we call touch-based tracking. We develop an analytical framework that measures the amount of identifying information (in bits) contained in these gestures, represented as feature vectors, at different levels of granularity. At the finest level, our framework quantifies the information carried by individual features, e.g., pressure on screen. At the second level, we quantify the information carried by a gesture sample, e.g., a single swipe. At the third level, our framework calculates the amount of information carried by multiple samples of the same gesture, e.g., a collection of swipes. Lastly, we measure the information carried by a collection of samples from multiple gestures, e.g., swipes and taps. We apply our framework on four widely used touch screen gestures: i) swipes, ii) taps, iii) keystrokes, and iv) handwriting.

We develop and deploy a "game-like" Android app called "TouchTrack" which consists of three well known open source games and one purpose-built handwriting module. We test our framework on a total of 40,600 gesture samples collected from 89 participants and identified features that contain high amount of identifying information using the *maximum-relevancy minimum-redundancy* (mRMR) algorithm [4]. With the same dataset, we measured the amount of information contained in samples from the same gesture and from multiple gestures. We found that 50 features in a single handwriting sample contribute 68.71% of information about users, which increases to 73.7% with multiple samples. We further identified that different gestures combined together reveal more information about users. For instance swipes, handwriting, and keystrokes carry 98.5% of information. Among users who performed all the four gestures, our framework showed 98.89% of information about users.

We also validated our framework in terms of correctly identifying a returning user. We found that with multiple samples, swipes and handwriting show a TPR of 90.0% and 91.0%, respectively. For a

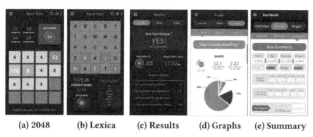

| (a) 2048 | (b) Lexica | (c) Results | (d) Graphs | (e) Summary |

Figure 1: TouchTrack Result Screens

combination of gestures we found that swipes and handwriting combined together had a TPR of 93.75%.

2 DATA COLLECTION

To illustrate the potential of touch-based tracking, our *TouchTrack* app collects gesture samples as raw readings from the touch sensors, sends them to our server, and informs users about the uniqueness of their gestures by displaying the uniqueness results. The app is made up of four games, three of them are based on popular open-source games and a fourth game was purposely developed by us. These games are i) 2048[1] to collect up, down, left and right swipes, ii) Lexica[2] to collect taps, and iii) Logo Maniac[3] to collect keystrokes, and iv) "Write Something" (developed by us) to collect writing samples. The four games were selected so as to capture user touch interactions in a natural way. Screenshots of the TouchTrack App are displayed in Figure 1. When a new user uses TouchTrack, he/she is required to sign up using a unique username, which together with the device ID is hashed and stored in our database. Prior to data collection, we underwent and obtained ethics approval. The users were informed about the purpose of TouchTrack and what data is being collected.

The Raw Dataset and Statistics: We gathered raw touch and motion features from the `MotionEvent` and `SensorEvent` Android APIs of the device. From these raw features we derived more features to capture information such as averages, standard deviations, mins, maxs etc. These derived features are called extracted features. Examples of the extracted features are *median of first 5 acceleration points*, *80-percentile of pairwise x-tilt*, and *standard deviation of change of area position*. We extracted 229 features for swipes, 7 for taps, 8 for keystrokes, and 241 for handwriting. Table 1 shows the summary statistics of our data collection. There were a total of 89 users who downloaded and used our app, however, only 30 users used all four games and hence provided samples for all gestures.

Table 1: Touch Gesture Data Statistics

Gesture	No. of Users	No. of Samples	Gesture	No. of Users	No. of Samples
Swipes	81	16611	Up Swipes	78	3568
Down Swipes	71	4781	Left Swipes	63	4252
Right Swipes	65	4010	Handwriting	36	1291
Taps	89	16225	Keystrokes	49	6473
All Gestures:	30	25186			
Total:	89	40600			

[1] https://github.com/gabrielecirulli/2048
[2] https://github.com/lexica/lexica
[3] https://github.com/Luze26/LogoManiac

3 THE METHODOLOGY

Our quantitative methodology is based on relative mutual information. To illustrate this, we consider quantifying uniqueness of a single feature by fixing a gesture, say right swipe. Let $\mathbb{U}$ denote the set of users and let $\mathbb{F}$ denote the range of values of the feature. Let U and F denote the random variables associated with these sets. Then, the relative mutual information is defined as

$$I_R(U;F) = 1 - \frac{H(U \mid F)}{H(U)},$$

where $H(U) = \log_2 |\mathbb{U}|$, and $H(U \mid F)$ is defined as $H(U \mid F) = -\sum_{f \in \mathbb{F}} \Pr(F = f) H(U \mid F = f)$. Finally,

$$H(U \mid F = f) = -\sum_{u \in \mathbb{U}} \Pr(U = u \mid F = f) \log_2 \Pr(U = u \mid F = f).$$

It boils down to quantifying the probabilities in the above two equations, which we do empirically through our dataset. Given a feature value f, $\Pr(U = u \mid F = f)$ is calculated by counting the number of times f has been exhibited by user u divided by the number times f appears in the dataset. $\Pr(F = f)$ is calculated from the empirical distribution of F. The methodology for quantifying uniqueness of gesture samples, modelled as featue vectors, is different. This is because due to high dimensionality of the feature vector, it is unlikely that any two feature vectors from the same user will be exactly the same. Thus, the probabilities are calculated differently using "fuzzy" matching (as opposed to exact). A similarity metric (in our case cosine similarity) is used to decide whether a received feature vector is similar to a given feature vector in the dataset. The rest of the calculation of the relative mutual information is similar to above.

4 RESULTS

In this section, we present the results of applying our framework on the touch gestures. We identify a set of features for each gesture type, and apply our methodology on the selected features to show uniqueness results.

Feature Subset Selection (FSS): We intend to find the uniqueness of gestures as a function of increasing number of features. To do this, we needed a ranking of features in terms of their distinguishing capacity. We use the maximum-relevance-minimal-redundancy (mRMR) algorithm that attempts to constrain features to a subset which are mutually as dissimilar to each other as possible, but as similar to the classification variable as possible [4]. We used sets of top i features from each gesture according to their mRMR rank, where i was incremented in discrete steps until m (the total number of features). We then evaluated their relative mutual information using our framework for the uniqueness of a single gesture sample and multiple samples from the same gesture.

We note that for all gestures, the relative mutual information increases with increasing number of features. Also, the uniqueness of a set of gesture samples is generally higher than single samples, and in all cases surpasses the uniqueness of single samples as we increase the number of features. The uniqueness of multiple swipe samples is the highest, with 92.01%, followed by handwriting (85.93%) and downward swipes (77.52%). On the other hand, samples of taps and keystrokes exhibit least uniqueness carrying 34.73% and 41.02% of information. We observe that given a single

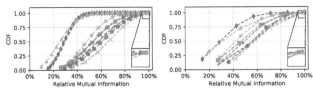

(a) CDF of a Gesture Sample   (b) CDF of Set of Gesture Samples

Figure 2: CDF of a Gesture Sample and a Set of Gesture Samples on a Single Device. Relative Information of Respective Categories (sample, set of samples) are: -•- Swipes: (57.7%, 63.3%), -○- Up Swipes: (48.5%, 50.23%), -■- Down Swipes: (52.2%, 54.5%), -+- Left Swipes: (53.9%, 68.6%), -*- Right Swipes: (53.3%, 57.4%), -♦- Taps: (29.5%, 34.7%), -▲- Keystrokes: (26.2%, 41.0%), -×- Handwriting: (68.7%, 73.7%)

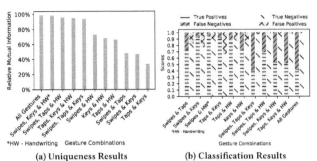

(a) Uniqueness Results   (b) Classification Results

Figure 3: Uniqueness and Classification Results for Gesture Combinations.

gesture sample, handwriting provides 79.49% of information about the user and a keystroke gives the least amount of information i.e. 28.76%.

Uniqueness of Features: Before assessing the uniqueness of features we binned any continuous features or features with a large domain. We found that *80-percentile of area* in left swipe reveals 56.10% of information about a user, followed by *20-percentile of area* in down swipe 55.50%. Among features which are shared among all gestures, *start area* contains 52.5% of information, followed by *start pressure* yielding 45.4% of information. On the other extreme, *inter-stroke time* for a keystroke reveals minimum amount of user information, i.e,. 7%. We observe no trend (in terms of dependency) among features, except that relative information decreases in descending order of the features.

Uniqueness of a Gesture Sample: Once we have fixed the set of features, we need to find the threshold τ of the cosine similarity metric that balances uniqueness of gesture samples and correctly (and uniquely) identifying a returning user. To do this, we split the data into an 80-20 partition, and then evaluated the equal error rate (EER). We observe that our methodology correctly re-identifies a returning user up to 81% (19% EER) of the time if given a handwriting sample. The worst performance is a TPR of 61% (39% EER) when a sample of keystroke is provided. After fixing the threshold, we computed the uniqueness through our relative mutual information metric. The results showed that a handwriting sample reveals the highest amount of information (68.71%), followed by swipes (57.77%). The four types of swipes, i.e., left, up, down, and right swipes, yield 53.9%, 52.2%, 52.2%, and 48.5% of information, respectively. However, taps and keystroke reveal only 29.5% and 26.2% of information. Figure 2a shows the CDF of a gesture sample. We observe a considerable difference in the range of information revealed by different gestures, with handwriting exposing more than 60% of information for half of the users in the database. Following this, the swipes also show high uniqueness, revealing 30% to 65% of information about 75% of users.

Uniqueness of a Set of Gesture Samples: We computed a different threshold of the cosine similarity metric for this category, and chose the one which resulted in the best EER. We found that the rate of re-identifying a returning user is higher reaching up to 91% (9% EER) for handwriting. This means that combining a few samples of the same gesture may allow for more accurate tracking.

We then calculated relative mutual information and found that handwriting reveals 73.7% of information, followed by left swipe which yields 68.6% of information of user gestures. In accordance with previous results, taps and keystrokes reveal minimum amount of information about users, i.e., 34.71% and 41.0%, respectively. The CDF is shown in Figure 2b.

Uniqueness of Combination of Gestures: Figure 3a shows the quantification results of multiple gestures in different combinations. We found that a combination of all gestures reveal a maximum 98.89% of information about users, followed by the combination of swipes, handwriting & keystrokes that yield 98.5% of information. We also tested these gesture combinations in terms of re-identifying returning users. Figure 3b shows the TPR and FPR of the different combinations of gestures. We see that as we increase the number of gestures in our combination, the FPR drastically decreases, but so does the TPR. For instance, all gestures together yields the 0.99% FPR but also a low TPR (just above 40%). The lowest FPR was recorded by the combination of swipes, handwriting and keystrokes (0.85%). The main reason for a big drop in TPR as compared to the rate of single gestures, is mainly due to the rather strict metric of only labelling a given combination as being from a user if the predicate for each gesture evaluates to 1.

5 FUTURE WORK

In the future we intend to extend our methodology to scenarios such as *single-device multi-user tracking* and *multi-device single-user tracking*. The first scenario distinguishes between multiple users accessing the same device. The second scenario is the tracking of the same user across multiple devices.

REFERENCES

[1] Peter Eckersley. 2010. How Unique Is Your Browser? *Proc. of the Privacy Enhancing Technologies Symposium (PETS)* (2010), 1–18. https://doi.org/10.1007/978-3-642-14527-8_1

[2] Pierre Laperdrix, Walter Rudametkin, and Benoit Baudry. 2016. Beauty and the Beast: Diverting Modern Web Browsers to Build Unique Browser Fingerprints. *Proceedings - 2016 IEEE Symposium on Security and Privacy, SP 2016* (2016), 878–894. https://doi.org/10.1109/SP.2016.57

[3] Łukasz Olejnik, Claude Castelluccia, and Artur Janc. 2012. Why Johnny Can't Browse in Peace: On the Uniqueness of Web Browsing History Patterns. *5th Workshop on Hot Topics in Privacy Enhancing Technologies (HotPETs 2012)* (2012), 1–16. http://hal.archives-ouvertes.fr/hal-00747841/

[4] Hanchuan Peng, Fuhui Long, and Chris Ding. 2005. Feature selection based on mutual information: Criteria of Max-Dependency, Max-Relevance, and Min-Redundancy. *IEEE Transactions on Pattern Analysis and Machine Intelligence* 27, 8 (2005), 1226–1238. https://doi.org/10.1109/TPAMI.2005.159 arXiv:f

POSTER: PenJ1939: An Interactive Framework for Design and Dissemination of Exploits for Commercial Vehicles

Subhojeet Mukherjee
Colorado State University
Subhojeet.Mukherjee@colostate.edu

Noah Cain
Colorado State University
noahcain@rams.colostate.edu

Jacob Walker
Colorado State University
jksctwkr@rams.colostate.edu

David White
Colorado State University
dwhite54@colostate.edu

Indrajit Ray
Colorado State University
Indrajit.Ray@colostate.edu

Indrakshi Ray
Colorado State University
Indrakshi.Ray@colostate.edu

ABSTRACT

Vehicle security has been receiving a lot of attention from both the black hat and white hat community of late. Research in this area has already led to the fabrication of different attacks, of which some have been shown to have potentially grave consequences. Vehicle vendors and original equipment manufacturers (OEM)s are thus presented with the additional responsibility of ensuring in-vehicular communication level security. In this poster paper, we present a framework, which allows any individual to write, test, and store exploit scripts which could then be run by any interested party on in-vehicular networks of commercial vehicles like trucks and buses.

KEYWORDS

CAN; J1939; Exploit; Script; Development; Interactive; Download

1 INTRODUCTION

Back in the 70's vehicles were driven purely by physical and mechanical interactions. Today, much of the human-mechanical interaction is mediated through embedded devices also referred to as Electronic Control Units (ECU)s. These devices are often intelligent and can ensure smooth driving, safety and comfort. The computerization of vehicles has, however, led to the advent of newer exploits which target these embedded devices and the underlying network they communicate with. Hackers and security professionals have shown that embedded networks in passenger cars can be compromised to cause large scale damage [2]. These networks primarily rely on the Controller Area Network (CAN) protocol for message exchange. While CAN ensures reliable message delivery across ECUs, it does not specify how messages on the network are utilized by ECUs. While passenger vehicles mostly use proprietary specifications to make such decisions, commercial vehicles use a common set of standards (SAE J1939 [1]) specified by SAE International. This makes commercial vehicles increasingly more susceptible to attacks which target the ubiquitously used SAE J1939 protocol stack.

CCS'17, Oct. 30–Nov. 3, 2017, Dallas, TX, USA.
© 2016 Copyright held by the owner/author(s). ISBN 978-1-4503-4946-8/17/10.
DOI: https://doi.org/10.1145/3133956.3138844

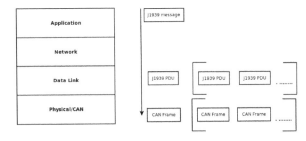

Figure 1: SAE J1939 Protocol Stack

Recently, security researchers [5, 6] have shown that attacks can be launched at different layers of the SAE J1939 protocol stack.

Since commercial vehicles expose almost the same set of attack surfaces as passenger vehicles, these attacks can be realized using similar tool-sets and can have severe consequences. In this poster paper, we present a framework which can be used to develop, test (on a built-in testbed setup) and store exploits written by any individual with J1939/CAN or relevant security related experience. These scripts can then be downloaded by a plethora of interested individuals including industry professionals, mechanics and garage technicians, and other tech-savvy users. Eventually, we aim to create an easily accessible framework which can benefit the heavy vehicle security community by making exploits accessible readily and expediently, thereby accelerating the process of penetration testing.

2 BACKGROUND

CAN [4] is an arbitration-based protocol that facilitates highly reliable communication over a multi-master broadcast serial bus. The SAE J1939 [1] protocol runs on top of CAN, i.e. it utilizes the physical communication standards exposed by the CAN protocol. The J1939 protocol stack is organized based on the seven layer OSI networking model. Currently, SAE standards are specified for 4 of the 7 layers[1]. These layers are shown in Fig. 1. A J1939 message is composed by an ECU at the *Application* layer and transmitted as a sequence of bits at the *Physical*/CAN layer after being bundled into fixed size *Protocol Data Units* (PDU)s. A typical J1939 PDU consists of a 29 bit *Identifier Field* and a 64 bit *Data Field*. A single J1939 message is uniquely identified using a *Parameter Group Number* or PGN. For example, messages related to torque or speed control

---

[1]http://www.sae.org/standardsdev/groundvehicle/j1939a.htm

correspond to PGN 0 (0000_{16}). Information required to generate a PGN for a message is embedded in the *Identifier* field. Vehicle specific parameters are embedded within the *Data* field. When an ECU receives a J1939 message, it first obtains the PGN from the identifier field. It then refers to the SAE standards [1] to obtain a set of parameter identifiers known as *Suspect Parameter Numbers* (SPNs) assigned to each PGN. Each SPN is assigned to a set of attributes (*starting position , length, resolution, offset* and *name*) that can be used to interpret the contents of the *Data* Field. As an hypothetical example, in the following bit sequence (representing the contents on the *Data* field), $00011100..._2$, SPN 789, *starting at bit position* 2 from left and extending for 4 bit of *length*, could signify percentage of torque applied when the decimal equivalent of the sequence of 4 bits is multiplied by the resolution 0.125% and added to the offset 0 i.e $0011_2 * 0.125_{10} \rightarrow 3_{10} * 0.125_{10}$.

3 PENJ1939 FEATURES

PenJ1939 is generally designed as an interactive framework which can be used by professionals to design and access existing attacks on J1939 based networks. However, designing attacks is often accompanied by other helpful and often necessary activities like monitoring bus traffic, interpreting J1939 messages, etc. With PenJ1939, we make an effort to integrate such features into one framework so as to ease the process of development and testing of attacks. Mentioned below are the salient features of PenJ1939:-

- **Attack Scripting**: Currently PenJ1939 allows attacks to be scripted in the Python scripting language. We provide a development interface, which could be used to write python code. As scripts could sometimes involve threaded executions, we allow users to split the scripting interface and develop/execute multiple programs in parallel. Users are also allowed to *upload* previously written and tested scripts on the PenJ1939 database.
- **Script Testing**: Each test script is executed on embedded controllers connected to a physical testbed. Test outputs and associated errors or warnings are presented to the user in order to aid in development. To test their scripts, users are required to obtain access to dedicated node controllers which act as gateways to the CAN network.
- **Library Access**: Script developers are also granted access to modules developed previously. This is done to avoid redundancy and speed up the process of exploit writing. Currently, all modules included as a part of a script are stored in the *Module* database.
- **Traffic Sniffing**: We provide restricted access (via a *TestBed Manger*) to the PenJ1939 experiment testbed. Script writers or users can test scripts by running their code and observing relevant outputs in hexadecimal format. Obtained outputs can also be interpreted at runtime using an inbuilt J1939 interpreter. This allows users to see actual vehicle parameters, some of which might be intended targets of the attack.
- **Script Verification**: Scripts being written on or uploaded to the PenJ1939 framework are passed through a final verification phase before being committed to the database. Albeit some scripts might not be supported for execution on our testbed. We still archive such scripts but notify end-users about the status. Verifying a script only ensures it executes without errors or warnings. Verification does not ensure the eventual correctness of the attack, i.e. whether it was successful in achieving the final goal.

- **Script Annotation**: Before exploits are committed to the PenJ1939 database, the exploit developers are encouraged to annotate their scripts with metadata to be used later as search fields. Currently, we support the following fields: a simple *Documentation* of what the exploit does, five default *Tags*: *J1939 layer, type of attack, affected ECUs, PGNs used* and *SPNs used* and *Pre-Requisites* like *ARM operating systems for node controllers, necessary ECUs connected to the bus, bus baud-rate* etc.
- **Regex-based Filtering**: PenJ1939 exposes a number of regular expression-based filtering interfaces. Script writers can filter traffic sniffed off the J1939 network. PenJ1939 supports message filtering based on *PGNs, SPNs, SPN interpreted values* and regex-based filtering on raw hexadecimal expressions for both the *ID* and *Data* fields. Modules and scripts can be filtered on the contents of their documentation, or associated tags and pre-requisites using regular expressions.
- **Downloading Scripts**: End-users can download previously uploaded scripts by either browsing the script directories or executing search regular expression-based queries. Before downloading a script, the user can verify the script's execution to see if it achieves the desired results, and the user can also access information about the developer of the script.

4 ARCHITECTURE AND COMPONENT INTERACTION

Fig. 2 shows the interactions between the architectural components of PenJ1939. The thick solid boxes represent web-pages accessible to the user. In order to write or download exploits, users need to be logged into the PenJ1939 system. The *Login-Manager* is responsible for verifying user credentials and/or signing up new users. Users can also take a brief tutorial of the system before creating user accounts. Both scripts written and uploaded on the system are sent to the *TestBed Manager* for final verification. The status of the script is accordingly updated to "Yes" if it had an error free execution or "N/A" if the testbed platform does not have adequate resources to run the script. Failed scripts are rejected and the user is notified accordingly. Once a script is ready to be uploaded to the *DB-Manager*, the *Scripting-Manager* asks the user to annotate scripts and modules by populating metadata search fields. The *DB-Manager* is also responsible for executing regular expression queries on search fields and return relevant scripts and modules. Users can select modules from the module browser, and read the module's documentation before using such modules. Once scripts are ready to be tested, users can request nodes. The *TestBed-Manager* is responsible for returning node handles, if a free node is found. The testbed is modeled on a previously published work from our group [3]. Currently, the *ECU Layer* has 3 ECUs (Engine Controller, Retarded, Brake Controller) attached to it. The *Sensor and Simulator Layer* is currently disabled. The testbed thus generates traffic as obtainable from a standalone truck. Two BeagleBone black devices, acting as *Node Controllers* are attached to the CAN network. Users can reserve these nodes to execute their scripts via the *TestBed-Manager*.

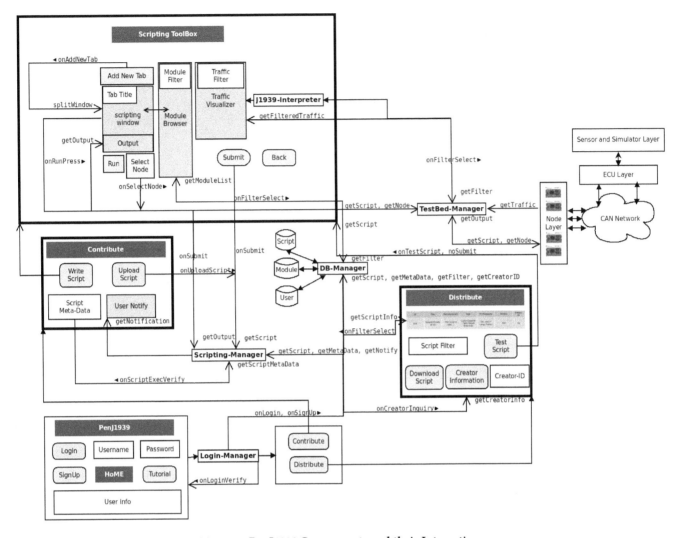

Figure 2: PenJ1939 Components and their Interactions

5   CURRENT IMPLEMENTATION AND FUTURE WORK

We have started the implementation process for PenJ1939. As mentioned earlier the testbed was a part of previous research and hence was set up at the beginning. All managers (Fig. 2) and associated databases have been set up. A J1939 decoder was designed as a part of our previous work [3]. Core functional modules of that the decoder were integrated into the PenJ1939 system in order to design the *J1939-Interpreter*. We are currently in the process of designing the web-based front-ends.

In future, we aim to improve some security critical aspects of our system. In particular, we believe that by integrating proper authentication and authorization mechanisms it may be possible for security professionals and researchers to alert specific OEMs about security issues in their J1939 implementations. We also aim to add additional features like authorized editing of code and patch management as a vision for of making PenJ1939 more usable.

ACKNOWLEDGEMENT

The work was supported in part by NSF under award numbers CNS 1619641 and CNS 1715458.

REFERENCES

[1] 2013. Serial Control and Communications Heavy Duty Vehicle Network - Top Level Document. (2013). http://standards.sae.org/j1939_201308
[2] C. Miller and C. Valasek. 2014. A Survey of Remote Automotive Attack Surfaces. *Black Hat USA* 2014 (2014).
[3] J. Daily, R. Gamble, S. Moffitt, C. Raines, P. Harris, J. Miran, I. Ray, S. Mukherjee, H. Shirazi, and J. Johnson. 2016. Towards a Cyber Assurance Testbed for Heavy Vehicle Electronic Controls. *SAE International Journal of Commercial Vehicles* 9, 2 (2016), 339–349.
[4] R. Bosch. 1991. CAN specification version 2.0. *Rober Bosch GmbH, Postfach* 300240 (1991).
[5] S. Mukherjee, H. Shirazi, I. Ray, J. Daily and R. Gamble. 2016. Practical DoS Attacks on Embedded Networks in Commercial Vehicles. In *Proceedings of 12th International Conference on Information Systems Security*. 23–42.
[6] Y. Burakova, B. Hass, L. Millar, A. Weimerskirch. 2016. Truck Hacking: An Experimental Analysis of the SAE J1939 Standard. In *Proceedings of 10th USENIX Conference on Offensive Technologies*. 211–220.

POSTER: Cyber Attack Prediction of Threats from Unconventional Resources (CAPTURE)*

Ahmet Okutan
Computer Engineering
Rochester Institute of Technology
Rochester, NY, USA
axoeec@rit.edu

Gordon Werner
Computer Engineering
Rochester Institute of Technology
Rochester, NY, USA
gxw9834@mail.rit.edu

Katie McConky
Industrial and Systems Engineering
Rochester Institute of Technology
Rochester, NY, USA
ktmeie@rit.edu

Shanchieh Jay Yang
Computer Engineering
Rochester Institute of Technology
Rochester, NY, USA
jay.yang@rit.edu

ABSTRACT

This paper outlines the design, implementation and evaluation of CAPTURE - a novel automated, continuously working cyber attack forecast system. It uses a broad range of unconventional signals from various public and private data sources and a set of signals forecasted via the Auto-Regressive Integrated Moving Average (ARIMA) model. While generating signals, auto cross correlation is used to find out the optimum signal aggregation and lead times. Generated signals are used to train a Bayesian classifier against the ground truth of each attack type. We show that it is possible to forecast future cyber incidents using CAPTURE and the consideration of the lead time could improve forecast performance.

CCS CONCEPTS

• **Security and privacy** → *Intrusion detection systems*;

KEYWORDS

Cyber-security, Unconventional signals, Bayesian Networks

1 INTRODUCTION

As computing and networking technologies are being embedded into our professional and personal activities, the impact of various and evolving cyber attacks continues to rise. This calls for an anticipatory capability to forecast potential cyber attacks before they happen [5, 6]. Such a capability requires examining beyond the traditional observables of malicious activities as they occur. This paper develops an automated, 24x7 system named CAPTURE that uses a broad range of unconventional signals from public data sources, including GDELT and Twitter, as well as reported cyber

incidents, to forecast different types of cyber attacks. Signals are named unconventional as they are not necessarily specific to a target entity or any cyber attack, but might be indicative for potential future cyber incidents towards the entity.

Sometimes an attacker is angered by a news release and motivated to launch a cyber attack towards a target entity [1]. Once the attacker has the intent, it might take some time to have the opportunity to execute it. This time could be different for each attack type due to the reconnaissance needed in the exploration phase or the responsiveness of the attacker. CAPTURE defines the lead time (Lt) as the time elapsed between the most recent observation of a significant signal correlation and the execution of a cyber attack. On the other hand, using different aggregation periods (At) for a signal, *i. e.*, aggregating over the last day, week or month could affect its predictive power.

CAPTURE uses a novel and systematic methodology to determine appropriate Lt and At for each unconventional signal with respect to each attack type and each target entity. This paper applies ARIMA [8] to the reported binary cyber incident data for each attack type. Whether a specific type of cyber attack occurs each day is treated as a time series and CAPTURE considers the forecasted occurrence of each attack type and its associated probability as base signals to reflect the potential pattern of attack occurrences. The ARIMA-based signals along with other unconventional signals configured with various Lt and At parameters are used by CAPTURE to perform an ensemble forecasting of future cyber incidents. CAPTURE uses these signals along with the reported cyber incidents to train a Bayesian model for each attack type of each target entity. It continually monitors and aggregates the signal data based on the systematically selected Lt and At, and forecasts future cyber incidents.

2 SYSTEM ARCHITECTURE

Figure 1 shows the overall system architecture of CAPTURE. Consider a set of attack types $A = \{A_1, A_2, ...A_m\}$, a set of target entities $E = \{E_1, E_2, ...E_t\}$, a set of unconventional signals $U = \{U_1, U_2, ...U_n\}$, and a set of Time Series signals $V = \{V_1, V_2, ...V_{2m}\}$. Using binary observations B_i of each A_i as time series until day d, ARIMA is applied to forecast the number of cyber attacks that

---
*This research is supported by the Office of the Director of National Intelligence (ODNI) and the Intelligence Advanced Research Projects Activity (IARPA) via the Air Force Research Laboratory (AFRL) contract number FA875016C0114.

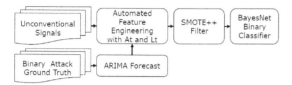

Figure 1: The brief overall architecture of CAPTURE.

will occur during the day $d + 1$. For each forecast a confidence value in the 95% confidence interval is generated. For each m attack types, forecasted daily counts and the associated confidences are used as signals to predict cyber attacks generating $2m$ Time Series signals in V. An instance of the CAPTURE architecture as shown in Figure 1 is created for each A_i and E_i combination. A key to the CAPTURE design is the ability to identify the optimal lead time and aggregation level for each signal. To perform this automated feature configuration a cross correlation is applied between the daily binary observations of B_i and each signal and the time lags for each signal are found in terms of days. Using the largest negative time lag as the lead time (Lt_i) and the difference between the largest negative lag and the smallest negative lag as aggregation time (At_i), the values of each signal are recalculated for each day. If there is no significant negative time lag, the signal is not used to predict attacks for A_i. If there is only one negative lag, the lag is used as At and Lt is set to 0 (See Figure 2). Repeating this process for each signal in U and V, a new set of signals say $Z = \{Z_1, Z_2, ...Z_k\}$ are generated for each attack type A_i where $k <= n + 2m$. A Bayesian network is a directed acyclic graph that is composed of k random variables and e edges that show the dependencies among these variables.

Let $Z = \{Z_1, Z_2, ...Z_k\}$ be k random variables (unconventional signals plus time series signals) with nominal or numeric values for a Bayesian network. The CAPTURE system trains a Bayesian classifier for each attack type A_i, using the set of aggregated signals in Z. Due to the nature of the cyber data, the data sets for some

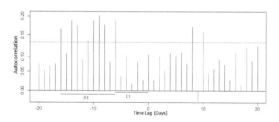

Figure 2: An example cross correlation that shows how the aggregation (At) and lead (Lt) times are found.

attack types are highly imbalanced. CAPTURE uses a novel filtering technique that is applied to the highly imbalanced data sets to make the data sets more balanced. The technique is named SMOTE++ and is built upon a previous technique called SMOTE [2]. It uses a combination of the majority under sampling, instance weighing, and minority over sampling (synthetic instance generation) techniques together. It uses k-means clustering starting with $k = 2$, and increments k until a cluster with minority instances is found. Then, it removes p percent of majority instances that are nearest to the

center of the minority cluster in terms of the Euclidean distance where the parameter p is tuned. SMOTE++ improves the prediction performance of the CAPTURE system significantly on some highly skewed cyber data sets.

2.1 Signals Used

2.1.1 GDELT Signals. GDELT [3] provides the mentions of events across all of its source documents. Each event has an associated average tone and it can take a value between -100 (extremely negative) and +100 (extremely positive).

- **GDELT Event Mentions (GEM)**: The mentions of all events that have a negative average tone are counted.
- **GDELT Event Tone (GET)**: The negative event tones in GDELT are summed up for the requested date interval.
- **GDELT Event Articles (GEA)**: The number of GDELT documents containing one or more mentions of a negative event are counted.

In GDELT, a numeric score is assigned to each event to capture the potential impact of the event on the stability of the country where it occurred (Goldstein scale). Four instability signals are calculated based on the Goldstein scale, with the hypothesis that an increase in the instability may result in an increase in the cyber attack probability. All instability signals are calculated for a given date interval and the country where the target entity operates.

- **Goldstein Event Count (GGC)**: The number of events associated with a negative Goldstein score.
- **Goldstein Score Average (GGA)**: The average of the Goldstein scores.
- **Goldstein Score Less Than Zero (GLZ)**: The average of scores that are less than zero.
- **Goldstein Score Less Than Minus Five (GLF)**: The average of scores that are less than minus five.

2.1.2 Twitter Events (TEC). The number of significant malicious events are counted based on the data from a previous study by Ritter *et al.* [7].

2.1.3 Level of Mentions of Entities (LME). Increased discussion of a target entity may indicate an increased surveillance towards the entity and could lead to increase in the likelihood of cyber attack towards it. To generate LME, the number of mentions of the target entity and its related keywords are counted in Twitter.

2.1.4 Sentiment Signals. According to Baumeister *et al.* a threat actor could be motivated to launch an attack based on anger [1]. Indications of outrage towards a target entity could be predictive for cyber incidents towards that entity. Two sentiment scores (named Affect (AFF) and Intensity (INT)) are used that are calculated by a private company in the industry for each of the three target entities, *i. e.*, anonymized K5 company, Defense, and Banking sectors. Six sentiment signals are used (two for each of the three targets) represented as *K5_AFF*, *K5_INT*, *DEF_AFF*, *DEF_INT*, *BANK_AFF*, and *BANK_INT*.

2.1.5 Time Series Signals. Applying ARIMA to the previously observed binary ground truth data of a given attack type, we forecast whether a cyber attack will occur at a future date. Using ARIMA forecasting, two values are generated for the future date,

i. e., the forecasted number of attacks (F) and the confidence associated with the forecast (C). These two values are generated daily for each attack type and used as signals for each trained Bayesian prediction model.

3 EVALUATION RESULTS

The CAPTURE system is evaluated based on the binary ground truth data of an anonymized company aliased as K5. The signals defined in 2.1 are used as inputs for the Bayesian classifier which is trained against the K5 ground truth on a daily basis. The signals until a date d are used with a Bayesian classifier to forecast the cyber attacks for the date $d + 1$. A separate Bayesian classifier is trained for each attack type defined for K5, *i. e.*, Malware (MW), Scan, Defacement (Def), Malicious Email (ME), Malicious URL (MU), and Denial of Service (DoS). The signals described in 2.1 are generated daily for all dates between July 1 2016 and Jan 1 2017. For each defined attack type, an auto cross correlation (CCR) analysis is carried out between each signal and the binary ground truth of the attack type. Using the CCR results, statistically significant time lags between the signal and the ground truth are determined. This process is repeated for each signal and attack type, and the optimum At and Lt parameters shown in Table 1 are found for each signal and attack type pair. We observe that different signals might have quite different aggregation and lead times for different attack types. The signals defined in 2.1

Table 1: At-Lt of signals found with cross correlation for each attack type. TS denotes Time Series signals (TS_MW_F and TS_MW_C denote the forecasted count and confidence respectively for Malware attacks).

Signal	MW	Scan	Def	MU	ME	DoS
GEM		11-1		14-3		
GET		12-1		12-5		
GEA		11-1		14-3		
TEC		5-16	20-1	5-14		
LME		2-4			14-1	20-1
GGC	20-1	16-1		6-1	6-13	9-8
GGA	20-1	16-1		6-1	6-13	9-8
GLF	20-1	16-1		6-1	6-13	9-8
GLZ	20-1	16-1		6-1	6-13	9-8
DEF_AFF		19-1			20-1	12-1
DEF_INT		6-6	13-4		9-1	14-1
BANK_AFF	5-1	11-1	7-5	4-1	7-14	17-1
BANK_INT		5-5	11-5		8-1	
K5_AFF			11-6	4-1	5-2	1-1
K5_INT	7-1	6-4	13-4		3-7	8-12
TS_MW_F	15-16	7-5	9-1			16-5
TS_MW_C	8-4	15-6	17-4		8-11	17-3
TS_SCAN_F					20-1	17-4
TS_SCAN_C		4-1	4-1	5-1	17-4	15-6
TS_DEF_F		16-1	9-1		12-8	11-10
TS_DEF_C		16-1	15-1			8-13
TS_MU_F		2-1	4-15		18-3	16-3
TS_MU_C	20-1	17-1	12-7	7-1	17-4	12-3
TS_ME_F		1-1	20-1		1-1	13-7
TS_ME_C	3-1	3-1		6-1		20-1
TS_DOS_F			18-1		8-11	3-4
TS_DOS_C			12-8			6-15

are recalculated based on the found At and Lt for each attack type. The recalculated signals are then used to train a Bayesian classifier for each attack type using its corresponding binary ground truth. The area under the ROC curve (AUC) gets better, when the true positive rate is high and false positive rate is low. Therefore, AUC is used to check the performance of each Bayesian model for each attack type. FilteredClassifier in Weka [4] is used to apply SMOTE++ and train a Bayesian classifier for each attack type with 10×10 folds cross validation. When the aggregated signals (Signals with At and Lt) are used, the AUC values shown in the first row of Table 2 are found for each attack type. To check the significance of using

Table 2: The AUC values found for each attack type for two cases.

AUC	MW	Scan	Def	MU	ME	DoS
Signals with At and Lt	0.51	0.67	0.69	0.56	0.64	0.82
Signals with At	0.51	0.61	0.66	0.57	0.62	0.78

Lt, a new set of signals (Signals with At) were calculated based on the At found with CCR and $Lt = 0$. With these signals, the AUC values of the Bayesian models for each attack type are shown in the second row of Table 2. We apply a t-test with a p-value of 0.05 and observe that the differences in the AUC values are significant for the Scan, Def and DoS attack types. We observe that using a lead time for the aggregated signals could improve the performance for some attack types, but believe that further research with different data sets is needed to generalize our findings.

4 CONCLUSION

The evaluations with the ground truth data of the anonymized company K5 illustrates the capability of CAPTURE. The results show that unconventional signals that are not directly related to a target entity, could be used to forecast cyber attacks towards it. Furthermore, cross correlation analysis is useful in determining the aggregation and lead times of the signals and using a lead time could improve the forecast performance.

REFERENCES

[1] Roy F. Baumeister, Kathleen D. Vohs, C. Nathan DeWall, and Liqing Zhang. 2007. How Emotion Shapes Behavior: Feedback, Anticipation, and Reflection, Rather Than Direct Causation. *Personality and Social Psychology Review* 11, 2 (2007), 167–203.
[2] Nitesh V. Chawla, Kevin W. Bowyer, Lawrence O. Hall, and W. Philip Kegelmeyer. 2002. SMOTE: Synthetic Minority Over-sampling Technique. *Journal Of Artificial Intelligence Research* 16, 1 (June 2002), 321–357.
[3] GDELT. 2017. The GDELT Project. (2017). http://www.gdeltproject.org/ [Online; accessed 6-February-2017].
[4] M. Hall, E. Frank, G. Holmes, B. Pfahringer, P. Reutemann, and I. H. Witten. 2009. The WEKA Data Mining Software: An Update. *SIGKDD Explorations* 11, 1 (Nov. 2009), 10–18.
[5] B. Munkhdorj and S. Yuji. 2017. Cyber attack prediction using social data analysis. 23 (01 2017), 109–135.
[6] A. Okutan, S. Yang, and K. McConky. 2017. Predicting Cyber Attacks With Bayesian Networks Using Unconventional Signals. In *Proceedings of the 12th Annual Conference on Cyber and Information Security Research (CISRC '17)*. ACM.
[7] A. Ritter, E. Wright, W. Casey, and T. Mitchell. 2015. Weakly Supervised Extraction of Computer Security Events from Twitter. In *Proceedings of the 24th International Conference on World Wide Web (WWW '15)*. Geneva, Switzerland, 896–905.
[8] G. Werner, S. Yang, and K. McConky. 2017. Time Series Forecasting of Cyber Attack Intensity. In *Proceedings of the 12th Annual Conference on Cyber and Information Security Research (CISRC '17)*. ACM.

POSTER: Towards Precise and Automated Verification of Security Protocols in Coq

Hernan M. Palombo
University of South Florida
hpalombo@usf.edu

Hao Zheng
University of South Florida
haozheng@usf.edu

Jay Ligatti
University of South Florida
ligatti@usf.edu

ABSTRACT

Security protocol verification using commonly-used model-checkers or symbolic protocol verifiers has several intrinsic limitations. Spin suffers the state explosion problem; Proverif may report false attacks. An alternative approach is to use Coq. However, the effort required to verify protocols in Coq is high for two main reasons: correct protocol and property specification is a non-trivial task, and security proofs lack automation. This work claims that (1) using Coq for verification of cryptographic protocols can sometimes yield better results than Spin and Proverif, and (2) the verification process in Coq can be greatly alleviated if specification and proof engineering techniques are applied. Our approach is evaluated by verifying several representative case studies. Preliminary results are encouraging, we were able to verify two protocols that give imprecise results in Spin and Proverif, respectively. Further, we have automated proofs of secrecy and authentication for an important class of protocols.

CCS CONCEPTS

• Security and privacy → Logic and verification;

KEYWORDS

Security Protocols; Verification; Coq

ACM Reference format:
Hernan M. Palombo, Hao Zheng, and Jay Ligatti. 2017. POSTER: Towards Precise and Automated Verification of Security Protocols in Coq. In *Proceedings of CCS '17, Dallas, TX, USA, October 30-November 3, 2017,* 3 pages.
https://doi.org/10.1145/3133956.3138846

1 INTRODUCTION

Security protocols are an ubiquitous mechanism to establish secure communications over insecure networks. As new technologies emerge, new protocols with specific requirements are being actively developed, e.g. private authentication for IoT [9]. The design of such protocols, however, tends to be error-prone. Attacks have been found on protocols that were thought to be correct for many years [3]. In this context, verification is a useful approach to provide stronger assurances that a protocol design satisfies some desired security policies.

There are several approaches to formally verify that protocol designs are correct. Model checking uses state transition systems to model the behavior of a system and then uses state exploration to find if an undesired state is reachable (i.e. a counter-example). Symbolic protocol verifiers are tailored tools that usually allow specification in some form of process algebra, and use some –usually automated– proof technique to find counter-examples in a similar way as model-checkers. On the other hand, theorem proving involves defining logical inference rules that describe the semantics of a system, and then using mathematical tools (e.g. induction) to prove different security-related theorems.

Unfortunately, commonly-used model checkers and protocol verifiers may yield imprecise results. For example, since an unbounded message space cannot be verified in Spin, verification may have to be reduced to single session configurations or restricted attacker models, which may lead to unsound results [2]. Further, Proverif sometimes reports false attacks due to its internal approximations [4].

On the other hand, theorem-proving does not have any of the aforementioned problems but involves greater verification effort in general. For example, the proof assistant Coq has a powerful specification language that is highly extensible but lacks built-in automation [1]. To the best of our knowledge, no previous work has used Coq to address Spin and Proverif's impreciseness problems, or explained how the process of verifying security protocols in Coq could be improved. This work fills this gap making two claims about verification of security protocols in Coq.

First, Coq can yield precise results for an important class of protocols that neither Spin nor Proverif can provide. Second, the verification process can be greatly alleviated if specification and proof engineering techniques are applied. To support our claims, we show two examples that give imprecise results in Spin and Proverif, respectively, and report the results of applying an iterative and incremental approach to achieve precise and automated verification of secrecy and authentication properties of several case studies.

Outline. Section 2 presents two examples of imprecise protocol verification in Spin and Proverif, respectively, that motivate our work. Section 3 gives a brief overview of our verification approach in Coq. Section 4 summarizes the results of several case-studies. Section 5 concludes the paper and outlines future work.

2 MOTIVATING EXAMPLES

We present two motivating examples of simple protocols yield imprecise results in Spin and Proverif, respectively.

NSPK in Spin. The NSPK protocol aims to provide mutual authentication between two parties communicating over an insecure network [11]. The protocol involves three parties, the two authenticating clients and a server which distributes public keys to the clients. Spin cannot verify the full version of the protocol, and finds an attack on a reduced version of the protocol but the attacker model is unsound. [2]. We specify the protocol in Coq and confirm that an impersonation attack is possible. Further, we fix the protocol using a timestamp and prove that the attack is no longer possible.

NSSK in Proverif. The NSSK protocol aims to generate a session key between two parties communicating over an insecure network [11]. When the NSSK protocol is composed with a symmetric encryption scheme to generate and transmit a secret, Proverif reports a false attack [5]. We specify the protocol in Coq and verify that the attack reported by Proverif is indeed false, i.e. the secret is not leaked to an attacker.

More generally, the two examples presented here expose some intrinsic limitations Spin and Proverif that affect verification of a wide class of protocols, properties, and configurations. Table 1 summarizes how the tools are compared in terms of preciseness and automation.

Table 1: Verification of Unbounded Number of Sessions

	SPIN	Proverif	Coq
Sound		✓	✓
No false attacks	✓		✓
Automated	✓	✓	

An unbounded number of sessions cannot be verified in Spin, and only a restricted class of attackers can be verified, i.e. those with very limited storage capabilities. These limitations may lead to results that are unsound, i.e. the verification process succeeds despite attacks are possible.

In Proverif, unbounded number of sessions can be verified but its internal abstractions may generate false attacks. Although an encoding approach using phases was proposed to reduce false attacks, it is guaranteed to be sound for a limited class of protocols, e.g. it does not work for multiparty protocols, and it has not been proven to work for correspondence assertions [5]. Further, it is difficult to know a priori if Proverif's output correspond to a false attack and phases need to be inserted into the encoding, and interpreting Proverif's outputs to rule out false attacks is sometimes nontrivial [10].

3 VERIFICATION IN COQ

A high level view of the verification process in Coq is shown in Figure 1. We follow a modular and incremental approach for developing specifications and proofs. We start with a base specification describing the protocol, attacker, and security properties that we want to prove. If the proofs succeed, we refine the specification and prove the security properties of the refinement. The process continues incrementally until either the specification is complete and all properties have been proved, or some property fails to hold and we conclude that the property is insecure. Note that the properties being proved are decidable, so in every case we can reach a conclusion.

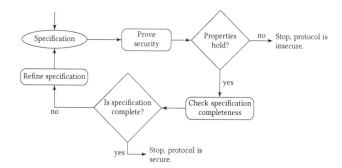

Figure 1: Incremental Verification in Coq.

Next, we discuss some general principles that guide our specification and proof development process.

3.1 Specifications

The specification process entails formalizing three main components: (1) the protocol, (2) an attacker model, and (3) the security properties.

3.1.1 Protocols. Informal protocol specifications describe a sequence of steps of the expected interactions between participants. There are several implicit assumptions in informal specifications that a formalization must disambiguate, e.g. the initial knowledge of the protocol's participants.

Our specification in Coq relies heavily on inductive definitions. First, we define the agents participating in the protocol. Second, we define messages, which can be primitives, e.g. names, nonces, and keys, or compositions of other messages, e.g. pairs or encrypted messages. Third, we define the expected protocol events, i.e. transitions. Because we are modeling an insecure network, send and receive operations are defined non-atomically as mutually inductive propositions.

3.1.2 Attacker Models. An attacker model must specify the attacker's initial knowledge and possible actions. Dolev-Yao attackers [8] have been widely used in the symbolic model. A Dolev-Yao attacker is one who may be able to spy, intercept, or inject messages at will. Weaker attacker models, e.g. a passive eavesdropper, are also sometimes desired.

In Coq, the attacker can be modeled by adding her capabilities to the mutually inductive definition of send and receive operations. Our definition contains rules for attacker's possible actions, e.g. constructors for names, nonces, cryptographic operations, and (de)composition of messages.

3.1.3 Security Properties. Two main properties that are usually requirements of security protocols are secrecy and authentication. Both can be formulated as safety properties.

Secrecy ensures that secret data can only be seen by authorized users. More precisely, secrecy is an invariant asserting that a token marked as secret cannot be learned by an attacker. In Coq, secrecy is formalized as a theorem stating that the attacker can never learn the secret.

The goal of authentication is to assert that an agent is really who he claim to be. An authentication protocol satisfies the property iff every time the authentication of a requester succeeds, the requester is whomever the authenticator expects to have authenticated. In Coq, it is an implication stating that if the protocol ends (and authentication succeeds), the authenticator has not authenticated the attacker.

3.2 Proofs

The proofs for secrecy and authentication properties are completed in several steps.

First, we specify a separate inductive definition of the attacker's knowledge that is used in the proofs of secrecy and authentication. This definition is different from the attacker's model described in Section 2 in that it indicates what the attacker may eventually learn as opposed to her capabilities.

Next, we prove several related lemmas; one stating that anything that is received can be learned by the attacker; a second one saying that the attacker learns everything that follows from the attacker model; and a third one asserting that what cannot be learned by the attacker is outside the attacker model. With these lemmas in hand, secrecy and authentication theorems are then proved using case analysis.

4 OTHER CASE-STUDIES

Apart from the examples presented in Section 2, we verify a representative sample of authentication and key-establishment protocols, namely the DS [6], TMN [12], and DH [7]. Our case-study selection is motivated by the relevance of the protocols and the observation that many security protocols use a common set of cryptographic primitives, which are present in the cases analyzed here.

For instance, the DS protocol, proposed as a fix to the NSPK protocol, is chosen to exercise the tools with a protocol that uses signatures, timestamps, and symmetric encryption. The TMN protocol serves as an interesting example for its use of Vernam encryption techniques, i.e. XOR functions, a technique commonly used in cryptography. Finally, DH is chosen because many protocol families, e.g. TLS, rely on the use of exponentiation for an unauthenticated agreement of a shared key between two parties.

4.1 Results

In most cases, we are able to prove that secrecy and authentication hold. However, some versions of the protocols are flawed and the proofs do not go through.

For example, for the DS protocol, we start with the original version described by Dennim and Sacco [6] which is known to be insecure. The proof of secrecy fails because an attacker can perform a MITM attack and the protocol may end with Bob sending the secret nonce to the attacker. To confirm the protocol's insecurity, the negation of the secrecy lemma is proved, which states that the attacker may be able to learn the secret nonce.

Finally, we fix the protocol specification and attempt to prove secrecy again. This time both proofs succeed as the MITM attack is no longer possible.

4.2 Automation

In all cases, the proofs follow a similar pattern. Based on this observation, the next step is to automate the proofs to increase the robustness and generality of our approach. For secrecy, we add the constructors of the attacker's knowledge-vector to the Hint database and then use the auto tactic to complete the proof. For authentication, we define a new tactic solve_auth in *Ltac* which pattern matches on the current goal.

5 CONCLUSION AND FUTURE WORK

This work shows that Coq provides precise results for verification of security protocols that cannot be directly obtained in Spin or Proverif. A second contribution is that the verification process in Coq can be significantly improved if specifications are developed modularly and incrementally, and proofs are automated. Towards this end, we explained general specification principles and automated proofs of secrecy and authentication properties for an important class of authentication and key-establishment protocols. Our ongoing work is to make the approach more general by verifying other types of protocols, e.g. those with privacy-related properties, adding more automation, and analyzing larger case studies.

REFERENCES

[1] Bruno Barras, Samuel Boutin, Cristina Cornes, et al. 2002. *The Coq proof assistant reference manual–version 7.2.* Technical Report. Technical Report 0255, INRIA.
[2] Noomene Ben Henda. 2014. Generic and efficient attacker models in SPIN. In *Proceedings of the 2014 International SPIN Symposium on Model Checking of Software.* ACM, 77–86.
[3] Karthikeyan Bhargavan, Bruno Blanchet, and Nadim Kobeissi. 2017. *Verified models and reference implementations for the TLS 1.3 standard candidate.* Ph.D. Dissertation. Inria Paris.
[4] Bruno Blanchet, Ben Smyth, and Vincent Cheval. 2016. ProVerif 1.94 pl1: Automatic Cryptographic Protocol Verifier, User Manual and Tutorial. (2016).
[5] Tom Chothia, Ben Smyth, and Chris Staite. 2015. Automatically checking commitment protocols in proverif without false attacks. In *International Conference on Principles of Security and Trust.* Springer, 137–155.
[6] Dorothy E Denning and Giovanni Maria Sacco. 1981. Timestamps in key distribution protocols. *Commun. ACM* 24, 8 (1981), 533–536.
[7] Whitfield Diffie and Martin E Hellman. 1976. New directions in cryptography. *Information Theory, IEEE Transactions on* 22, 6 (1976), 644–654.
[8] Danny Dolev and Andrew C Yao. 1983. On the security of public key protocols. *Information Theory, IEEE Transactions on* 29, 2 (1983), 198–208.
[9] Mohamed Amine Ferrag, Leandros A Maglaras, Helge Janicke, and Jianmin Jiang. 2016. Authentication Protocols for Internet of Things: A Comprehensive Survey. *arXiv preprint arXiv:1612.07206* (2016).
[10] Murat Moran and Dan S Wallach. 2017. Verification of STAR-Vote and Evaluation of FDR and ProVerif. *arXiv preprint arXiv:1705.00782* (2017).
[11] Roger M Needham and Michael D Schroeder. 1978. Using encryption for authentication in large networks of computers. *Commun. ACM* 21, 12 (1978), 993–999.
[12] Makoto Tatebayashi, Natsume Matsuzaki, and David B Newman. 1989. Key distribution protocol for digital mobile communication systems. In *Conference on the Theory and Application of Cryptology.* Springer, 324–334.

POSTER: Probing Tor Hidden Service with Dockers

Jonghyeon Park
Chungnam National University
Daejeon, Republic of Korea
pjh000901@cnu.ac.kr

Youngseok Lee
Chungnam national University
Daejeon, Republic of Korea
lee@cnu.ac.kr

ABSTRACT

Tor is a commonly used anonymous network that provides the hidden services. As the number of hidden services using Tor's anonymous network has been steadily increasing every year, so does the number of services that abuse Tor's anonymity. The existing research on the Tor is mainly focused on Tor's security loopholes and anonymity. As a result, how to collect and analyze the contents of Tor's hidden services is not yet in full swing. In addition, due to the slow access speed of the Tor browser, it is difficult to observe the dynamics of the hidden services. In this work, we present a tool that can monitor the status of hidden services for the analysis of authentic hidden service contents, and have automated our tool with the virtualization software, Docker, to improve the crawling performance. From August 12, 2017 to August 20, 2017, we collected a total of 9,176 sites and analyzed contents for 100 pages.

KEYWORDS

Tor; Deep Web; Dark Web; Hidden Service; Docker;

1 INTRODUCTION

Tor is an anonymous communication tool that uses a special communication method called Onion routing to ensure high anonymity to the user. The high anonymity of Tor applies to web services as a hidden service, and Tor's hidden service has helped people who need freedom and privacy on the Internet. However, the illegal hidden services by abusing Tor are steadily increasing. Because of the anonymity feature of Tor, it is difficult to identify the seller even if illegal goods are traded.

Compared to the increase in these illegal hidden services, previous research has concentrated on the technical aspects of Tor. Tor's classic work has focused on attacking at the network and anonymity [2, 4, 7]. They studied on attack methods using Tor's security defects and factors that can remove anonymity. A research on the contents includes the discovery of the Tor hidden service at the protocol level [4] and it observed the usage of the Tor service through the port scan [2]. This study examined how to discover unknown hidden services using Tor's network weakness or system defects, rather than analyzing the contents of hidden services.

The recent Ransomware incident also uses Tor hidden services for the Bitcoin transaction. A few Tor studies have begun to concentrate on the content analysis and overall scale of hidden service. A

study [8] created a special crawler called Dark Crawler. This Dark Crawler was used to analyze the connections between illegal hidden services and the content of extremists and terrorists operating under hidden services at Tor. In [6], they analyzed the content of the hidden service and found the connection point between the normal network and the hidden service through the domain and the resource, and discovered the appearance rate and characteristics of the web tracking through the script used by the hidden service. [1] conducted a two-month intensive analysis of Tor's large illegal marketplace, Agora. They investigated the illegal goods sold in Agora and the country of the seller, and found out the possibility of organized crime. Thus, the recent Tor research is toward the analysis of the content of the large-scale hidden service and the analysis of the ecosystem of the hidden service.

Generally, it is not easy to crawl many Tor hidden services quickly. Hidden service providers open their services for a short time to avoid monitoring and tracking. They occasionally operate most of the hidden services, and often change the address of the hidden service. In addition, due to encryption and peer-to-peer connection of Tor, the access to the Tor hidden service is slow, which is also applied to the Tor crawler. Because of these two features, it is difficult for researchers to collect and analyze the hidden services contents. One the interesting cloud computing environment is to virtualize the computing resource and to automate the job process. As the Tor web browsing is slow, we need a lot of computing resources to collect many Tor hidden service quickly. Due to the popular virtualization software such as Docker, we can easily deploy virtualized computing resources on the cloud. Docker [5] provides containers of abstraction and automation of operating system images, which is contributed to improve the computing resource utilization. Thus, we present a Docker-based Tor hidden service crawler to collect and analyze the hidden services automatically and to monitor them quickly. From experiments, we observed that distributed processing with Docker improves the crawling speed of hidden service pages against Tor's slow communication speed. We also found that a lot of Tor marketplaces and communities are related with illegal trading and Bitcoins.

2 TOR CRAWLER AND ANALYSIS SYSTEM

Figure 1 shows the Tor crawler and analysis system. After we initiate the virtual computing resource on the cloud services such as Microsoft Azure or Amazon EC2, we run one or more Docker container on a cloud computing instance. Each Docker container, a virtualized Linux server, performs as a Tor crawler. To improve the scalability, we load multiple containers of the Docker virtual machine on one instance. We create an image of a dedicated Docker to facilitate configuration and deployment for the crawler. Each Docker container has a set of Tor hidden service addresses to be crawled and it starts to collect Tor hidden services of the whole

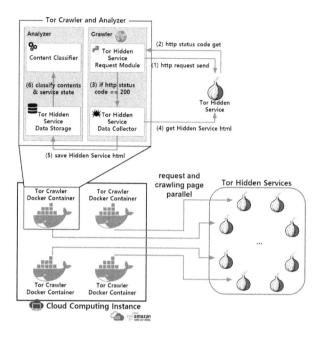

Figure 1: Tor crawling and analysis system architecture

Table 1: Tor http return value for classification

Return Value	State	Result
200	Live	html file
401, 403	Live	-
4XX, 5XX	Dead	-
Req or Sel TimeOut/ConnectError	Dead	-

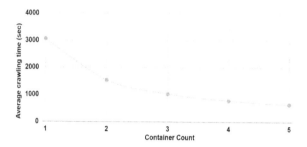

Figure 2: Crawling time by the number of Docker containers.

address set. We collected 16,683 Tor hidden service addresses from June to July 2017 with our implementation using an out-of-band hidden service address collection method [3].

We explain the Tor hidden service crawler in each Docker container in Fig. 1. The Tor crawler running on the Docker consists of two processes. One is a Tor hidden service request module that sends a request message, and the other is a Tor hidden service data collector that gathers html files from a hidden service page.

The request module sends a request message to the Tor hidden service server. The request module receives a reply message from the hidden service server and reads the http status code from the reply within a time limit of 30 seconds[1]. If the request is not received, TimeOut or ConnectionError occurs. In this case, we consider the hidden service as dead.

When the request module process finishes, the hidden service data collector checks the http status code and gathers the corresponding html files. We make the Tor crawler collect the hidden service page that actually operates the web page. Thus, the Tor hidden service data collector works only when the http status code is 200. For the address identified as http status code 200, we use the Tor hidden service data collector to access the hidden service page and to save the page's html files. This process, like the request module, has a time limit of 30 seconds.

The Tor analyzer classifies the state of the hidden service measured through the Tor crawler into live or dead states according to the log in Table 1. The Tor crawler actually judges that the hidden service can be accessed in the live state with the http status code of 200. Among the hidden services, there are web pages that request a password for access. These pages return the status code of 401 or 403 because they are not authorized, but the service is operating normally.

---

[1] 30 seconds is the average time when a hidden service request triggers an exception.

3 EXPERIMENT RESULT

We have configured five Microsoft Azure instances to test the Tor hidden service's crawling and observing experiment. We used the instance with 2 core and 7GB memory, and Ubuntu 16.04 LST OS. We ran 4 Docker containers on each instance, executing a total of 20 Containers in parallel. The experiment was conducted over 9 days from August 2, 2017 at 2:00 AM UTC to August 20, 17:00 UTC. The number of Onion addresses in this experiment was 16,683, and the addresses were crawled twice a day at 12-hour intervals. Of the total of 20 containers, 11 Docker containers succeeded in collecting data normally. We analyzed 9,176 addresses out of a total of 16,683 addresses.

First, we examine how the virtualization with Docker can improve the Tor hidden service crawling time. To observe the crawling time while the number of containers varies, we select 100 addresses randomly, run each instance from one to five containers, test 100 addresses, and measure the crawling response time. Figure 2 shows the average crawling time as the number of containers increases. For one container, it takes 3,062 seconds to crawl 100 addresses. With five Docker containers, it needs an average of 640 seconds, which is about 4.78 times fast than one container.

Second, we dissect the hidden service contents. We look into the hidden service contents of randomly selected 100 hidden services and extract feature values of words from the collected Tor hidden service. After saving 100 hidden service pages, we classify the contents into 11 categories in Table 2. We classify hidden service contents based on words in the html file. The largest content category is the marketplace of 20%, which is a commodity transaction site for Tor users. In the marketplace, illegal transaction services for prohibited goods such as hacking requests, hitman service, cloned credit cards, and drugs take 16%. In Fig. 3, the upper two sites are the examples of the Tor marketplace hidden service. In the case of the community of 14%, there are communities about the illegal themes such as drug dealers and pedophilia. One unusual category

Table 2: Classification of 100 Tor hidden service samples

Contents Category	Percentage(%)
Marketplace	20
Community	14
Hidden Service directory	12
Personal Blog	9
Onion address sales page	9
Unknown page	9
Bitcoin laundering	6
Wiki	5
Apache default setting page	5
Journalist, Movement organization	4
Software distribution, sales	4
Illegal file sharing	3

Figure 3: Examples of Tor hidden service pages: hacking request service, cloned credit card market, Bitcoin laundry service and Hidden Service directory

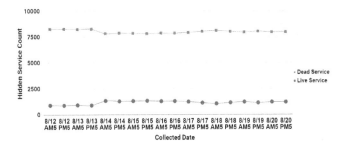

Figure 4: Hidden service state dynamics over 9 days: live or dead

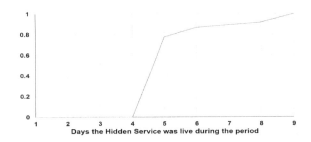

Figure 5: CDF of Tor hidden service live state (day).

is Bitcoin laundry service of 6%, where users may send Bitcoin with the promotion to receive the returns of 10x to 100x coins. The site at the bottom left of Fig. 3 is a Bitcoin laundry example. Further research is necessary to undermine the usage of the Bitcoin laundry service's Bitcoin transaction. During the collection of these pages, 9% of pages are unknown.

Third, we investigate how Tor hidden services of 9,176 addresses change their states under 18 runs of experiments over 9 days. We crawl Tor hidden services twice a day during period and record the live or dead state of the service. We plot the number of live and dead hidden services for each measurement in Fig. 4. During the observation period, the hidden service averaged 1,166 alive during the whole period and 8,010 services were dead.

8,157 services out of 9,176 were always dead state. We count how often the Tor crawler finds the live state of the target hidden service over 9 days. We observe that 1,019 hidden services were always alive during the observation period. In Fig. 5, 77.2% of the total hidden services were maintained alive at least five days.

4   CONCLUSION AND FUTURE WORK

In this work, we proposed a virtualized Tor crawling and analysis system to monitor the status of Tor hidden services and to classify their contents. We have implemented our tool with Docker on the MS Azure cloud computing platform and have analyzed Tor hidden services. Based on the results of content analysis, we have shown that illegal Tor hidden services are popular. Our research will contribute to the early discovery of illegal services through scalable Tor hidden service crawling and analysis.

ACKNOWLEDGMENTS

This research was supported by the MSIP(Ministry of Science, ICT and Future Planning), Korea, under the ITRC(Information Technology Research Center) support program (IITP-2017-2016-0-00304) supervised by the IITP(Institute for Information & communications Technology Promotion)

REFERENCES

[1] Andres Baravalle, Mauro Sanchez Lopez, and Sin Wee Lee. 2016. Mining the Dark Web: Drugs and Fake Ids. In *Data Mining Workshops (ICDMW), 2016 IEEE 16th International Conference on*. IEEE, 350–356.
[2] Alex Biryukov, Ivan Pustogarov, Fabrice Thill, and Ralf-Philipp Weinmann. 2014. Content and popularity analysis of Tor hidden services. In *Distributed Computing Systems Workshops (ICDCSW), 2014 IEEE 34th International Conference on*. IEEE, 188–193.
[3] Kang Li, Peipeng Liu, Qingfeng Tan, Jinqiao Shi, Yue Gao, and Xuebin Wang. 2016. Out-of-band discovery and evaluation for tor hidden services. In *Proceedings of the 31st Annual ACM Symposium on Applied Computing*. ACM, 2057–2062.
[4] Zhen Ling, Junzhou Luo, Kui Wu, and Xinwen Fu. 2013. Protocol-level hidden server discovery. In *INFOCOM, 2013 Proceedings IEEE*. IEEE, 1043–1051.
[5] Dirk Merkel. 2014. Docker: lightweight linux containers for consistent development and deployment. *Linux Journal* 2014, 239 (2014), 2.
[6] Iskander Sanchez-Rola, Davide Balzarotti, and Igor Santos. 2017. The Onions Have Eyes: A Comprehensive Structure and Privacy Analysis of Tor Hidden Services. In *Proceedings of the 26th International Conference on World Wide Web*. International World Wide Web Conferences Steering Committee, 1251–1260.
[7] Matthew Thomas and Aziz Mohaisen. 2014. Measuring the Leakage of Onion at the Root. *ACM WPES* (2014).
[8] Ahmed T Zulkarnine, Richard Frank, Bryan Monk, Julianna Mitchell, and Garth Davies. 2016. Surfacing collaborated networks in dark web to find illicit and criminal content. In *Intelligence and Security Informatics (ISI), 2016 IEEE Conference on*. IEEE, 109–114.

POSTER: Evaluating Reflective Deception
as a Malware Mitigation Strategy

Thomas Shaw
The University of Tulsa
thomas-shaw@utulsa.edu

James Arrowood
Haystack Security, LLC
jim.arrowood@haystacksecurity.com

Michael Kvasnicka
The University of Tulsa
ttk164@utulsa.edu

Shay Taylor
The University of Tulsa
sat763@utulsa.edu

Kyle Cook
The University of Tulsa
kac330@utulsa.edu

John Hale*
The University of Tulsa
john-hale@utulsa.edu

CCS CONCEPTS

• **Security and privacy** → **Malware and its mitigation**;

KEYWORDS

Deception Technology; Reflective Deception; Malware

ACM Reference Format:
Thomas Shaw, James Arrowood, Michael Kvasnicka, Shay Taylor, Kyle Cook, and John Hale. 2017. POSTER: Evaluating Reflective Deception as a Malware Mitigation Strategy. In *Proceedings of CCS '17, Dallas, TX, USA, October 30-November 3, 2017,* 3 pages.
https://doi.org/10.1145/3133956.3138833

1 INTRODUCTION

Deception is a defensive technique that influences attacker behavior through misinformation or concealment of information [5, 8, 11, 13]. It may be used to forestall an attack, lead an attacker away from a target, and learn about an attacker's motives and capabilities.

This poster describes a defensive deception technique – Reflective Deception – along with an experimentation platform to evaluate its efficacy and performance in mitigating malware. Techniques such as this hold promise for extending the role of deception as a highly integrated cyber defense strategy. Moreover, the platform presented here constitutes a blueprint for the safe and systematic assessment of deception-based malware mitigation strategies.

2 REFLECTIVE DECEPTION

Reflective Deception blends traits from two established deception techniques – honeypots and interdiction. Honeypots expose vulnerable systems to attackers, enticing them to reveal their intent and tactics [3, 10, 12]. A honeypot requires an "operational cover story" sensitive to the context of surrounding system elements. The services it exposes should blend in with neighboring systems,

while offering an attractive target to attackers. One benefit of honeypots (and defensive deception techniques, in general) is that they increase the workload of an attacker.

Deception has also played a role in the protection of digital content online. File spoofing technologies emerged shortly after the turn of the century, flooding P2P networks with decoy media [4, 7]. Interdiction based on file spoofing relies on: (1) fabricating decoys with meta data and file characteristics identical to authentic source media, and (2) the ability to saturate a target network with a robust population of decoys. The principal objectives in such a strategy are to conceal the authentic media, while increasing the burden and work required by the attacker to locate it.

Several efforts promote the use of deception to disrupt various phases of what has become known as the intrusion or cyber "kill chain" [1, 3, 9]. Deception has assisted with manipulating an attacker's C2 infrastructure via DNS redirection and by manipulating the actions on objectives phase through honeypots. Other work extends deceptive capabilities in this phase by deceiving the attacker as they interact with the operating system [6].

However, many of these applications require detecting an intruder before the deception can be deployed. Reflective Deception is a variant of deception with no such constraint [2]. A core tenet of Reflective Deception is to manufacture and amplify decoy responses to malware before it is even detected, thereby overwhelming an attacker with spurious feedback. For example, when combating malware distributed through attachments and links, a Reflective Deception strategy would be to open and execute the malware in a secure sandbox a multitude of times. This creates the illusion of dozens, hundreds, or potentially thousands of malware infected systems that call back to the attacker to produce volumes of command and control channels as illustrated in Figure 1. During this time, if a user genuinely falls prey to the malware, their callback traffic is buried within the decoy callbacks distributed over time, thus protecting the infected user as seen in Figure 2.

3 EXPERIMENTATION PLATFORM

The experimentation platform we propose comprises: (i) a physical infrastructure, (ii) a virtual infrastructure, (iii) a victim domain, and (iv) an attacker domain (Figure 3). This platform provides a secure, agile and highly automated solution for exploring the properties and performance of deception and related malware mitigation strategies. It can be deployed and operated in a manner completely disconnected from the Internet or with extremely limited and tightly controlled access to it.

---

*To Whom Correspondence Should Be Addressed

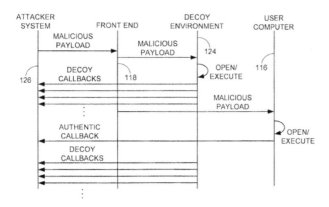

Figure 1: Reflective Deception Callbacks.

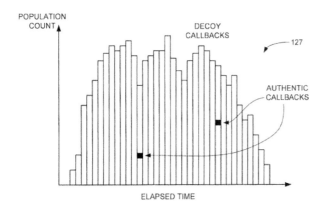

Figure 2: Temporal Distribution of Decoy Callbacks.

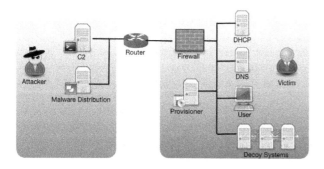

Figure 3: Reflective Deception Experimentation Platform.

3.1 Physical Infrastructure

The physical infrastructure constitutes hardware that hosts the virtual infrastructure. A minimal configuration accommodates one attacker machine, two infrastructure machines, and three victim machines. The physical infrastructure should be capable of running a hypervisor to support multiple internal networks and machines with multiple network interface cards (NICs). (Most virtualization clusters should be able to handle these minimum requirements.) A reference solution has been fielded within a VMWare Cluster at the University of Tulsa. This cluster consists of 18 physical machines totaling 128 cores (300 GHz of aggregate processing power), 464 GBs of RAM, and 8.7 TBs of storage. VMware's VCenter seamlessly balances virtual machines across the physical systems.

3.2 Virtual Infrastructure

The virtual infrastructure consists of support systems not participating as attacker or victim. These include a router, firewall, DNS server, DHCP server, and the provisioning and deployment servers.

3.2.1 Router and Firewall. The router is the backbone of the virtual infrastructure, linking victim and attacker domains. Placing the attacker and victims on separate networks facilitates monitoring all traffic passing between the two. Installing a firewall creates additional options for logging and increased realism. The firewall can be used to watch for connections and block certain traffic to more faithfully represent a real-world environment.

The router in our solution is a VM running FreeBSD with two NICs to bridge two separate VMware virtual switches – one for the attacker domain and one for the victim domain. This router also doubles as the firewall. It only has access to the internal networks, with no outside connection to ensure the malware cannot escape the controlled environment. Both virtual networks are NAT'd, and require manual port-forwarding. This increases the complexity of configuring an attack, but ensures that the experimenter has full knowledge of the requirements of the attack and the environment.

3.2.2 Provisioning and Deployment Server. The provisioning and deployment machine is the most complex part of the infrastructure due to scalability requirements. There are several provisioning options, including scripting the duplication of VM templates and re-imaging existing VMs through a provisioning server. All victim machines must tie into this deployment server, which distributes the malware. It must accept an executable to be pulled and executed by all VMs. After an experiment, these machines must be destroyed or re-imaged to prevent contamination across experiments.

A local host executes a PowerShell/PowerCLI script connected to vCenter. It takes arguments to configure the experiment and set names for cloned decoys. A Windows VM acts as a template to create a snapshot and use VMWare's Linked Clones to produce a volume of decoys. The script then downloads the malware from the Malware Distribution Server, and runs PSExec to execute it across all decoys. The script waits a fixed period of time, then removes the VMs and the machines from the domain, erasing their DNS records.

3.2.3 DHCP AND DNS Servers. The DHCP server mainly applies to the victim domain, but is optional on the attacker side. It promotes scalable automated automated deployment. While static addresses can be assigned to victims, it is safer to assign them dynamically.

The role of DNS depends on the configuration of the provisioning and deployment server. Some require a fully qualified domain name, and thus internal DNS. The DNS server can also host an internal email server to test automated email and attachment scanning. The DNS server supports an intranet for the victim domain, and should not be publicly accessible. For simplicity, attacker domain machines in our solution have manually set static IP addresses.

3.3 Victim Domain

The victim domain comprises systems that are directly attacked or are used in the Reflective Deception response. This domain fielded by the provisioning and deployment server with a few static machines acting as legitimate targets of an attack. All other victim machines (decoy clones) are deployed as needed.

Incorporating diversity into the decoy population improves the efficacy of the Reflective Deception response. *Victim Masquerading* techniques such as synthetic web browsing, mouse movement and forged credentials can increase the amount of time it takes for an attacker to discern whether a system is a viable target. Automated credential generation can also be used to confuse credential harvesters designed to scrape credentials passing through the machine, such as those for bank accounts or e-commerce sites. Our primary technique is an automated credential generation tool connected to an internal web address. This site can be quickly themed based on the kind of credential, for example appearing as a banking website or e-commerce site. With the internal DNS server, these sites can be resolved to real, external domain names, further confusing an automated credential harvester (e.g. amazon.com).

3.4 Attacker Domain

The attacker domain only requires a few machines, depending on the malware under test. These include systems to launch attacks, monitor incoming and outgoing traffic, and house command and control operations. A separate host is responsible for the distribution of malware as it acts as a middle-man between domains to prevent the malware from leaking. The attacker domain may incorporate a malicious web server that encompasses these and other functions. In short, the systems in this domain must be configured to support a realistic manifestation of the malware's ecosystem.

3.4.1 Packet Capture Server. To determine whether Reflective Deception counter measure is effective, a packet capture server logs traffic from victim and attacker domains. It sits on the attacker domain, but is configured using port-mirroring to see traffic from the victim domain as well. Port mirroring on a switch copies and forwards data from source to destination ports. The source can be one or more VLANs/ports as long as the source port is not the same as the destination port. The server's interface is set to promiscuous mode to capture traffic intended for other machines. Since the switch sends packets directly to the packet capture's port it has no need for an IP address. Captured traffic is stored in PCap files and processed through a packet analyzer for analysis.

3.4.2 Malware Distribution Server. To prevent malware leaks, an air-gapped malware distribution server (MDS) runs an SSH server and a web server. A PowerCLI script switches the MDS between domains – neither domain is ever connected from anything other than the router/firewall. For matters of convenience, the malware is uploaded to the SSH server by secure copy, and downloaded from the HTTP server. Data can only be uploaded from the attacker domain and only downloaded from the victim domain. This inhibits leaks through the MDS and admits superior access control.

3.4.3 Command and Control Center. The command and control (C2) center hosts remote administration tools (RATs) used to take control of victims. Under a standard firewall ruleset ('block all in' and 'allow all out'), a victim can connect to an attacker, but not vice versa. Thus, malware commonly 'phones home' to the attacker, creating a connection. RATs have the capability of seeing all machines connected to them simultaneously with the ability to manipulate multiple machines at once, giving rise to a botnet.

4 ON-GOING WORK

On-going work targets multiple objectives, including: (i) development of metrics for Reflective Deception, (ii) evaluation and refinement of our experimentation platform, and (iii) evolution of Reflective Deception tactics. A test using Dark Comet as a representative malware specimen has been conducted, with post-analysis efforts underway. The test ran multiple scenarios using decoy volumes ranging from 1 - 100, generating in aggregate 836 MB of PCap files. Plans are in place to upgrade the infrastructure to support larger decoy volumes as analysis on the first data set begins.

The definition of performance and efficiency metrics remains a thorny subject. Ultimately, a constellation of measures will serve best to identify the right balance in employing Reflective Deception. In addition, the development and operation of the experimentation platform has yielded insights about its architecture. Nuances with automation and VM management confounded naive design thinking, while fundamental rules regarding minimal hardware footprint and capabilities emerged. Strategies for coping with physical and virtual limitations have inspired alternative solutions and potential trade-offs in the platform's implementation. Finally, as the experimenter's familiarity with the attacker's viewpoint grows, concepts for enhanced tactics in Reflective Deception are being cultivated.

REFERENCES

[1] M. H. Almeshekah, E. H. Spafford, and M. J. Atallah. Improving security using deception. Technical Report CERIAS Tech Report, 13, Center for Education and Research Information Assurance and Security, Purdue University, 2013.

[2] J. Arrowood. Cyber attack disruption through multiple detonations of received payloads. Technical Report U.S. Patent No. 8,943,594, USPTO, January 27, 2015.

[3] B. Cheswick. An evening with berferd in which a cracker is lured, endured, and studied. In *Proc. Winter USENIX Conference*, 1992.

[4] N. Christin, A. Weigend, and J. Chuang. Content availability, pollution and poisoning in file sharing peer-to-peer networks. In *Proceedings of the 6th ACM conference on Electronic commerce*, pages 68–77, 2005.

[5] F. Cohen. A note on the role of deception in information protection. *Computers & Security*, 17(6):483–506, 1998.

[6] F. Cohen, D. Rogers, and V. Neagoe. Method and apparatus providing deception and/or altered execution of logic in an information system. Technical Report U.S. Patent No. 7,296,274, USPTO, November 13, 2007.

[7] J. Hale and G. Manes. Method to inhibit the identification and retrieval of proprietary media via automated search engines utilized in association with computer compatible communications network. Technical Report U.S. Patent No. 6,732,180, USPTO, May 4, 2004.

[8] K. Heckman. et al. Denial and deception in cyber defense. *Computer*, 48(4):36–44, 2015.

[9] Hutchins, M. E. Cloppert, and R. Amin. Intelligence-driven computer network defense informed by analysis of adversary campaigns and intrusion kill chains. In *Proceedings of the 6th International Conference on Information Warfare and Security*, pages 113–125, March 17-18, 2011.

[10] C. Kreibich and J. Crowcroft. Honeycomb: creating intrusion detection signatures using honeypots. *ACM SIGCOMM Computer Communication Review*, 34(1):51–56, 2004.

[11] L. Pingree. Emerging technology analysis: Deception techniques and technologies create security technology business opportunities. Technical report, Gartner Inc., July 16, 2015.

[12] A. Yasinsac and Y. Manzano. Honeytraps, a network forensic tool. In *Sixth Multi-Conference on Systemics, Cybernetics and Informatics*, 2002.

[13] J. Yuill, D. Denning, and F. F. Using deception to hide things from hackers: Processes, principles, and techniques. Technical report, North Carolina State University, 2006.

POSTER: Improving Anonymity of Services Deployed Over Tor by Changing Guard Selection

Abhishek Singh

University of Oslo, Norway

ABSTRACT

Many P2P applications are emerging that use Tor to ensure anonymity of their users. Each user in such an application creates an onion service so that the user can receive requests from other users. Such large-scale use of onion services leak a lot of sensitive information to guards in Tor. The cause of these leaks is diversity in guards' resources and the guard selection algorithm in Tor that is designed to use guards' resources efficiently. We describe a preliminary approach for selecting guards which reduces the amount of sensitive information leaked to guards while using guards' resources with same efficiency. Experiments in the context of a P2P publish/subscribe application shows that the approach reduces information leaked to guards by 25%.

CCS CONCEPTS

• **Security and privacy** → **Pseudonymity, anonymity and untraceability**; *Privacy-preserving protocols*; Economics of security and privacy;

KEYWORDS

Tor; Onion Services; Guard Selection

1 INTRODUCTION

Tor hosts a large number of anonymous services which are referred to as *onion services*. There were nearly 60 thousands onion services in the beginning of August 2017 [6]. These services are used for various applications; for example, file sharing [1], chat [2], VoIP [3] and censorship avoidance [4]. There are emerging class of P2P applications (such as BitTorrent [7] and P2P publish/subscribe [8]) where each user creates an onion service.

A user sends a message using Tor to its destination by forwarding it through an *onion circuit* which consists of a chain of randomly selected relays. The message is encrypted in multiple layers at the source and a layer of encryption is removed at each hop of the onion circuit. The relay at the first hop of an onion circuit C created by a user U is referred to as the *entry guard* for U in C. An entry guard plays a crucial role in preserving user's anonymity as the

[1] https://github.com/Tribler/tribler, https://wiki.vuze.com/w/Tor_HowTo
[2] https://github.com/prof7bit/TorChat
[3] https://trac.torproject.org/projects/tor/wiki/doc/TorifyHOWTO/Mumble
[4] https://www.facebook.com/facebookcorewwwi/

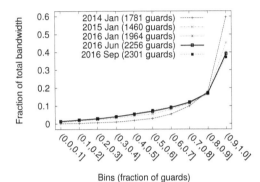

Figure 1: Fraction of total bandwidth contributed by different set of guards over a period of time. Guards are sorted by their bandwidth and then they are grouped together into bins.

entry guard knows user's IP address. A user selects an entry guard from a publicly available list of potential guards called *Tor consensus*. Each user does the selection independently of other users and does not disclose the entry guard identity to them.

There are guards with malicious intent of deanonymizing users of Tor. Such malicious guards have been used to identify an onion service provider [1] and to learn which onion services are of interest to a specific user [5]. The risks of exploits become especially severe when the same malicious guard is selected both by the user and by the onion service provider for the onion circuit between them. In this case, the guard can identify this situation and monitor communication patterns between the user and the service. This can be further correlated with additional information and exploited in the context of various applications [9].

In this work, we show experimentally that the currently used guard selection mechanism in Tor is deficient because it results in relatively many instances when a guard is selected by both ends of an onion circuit. The probability of selection in Tor is proportional to the amount of bandwidth contributed by the guard [2]. Biasing the selection towards guard's bandwidth helps Tor to scale and support a higher number of users. The fundamental problem, however, is that it increases the probability for an onion service and a service user to select the same bandwidth-rich guard. The problem is exacerbated by the fact that the bandwidth contributed by guards is highly skewed. Figure 1 shows this skewness: 10% of guards with most bandwidth provide 39% of all bandwidth in the Tor infrastructure in June 2016.

We propose an improved guard selection algorithm for Tor that reduces the probability of a guard being selected by both ends of a circuit. The algorithm retains the selection bias by the amount of bandwidth contributed by the guard, which is important for scalability.

In Section 2, we describe the case when a guard is likely to be selected by both ends of an onion circuit, and we discuss trade-offs between scalability of the Tor infrastructure and the anonymity for selection of entry guards by onion services. We outline requirements for modifying the guard selection algorithm in Section 3. We present the intuition behind our approach in Section 4. The key idea is to change the guard selection algorithm for an onion service to take into account number of users accessing it. Experiments in case of a P2P publish/subscribe application show that the approach reduces the amount of information leaked to guards by 25%.

2 PROBLEMS AND CHALLENGES

Disclosure of Vulnerable Communication Links. Guards learn of a large number of users' access to onion services with P2P applications that use Tor. This is because: 1) a peer-to-peer connection from user A to user B is implemented as user A accessing user B's onion service, and 2) each user establishes peer-to-peer connections with many users. Consider an example of a P2P publish/subscribe application that disseminates micro-news from a popular user U to 2256 users. This scenario runs on a Tor network from June 2016 consisting of 2256 guards. Due to bias in selection of guards in Tor, guard G_l with the largest bandwidth in Tor contains 14 users and it learns of any circuit among these 14 users. In contrast, only 1 user selects G_l with the optimal strategy and guard G_l does not learn of both ends of any circuit created by the user.

We use *vulnerable communication link* to refer to disclosure of a circuit between two users using same entry guard. Specifically, two users have a vulnerable communication link between them if: 1) they use the same entry guard, and 2) there is a non-zero probability of them communicating. In the above example, $\binom{14}{2}$ vulnerable communication links are exposed to guard G_l. The actual use of a vulnerable communication link between two users depends on the application. In general, a vulnerable communication link between two users is used earlier (which reveals the link to their entry guard), in following situations: 1) when a user changes its communication partners frequently (for example, to fetch a missing chunk from a newly discovered peer in a BitTorrent session), 2) when users are not available all the time, and when a user uses the application for a long duration (as in the case of P2P publish/subscribe).

Challenges in Reducing Vulnerable Communication Links. The challenge in providing the reduction is to ensure following goals at the same time: scalability of Tor infrastructure and high randomness for the selection of a user's entry guard. We discuss few naive approaches to demonstrate the difficulty in satisfying both goals.

Using the optimal strategy of selecting guards provides high randomness for selection of a user's entry guard and it minimizes vulnerable communication links. However, the strategy limits scalability of Tor as a guard with low bandwidth will exceed its resource limits with relatively small increase in number of users.

Another approach for the reduction is to: 1) partition users in to sets such that users in a set do not communicate with any user in the set, and 2) assign users in a set to the same entry guard. Achieving such a partitioning in a deterministic way is difficult as it requires users to disclose their communication partners. Thus, we focus on a probabilistic approach to partition users in a set that have a low probability of communicating among them.

Probability of two users to communicate is low if the users communicate with few other users. The heuristic is used to partition users such that number of users selecting a guard is proportional to the guard's bandwidth. This approach has following steps: 1) sort users in increasing order of number of their communication partners, 2) sort guards in decreasing order of bandwidth provided by them, and 3) first C_{g1} users select the first guard $g1$ where C_{g1} is proportional to guard $g1$'s bandwidth, and 4) next C_{g2} users select second guard $g2$, and so on. A drawback of the approach is that selection of a user's entry guard is not random. This makes it trivial to locate the entry guard if an estimate for number of communication partners for the user is known.

3 REQUIREMENTS

Our goal is to design a guard selection algorithm that reduces the total amount of vulnerable communication links while adhering to following constraints. First, a user selects his entry guard independently of other users and this is done without communicating with other users. Second, randomness associated with the selection of a user's entry guard should be large enough to prevent the adversary from guessing easily the selected entry guard. Third, in order to avoid load imbalances in Tor infrastructure the number of users that select a guard should be proportional to the guard's bandwidth.

4 PROPOSED APPROACH

We propose a new approach for guard selection where a user takes into account relative popularity of his onion service to select his entry guard. Popularity of a user's onion service provides an estimate of number of users that communicate with the user. This allows partitioning of users into different sets of users such that there is a low probability of users in a set to communicate among them. The approach uses following globally-defined constraints: the lower limit for randomness associated with the selection of entry guard for a user, and the upper limit for maximum probability of selection of a guard to prevent overloading it. The approach requires a user to estimate the fraction of onion services that are less popular than his onion service. One way to estimate this fraction is to adapt the monitoring system [3, 6] which measures number of onion services in Tor. A user uses this fraction to generate an appropriately skewed distribution containing selection probability of guards. A crucial aspect of the approach is that it satisfies the globally defined constraints even though users use different probability distributions for selecting their entry guards.

Intuition. Our idea is for users to generate different probability distributions for selecting their entry guards such that the bias towards guards with large bandwidth in a user's probability distribution decreases monotonically with increase in popularity of his onion service. This is in contrast to Tor where all users use the same probability distribution (refer to the curve labeled "Tor" in Figure 2). The approach ensures that average selection probability across all guards (refer to the curve labeled "Average" in Figure 2) is similar to the probability distribution with Tor; that is, the number of users selecting a guard in the approach is similar to that in Tor. Reduction in vulnerable communication links happens due to following reasons: First, there is a reduction in the number of vulnerable communication links for user U_l having a popular onion service as user

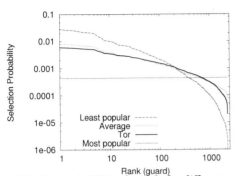

Figure 2: Selection probability of guards for different users with the proposed approach. Guards are ranked in decreasing order of their bandwidth.

U_l is likely to select a guard with small bandwidth. This is because there is a small (or no) bias towards guards with large bandwidth in probability distribution for user U_l (refer to the curve labeled "Most popular" in Figure 2) and there are more guards with small bandwidth in Tor (refer to Figure 1). Second, number of vulnerable communication links disclosed to guard G_l having large bandwidth is reduced as G_l is selected mostly by users with less popular onion services. This is because probability distribution for a user with less popular onion service is skewed towards guards with large bandwidth (refer to the curve labeled "Least popular" in Figure 2). Probability of communication among users that selected guard G_l is low as they are less likely to communicate as they communicate with few partners.

Results. We measured reduction in vulnerable communication links with the proposed approach in the context of a P2P publish/subscribe application [8] which uses Tor to hide communication between users. This publish/subscribe application distributes micro-news messages (such as Tweets in Twitter) from a publisher to all its subscribers. A user and his subscribers form a group. The P2P overlay for the group is constructed independently of other groups. An experiment consists of following steps: 1) users select their entry guards and they construct P2P overlays for distributing micro-news messages, and 2) given an assignment of users to entry guards, we measure the number of vulnerable communication links.

Workload for the experiment consists of 10,000 users which in turn means that there are 10000 groups. Each user has subscriptions (same as followees in Twitter) and a set of users (same as the user's followers in Twitter) that are interested in the user's micro-news messages. The distribution of subscriptions and the distribution of followers in the workload is similar to the one observed in Twitter [4]. Guards and distribution of their bandwidth is taken from the Tor consensus from June 2016 containing 2256 guards.

We measure vulnerable communication links over 10 runs. There were 16147 vulnerable communication links on average with Tor and these links leak information for 5200 groups. There was a reduction of 25% in vulnerable communication links with our approach and the number of groups which can be observed was 18% fewer than in case of Tor.

5 DISCUSSION

A malicious guard can increase the amount of bandwidth it provides so that it can observe more users. The malicious guard will observe more number of vulnerable communication links in Tor than in the proposed approach. This is because with with our approach increasing a guard's bandwidth increases the probability of selection of the guard by users that have less popular onion services. This makes the strategy sub-optimal as the cost of additional bandwidth does not yield proportional amount of disclosures.

In practice, an attacker controls multiple guards [1]. Tor assumes that an attacker controls guards only in a /16 subnet of the Internet as there is no reliable way in Tor to identify if two guards are being controlled by same attacker. This assumption is used in Tor to select relays in an onion circuit and to select multiple entry guards for a user. We outline a way to adapt our approach for handling attackers assumed in Tor's threat model. Guards in a /16 subnet are treated as a single logical entity referred to as *meta guards*. Selection of a user's entry guard is done in two steps: first a meta guard is selected and then a guard from the corresponding /16 subnet is selected. Selection of a meta guard is done in the same way as the selection of a guard in Section 4. Probability of selecting a guard from a meta guard is proportional to its bandwidth in the meta guard. The modification ensures that an attacker does not obtain disproportionate number of vulnerable communication links by increasing bandwidth of its guards in a /16 subnet or by adding more guards in the same /16 subnet.

REFERENCES

[1] Alex Biryukov, Ivan Pustogarov, and Ralf-Philipp Weinmann. 2013. Trawling for Tor Hidden Services: Detection, Measurement, Deanonymization. In *Proceedings of the 2013 IEEE Symposium on Security and Privacy.*

[2] Tariq Elahi, Kevin Bauer, Mashael AlSabah, Roger Dingledine, and Ian Goldberg. 2012. Changing of the Guards: A Framework for Understanding and Improving Entry Guard Selection in Tor. In *Proceedings of the Workshop on Privacy in the Electronic Society (WPES 2012).* ACM.

[3] George Kadianakis and Karsten Loesing. 2015. *Extrapolating network totals from hidden-service statistics.* Technical Report. Tor Project. https://research.torproject.org/techreports/extrapolating-hidserv-stats-2015-01-31.pdf.

[4] Haewoon Kwak, Changhyun Lee, Hosung Park, and Sue Moon. 2010. What is Twitter, a Social Network or a News Media?. In *Proceedings of the 19th International Conference on World Wide Web (WWW '10).* ACM, 10.

[5] Albert Kwon, Mashael AlSabah, David Lazar, Marc Dacier, and Srinivas Devadas. 2015. Circuit Fingerprinting Attacks: Passive Deanonymization of Tor Hidden Services. In *Proceedings of the 24th USENIX Conference on Security Symposium (SEC'15).* USENIX Association, 16.

[6] Karsten Loesing, Steven J. Murdoch, and Roger Dingledine. 2010. A Case Study on Measuring Statistical Data in the Tor Anonymity Network. In *Proceedings of the Workshop on Ethics in Computer Security Research (WECSR 2010) (LNCS).* Springer. https://metrics.torproject.org/hidserv-dir-onions-seen.html.

[7] Ruigrok R.J. 2015. *BitTorrent file sharing using Tor-like hidden services.* Master's thesis.

[8] Abhishek Singh, Guido Urdaneta, Maarten van Steen, and Roman Vitenberg. 2012. On Leveraging Social Relationships for Decentralized Privacy-preserving Group Communication. In *Proceedings of the Fifth Workshop on Social Network Systems (SNS '12).* ACM, New York, NY, USA, Article 5, 6 pages.

[9] Xinyuan Wang, Shiping Chen, and Sushil Jajodia. 2005. Tracking Anonymous Peer-to-peer VoIP Calls on the Internet. In *Proceedings of the 12th ACM Conference on Computer and Communications Security (CCS '05).* ACM.

POSTER: Inaudible Voice Commands

Liwei Song, Prateek Mittal

Department of Electrical Engineering, Princeton University

liweis@princeton.edu, pmittal@princeton.edu

ABSTRACT

Voice assistants like Siri enable us to control IoT devices conveniently with voice commands, however, they also provide new attack opportunities for adversaries. Previous papers attack voice assistants with obfuscated voice commands by leveraging the gap between speech recognition system and human voice perception. The limitation is that these obfuscated commands are audible and thus conspicuous to device owners. In this poster, we propose a novel mechanism to directly attack the microphone used for sensing voice data with *inaudible voice commands*. We show that the adversary can exploit the microphone's non-linearity and play well-designed *inaudible ultrasounds* to cause the microphone to record normal voice commands, and thus control the victim device inconspicuously. We demonstrate via end-to-end real-world experiments that our inaudible voice commands can attack an Android phone and an Amazon Echo device with high success rates at a range of 2-3 meters.

KEYWORDS

Microphone; non-linearity; intermodulation distortion; inaudible ultrasound injection

1 INTRODUCTION

Voice is becoming an increasingly popular input method for humans to interact with Internet of Things (IoT) devices. With the help of microphones and speech recognition techniques, we can talk to voice assistants, such as Siri, Google Now, Cortana and Alexa for controlling smartphones, computers, wearables and other IoT devices. Despite their ease of use, these voice assistants also provide adversaries new attack opportunities to access IoT devices with voice command injections.

Previous studies about voice command injections target the speech recognition procedure. Vaidya et al. [1] design garbled audio signals to control voice assistants without knowing the speech recognition system. Their approach obfuscates normal voice commands by modifying some acoustic features so that they are not human-understandable, but can still be recognized by victim devices. Carlini et al. [2] improve this black-box approach with more realistic settings and propose a more powerful white-box attack method based on knowledge of speech recognition procedure. Although not human-recognizable, these obfuscated voice commands

are still conspicuous, as device owners can still hear the obfuscated sounds and become suspicious.

Figure 1: The attack scenario for inaudible voice commands.

In contrast, we propose a novel *inaudible* attack method by targeting the microphone used for voice sensing by the victim device. Due to the inherent non-linearity of the microphone, its output signal contains "new" frequencies other than input signal's spectrum. These "new" frequencies are not just integer multiples of original frequencies, but also the sum and difference of original input frequencies. Based on this security flaw, our attack scenario is shown in Fig. 1. The adversary plays an ultrasound signal with spectrum above $20kHz$, which is inaudible to humans. Then the victim device's microphone processes this input, but suffers from non-linearity, causing the introduction of new frequencies in the audible spectrum. With careful design of the original ultrasound, these new audible frequencies recorded by the microphone are interpreted as actionable commands by voice assistant software.

In this poster, we put forward a detailed attack algorithm to obtain inaudible voice commands and perform end-to-end real-world experiments for validation. Our results show that the proposed inaudible voice commands can attack an Android phone with 100% success at a distance of 3 meters, and an Amazon Echo device with 80% success at a distance of 2 meters.

2 RELATED WORK

Recently, a few papers have proposed attacks against data-collecting sensors. Son et al. [3] show that intentional resonant sounds can disrupt the MEMS gyroscopes and cause drones to crash. Furthermore, by leveraging the circuit imperfections, Trippel et al. [4] achieve control of the outputs of MEMS accelerometers with resonant acoustic injections. Different from these approaches, we consider the microphone's non-linearity, so we do not need to find the resonant frequency. Instead, we need to carefully design ultrasounds that are interpreted by microphones as normal voice commands.

Roy et al. [5] conduct a similar work, where the non-linearity of the microphone is exploited to realize inaudible acoustic data communications and jamming of spying microphones. However, their data communication method needs additional decoding procedures after the receiving microphone, and their jamming method injects strong *random* noises to spying microphones. In contrast, we consider a completely different scenario, where the target microphone needs no modification and its outputs have to be interpreted as target voice commands.

3 ULTRASOUND INJECTION ATTACKS

In our attack scenario, the goal is to obtain well-designed ultrasounds which are inaudible when played but can be recorded similarly to normal commands at microphones. The victim can be any common IoT device with an off-the-shelf microphone, and it does not need any modification, except adopting the always-on mode to continuously listen for voice input, which has been used in many IoT devices such as Amazon Echo. To perform an attack, the adversary only needs to be physically proximate to the target and have the control of a speaker to play ultrasound, which can be achieved by either bringing an inconspicuous speaker close to the target or using a position-fixed speaker to attack nearby devices.

3.1 Non-Linearity Insight

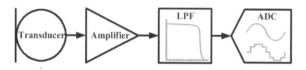

Figure 2: Typical diagram of a microphone.

As shown in Fig. 2, a typical microphone consists of four modules. The transducer generates voltage variation proportional to the sound pressure, which passes through the amplifier for signal enlargement. The low-pass filter (LPF) is then adopted to filter out high frequency components. Finally, the analog to digital converter (ADC) is used for digitalization and quantization. According to the Nyquist sampling theorem, the cut-off frequency of LPF should be less than the half of ADC's sampling rate. Since the audible sound frequency ranges from $20Hz$ to $20kHz$, a typical sampling rate for ADC is $48kHz$ or $44.1kHz$, and the filter's cut-off frequency is usually set about $20kHz$.

To obtain a good-quality sound recording, the transducer and the amplifier should be fabricated as linear as possible. However, they still exhibit non-linear phenomena in practice. Assume the input sound signal is S_{in}, the output signal after amplifier S_{out} can be expressed as

$$S_{out} = \sum_{i=1}^{\infty} G_i S_{in}^i = G_1 S_{in} + G_2 S_{in}^2 + G_3 S_{in}^3 + \cdots, \qquad (1)$$

where $G_1 S_{in}$ is the linear term and dominates for input sound in normal range. The other terms reflect the non-linearity and have an impact for a large input amplitude, usually the third and higher order terms are relatively weak compared to the second-order term.

The non-linearity introduces both *harmonic distortion and intermodulation distortion* to the output signal. Suppose the input signal is sum of two tones with frequencies f_1 and f_2, i.e., $S_{in} =$

$\cos(2\pi f_1 t) + \cos(2\pi f_2 t)$, the output due to the second-order term is expressed as

$$
\begin{aligned}
G_2 S_{in}^2 = & G_2 + \frac{G_2}{2} \left(\cos\left(2\pi\left(2f_1\right)t\right) + \cos\left(2\pi\left(2f_2\right)t\right)\right) \\
& + G_2 \left(\cos\left(2\pi\left(f_1 + f_2\right)t\right) + \cos\left(2\pi\left(f_1 - f_2\right)t\right)\right),
\end{aligned} \qquad (2)
$$

which includes both harmonic frequencies $2f_1, 2f_2$ and intermodulation frequencies $f_1 \pm f_2$.

Our attack intuition is to exploit the intermodulation to obtain normal voice frequencies from the processing of ultrasound frequencies. For example, if we play an ultrasound with two frequencies $25kHz$ and $30kHz$, the listening microphone will record the signal with the frequency of $30kHz - 25kHz = 5kHz$, while other frequencies are filtered out by the LPF.

3.2 Attack Algorithm

Now, we present how this non-linearity can be leveraged to design our attack ultrasound signals. Assume the signal of normal voice command, such as "OK Google", is S_{normal}. Our attack algorithm contains the following steps.

Low-Pass Filtering

First we adopt a low-pass filter on the normal signal, with the cut-off frequency as $8kHz$ to remove high frequency components. Human speech is mainly concentrated on low frequency range, and many speech recognition systems, such as CMU Sphinx [6], only keep spectrum below $8kHz$. Therefore, the filtering step can allow us to adopt a lower carrier frequency for modulation, while still preserving enough data of the original signal. Denote the filtered signal as S_{filter}.

Upsampling

Usually, the normal voice command S_{normal} is recorded with sampling rate of $48kHz$ (or $44.1kHz$), the same as S_{filter}. This sampling rate only supports generating ultrasound with frequency ranging from $20kHz$ to $24kHz$ (or $22.05kHz$), which is not enough. To shift the whole spectrum of S_{filter} into inaudible frequency range, the maximum ultrasound frequency should be no less than $28kHz$. Thus, we derive an upsampled signal S_{up} with higher sampling rate.

Ultrasound Modulation

In this step, we need to shift the spectrum of S_{up} into high frequency range to be inaudible. Here, we adopt amplitude modulation for spectrum shifting. Assuming the carrier frequency is f_c, the modulation can be expressed as

$$S_{modu} = n_1 S_{up} \cos(2\pi f_c t), \qquad (3)$$

where n_1 is the normalized coefficient. The resulting modulated signal contains two sidebands around the carrier frequency, ranging from $f_c - 8kHz$ to $f_c + 8kHz$. Therefore, f_c should be at least $28kHz$ to be inaudible.

Carrier Wave Addition

Modulating the voice spectrum into inaudible frequency range is not enough, they have to be translated back to normal voice frequency range at the microphone for successful attacks. Without modifying the microphone, we can leverage its non-linear phenomenon to achieve demodulation by adding a suitable carrier wave, and the final attack ultrasound can be expressed as

$$S_{attack} = n_2(S_{modu} + \cos(2\pi f_c t)), \qquad (4)$$

where n_2 is used for signal normalization.

The above steps illustrate the entire process of obtaining an attack ultrasound. This well-designed inaudible signal S_{attack}, when played by the attacker, can successfully inject a voice signal similar to S_{normal} at the target microphone and therefore control the victim device inconspicuously.

4 EVALUATION

We perform real-world experiments to evaluate our proposed inaudible voice commands. All of the following tests are performed in a closed meeting room measuring approximately 6.5 meters by 4 meters, 2.5 meters tall. To play the attack ultrasound signals, we first use a text-to-speech application to obtain the normal voice commands and follow the described attack algorithm with $192kHz$ upsampling rate and $30kHz$ carrier frequency to get attack signals in our laptop. Then a commodity audio amplifier [7] is connected for power amplification, and the amplified signals are provided to a tweeter speaker [8]. A video demo is available at https://youtu.be/wF-DuVkQNQQ.

4.1 Attack Demonstration

We first validate the feasibility of our inaudible voice commands: the normal voice command is "OK Google, take a picture", and a Nexus 5X running Android 7.1.2 is placed 2 meters away from the speaker for recording.

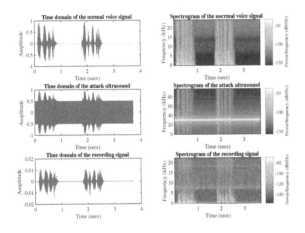

Figure 3: Time plots and spectrograms for the normal voice, the attack ultrasound and the recording signal.

Fig. 3 presents the normal voice command, the attack ultrasound and the recording sound in both time domain and frequency domain. We can see that the spectrum of attack ultrasound is above $20kHz$, and after processing this ultrasound, the microphone's recording sound is quite similar to the normal voice. When playing the attack ultrasound, the phone is successfully activated and opens the camera application.

4.2 Attack Performance

We further examine our ultrasound attack range for two devices: an Android phone and an Amazon Echo, where we try to spoof voice commands "OK Google, turn on airplane mode", and "Alexa, add milk to my shopping list", respectively. The following table shows the relationship between the attack range and the speaker's input power. We can see that the attack range is positively correlated to the speaker's power. The attack range of our approach is less for the Amazon Echo compared to the Android phone, since its microphone is plastic covered.

Table 1: The relationship between our attack range and the speaker's input power.

Input Power ($Watt$)	9.2	11.8	14.8	18.7	23.7
Range (Phone, cm)	222	255	277	313	354
Range (Echo, cm)	145	168	187	213	239

We also check the attack accuracy by setting input power as $18.7W$ and placing phone and Echo 3 meters and 2 meters away, respectively. For each device, we repeat the corresponding inaudible voice command every 10 seconds for 50 times. The attack success rates are 100%(50/50) for the Android phone and 80%(40/50) for the Amazon Echo.

5 CONCLUSION

Based on the inherent non-linear properties of microphones, we propose a novel attack method by transmitting well-design ultrasounds to control common voice assistants, like Siri, Google Now, and Alexa. By taking advantage of intermodulation distortion and amplitude modulation, our attack voice commands are *inaudible* and achieve high success rates on an Android phone more than three meters away and on an Amazon Echo device more than two meters away.

ACKNOWLEDGMENTS

This work was supported in part by NSF awards CNS-1553437, EARS-1642962 and CNS-1409415.

REFERENCES

[1] T. Vaidya, Y. Zhang, M. Sherr, and C. Shields. Cocaine noodles: exploiting the gap between human and machine speech recognition. In *USENIX Workshop on Offensive Technologies(WOOT)*, Washington, D.C., Aug. 2015.
[2] N. Carlini, P. Mishra, T. Vaidya, Y. Zhang, M. Sherr, C. Shields, D. Wagner, and W. Zhou. Hidden voice commands. In *USENIX Security*, pp. 513-530, Austin, TX, Aug. 2016.
[3] Y. Son, H. Shin, D. Kim, Y. S. Park, J. Noh, K. Choi, J. Choi, and Y. Kim. Rocking drones with intentional sound noise on gyroscopic sensors. In *USENIX Security*, pp. 881-896, Washington, D.C., Aug. 2015.
[4] T. Trippel, O. Weisse, W. Xu, P. Honeyman, and Kevin Fu. WALNUT: Waging doubt on the integrity of MEMS accelerometers with acoustic injection attacks. In *IEEE European Symposium on Security and Privacy (EuroS&P)*, pp. 3-18, Paris, France, April 2017.
[5] N. Roy, H. Hassanieh, and R. R. Choudhury. Backdoor: Making microphones hear inaudible sounds. In *Proceedings of the 15th Annual International Conference on Mobile Systems, Applications, and Services (MobiSys)*, pp. 2-14, New York, NY, June 2017.
[6] Open Source Speech Recognition Toolkit, CMUSphinx. https://cmusphinx.github.io/.
[7] R-S202 Natural Sound Stereo Receiver, Yamaha Corporation. https://usa.yamaha.com/products/audio_visual/hifi_components/r-s202/index.html.
[8] FT17H Horn Tweeter, Fostex. http://www.fostexinternational.com/docs/speaker_components/pdf/ft17hrev2.pdf.

POSTER: Is Active Electromagnetic Side-channel Attack Practical?

Satohiro Wakabayashi
Waseda University
Shinjuku, Tokyo, Japan
wakabayashi@goto.info.waseda.ac.jp

Seita Maruyama
Waseda University
Shinjuku, Tokyo, Japan
maruyama@nsl.cs.waseda.ac.jp

Tatsuya Mori
Waseda University
Shinjuku, Tokyo, Japan
mori@nsl.cs.waseda.ac.jp

Shigeki Goto
Waseda University
Shinjuku, Tokyo, Japan
goto@goto.info.waseda.ac.jp

Masahiro Kinugawa
National Institute of Technology,
Sendai College
Sendai, Miyagi, Japan
kinugawa@sendai-nct.ac.jp

Yu-ichi Hayashi
Nara Institute of Science and
Technology
Ikoma, Nara, Japan
yu-ichi@is.naist.jp

ABSTRACT

Radio-frequency (RF) retroreflector attack (RFRA) is an *active* electromagnetic side-channel attack that aims to leak the target's internal signals by irradiating the targeted device with a radio wave, where an attacker has embedded a malicious circuit (RF retroreflector) in the device in advance. As the retroreflector consists of small and cheap electrical elements such as a field-effect transistor (FET) chip and a wire that can work as a dipole antenna, the reflector can be embedded into various kinds of electric devices that carry unencrypted, sensitive information; e.g., keyboard, display monitor, microphone, speaker, USB, and so on. Only a few studies have addressed the basic mechanism of RFRA and demonstrated the success of the attack. The conditions for a successful attack have not been adequately explored before, and therefore, assessing the feasibility of the attack remains an open issue. In the present study, we aim to investigate empirically the conditions for a successful RFRA through field experiments. Understanding attack limitations should help to develop effective countermeasures against it. In particular, with regard to the conditions for a successful attack, we studied the distance between the attacker and the target, and the target signal frequencies. Through the extensive experiments using off-the-shelf hardware including software-defined radio (SDR) equipment, we revealed that the required conditions for a successful attack are (1) up to a 10-Mbps of target signal and (2) up to a distance of 10 meters. These results demonstrate the importance of the RFRA threat in the real world.

CCS CONCEPTS

• **Security and privacy** → **Hardware attacks and countermeasures**;

CCS '17, October 30-November 3, 2017, Dallas, TX, USA
© 2017 Copyright held by the owner/author(s).
ACM ISBN 978-1-4503-4946-8/17/10.
https://doi.org/10.1145/3133956.3138830

KEYWORDS

Active electromagnetic side-channel attack, Hardware security, RF retroreflector attack

1 INTRODUCTION

Electromagnetic side-channel attacks are attacks performed by passively measuring the electromagnetic emanation originating from a target device. An attacker can reconstruct the original signal by analyzing the measured radio wave. Although there have been many studies on *passive* electromagnetic side-channel attacks, few works have been performed on *active* electromagnetic side-channel attacks [1, 2]. In Ref. [1], Anderson mentioned that some of these methods were already known to the intelligence community; in particular, he mentioned reports of the CIA using software-based radio-frequency (RF) exploits in economic espionage against certain European countries.

The NSA advanced network technology (ANT) catalog is a classified document that lists several surveillance technologies used by the United States National Security Agency (NSA). The catalog was included in the series of documents leaked by Edward Snowden in December 2013. Among the technologies listed in the catalog, the technology called ANGRYNEIGHBOR and its variants are attack methods based on the principle of the *RF retroreflector attack (RFRA)*, which is an active electromagnetic side-channel attack. An attacker actively irradiates the target device with a radio wave at a resonant frequency and passively monitors the reflected radio wave from the target device. As the attacker has embedded a malicious circuit (retroreflector) into the target device, the reflected wave is modulated by the target signal, and the attacker can read the target signal from the reflected wave.

After the NSA ANT catalog was leaked, several hackers started recreating the surveillance tools using open-source hardware and software [3]. In DEF CON 22 [4], Michael Ossmann successfully demonstrated that RFRA can be implemented with an off-the-shelf SDR (HackRF One) and a simple RF retroreflector, and an attacker can read the keystroke remotely by applying the attack to a PS/2 keyboard. Although these prior works have successfully demonstrated the threat of RFRA, an empirical research approach has not been applied to understanding the attack mechanism. Given this background, we aim to answer the following simple research question: **RQ** "*Is RFRA a practical attack?*" To answer this question, we first create a simple RF retroreflector that is made from coaxial cable. We embed a field-effect transistor (FET) chip in the cable and make its woven copper shield work as a dipole antenna. This setup can be seen as a generic form of a RF retroreflector. We then generate electric waveforms in the retroreflector using a function generator connected to it. Finally, using SDR, we irradiate the retroreflector with a radio wave at a resonant frequency of the reflector's antenna and analyze the reflected radio wave from the reflector.

The key findings we derived through the field experiments with an off-the-shelf SDR (USRP N210) and a laptop PC are summarized as follows:

- RFRA succeeded with the distance of 10 m between an attacker and a target device.
- RFRA succeeded to read the internal signal of 10 Mbps, which was roughly half of the maximum rate of the SDR processing capability.

These findings suggest that the RFRA threat is real, and we need to develop effective countermeasures against it. Through our experiments, we conjecture that an attacker equipped with hardware device instead of SDR will be able to target higher frequency of internal signals, e.g., USB high-speed.

2 RFRA MECHANISM

The core of an RFRA lies in the retroreflector embedded into the target device. Figure 1 shows the structure of a retroreflector, which includes a FET chip and a dipole antenna. Figure 2 presents its actual implementation using a coaxial cable, where the gate of the FET is attached to the copper core, and the source and drain of the FET are connected to a woven copper shield, which works as a dipole antenna. The victim's target signal will go through the copper core, which is received by the gate of FET.

As shown in Figure 3, an attacker irradiates radio waves to the circuit and attempts to analyze the reflected radio wave, which is AM-modulated with the target signal. Let's see why the reflected radio wave is AM-modulated with the target signal. First, current is induced when the dipole antenna receives the carrier wave, which is transmitted by an attacker. The FET controls the induced current in proportional to the voltage of the target signal applied to the gate. Therefore, the generated current on the antenna becomes an AM signal modulated by the target signal. The dipole antenna radiates radio waves according to the AM signal. Finally, the attacker will demodulate the AM signal to revert the original target signal. We note that the resonant frequency is determined by the length of dipole antenna; i.e., when any odd multiple of half wavelength equals to the length of antenna. In our experiments, the length of the dipole antenna was set to 1 m, which corresponds to the resonant frequency of 599.6 MHz.

3 EXPERIMENTS

3.1 Setup

Figure 4 shows the experimental setup. The RF reflector is connected to a function generator, which generates the target's signal. Two directional antennas are connected to an SDR (USRP). The antennas and the target reflector are placed on cardboard boxes

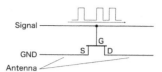

Figure 1: A RF retroreflector that includes a FET chip and a dipole antenna. An internal signal is applied to the gate of FET.

Figure 2: An implementation of the RF retroreflector using a coaxial cable.

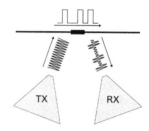

Figure 3: Overview of an RFRA attack.

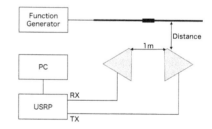

Figure 4: Experimental setup (overview).

with controlled distances. The reflector's antenna cable is set up straightened. Table 1 summarizes the instruments used in our experiments, and Table 2 lists the software and specs PC used for SDR.

3.2 Distance between the attacker and the target

We first investigate the effective distance for an RFRA. To this end, we change the distance between the TX/RX antennas (on the attacker's side) and the reflector. The power of the irradiated radio waves is set to the maximum intensity of USRP. The frequency of the irradiated wave ranges from 590 MHz to 680 MHz, roughly

Table 1: Instruments used in the experiments.

Instrument	Model
Antenna	Ettus Research LP0410
Software Radio Peripheral (USRP)	USRP N210
Function generator	AFG3102
Oscilloscope	MSO4054
Attacker PC	ASUS ROG G752VS
FET (attached to the target)	ATF-54143

Table 2: List of software and PC used for SDR.

OS	Windows 10
SDR software toolkit	GNU Radio 3.7.11
CPU	Core i7 7700HQ 2.8GHz/4 Core
RAM	32GB

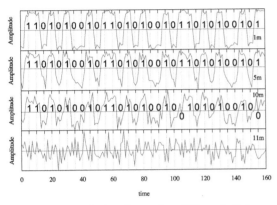

Figure 5: Measured signals under different distances between the attacker and the target.

corresponding to the resonant frequency of the target's antenna[1]. We let the target signal be a digital signal that repeats the 10-bits pattern "1101010010." The voltage of the signal is set to 3 Vpp. The transmission rate of the target signal is set to 2 Mbps, and the sampling rate of USRP is set to 10 MS/s.

Figure 5 shows the measured waveforms for the distances of 1 m, 5 m, 10 m, and 11 m. '0's and '1's present the decoded bits. The numbers shown above/below the middle line indicate the correctly/incorrectly estimated bits. The attack succeeds when the distance is less than or equal to 10 m. Note that for the case of 10 m, we show the result where 2 of 31 bits are detected as errors. However, the attack succeeds to read most of the original signals in the 10 m case. At the distance of 11 m, however, we observe no signals. From these results, we conclude that RFRA is effective within the distance of 10 m, which is long enough to make the attack practical in many scenarios.

3.3 Transmission rate of the target signal

Next, we examine the highest transmission rate of the target signal, at which the RFRA attack is effective. The distance between the antennas and the target reflector is fixed to 1 m. The USRP sampling

rate is set to 25 MS/s. The transmission rate of the target signal is set to 1 Mbps, 5 Mbps, 10 Mbps, and 20 Mbps. Figure 6 shows the results (the case for 20 Mbps is omitted due to space limitation). The frequency of the irradiated wave is set to 771.2 MHz.

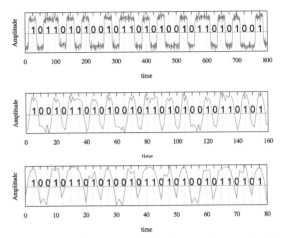

Figure 6: Measured waveforms for the target signals with the frequencies of 1 Mbps (top), 5 Mbps (middle), and 10 Mbps (bottom).

After several trials, we find that RFRA can read signals up to 10 Mbps. USRP N210 has the maximum sampling rate of 25 MS/s[2]. Theoretically, with this sampling rate, it is possible to read a signal below 12.5 MHz, which corresponds to a transmission rate of 25 Mbps. However, our setup fails to read the 20 Mbps signal. Although not conclusive, we conjecture that this limit is due to hardware performance; i.e., using high-performance hardware can extend the limitation of RFRA. We leave this issue for our future work. We note that the FET chip we used is capable of switching to the 6 GHz frequency.

4 SUMMARY

Through the field experiments, we demonstrated that the threat of RFRA is practical; the implementation with an off-the-shelf SDR and a laptop PC successfully reads the target's internal signal at 10 m distance. To the best of our knowledge, this work is the first to characterize the limitation of RFRA in a systematic way. The following issues are left for future study. What kind of devices/signals could be targeted with RFRA? Can hardware-implemented RFRA read high-speed signals such as 1 G+ bps? How can we detect RF retroreflectors? How can we mitigate RFRA?

REFERENCES

[1] Ross J. Anderson. 2008. *Security Engineering: A Guide to Building Dependable Distributed Systems* (2 ed.). Wiley Publishing.
[2] Markus G. Kuhn and Ross J. Anderson. 1998. Soft Tempest: Hidden Data Transmission Using Electromagnetic Emanations. In *Information Hiding (LNCS)*, Vol. 1525. Springer, 124–142.
[3] M. Ossman and D. Pierce. 2014. The NSA Playset. In *ToorCamp*. https://archive. org/details/nsaplayset-toorcamp2014.
[4] Michael Ossmann. 2014. The NSA Playset: RF Retroreflectors. (2014). DEF CON 22.

---

[1] As the actual resonant frequency was sensitive to the placement of the target, we manually adjusted the frequency for each distance.

[2] The sampling rate can be configured up to 50 MS/s with the low dynamic range. However, we could not observe any signals in the low dynamic range.

POSTER: BGPCoin: A Trustworthy Blockchain-based Resource Management Solution for BGP Security

Qianqian Xing, Baosheng Wang, Xiaofeng Wang
College of Computer, National University of Defense Technology
Changsha, Hunan, China 410073
xingqian0110@hotmail.com,bswang@nudt.edu.cn,xf_wang@nudt.edu.cn

ABSTRACT

Origin authentication is one of the most concentrated and advocated BGP security approach against IP prefix hijacking. However, the potential risk of centralized authority abuse and the fragile infrastructure may lead a sluggish deployment of such BGP security approach currently. We propose BGPCoin, a trustworthy blockchain-based Internet resource management solution which provides compliant resource allocations and revocations, and a reliable origin advertisement source. By means of a smart contract to perform and supervise resource assignments on the tamper-resistant Ethereum blockchain, BGPCoin yields significant benefits in the secure origin advertisement and the dependable infrastructure for object repository compared with RPKI. We demonstrate through an Ethereum prototype implementation that the deployment incentives and increased security are technically and economically viable.

CCS CONCEPTS

• Security and privacy → Security protocols;

KEYWORDS

Blockchain; BGP security; Origin authentication; RPKI

ACM Reference format:
Qianqian Xing, Baosheng Wang, Xiaofeng Wang. 2017. POSTER: BGPCoin: A Trustworthy Blockchain-based Resource Management Solution for BGP Security. In *Proceedings of CCS'17, Oct. 30–Nov. 3, 2017, Dallas, TX, USA.*, , 3 pages.
DOI: http://dx.doi.org/10.1145/3133956.3138828

1 INTRODUCTION

RPKI [3] and ROVER [7] both provide a PKI-based trusted mapping method from an IP prefix to the Autonomous System(s) (ASes). Although RPKI has been advocated and standardized of the relevant protocols by IETF, the potential misconfigured, faulty or compromised RPKI authorities may result to its disappointingly sluggish adoption [2]. ROVER claims a "fail-safe" mode to protect BGP from misconfigurations, but it has no help to hinder the misbehavior of centralized authorities. Despite the efforts of appending logs to visualize and alarm changes to the RPKI passively, and providing consent for revocations to balance the power of RPKI authorities positively [3], they still suffers from the following problem: (1) RPKI

and ROVER do not sufficiently incentivize recording or monitoring authority behavior, (2) to achieve the revocation consent in RPKI or ROVER requires such a complicated and burdened collaboration between RC issuers(to sign) and relying parties(to validate) that may also lead to its passive application, (3) RPKI's infrastucture is fragile to resist the deleting and overwriting of objects from malicious authorities and maintain a consistent view of information (RCs, ROAs, manifests).

In summary, we have reasons to debate that RPKI or ROVER neither gives an efficient and reliable solution to extricate ISPs from IP hijackings or takedowns.

For the inherently untrusted and error-prone Internet, the blockchain is an ideal trustworthy and reliable infrastructure [1] supporting security architectures. We propose BGPCoin, a trustworthy blockchain-based resource management solution. Concretely, (1) BGPCoin compels every authority organisation to operate compliant resource assignments and revocations(under consent) by a smart contract, thus primarily precludes the misconfigurations and entity misbehaviors (that violate to the contract), (2) the append-only ledger on the blockchain maintains a consistent view of information in BGPCoin, which not only avoids mirror world attack like in RPKI, but also forbids reversing or overwriting the resource assignments.

2 BGPCOIN DESIGN

BGPCoin is a system hosted on the Ethereum blockchain and controlled by a smart contract, that allows entities to manage (such as storing, allocating, assigning and revoking) Internet address and Autonomous System Number resources of itself and other participants, i.e., the Internet Assigned Numbers Authority(IANA), Regional/National/Local Internet Registries, Internet Service Providers(ISPs) and Autono-mous Systems(ASes). Instead of origin authorization by RCs and ROAs, BGPCoin records resource assignments and authorizations in transactions on the Ethereum blockchain [5]. By tracking changes of the ownerships and usufructs of resource assets through a public ledger created and maintained through network consensus, every resource is solely owned or leased.

BGPCoin Infrastructure: In contrast with RPKI that requires different components to sign/store/verify origin attestations, BGPCoin only need the existing Ethereum system as its infrastructure, including its Ethereum blockchain and the miners. We retain the Bitcoin notion of addresses, peers, miners, transactions, blockchains. Every participated entity peer with its address as its public key has it own private keys (as a key-pair with its address).

(1) BGPCoin Miner vs. Relying Party: Compared with that RPKI objects are cryptographically verified by their relying parties, the

task of verifing a transaction is in charge of the BGPCoin contract and the miners. Once a transaction is added to the blochchain, its verification has been confirmed. Compared with that RPs push origin validation results to edge routers to inform routing decisions in BGP, BGPCoin allows an edge router to directly request IP resource mappings from the Ethereum client in its own AS.

(2) Blockchain vs. Repository: Different with the distributed repositories which are undertaken by their authories without supervision, the Ethereum blockchain provides a distrubuted and tamper-resistant log of all transactions, leading to transaction non-repudiability and the ability to retrace the history of any transaction. Thus the global consistent view of information in BGPCoin avoids mirror world attack[3] like in RPKI.

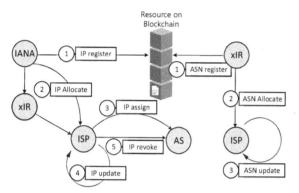

Figure 1: Operators for IP and AS number resource in BG-PCoin. xIR represents RIR, NIR and LIR which are respectively short for Regional/National/Local Internet Registry.

BGPCoin Components: The design of BGPCoin contains two primary components: the smart contract which dictates the protocol of the system and acts as an interface to the blockchain for the resource management, and the client which interacts with the smart contract to allow users to fully utilize the system by allowing them to search for resource. The contract of BGPCoin contains two primary functions, **resource trading** and **resource searching**, with one characteristics: **aggregated Internet Address repositing&updating**. The resource management protocol for BGP security is implemented by operating the BGPCoin resource trading function. The client of BGPCoin complishes every IP validation according to the IP ownership record on the blockchain by operating the resource searching function. For the efficient storage by compressing the amount of resource entries on blockchain, BGPCoin aggregates the IP-Prefixes that are contiguous and have the same owner and the same leasee (in the case that they are leased).

2.1 Smart Contract

The smart contract defines all operations that the participated entities can take upon the assets and also the precondition and the result of those operations. An entity refers to any participant in the system, i.e., IANA, xIPs and ISPs. BGPCoin has two types of assets: *Internet Address resource* and *AS numbers resource*. Every asset has its fields to represent its assignment and authorized status, shown in Fig.1, which as the origin attestation supports IP announcement validation in BGP updating.

```
struct IPB{               struct ASNData
   uint32  IP_start;         {
   uint8   wildnum;           address owner;
   State   state;            uint    IPBindex;
   address owner;            uint    stime;
   address leasee;           uint    validperiod;
}                            }
   mapping (uint24 => ASNData) public ROA;
```

Figure 2: Data Structures of BGPCoin Assets.

BGPCoin has three types of *entities* and five types of *trading operations* for *Internet Address resource*: IANA for registering IP resources and allocating to xIRs, xIRs for allocating IP resources to its sub xIRs and then to ISPs, ISPs for allocating IP resources to its sub ISPs or assigning them to ASes, and three types of *trading operations* for *AS numbers resource*: RIRs for registering ASN resources and allocating to its sub xIRs or ISPs, as shown in Table.1 and Fig.1. We note that an IP resource assignment means an established lease with its period of validity. The owner of some resource has the right to update the resource after its period of validity. IP revoke operated by its owner in its period of validity is only allowed on the condition that a consent signature of the resource leasee is appended.

Table 1: Semantics of BGPCoin trading operations

Operation	Example
IP register	IANA:$< IPB, \varnothing >$
IP allocate	IANA/xIR→xIR: $< IPB, \varnothing >$
IP assign	xIR:$< IPB, ASN >$
IP update	xIR:$< IPB, ASN_1 > \rightarrow < IPB, ASN_2 >$
IP revoke	xIR:$< IPB, ASN > \rightarrow < IPB, \varnothing >$
ASN register	xIR:$< ASN, -, - >$
ASN allocate	xIR→ISP:$< ASN, stime, period >$
ASN update	ISP:$< ASN, stime', period >$

2.2 Client

Every resource authority organization maintains an Ether-eum client to interact with the smart contract to not only take operations upon its own resource, but also retrieve resource data from the blockchain.

Prior-setting. As the deployer of BGPCoin, IANA firstly collects the mappings from all resource authority organizations to their Ethereum account addresses. The mappings authorized by every participated organization (IANA, xIRs and ISPs) are collected as a profile in the contract before BGPCoin is launched. As a result, one transaction between Ethereum accounts, as an attestation, could be mapped to a resource allocation from its present owner to its next owner, or a resource assignment from its owner to the leasee.

Route Origin Advertisement. Every AS maintains an Ethereum client to the contract. Compared with the method of downloading the validated ROAs list from rely parties in RPKI, ours allows an edge router to directly request IP resource mappings from the Ethereum client in its own AS.

3 BGPCOIN TRANSACTION VS. RC/ROA IN RPKI

The BGPCoin and RPKI both protect against prefix and subprefix hijacks by providing a trusted mapping from an IP prefix to an AS

Table 2: BGPCoin Transaction vs RC/ROA

Transaction in BGPCoin		RC/ROA in RPKI	
History-based trustworthiness	Sequential Transparency	Certificate-based trustworthiness	Log-appending Transparency
	Hash-chained Integrity		Menifest-signed Integrity
Transaction Audit	Miner Verification	Unbridled Authority Misbehavior	Misconfiguration
	Immutable Ledger		Stealthy Deleting/Overwriting
	Muti-signature Consent		Unilateral Revoke/Reclaim
Explicit Resource Ownership	Sole Usufruct of IP prefix	Overflexible Resource Attestation	Double-cover IP prefix
	Reallocation after Withdrawal		Targeted Whacking

authorized to originate the prefixes in BGP. In contrast to RC/ROA in RPKI, BGPCoin transaction yields significant benifits with three properties detailed in Table 2.

History-based trustworthiness: The history-based trustworthiness supported by the blockchain not only frees BGPcoin from certificate management, but also essentially plays a role of the monitor and log system which comparatively is an additional assembly in RPKI.

Inherent transaction audit: The conduction of BGPCoin smart contract with the miner verication eradicates the misconfigurations and entity misbehaviors that violating to the contract like stealthy deleting/overwriting objects. The immutable ledge on blockchain guarantees that once a resource transaction is successfully validated by miners, it is impossible to reverse or overwrite it. Moreover, muti-signature consent precludes the unilateral revoke. Those inherent transaction audit property enables BGPRoin to eliminate the risk from authorities.

Explicit resource ownership: Explicit resource ownership indicated by the transaction ledger eliminates the circular dependency[2] in issuing RCs(or ROAs), since a transaction concurrently displays an allocation(or assignment) and its authorization.

4 EVALUATION

We has implemented a working prototype of BGPCoin. We implement the smart contract in Solidity[1], a high-level Ethereum language that resembles JavaScript for writing smart contracts that are compiled to EVM code. We demonstrate the preliminary experiment upon Truffle[2], a development environment and testing framework for Ethereum.

Preliminary Results: We estimated the approximate computational steps (in Ethereum's gas) and approximate costs (in US dollars, for creating the BGPCoin contract and for each trading operation supported by the BGPCoin contract in Table 3.As in May 2017, 1 ether =$92.43 and 1 gas= 1.8×10^{-8} ether [3]. We note that the cost of the operations in Ethereum is relatively low compared with the fee-of-service internet resource management. Moreover, the participated organization motivates the mining and validation by increasing the mining reward and fee on demand when submitting a resource transaction.

Scalability. A BGP peer receives 4.94 average prefix updates/s [4]. Since Ethereum has 7-15 trans/s[4] and moreover, adavanced consensuses[5] are in progress to promote the Ethereum's thrughputs

Table 3: Cost of BGPCoin trading operations

Operation	Gas	USD	Operation	Gas	USD
IP register	155448	0.259	IP revoke	72960	0.121
IP allocate	188113	0.313	ASN register	42411	0.071
IP assign	183246	0.305	ASN allocate	68876	0.114
IP update	69101	0.115	ASN update	27691	0.046
BGPCoin Contract Creation				3985649	6.631

to thousands transactions per second, that is viable to have BGPCoin averagely 5 tran/s throughput for BGP advertisement.

5 CONCLUSION AND FUTURE WORK

In this work, we introduce a novel Internet resource management solution for BGP security. We design the BGPCoin system consisted with a smart contract-based resource assignment attestation and a blockchain-based dependable repository infrastructure. We demonstrate through a preliminary analysis that the deployment incentives and increased security are technically and economically viable. We are conducting extensive experiments to study the scalability of the global deployment of BGPCoin and the security enhancement [6] of the smart contract of BGPCoin. We believe BGPCoin poses the feasible and credible BGP security solution on the condition of the security of Ethereum blockchain itself and the smart contract programming. Other security threat similar of vulnerable loose ROAs [2] in RPKI are considering to be forbidden in the future by a rigorous route policy for BGP adversments in BGPCoin.

ACKNOWLEDGMENT

This research is supported in part by the project of National Basic Research and Development Program of China (2012CB315906), and National Key Research and Development Program of China (2017YFB0802301).

REFERENCES

[1] Joseph Bonneau, Andrew Miller, Jeremy Clark, Arvind Narayanan, Joshua A. Kroll, and Edward W. Felten. 2015. SoK: Research Perspectives and Challenges for Bitcoin and Cryptocurrencies. In *Security and Privacy*. 104–121.
[2] Yossi Gilad, Avichai Cohen, Amir Herzberg, Michael Schapira, and Haya Shulman. 2017. Are We There Yet? On RPKI's Deployment and Security. In *NDSS*.
[3] Ethan Heilman, Danny Cooper, Leonid Reyzin, and Sharon Goldberg. 2014. From the consent of the routed: Improving the transparency of the RPKI. In *Proceedings of the 2014 ACM conference on SIGCOMM*. ACM, 51–62.
[4] Geoff Huston. 2017. The BGP Instability Report. (2017). http://bgpupdates.potaroo.net/instability/bgpupd.html.
[5] Daniel Kronovet. 2017. A next-generation smart contract and decentralized application platform. (2017). https://github.com/ethereum/wiki/wiki/White-Paper.
[6] Loi Luu, Duc Hiep Chu, Hrishi Olickel, Prateek Saxena, and Aquinas Hobor. 2016. Making Smart Contracts Smarter. In *ACM Sigsac Conference on Computer and Communications Security*. ACM Press, 254–269.
[7] Aanchal Malhotra and Sharon Goldberg. 2014. RPKI vs ROVER: comparing the risks of BGP security solutions. In *SIGCOMM 2014 ACM conference*. ACM Press, 113–114.

---

[1] http://solidity.readthedocs.io/en/develop/index.html
[2] https://github.com/trufflesuite/truffle
[3] https://ethstats.net/, https://coinmarketcap.com/.
[4] https://en.wikipedia.org/wiki/Ethereum
[5] https://github.com/ethereum/EIPs/issues/225

POSTER: **Who was Behind the Camera?**

— Towards Some New Forensics

Jeff Yan
Linköping University, Sweden
jeff.yan@liu.se

Aurélien Bourquard
Massachusetts Institute of Technology, USA
aurelien@mit.edu

ABSTRACT

We motivate a new line of image forensics, and propose a novel approach to photographer identification, a rarely explored authorship attribution problem. A preliminary proof-of-concept study shows the feasibility of our method. Our contribution is a forensic method for photographer de-anonymisation, and the method also imposes a novel privacy threat.

KEYWORDS

Forensics, privacy, photographer identification, photographer de-anonymisation, inverse problems

1 INTRODUCTION

We consider such a research problem: given a *single* photo, how to determine who was the cameraman? This is in general a hard problem, except for selfies and except if the photographer's shadow became visible in the photo or her image was captured by a reflective object in the photo, such as a subject's eyes.

This problem is interesting to intelligence agencies. For example, a photo of a secret military facility in Russia can be valuable to the Central Intelligence Agency of USA. However, when the photo gets leaked by a mole inside the CIA, Russia's anti-spy operatives would be keen to work out who took the photo in the first place.

The problem is interesting to law enforcement agencies, too. For example, when the Scotland Yard are tipped off by a photo from an anonymous source that offers clues to a criminal investigation, it is likely to gain further information to accelerate their investigation by identifying the person behind the camera.

Moreover, the problem is also interesting to privacy researchers. The answer to the research question will likely provide novel methods of privacy intrusion by de-anonymising a photographer of any concerned photo on the Internet, and motivate novel research for protecting photographers' anonymity.

Not all photographers care that it is public knowledge that some photos are taken by them. But in some circumstances, some photographers would care if some photos are linked to them as the people behind the camera.

From the forensic perspective, a technique that does not identify the photographer 100% of the time can still be practically useful,

This work is partially supported by the Knut and Alice Wallenberg Foundation.
Permission to make digital or hard copies of part or all of this work for personal or classroom use is granted without fee provided that copies are not made or distributed for profit or commercial advantage and that copies bear this notice and the full citation on the first page. Copyrights for third-party components of this work must be honored. For all other uses, contact the owner/author(s).
CCS '17, October 30-November 3, 2017, Dallas, TX, USA
© 2017 Copyright is held by the owner/author(s).
ACM ISBN 978-1-4503-4946-8/17/10.
https://doi.org/10.1145/3133956.3138848

since it will narrow down suspects to a small number. Complemented with other means such as surveillance, it is highly likely for intelligence agencies or law enforcements to pin down the concerned photographer accurately.

We first review related work, and show that existing approaches do not resolve the research question we are asking. Then, we propose a new approach, and demonstrate its feasibility by a proof-of-concept but realistic simulation study. Our method is applicable to both digital and film photography, in theory.

2 RELATED WORK

Visual stylometry. Artists like Claude Monet and Vincent van Gogh demonstrate distinctive styles in their paintings. In the past hundreds of years, people relied on stylistic analysis to tell apart genuine fine art from fakes. It became an emerging research area in recent years to apply signal processing and machine learning methods to analyse painting images for artist identification [1, 2].

Similarly, some photographers display peculiar styles in the photos they produce. For example, widely regarded as one of the best portrait photographers of all time, Yousuf Karsh is known for distinctive features in his portraits due to lighting, composition and posture. Ernst Haas showed a distinctive personal style in his impressionist colour photography, too. Therefore, it is a natural extension to develop photographer identification methods from painting artist identification.

However, a training set of photos a priori, usually of a large size, is needed for each concerned photographer to make machine learning methods to work. This approach will hardly work if the given photo is the only available one taken by a suspect photographer, since it is impossible to collect a training set of photos for the photographer. On the other hand, if a photographer's style is not sufficiently sophisticated, it is easy for somebody else to emulate. This can be exploited to fool machine learning algorithms, and to frame a photographer.

Camera fingerprint [3,4]. CCD or CMOS imaging sensors are a digital camera's heart. Due to sensor design and imperfections of the sensor manufacturing process, systematic artefacts (usually known as sensor pattern noises) form an equivalent of a digital fingerprint that can identify a camera. Such fingerprints are intrinsically embedded in each image and video clip created by a digital camera. Forensic applications of camera fingerprints include 1) source camera identification (which camera was used to produce this image?), and 2) device linking (were two images produced by the same camera?).

Camera fingerprint, in theory, can link a photo to a specific camera, if a reference fingerprint can be established for the camera, e.g. when the camera is physically accessible, or a set of photos taken by the same camera is otherwise available. However, camera fingerprint does not link a photo to a specific user of the camera. This is an issue when the same camera has been used by many people. Moreover, camera fingerprint can be easily removed from each photo, entirely disabling its forensic applications. The camera fingerprint technique has been developed for digital cameras, and it does not work for traditional film photography.

Image metadata has a limited forensic application. For example, it can link a digital image to a camera model at most, not to a specific camera, let alone a photographer. On the other hand, film photography does not produce any such metadata.

All the methods discussed above do not really provide a solution to our research question.

3 A NOVEL METHOD

When a scene is photographed, a photographer's body often deflects light (via reflection and refraction) into the scene, leaving an impact on a photo created thereafter. Our hypothesis is that light rays deflected by a photographer into the photo that she is taking will give away some physical characteristics of herself.

We refine our research problem as follows. Photo P_1 was taken of a scene by a photographer at will, i.e. its acquisition is non-controlled; our task is to work out who took the photo. We have access to the same physical scene, and we take a photo P_2 similar to P_1, while all acquisition parameters are reproduced in a controlled manner to be the same as used for producing P_1, except that the photographer is absent. Our research questions are: 1). What differences in P_1 and P_2 can be exploited to deduce the photographer's physical characteristics? 2). Under what conditions the above measurement will work for the purpose?

We choose to answer these questions via a realistic simulation, rather than an empirical lab study, since the latter involves with experiments that are more expensive and sophisticated to set up. Specifically, we use photon mapping, a well-established ray tracing technique, to conduct a proof-of-concept feasibility study. Photon mapping realistically simulates the interaction of light with different objects. In this approach, light rays from a light source and rays from a camera are traced independently until some termination criterion is met. Then, they are connected in a second step to produce a radiance value.

3.1 Experimental Design

We use the popular POVRay software[1] for scene definition and rendering, as well as photon mapping.

3.1.1 Scene Definition. Fig. 1 illustrates the scene that we use for this study, as viewed from the camera. The ground consists of a brown surface of unit-normalized RGB colour (0.80, 0.55, 0.35). The camera capturing the scene is placed 1.5m above the ground, and 2m away from a dark wall that is modelled as a non-reflective rectangular object of 1m width and 1.9m height. This wall casts a shadow on the floor, because of a light source 3m high and 1m

---

[1] http://www.povray.org

behind the wall. The camera's angle of view is 90°, which many lenses can achieve in photography, and the camera is oriented towards the corner formed by the floor and the wall.

The ground and wall surfaces are flat and modelled with ambient-light and diffuse-light coefficients of 0.1 and 0.9, respectively. The resolution of the rendered scene is 1600x900 pixels. The bit depth is 16 bits per colour channel, in RGB format; this allows minimizing numerical errors.

The photos P_1 and P_2 are acquisitions of the underlying 3D scene described above, from the point of view of the camera, taken with and without the presence of the photographer, respectively. Accordingly, every picture is a rendered version of the scene computed through the POVRay software.

Fig. 1: Scene as viewed from the camera, without the presence of the photographer, as defined in Sect. 3.1.1. The wall (black) and its shadow on the floor (brown) are visible in the picture.

3.1.2 Photographer. When present, the photographer faces the wall in the scene and stands together with the camera. The photographer's jacket is modelled as a reflective rectangular object whose width and height are free parameters. The jacket exhibits surface irregularities in form of bumps, whose characteristic widths parallel to the surface is 30cm, and whose depth normal to the surface is left as a free parameter, as for the case of the jacket colour. Accordingly, the jacket material reflects light from the light source onto the floor of the scene.

The jacket-surface bumps are modelled by the so-called bump-mapping technique with a smooth-random-noise function. This approach allows simulating accurate surface properties without increasing the complexity of the underlying surface geometry. The light reflections from the body surface onto the floor and the wall are simulated using photon mapping with a count of 20×10^6 photons, a figure that is empirically determined to be sufficient to converge to a high-quality scene rendering. Photon mapping is essential to model the effect of reflected light from the complex jacket surface onto the rest of the scene (especially the floor) by simulating trajectories of individual photons emitted from the light source and infer their distribution accordingly.

Based on the pair of photographs P_1 and P_2, the parameters that are estimated with our method are the (a) height, (b) width, and (c) colour of the photographer's jacket, where the jacket dimensions are assumed to match the photographer's dimensions, and (d) the presence of bumps of distinct depths on the jacket surface. A non-flat surface typically exhibits bumps, whose size and depth normal to the surface may vary; a zero depth is equivalent to a flat surface. In conjunction with colour, the presence and dimensions of bumps characterize the type or class of material used. Indeed, fibres composed of different fabrics are expected to modulate light-reflection properties differently through their surface irregularities. The observed light-brightness distribution on the photo P_1 used for estimation is thus expected to vary accordingly, which can be used for estimation.

Each of the parameters (a)-(d) is varied within a certain range and compared to corresponding estimates, using 8 data points in total, and using preassigned default values for the other parameters. The jacket width ranges from 0.5m to 1.5m. The jacket height ranges from 1m to 2m. The depth of bumps normal to the jacket surface ranges from 0 to 20cm. Following the RGB convention, the jacket colour ranges from 0 to 1 for the G channel, the other colour channels being left to their default values.

In our study, each parameter of interest is varied and estimated independently while other parameters stay constant at their default values. This allows inferring preliminary yet indicative proof-of-principle results where confounding factors are minimized.

3.1.3 Noise levels. For every parameter and estimations we work on, we consider several simulated noise levels in rendered scenes, both with and without the photographer, corresponding to various signal-to-noise ratio (SNR) levels (defined as the ratio between the energies of the signal and of the noise) for the photographs in decibels (dB). Specifically, we consider cases with 25, 30, 35, 40, 45, 50, and +∞ dB. The noiseless case corresponds to a perfect replication of photo acquisition conditions, including the camera being the same model. Other noise levels help to lessen our tight control, by allowing for example a camera different from the one used by the original photographer, and by accounting for the presence of sensor noise.

3.3 Results and Discussions

Due to space limits, we only present selected results but omit details of our estimation methods. Figs. 2-3 show that the photographer's width and height can be estimated based on the rendered scene (estimates in pixels, according to the resolution of the rendered scenes), even though the relationship is not linear. In particular, the increase in the estimated values is monotonic with respect to the original scene-parameter values for these geometric features, which allows for further calibration. The estimation starts to break down below a certain SNR level due to noise.

Finally, Fig. 4 shows that the estimated bump depth value (determined using normalized gradients on the rendered scenes) increases with the corresponding scene parameter. Noise also affects the estimation results because it increases the perceived surface irregularity viewed from the rendered scene, even though Gaussian filtering was used to mitigate the effect. From a forensic perspective, the bump-depth estimate could provide information on fabric materials of the clothes the photographer was wearing. While it may be hard to pinpoint exact materials, our method could potentially classify them into several categories.

REFERENCES

[1] C. R. Johnson Jr, E. Hendriks, I. J. Berezhnoy, E. Brevdo, S. M. Hughes, I. Daubechies, J. Li, E. Postma, and J. Z. Wang. Image processing for artist identification. IEEE Signal Processing Magazine, 25(4):37–48, 2008.

[2] K Alfianto Jangtjik, M-C Yeh, K-L Hua. Artist-based Classification via Deep Learning with Multiscale Weighted Pooling. ACM Multimedia 2016: 635-639

[3] J. Lukas, J. Fridrich, and M. Goljan. Digital camera identification from sensor pattern noise. IEEE Trans. Inf. Forensics & Security, 1(2):205 214, 2006.

[4] J Yan. Novel security and privacy perspectives of camera fingerprints. Twenty-fourth International Workshop on Security Protocols, Apr 2016. Springer LNCS.

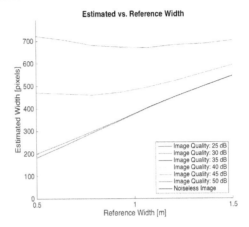

Fig. 2: Estimated vs. reference width (0.5~1.5m range)

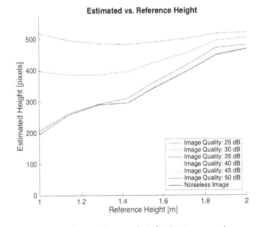

Fig. 3: Estimated vs. reference height (1~2m range)

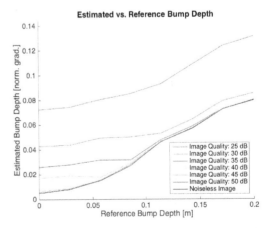

Fig. 4: Estimated vs. reference bump depth (0~20cm range)

POSTER: A PU Learning based System for Potential Malicious URL Detection

Ya-Lin Zhang[†,‡], Longfei Li[‡], Jun Zhou[‡], Xiaolong Li[‡], Yujiang Liu[‡], Yuanchao Zhang[‡],Zhi-Hua Zhou[†]
[†]National Key Lab for Novel Software Technology, Nanjing University, China
[†]{zhangyl, zhouzh}@lamda.nju.edu.cn
[‡]Ant Financial Services Group, China
[‡]{longyao.llf, jun.zhoujun, xl.li, yujiang.lyj, yuanchao.zhang}@antfin.com

ABSTRACT

This paper describes a PU learning (Positive and Unlabeled learning) based system for potential URL attack detection. Previous machine learning based solutions for this task mainly formalize it as a supervised learning problem. However, in some scenarios, the data obtained always contains only a handful of known attack URLs, along with a large number of unlabeled instances, making the supervised learning paradigms infeasible. In this work, we formalize this setting as a PU learning problem, and solve it by combining two different strategies (two-stage strategy and cost-sensitive strategy). Experimental results show that the developed system can effectively find potential URL attacks. This system can either be deployed as an assistance for existing system or be employed to help cyber-security engineers to effectively discover potential attack mode so that they can improve the existing system with significantly less efforts.

KEYWORDS

URL Attack Detection, Machine Learning, PU Learning

1 INTRODUCTION

With the rapid development of internet, more and more kinds of URL attacks have arisen, becoming a serious threat to cyber-security. Traditional URL attack detection systems are mainly constructed through the use of blacklists or rule lists. These lists will gradually become much longer, and it is impracticable to cover all attacks by these ways. More severely, these kinds of methods lack the ability of detecting potential attacks, making it awkward for cyber-security engineers to efficiently discover newly generated URL attacks.

To provide better generalization performance, machine learning based approaches have been employed to this task. These approaches mainly fall into two categories: most formalize it as a supervised learning problem, in which labeled data are needed [6], while the rest try to solve the problem in an unsupervised manner, e.g., by anomaly detection techniques [5], with no label information required. When the labeled data can be obtained, supervised learning methods can always provide better generality. However, in

some conditions, the exact label information is difficult to acquire. For example, we may only get a small set of malicious URLs and a large amount of unlabeled URL records, which means that the aforementioned supervised learning methods can not be directly employed, as we have no labeled negative instances. On the other hand, if we simply solve it in an unsupervised manner, the label information of the known malicious URLs will be terribly wasted, and the performance may be extremely unsatisfactory.

In this paper, we formalize the aforementioned setting as a PU learning (Positive and Unlabeled learning) problem [3], which can naturally make better use of the detected malicious URLs, along with the unlabeled URLs, and provide better performance. Furthermore, we develop a potential URL attack detection system based on PU learning methods. There are many strategies which can be employed to handle PU learning problem, such as two-step strategy [4], cost-sensitive strategy [2], etc. In this work, we combine the models of two-step strategy and cost-sensitive strategy to construct our system. We empirically evaluate the developed system, and the results show that it can effectively find potential URL attacks and significantly reduce the efforts of cyber-security engineers, making it useful in real scenarios of URL attack detection.

The rest of this paper is organized as follows. In Section 2 we describe the developed system. In Section 3 we empirically evaluate the developed system based on the scenario we encountered in Ant Financial[1]. Finally, in Section 4 we conclude the work.

2 THE SYSTEM ARCHITECTURE

In this section, we present the architecture of the developed system. As shown in Figure 1, our system mainly contains 3 modules: (i) **Feature Extraction**, which transforms original URLs into numerical feature vectors; (ii) **Model Training**, which trains PU learning models using the extracted features of training URLs; (iii) **Prediction**, which makes prediction for the new-coming URLs, and a candidate malicious URL set will be outputted by the system.

2.1 Feature Extraction

The original URLs are first transformed to numerical feature vector representations, which can be conveniently used in the subsequent machine learning algorithms. Below, we briefly explain the points of focus of our developed system and present the details of feature extraction process that we use in the system.

---

[1]Ant Financial is a technology company that brings inclusive financial services to the world. It operates Alipay, the world's largest mobile and online payments platform.

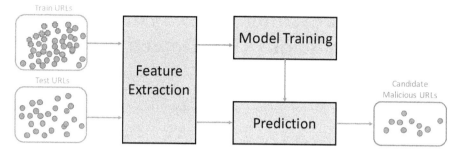

Figure 1: Overview of the proposed system

scheme:[//[user[:password]@]host[:port]][/path][?query][#fragment]

Figure 2: The generic syntax of URLs

Generally speaking, a URL can be separated into several parts, including the scheme part, the authority part, the path part, the query part and fragment part, as shown in Figure 2. A vicious user can modify any of these parts for malicious purpose. In our scenario, the first few parts are restricted, and the attacks mainly come from the fragment part, so we mainly focus on the situation that the attack is executed based on the malicious modification of the fragment parts. Specifically, the fragments are always formed as '$key_1 = value_1 \& \cdots \& key_n = value_n$', and the value may be arbitrarily modified by the attackers to make an attack. Thus, our system mainly deals with this setting, and the feature extraction process directly extracts features from the key-value pairs of the fragment parts.

To be more specific, given a set of URLs, we first separate each of them into the aforementioned parts, and key-value pairs are extracted from the fragments of each URL. Second, since we are focused on discovering the trait of *malicious* URLs, we filter the key-value pairs and only keep the top-N keys that appear mostly in the *malicious* URLs, while the rest of the key-value pairs for each URL are collected together as one key-value pair, thus there will be at most $(N + 1)$ key-value pairs extracted from each URL. Finally, we heuristically extract 8 different statistical information from each filtered value, including the count of *all* characters, letters, numbers, punctuations in the value, and the count of *different* characters, letters, numbers, punctuations in the value. Thus each URL will be described by a $(N + 1) * 8$ dimensional feature vector.

2.2 Model Training

Note that traditional supervised learning techniques can not be directly used in our scenario, as negative labels are unaccessible. In this work, we formalize this problem as a PU learning (Positive and Unlabeled learning) problem.

PU learning [3] is a special case of semi-supervised learning [1, 7], which deals with the tasks where only positive and unlabeled instances are provided, while no negative instance is given. Many strategies have been proposed to solve it. To bypass the embarrassment of lacking labeled negative instances, two-step strategy attempts to first excavate some reliable negative instance, and then transforms the problem into a traditional supervised or semi-supervised learning problem. On the other hand, cost-sensitive learning techniques for binary classification with unequal misclassification cost are readily available for handling PU learning problem [2]. In our developed system, these two strategies are both employed and combined further to form the final prediction model.

Two-Stage Strategy: We select reliable negative instances from unlabeled instances in the first stage, the details of the algorithm are showed in Algorithm 1. In stage two, with the positive instances and selected reliable negative instances, a traditional supervised model is trained and will be further used for predicting new instances.

In this work, with the consideration of efficiency, we employ logistic regression to train the classification model.

Algorithm 1 Reliable Negative Instances Selection

Input: Positive Instance Set P, Unlabeled Instance Set U, Sample Ratio s.
Output: Reliable Negative Instance Set RN.
1: Set $RN = \emptyset$
2: Sample $s\%$ of the instances from P as S
3: Set $P_s = P - S$ with label 1, $U_s = U \cup S$ with label -1
4: Train a classifier g with P_s and U_s
5: Classify instances in U using g, output the class-conditional-probability

6: Select a threshold θ according to the class-conditional-probability of instances in S
7: **for** $d \in U$ **do**
8:    if $Pr(1|d) \leq \theta$, $RN = RN \cup d$
9: **end for**
10: Output RN.

Cost-Sensitive Strategy: We assume that there are very few positive instances in unlabeled instances. By attaching all unlabeled instances with negative labels, the following objective function is minimized:

$$C_+ \sum_{y_i=1} l(y_i, f(x_i)) + C_- \sum_{y_i=-1} l(y_i, f(x_i)) + \lambda R(w), \quad (1)$$

in which C_+ and C_- denote the penalty factor for misclassification of positive and negative instances, respectively. $l(y_i, f(x_i))$ is the loss, such as log-loss and hinge-loss. λ is the regularization coefficient and $R(w)$ is the regularization term, like $L1-$norm and $L2-$norm. In this work, we set the loss to be log-loss and the regularization term to be $L2-$norm. The specific objective function is as:

$$C_+ \sum_{y_i=1} LL(y_i f(x_i)) + C_- \sum_{y_i=-1}' LL(y_i f(x_i)) + \lambda \|w\|^2, \quad (2)$$

in which $LL(z) = \log(1 + \exp(-z))$ is the log-loss. In practice, C_+ and C_- are selected via a validation set, and C_+ is always much bigger than C_-, which means that the penalty of misclassifying a positive instance is much bigger than misclassifying a negative one. The learned model will pay more attention on correctly classifying malicious URLs.

2.3 Prediction

In prediction phase, a new-coming URL will be firstly delivered to the feature extraction module to transfer the original URL into a $(N + 1) * 8$ dimensional vector. Then the extracted feature vector is fed into the two obtained models (by using two-stage strategy and cost-sensitive strategy) described before, and each model will output a score to denote the probability of the URL being malicious. The higher the score is, the more likely the URL is a malicious one. We simply average the two scores as the final score of an URL. The URLs with higher scores are selected to construct the candidate malicious URL set.

In practice, we will filter a set of K URLs based on the candidate malicious URL set, and the filtered URLs will be manually checked by the cyber-security engineers to verify the result.

3 EMPIRICAL EVALUATION

3.1 Dataset and Setup

The dataset is sampled from the daily-arrived URL requests in Ant Financial. Note that the data mainly contains two parts: a large set of unlabeled URLs and a handful of malicious URLs which have been already marked by the existing system, and different attack types may appear among the malicious ones, including XXE (XML External Entity Injection), XSS (Cross SiteScript) and SQL injection, etc. We simply regard all these types as malicious URLs with no subdivision. Since the total dataset is too large, we sample 1 billions of URLs from each day's requests, in which the number of detected malicious URLs by the existing system varies from tens of thousands to hundreds of thousands. The model is trained using data collected in 7 consecutive days, and will be used to predict the scores of each day's new-coming *unlabeled* URLs.

When extracting key-value pairs, N is set to be 99, so that each URL is described by a 800 dimensional vector. Min-max normalization is used to process the features to the same scale. As we explained in the model training section, logistic regression based methods are employed to train the PU learning models. The parameters such as C_+, C_- and λ are selected via a validation set.

3.2 Empirical Results

Since we have no label information of the daily-arrived unlabeled URLs, we use the help of the cyber-security engineers to check the results and verify the effectiveness of our system.

It is very time-consuming to check the results, so we set the size K of the candidate malicious URL set to be at most 150, and cyber-security engineers will manually check whether the selected URLs are malicious or benign. Table 1 summarizes the details of three day's results. As we can see from the table, the accuracy of the filtered candidate set can be up to 90%, indicating that the proposed system can effectively discover the potential malicious URLs, which can not be captured by the existing system. What should be specially

mentioned is that new attack modes have been discovered based on the candidate malicious URL set, and the cyber-security engineers in Ant Financial have already improve the existing system with this help. At the same time, the developed system can also be used together with the existing system to improve the ability of the whole system.

Table 1: Evaluation results of the candidate malicious URLs. The number of selected candidate URLs, the number of confirmed malicious URLs and the accuracy (%) are presented.

	Date A	Date B	Date C
# Candidate Ins.	113	103	141
# Malicious Ins.	91	97	130
Accuracy	80.5	94.2	92.2

4 CONCLUSIONS

In this work, we develop a potential URL attack detection system based on PU learning. Compared to supervised learning based approaches, our method only needs a handful of malicious URLs, along with the unlabeled URLs, which is suitable for the real situation that we encounter.

The developed system mainly contains three parts: firstly, a feature extraction process is executed to transfer the original URLs into numerical feature vectors; Secondly, two-stage strategy and cost-sensitive strategy are employed to train the classification models; Finally, each new-coming URL will be first transformed into numerical feature vector and then be fed into the learned models, those URLs with high scores will be regarded as potential malicious URLs with high probability.

Empirical results show that our developed system can effectively discover potential URL attacks. This system can either be deployed as an assistance for the existing system or be employed to help cyber-security engineers to effectively discover potential attack mode.

ACKNOWLEDGMENTS

Partially supported by NSFC (61333014) and the Collaborative Innovation Center of Novel Software Technology and Industrialization.

REFERENCES

[1] Olivier Chapelle, Bernhard Scholkopf, and Alexander Zien. 2009. Semi-Supervised Learning. *IEEE Transactions on Neural Networks* 20, 3 (2009), 542–542.
[2] Marthinus C du Plessis, Gang Niu, and Masashi Sugiyama. 2014. Analysis of Learning from Positive and Unlabeled Data. In *Advances in Neural Information Processing Systems 27*. 703–711.
[3] Charles Elkan and Keith Noto. 2008. Learning Classifiers from Only Positive and Unlabeled Data. In *Proceedings of the 14th ACM SIGKDD International Conference on Knowledge Discovery and Data Mining*. 213–220.
[4] Bing Liu, Yang Dai, Xiaoli Li, Wee Sun Lee, and Philip S Yu. 2003. Building Text Classifiers Using Positive and Unlabeled Examples. In *Proceeding of the 3rd IEEE International Conference on Data Mining*. 179–186.
[5] Fei Tony Liu, Kai Ming Ting, and Zhi-Hua Zhou. 2008. Isolation Forest. In *Proceeding ot the 8th IEEE International Conference on Data Mining*. 413–422.
[6] Justin Ma, Lawrence K Saul, Stefan Savage, and Geoffrey M Voelker. 2009. Beyond Blacklists: Learning to Detect Malicious Web Sites from Suspicious URLs. In *Proceedings of the 15th ACM SIGKDD International Conference on Knowledge Discovery and Data Mining*. 1245–1254.
[7] Zhi-Hua Zhou and Ming Li. 2010. Semi-Supervised Learning by Disagreement. *Knowledge and Information Systems* 24, 3 (2010), 415–439.

Identity related Threats, Vulnerabilities and Risk Mitigation in Online Social Networks*

A Tutorial

Leila Bahri
Royal Institute of Technology - KTH
Stockholm, Sweden
lbahri@kth.se

ABSTRACT

This tutorial provides a thorough review of the main research directions in the field of identity management and identity related security threats in Online Social Networks (OSNs). The continuous increase in the numbers and sophistication levels of fake accounts constitutes a big threat to the privacy and to the security of honest OSN users. Uninformed OSN users could be easily fooled into accepting friendship links with fake accounts, giving them by that access to personal information they intend to exclusively share with their real friends. Moreover, these fake accounts subvert the security of the system by spreading malware, connecting with honest users for nefarious goals such as sexual harassment or child abuse, and make the social computing environment mostly untrustworthy. The tutorial introduces the main available research results available in this area, and presents our work on collaborative identity validation techniques to estimate OSN profiles trustworthiness.

KEYWORDS

Sybil accounts, OSN identity validation, Profile trustworthiness, Sybil marking

ACM Reference Format:
Leila Bahri. 2017. Identity related Threats, Vulnerabilities and Risk Mitigation in Online Social Networks. In *Proceedings of CCS '17, Dallas, TX, USA, October 30-November 3, 2017*, 3 pages.
https://doi.org/10.1145/3133956.3136066

1 INTRODUCTION

Identity management in the realms of Online Social Networks (OSNs) is one of the most critical elements in discussing their security. The ability to reliably identify a profile on an OSN is the first building block towards ensuring the protection of both the users (and their data), and the OSN provider's resources and reputation. Unfortunately, this ability is not easily achieved, and/or is not provided in today's major OSNs. The looseness in obtaining a digital identity (i.e., a profile) on an OSN, where only a valid email account is required, facilitates their joining as open socializing platforms, but also makes them exposed to identity related attacks and threats. As a matter of fact, the percentage of fake accounts existing in today's major OSNs is continuously increasing regardless of the efforts put into detecting them, and is reported to have increased from 5.5% in 2012 to about 12% in 2015 on Facebook, for instance.[1]

There is a huge body of work in the area of detecting fake accounts in OSNs, mostly under the research topic known as Sybil detection [7]. A Sybil account represents a forged fake identity that could have been one of million others created, at scale, by a bot, or manually at a smaller scale, but with generally common malicious aims, such as spreading malware, spying on users activity and/or stealing their personal information, or infecting the environment with fake content. Sybil detection algorithms aim at discriminating between fake and real accounts based on Sybils behavior and/or features in the network, or after they have demonstrated detected malicious activity.

Generally, most works on Sybil detection adopt one of two main appraoches. The first one is a graph based appraoch, which assumes that Sybil nodes exhibit different connection patterns in the social network compared to real ones. The second approach relies on a behavioral premise, assuming that Sybil nodes behave in ways that are easily differentiable from honest activity. However, Sybil accounts are getting more sophisticated and are moving towards getting social: i.e., Sybil accounts target misleading as many honest users as possible into befriending them, gaining as such their trust in the network and looking as good profiles to detection mechanisms. Moreover, when Sybils succeed at befriending honest users, the privacy of these latters is at stake as personal information that is supposed to be shared with real friends becomes available to fake entities that might have malicious intentions (such as spreading malware, engaging in sexual embarrassment or child abuse activities, etc.).

To address this issue, we have worked on exploring identity validation solutions from a social, collaborative perspective. We have explored how the collective wisdom of honest users in a social network could be explored to analyze new profiles based only on the content they contain. We have found that honest profiles exhibit content correlations that could be learned, both using crowdsourcing techniques [2][3], and using unsupervised decentralized machine learning techniques [10] [12] [11], and that could be effectively used to flag fake profiles early on, based only on their content.

---

*All the work conducted by the author under this topic has taken place at the University of Insubria in Varese, Italy, mainly in collaboration with Prof. Elena Ferrari and to Ass. Prof. Barbara Carminati.

CCS '17, October 30-November 3, 2017, Dallas, TX, USA
© 2017 Copyright held by the owner/author(s).
ACM ISBN 978-1-4503-4946-8/17/10.
https://doi.org/10.1145/3133956.3136066

---

[1] According to statistics published on www.statisticbrain.com

The objective of the tutorial is to initiate the audience to this topic of Sybil detection in OSNs, to its main techniques, and to the challenges facing it. A synthesis of the related literature will shed the light on the main adopted techniques and on the main challenges facing this research field. The main focus would be on user-centric and community-sourced identity validation techniques, as a promising approach to face social Sybil threats. The main goal would be to open new research directions and questions under this important area.

2 SYBIL DETECTION

Given the importance of the problem of detecting Sybils, the literature has a plethora of related research works. In general, these could be discussed under two main categories: 1) graph-based Sybil detection, and 2) behavior-based Sybil deception. For the first category, the focus is on observations made from topological structures of the underlying social network graph, showing that Sybil accounts exhibit connection patterns that could be differentiable from real ones. For instance, works such as [19][18], [17], [4], [5], and [1] have leveraged on the observation that Sybil accounts tend to mix much faster in the graph compared to real accounts.

Under the second category, the focus is more on detecting behavioral features related to accounts activities in the social network for which Sybil accounts exhibit clearly differentetiable patterns compared to real users. For instance, features related to the frequency of sending friend requests and frequency of making new friends (e.g., [16]), to accounts names structures (e.g., [15]) or to the ratio of outgoing to incoming activity and clickstream in the network (e.g., [13]), or combinations of these have been explored. In addition to that, there is also a third category that adopts a hybrid approach and tries to use both graph-based and behavioral-based features, such as the works in [6], [8], or in [9].

These automated techniques for Sybil detection face challenges mostly related to the countinuous sophisitication of Sybil accounts that adapt themselves to the used features and can manage to look or to behave as normal acounts do. To overcome these limitations, the exploitation of the human factor, as a second layer of protection, remains one of the most effective solutions, such as argued in [14].

3 IDENTITY VALIDATION

Without denying the importance of automated Sybil detection techniques, collaborative identity validation is also important as another layer of protection against more sophisticated Sybil accounts. Identity validation refers to labelling accounts with metrics that represent their estimated trustworthiness in the social network, mostly as perceived by the general users. We have conducted several research works on this topic, starting by a crowd-sourcing based technique for analyzing social network profiles and detecting those looking uncoherent and suspicsious compared to normal trends exhibited in mormal profiles [2]. In [2], we have proposed a semi-supervised learning strategy to detect correlations between attributes in a profile schema. The learned correlations were later used to parse new profiles and detect the levels of coherence they exhibit compared to other real profiles among the social group they try to connect with.

In [3], we have shown how the learning of correlations between profile attributes and the evaluation of new profiles for coherence can be achieved in a privacy preserving manner, uwing anonymization techniques. Then, in [10] and [11] we have achieved the same outcome using fully unsupervised learning within a fully dencetralized architecture where every user in the social network is only aware of her/his direct friends. We have also found that profiles trustworthiness depends on the social community they belong to. That is, it might be easier for a Sybil account to sophisticate the account to generally look real, but it can be detected within given social communities, as members of each community tend to exhibit hidden local profile patterns that can rather not be easily detected by Sybils.

4 CONCLUSION

Fighting against Sybil accounts in online social networks is a dual infinite race between detector mechanisms and the designers of the attacks. Understanding and containing identity related threats and vulnerabilities, especially in open general social networks where it is easy to sign up for a new profile, remains of utmost importance in ensuring environments of reliable information and safe social computing. The aim of this tutorial is to provide an understanding of these threats, of the existing work in the field, and to highlight the possible research direction that can be undertaken.

REFERENCES

[1] Lorenzo Alvisi, Allen Clement, Alessandro Epasto, Silvio Lattanzi, and Alessandro Panconesi. 2013. Sok: The evolution of sybil defense via social networks. In *Security and Privacy (SP), 2013 IEEE Symposium on*. IEEE, 382–396.

[2] Leila Bahri, Barbara Carminati, and Elena Ferrari. 2014. Community-based Identity Validation in Online Social Networks. In *Proceedings of the 34th international conference on Distributed Computing Systems*. IEEE.

[3] Leila Bahri, Barbara Carminati, and Elena Ferrari. 2016. COIPâĂŤContinuous, Operable, Impartial, and Privacy-Aware Identity Validity Estimation for OSN Profiles. *ACM Transactions on the Web (TWEB)* 10, 4 (2016), 23.

[4] Qiang Cao, Michael Sirivianos, Xiaowei Yang, and Tiago Pregueiro. 2012. Aiding the detection of fake accounts in large scale social online services. In *Presented as part of the 9th USENIX Symposium on Networked Systems Design and Implementation (NSDI 12)*. 197–210.

[5] George Danezis and Prateek Mittal. 2009. SybilInfer: Detecting Sybil Nodes using Social Networks.. In *NDSS*. San Diego, CA.

[6] Meng Jiang, Peng Cui, Alex Beutel, Christos Faloutsos, and Shiqiang Yang. 2014. Catchsync: catching synchronized behavior in large directed graphs. In *Proceedings of the 20th ACM SIGKDD international conference on Knowledge discovery and data mining*. ACM, 941–950.

[7] Krishna B Kansara and Narendra M Shekokar. 2015. At a Glance of Sybil Detection in OSN. In *2015 IEEE International Symposium on Nanoelectronic and Information Systems*. IEEE, 47–52.

[8] Naeimeh Laleh, Barbara Carminati, and Elena Ferrari. 2015. Graph Based Local Risk Estimation in Large Scale Online Social Networks. In *2015 IEEE International Conference on Smart City/SocialCom/SustainCom (SmartCity)*. IEEE, 528–535.

[9] Yixuan Li, Oscar Martinez, Xing Chen, Yi Li, and John E Hopcroft. 2016. In a World That Counts: Clustering and Detecting Fake Social Engagement at Scale. In *Proceedings of the 25th International Conference on World Wide Web*. International World Wide Web Conferences Steering Committee, 111–120.

[10] Amira Soliman, Leila Bahri, Barbara Carminati, Elena Ferrari, and Sarunas Girdzijauskas. 2015. Diva: Decentralized identity validation for social networks. In *Advances in Social Networks Analysis and Mining (ASONAM), 2015 IEEE/ACM International Conference on*. IEEE, 383–391.

[11] Amira Soliman, Leila Bahri, Sarunas Girdzijauskas, Barbara Carminati, and Elena Ferrari. 2016. CADIVa: cooperative and adaptive decentralized identity validation model for social networks. *Social Network Analysis and Mining* 6, 1 (2016), 1–22.

[12] Amira Soliman, Leila Bahri, Jacopo Squillaci, Barbara Carminati, Elena Ferrari, and Sarunas Girdzijauskas. 2016. BeatTheDIVa - Decentralized Identity Validation in OSNs. In *icde*. IEEE.

[13] Gang Wang, Tristan Konolige, Christo Wilson, Xiao Wang, Haitao Zheng, and Ben Y Zhao. 2013. You are how you click: Clickstream analysis for sybil detection. In *Proc. USENIX Security*. Citeseer, 1–15.

[14] Gang Wang, Manish Mohanlal, Christo Wilson, Xiao Wang, Miriam Metzger, Haitao Zheng, and Ben Y Zhao. 2012. Social turing tests: Crowdsourcing sybil detection. *arXiv preprint arXiv:1205.3856* (2012).

[15] Cao Xiao, David Mandell Freeman, and Theodore Hwa. 2015. Detecting Clusters of Fake Accounts in Online Social Networks. In *Proceedings of the 8th ACM Workshop on Artificial Intelligence and Security*. ACM, 91–101.

[16] Zhi Yang, Christo Wilson, Xiao Wang, Tingting Gao, Ben Y Zhao, and Yafei Dai. 2014. Uncovering social network sybils in the wild. *ACM Transactions on Knowledge Discovery from Data (TKDD)* 8, 1 (2014), 2.

[17] Haifeng Yu, Phillip B Gibbons, Michael Kaminsky, and Feng Xiao. 2008. Sybillimit: A near-optimal social network defense against sybil attacks. In *Security and Privacy, 2008. SP 2008. IEEE Symposium on*. IEEE, 3–17.

[18] Haifeng Yu, Michael Kaminsky, Phillip B Gibbons, and Abraham Flaxman. 2006. Sybilguard: defending against sybil attacks via social networks. In *ACM SIG-COMM Computer Communication Review*, Vol. 36. ACM, 267–278.

[19] Kuan Zhang, Xiaohui Liang, Rongxing Lu, and Xuemin Shen. 2014. Sybil Attacks and Their Defenses in the Internet of Things. *Internet of Things Journal, IEEE* 1, 5 (2014), 372–383.

Web Tracking Technologies and Protection Mechanisms

Nataliia Bielova
Université Côte d'Azur, Inria
Sophia Antipolis, France
nataliia.bielova@inria.fr

ABSTRACT

Billions of users browse the Web on a daily basis, leaving their digital traces on millions of websites. Every such visit, every mouse move or button click may trigger a wide variety of hidden data exchanges across multiple tracking companies. As a result, these companies collect a vast amount of user's data, preferences and habits, that are extremely useful for online advertisers and profitable for data brokers, however very worrisome for the privacy of the users.

In this *3-hours tutorial* we will cover the vide variety of Web tracking technologies, ranging from simple cookies to advanced cross-device fingerprinting. We will describe the main mechanisms behind web tracking and what users can do to protect themselves. Moreover, we will discuss solutions Web developers can use to automatically eliminate tracking from the third-party content they include in their applications. This tutorial will be of interest to a *general audience* of computer scientists, and *we do not require any specific prerequisite knowledge* for attendees.

We will cover the following tracking mechanisms:

- third-party cookie tracking, and other stateful tracking techniques that enables tracking across multiple websites [26, 28, 29],
- cookie respawning that is used to re-create deleted user cookies [7, 27],
- cookie synching that allows trackers and ad agencies to synchronise user IDs across different companies [13, 24],
- browser fingerprinting, including Canvas, WebRTC and AudioContext fingerprinting [6, 11, 13, 21]
- cross-browser device fingerprinting, allowing trackers to recognise users across several devices [10].

We will then demonstrate prevalence of such techniques on the Web, based on previous research [6, 13, 17, 22, 26, 31]. We will present the advertisement ecosystem and explain how Web technologies are used in advertisement, in particular in Real-Time-Bidding (RTB). We will explain how cookie synching is used in RTB and present recent analysis on how much a user's tracking data is worth [24]. We will discuss the

mechanisms the website owners use to automatically interact with the ad agencies [23], and explain its consequences on user's security and privacy.

To help users protect themselves from Web tracking, we will give an overview of existing solutions. We'll start with the browser settings, and show that basic third-party cookie tracking is still possible even in the private browser mode of most common Web browsers. We then present privacy-protecting browser extensions and compare how efficient they are in protection from Web tracking [19]. Then, we'll present possible protection mechanisms based on browser randomisation [15, 16] to protect from advanced fingerprinting techniques.

Finally, we will present solutions for Web developers, who want to include third-party content in their websites, but would like to automatically remove any tracking of their users. In particular, we will discuss simple solutions that exist today for social plugins integration [25], and propose more advanced server-side based solutions that are a result of our own research [30].

KEYWORDS

web tracking; surveillance; online privacy; big data

BIO

Nataliia Bielova is a Research Scientist at Inria, French National Institute for Research in Computer Science and Automation. Nataliia is internationally known for her work on applying formal methods to security and privacy of web browsers. Her main interest is privacy- and transparency-enhancing technologies for Web applications. She works on measurement, detection and prevention of web tracking, including advanced behaviour-based fingerprinting [14]. Nataliia received the French Doctoral Supervision and Research Award (PEDR) in 2017. Before obtaining her permanent position in 2013, Nataliia was a postdoctoral researcher at Inria Rennes from 2012 to 2013, where she worked on automatic detection of web tracking scripts using program analysis [8]. She received her PhD in Computer Science from the University of Trento, Italy in 2011.

1 HOW DOES WEB TRACKING WORK?

Web tracking is the practice when some content ("trackers") embedded in a webpage recognises the users visiting the page. Differently from analytics, trackers are usually

¹This work has been partially supported by the ANR project AJACS ANR-14-CE28-0008.

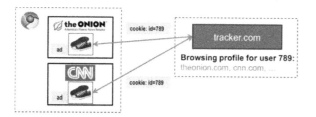

Figure 1: Basic cookie-based tracking from [17]. The third-party domain `tracker.com` recognises a user with a cookie "789" on sites that embed content from `tracker.com`.

"third-party" meaning that they belong to a different domain than the hosting webpage. Because trackers are originating from a third-party domain, they are able recognise user's across different websites where these trackers are embedded [17, 18, 26].

The basic tracking mechanism based on cookies is shown in Figure 1. When a user visits `theonion.com`, the browser loads additional third-party content from `tracker.com`. This content sets up a browser cookie with value "789" that is automatically stored in the browser. Upon a later request to a different website `cnn.com`, the third-party tracker `tracker.com` will recognise the same user "789" and thus will learn that this user has been to `theonion.com` and `cnn.com`.

Web tracking technologies are largely divided into two broad categories: *stateful* and *stateless*. Stateful tracking techniques store information on the user's computer and later retrieve it to recognise the user. Third-party cookies are the most prevalent online tracking technique, and in recent years researchers found out that cookies can be "respawned" even if the user deleted them [7, 27]. Moreover, cookies get synchronised among different data brokers in order to map and exchange user's profiles [13, 24]. Several groups of researchers have reported on the usage of different stateful trackers on popular websites [7, 17, 26, 28].

Stateless technologies allow trackers to recognise users without storing any information on the user's machine. Device fingerprinting collects information about the user's browser and OS properties, and can distinguish users by these characteristics [11]. In 2010, Eckersley first demonstrated that the technology is effective (see Panopticlick project [12]). Researchers later on have discovered that device fingerprinting started being used by tracking companies [6, 21]. Moreover, because of the advance of web standards and HTML5, new more advanced techniques became possible, that use Canvas API, WebRTC and AudioContext fingerprinting [13]. Recently, more fingerprinting techniques were discovered, that allow to track users across devices [9, 10]. In another recent project, researchers demonstrate that web browsers may be detected via the extensions that the user installs and websites where the user is logged in [14].

2 ADVERTISEMENT AND REAL-TIME-BIDDING

Real-Time-Bidding (RTB) is one of the main mechanisms that advertisement agencies are using to target users online. The advertisement ecosystem has substantially grown in the last 10 years, building on standard and more advanced web tracking technologies. We will show how fast this ecosystem has grown over the last years, and present main Web technologies used in advertisement. Researchers have detected that cookie synching is the main component of RTB and analysed how much a user's tracking data is worth in RTB: it is often sold for less than $0.0005 [24]. It was revealed that in RTB, the website owners and the ad agencies often tightly cooperate [23]. Such collaboration sometimes leads to bypassing basic Web security protections implemented by the browser, such as the Same-Origin-Policy. We discuss potential security issues raised by such collaboration.

3 PROTECTION FROM WEB TRACKING

The most common way to prevent most of the cookie tracking is to use the browser configuration and explicitly block third-party cookies. Even though research shows that in presence of other tracking techniques, cookies can be "respawned", the fact that the browser itself does not set, and moreover, does not send any third-party cookies, is already the first step to protect yourself. Private browsing modes in modern browser provide some protection as well, however they do not disable third-party cookies.

Another line of protection is by browser extensions. *AdBlock Plus* [1], *Ghostery* [3], *uBlock* [5], *Disconnect* [2] and *Privacy Badger* [4] are the most used privacy extensions in 2016 [19]. AdBlock Plus and uBlock rely on two community-driven rulesets that define whether a certain third-party content is a tracker. However, they do not provide full protection because if a tracker sets up a new domain not present in these rulesets, tracking via such domain will not be blocked. Ghostery and Disconnect create blocking rules internally. Differently from rule-based approaches, Privacy Badger uses heuristics to automatically detect third-party trackers on-the-fly. Even though none of these extensions can guarantee a 100% protection, they however disallow well-known companies to track you on the Web. Recently, researchers have measured the effectiveness of all these extensions on the top 200,000 websites [19].

Most of the solutions presented above do protect from a significant number of known trackers, but may be less effective against device fingerprinting. To protect yourself from this advanced stateless tracking, the simplest way is to disable JavaScript, however this may be not very practical. Several web browsers, proposed by researchers, aim at protecting from fingerprinting through the randomisation of browser properties [15, 16, 20].

Finally, website developers might also be interested in protecting their users from web tracking. This choice may be important either due to ethical reasons, or requirement for legal compliance, such as with upcoming EU ePrivacy regulation, which may make website owners liable for the third-party tracking present on their websites. *Social share privacy* platform [25] allows website developers to include social widgets, but disable any request to a third party until the used clicks on the button. Researchers have recently proposed *a server-side technique to protect against web tracking*: it's based on setting up two additional servers that rewrite and redirect the original web application requests so that third-party tracking is automatically removed from the third-party content [30].

REFERENCES

[1] 2017. Adblock Plus – Surf the web without annoying ads! (2017). https://adblockplus.org/.

[2] 2017. Disconnect. (2017). https://disconnect.me/.

[3] 2017. Ghostery. (2017). https://www.ghostery.com/.

[4] 2017. Privacy Badger - Electronic Frontier Foundation. (2017). https://www.eff.org/fr/privacybadger.

[5] 2017. uBlock Origin browser extension. (2017). https://www.ublock.org/.

[6] Gunes Acar, Marc Juárez, Nick Nikiforakis, Claudia Díaz, Seda F. Gürses, Frank Piessens, and Bart Preneel. 2013. FPDetective: dusting the web for fingerprinters. In *2013 ACM SIGSAC Conference on Computer and Communications Security, CCS'13, Berlin, Germany, November 4-8, 2013*, Ahmad-Reza Sadeghi, Virgil D. Gligor, and Moti Yung (Eds.). ACM, 1129–1140. https://doi.org/10.1145/2508859.2516674

[7] M. Ayenson, D. J. Wambach, A. Soltani, N. Good, and C. J. Hoofnagle. 2011. Flash cookies and privacy II: Now with HTML5 and ETag respawning. In *SSRN eLibrary*. http://papers.ssrn.com/sol3/papers.cfm?abstract_id=1898390.

[8] Frédéric Besson, Nataliia Bielova, and Thomas Jensen. 2013. Hybrid Information Flow Monitoring Against Web Tracking. In *CSF'13*. IEEE, 240–254.

[9] Károly Boda, Ádám Máté Földes, Gábor György Gulyás, and Sándor Imre. 2011. User Tracking on the Web via Cross-Browser Fingerprinting. In *Information Security Technology for Applications - 16th Nordic Conference on Secure IT Systems, NordSec 2011, Tallinn, Estonia, October 26-28, 2011, Revised Selected Papers (Lecture Notes in Computer Science)*, Peeter Laud (Ed.), Vol. 7161. Springer, 31–46. https://doi.org/10.1007/978-3-642-29615-4_4

[10] Yinzhi Cao, Song Li, and Erik Wijmans. 2017. (Cross-)Browser Fingerprinting via OS and Hardware Level Features. In *24th Annual Network and Distributed System Security Symposium, NDSS 2017, San Diego, California, USA, 26 February - 1 March, 2017*. To Appear.

[11] P. Eckersley. 2011. How unique is your browser? *(LNCS)*, Vol. 6205. Springer, 1–18.

[12] P. Eckersley. 2017. The Panopticlick project. (2017). https://panopticlick.eff.org.

[13] Steven Englehardt and Arvind Narayanan. 2016. Online Tracking: A 1-million-site Measurement and Analysis. In *Proceedings of the 2016 ACM SIGSAC Conference on Computer and Communications Security, Vienna, Austria, October 24-28, 2016*, Edgar R. Weippl, Stefan Katzenbeisser, Christopher Kruegel, Andrew C. Myers, and Shai Halevi (Eds.). ACM, 1388–1401. https://doi.org/10.1145/2976749.2978313

[14] Gábor György Gulyás, Dolière Francis Somé, Nataliia Bielova, and Claude Castelluccia. 2017. Browser Extension and Login-Leak Experiment. (2017). https://extensions.inrialpes.fr/.

[15] Pierre Laperdrix, Walter Rudametkin, and Benoit Baudry. 2015. Mitigating Browser Fingerprint Tracking: Multi-level Reconfiguration and Diversification. In *10th IEEE/ACM International Symposium on Software Engineering for Adaptive and Self-Managing Systems, SEAMS 2015, Florence, Italy, May 18-19, 2015*, Paola Inverardi and Bradley R. Schmerl (Eds.). IEEE Computer Society, 98–108. https://doi.org/10.1109/SEAMS.2015.18

[16] Pierre Laperdrix, Walter Rudametkin, and Benoit Baudry. 2016. Beauty and the Beast: Diverting Modern Web Browsers to Build Unique Browser Fingerprints. In *IEEE Symposium on Security and Privacy, SP 2016, San Jose, CA, USA, May 22-26, 2016*,

IEEE Computer Society, 878–894. https://doi.org/10.1109/SP.2016.57

[17] Adam Lerner, Anna Kornfeld Simpson, Tadayoshi Kohno, and Franziska Roesner. 2016. Internet Jones and the Raiders of the Lost Trackers: An Archaeological Study of Web Tracking from 1996 to 2016. In *25th USENIX Security Symposium (USENIX Security 16)*. USENIX Association.

[18] Jonathan R. Mayer and John C. Mitchell. 2012. Third-Party Web Tracking: Policy and Technology. In *IEEE Symposium on Security and Privacy, SP 2012, 21-23 May 2012, San Francisco, California, USA*. IEEE Computer Society, 413–427. https://doi.org/10.1109/SP.2012.47

[19] Georg Merzdovnik, Markus Huber, Damjan Buhov, Nick Nikiforakis, Sebastian Neuner, Martin Schmiedecker, and Edgar Weippl. 2017. Block Me If You Can: A Large-Scale Study of Tracker-Blocking Tools. In *2nd IEEE European Symposium on Security and Privacy*. Paris, France. To appear.

[20] Nick Nikiforakis, Wouter Joosen, and Benjamin Livshits. 2015. PriVaricator: Deceiving Fingerprinters with Little White Lies. In *Proceedings of the 24th International Conference on World Wide Web (WWW '15)*. International World Wide Web Conferences Steering Committee, Republic and Canton of Geneva, Switzerland, 820–830.

[21] Nick Nikiforakis, Alexandros Kapravelos, Wouter Joosen, Christopher Kruegel, Frank Piessens, and Giovanni Vigna. 2013. Cookieless Monster: Exploring the Ecosystem of Web-Based Device Fingerprinting. In *2013 IEEE Symposium on Security and Privacy, SP 2013, Berkeley, CA, USA, May 19-22, 2013*. IEEE Computer Society, 541–555. https://doi.org/10.1109/SP.2013.43

[22] Nick Nikiforakis, Alexandros Kapravelos, Wouter Joosen, Christopher Kruegel, Frank Piessens, and Giovanni Vigna. 2013. Cookieless Monster: Exploring the Ecosystem of Web-Based Device Fingerprinting. In *IEEE Symposium on Security and Privacy*. 541–555.

[23] Lukasz Olejnik and Claude Castelluccia. 2014. Analysis of OpenX-Publishers Cooperation. In *7th Workshop on Hot Topics in Privacy Enhancing Technologies (HotPETs 2014)*.

[24] Lukasz Olejnik, Minh-Dung Tran, and Claude Castelluccia. 2014. Selling off User Privacy at Auction. In *21st Annual Network and Distributed System Security Symposium, NDSS 2014, San Diego, California, USA, February 23-26, 2014*.

[25] Mathias Panzenböck. 2012. Social Share Privacy. (2012). http://panzi.github.io/SocialSharePrivacy/.

[26] Franziska Roesner, Tadayoshi Kohno, and David Wetherall. 2012. Detecting and Defending Against Third-Party Tracking on the Web. In *Proceedings of the 9th USENIX Symposium on Networked Systems Design and Implementation, NSDI 2012, San Jose, CA, USA, April 25-27, 2012*, Steven D. Gribble and Dina Katabi (Eds.). USENIX Association, 155–168. https://www.usenix.org/conference/nsdi12/technical-sessions/presentation/roesner

[27] A. Soltani. 2011. Respawn redux. (August 2011). Online. Available: http://ashkansoltani.org/docs/respawnredux.html.

[28] Ashkan Soltani, Shannon Canty, Quentin Mayo, Lauren Thomas, and Chris Jay Hoofnagle. 2010. Flash Cookies and Privacy. In *AAAI Spring Symposium: Intelligent Information Privacy Management*.

[29] Ashkan Soltani, Shannon Canty, Quentin Mayo, Lauren Thomas, and Chris Jay Hoofnagle. 2010. Flash Cookies and Privacy. In *AAAI spring symposium: intelligent information privacy management*. 158–163.

[30] Dolière Francis Somé, Nataliia Bielova, and Tamara Rezk. 2017. Control What You Include! Server-Side Protection against Third Party Web Tracking. In *International Symposium on Engineering Secure Software and Systems (ESSoS)*. To appear.

[31] Ting-Fang Yen, Yinglian Xie, Fang Yu, Roger Peng Yu, and Martin Abadi. 2012. Host Fingerprinting and Tracking on the Web: Privacy and Security Implications. In *Proc. of 19th Annual Network and Distributed System Security Symposium (NDSS)*. Internet Society.

Tutorial: Private Information Retrieval

Ryan Henry

Indiana University
School of Informatics and Computing
Bloomington, IN 47405, USA
henry@indiana.edu

ABSTRACT

Private information retrieval (PIR) is a cryptographic primitive that facilitates the seemingly impossible task of letting users fetch records from untrusted and remote database servers without revealing to those servers which records are being fetched. The research literature on PIR is vast; in the over two decades since its 1995 introduction by Chor, Goldreich, Kushilevitz, and Sudan, the cryptography, privacy, and theoretical computer science research communities have studied PIR intensively and from a variety of perspectives. Alas, despite a series of significant advances, most privacy practitioners and theoreticians alike fall into one of two camps: (i) those who believe that PIR is so inefficient and abstruse as to make it all-but-useless in practice, or (ii) those who remain blissfully unaware that PIR even exists. Indeed, to date not even one of the numerous PIR-based applications proposed in the research literature has been deployed at scale to protect the privacy of users "in the wild".

This tutorial targets both of the above camps, presenting a bird's-eye overview of the current state of PIR research. Topics covered will span the spectrum from purely theoretical through imminently applicable and all the high points in between, thereby providing participants with an awareness of what modern PIR techniques have (and do not have) to offer, dispelling the myth of PIR's inherent impracticality, and hopefully inspiring participants to identify practical use cases for PIR within their own niche areas of expertise. This introductory tutorial will be accessible to anyone comfortable with college-level mathematics (basic linear algebra and some elementary probability and number theory).

KEYWORDS

Private information retrieval; coding theory; applied cryptography; trusted hardware; function secret sharing

CCS'17, Oct. 30–Nov. 3, 2017, Dallas, TX, USA.
© 2017 Copyright held by the owner/author(s). ISBN 978-1-4503-4946-8/17/10.
DOI: http://dx.doi.org/0.1145/3133956.3136069

DESCRIPTION OF TUTORIAL

This tutorial provides participants with a broad overview of the current state-of-the-art with respect to a cryptographic primitive called *private information retrieval* (PIR). Information retrieval (IR)—roughly, the activity of locating and retrieving relevant information from a corpus (i.e., database) D of files or records—is among the most fundamental and ubiquitous tasks in computing. In "classical" IR settings, a client encodes its information needs in a query q, while the holder of D (whether a remote server or a service running on the client's local host) ranks the elements of D by relevance to the client's needs as expressed in q, and then it returns to the client one or more of the "top" matches.

PIR extends the classical IR setting with an interesting twist: it insists that the holder of D learns nothing about the information needs expressed in q (including the ranking it induces and the matches it returns). While intuition might insist that it is clearly *not* possible to realize such privacy for IR, the research literature contains numerous PIR protocols that do just that (albeit only for some very basic forms of IR), with known constructions based on information- and coding-theoretic primitives (e.g., secret sharing [3, 4] and error-correcting codes [9]), both public- and private-key encryption (e.g., partially homomorphic encryption [7] and function secret sharing [1, 11], anonymity [6, 10], and trusted hardware (e.g., TPMs [12] and SGX). As for what types of IR can be realized as PIR, the literature considers PIR constructions supporting physical position-based queries [3], keyword-based queries [2], simple SQL-based queries [8], statistical queries [11], and index-based queries [5].

Yet despite the ubiquity of IR, the ever-increasing quantity and sensitivity of information being digitized and made available online, and the veritable wealth of PIR techniques in the literature, *PIR has never been deployed at scale to protect the privacy of users "in the wild"*. This tutorial sets out with the lofty goal of changing that. It will cover topics spanning the spectrum from purely theoretical through imminently applicable and all the high points in between, thereby providing participants with an awareness of what modern PIR techniques have (and do not have) to offer, dispelling the myth of PIR's inherent impracticality, and hopefully inspiring participants to identify practical use cases for PIR within their own niche areas of expertise.

SCOPE OF TUTORIAL

The duration of the tutorial will be **three hours**, with each hour being devoted to a different "module" about PIR.

The first half-hour will motivate the PIR problem, illustrating why widely deployed primitives (like encryption and anonymous communications) cannot be relied upon to solve many, or even most, IR-based privacy problems. Following this, the second half-hour will be devoted to formally defining PIR as a cryptographic primitive, using the so-called "trivial PIR" protocol as an ideal (from a privacy perspective) yet impractical reference against which to base the definitions. Throughout the development of formal PIR definitions, participants will learn about some of the fundamental possibility and impossibility results these definitions imply. We will also take this opportunity to clarify the relationships PIR has to oblivious transfer (OT), oblivious RAM (ORAM), and secure multiparty computation (MPC).

The second hour will consist of a discussion about all of the major "flavours" of PIR in the research literature, including information-theoretic PIR (IT-PIR), computational PIR (C-PIR), function secret sharing-based PIR (FSS-PIR), anonymity-based PIR (A-PIR), trusted hardware-based PIR (TH-PIR), and various hybrids thereof. Throughout this discussion, participants will learn about the high-level idea underlying each flavour of PIR as well as their inherent strengths and weaknesses. In addition, we will walk through low-level details for a handful of representative PIR protocols.

The final hour will focus on a hodge-podge of practical considerations like Byzantine robustness, techniques for "batching" queries or batch-coding databases, how to realize expressive query types (e.g., keyword-, SQL-, and index-based PIR queries) or advanced functionality (e.g., ACLs and pricing) atop basic PIR, and open-source implementations.

INTENDED AUDIENCE

This tutorial is intended for a broad audience, including researchers and practitioners from academia, government, and industry. The material covered focuses primarily on technical aspects of PIR and will be most accessible to computer scientists and software developers—the tutorial will not address legal, ethical, sociological, or economic considerations; nonetheless, social scientists and policymakers are welcome and encouraged to participate.

Prerequisite knowledge: This is an *introductory level* tutorial and will be accessible to anyone comfortable with college-level mathematics (specifically, basic linear algebra and some elementary probability and number theory). It does not assume any prior knowledge about PIR or other advanced cryptographic primitives, although participants having some familiarity with cryptographic definitions and hardness assumptions will find a few of the "deep-dive" topics easier to grok.

REFERENCES

[1] Elette Boyle, Niv Gilboa, and Yuval Ishai. Function secret sharing. In *Advances in Cryptology: Proceedings of EUROCRYPT 2015 (Part II)*, volume 9057 of *LNCS*, pages 337–367, Sofia, Bulgaria (April 2015).

[2] Benny Chor, Niv Gilboa, and Moni Naor. Private information retrieval by keywords. Technical Report CS 0917, Technion-Israel Institute of Technology, Haifa, Israel (February 1997).

[3] Benny Chor, Oded Goldreich, Eyal Kushilevitz, and Madhu Sudan. Private information retrieval. In *Proceedings of FOCS 1995*, pages 41–50, Milwaukee, WI, USA (October 1995).

[4] Ian Goldberg. Improving the robustness of private information retrieval. In *Proceedings of IEEE S&P 2007*, pages 131–148, Oakland, CA, USA (May 2007).

[5] Syed Mahbub Hafiz and Ryan Henry. Querying for queries: Indexes of queries for efficient and expressive IT-PIR (October–November 2017).

[6] Yuval Ishai, Eyal Kushilevitz, Rafail Ostrovsky, and Amit Sahai. Cryptography from anonymity. In *Proceedings of FOCS 2006*, pages 239–248, Berkeley, CA, USA (October 2006).

[7] Eyal Kushilevitz and Rafail Ostrovsky. Replication is not needed: Single database, computationally-private information retrieval. In *Proceedings of FOCS 1997*, pages 364–373, Miami Beach, FL, USA (October 1997).

[8] Femi G. Olumofin and Ian Goldberg. Privacy-preserving queries over relational databases. In *Proceedings of PETS 2010*, volume 6205 of *LNCS*, pages 75–92, Berlin, Germany (July 2010).

[9] Nihar B. Shah, K. V. Rashmi, and Kannan Ramchandran. One extra bit of download ensures perfectly private information retrieval. In *Proceedings of ISIT 2014*, pages 856–860, Honolulu, HI, USA (June–July 2014).

[10] Raphael R. Toledo, George Danezis, and Ian Goldberg. Lower-cost ϵ-private information retrieval. In *Proceedings on Privacy Enhancing Technologies (PoPETs)*, volume 2016(4), pages 184–201, Darmstadt, Germany (October 2016).

[11] Frank Wang, Catherine Yun, Shafi Goldwasser, Vinod Vaikuntanathan, and Matei Zaharia. Splinter: Practical private queries on public data. In *Proceedings of NSDI 2017*, pages 299–313, Boston, MA, USA (March 2017).

[12] Peter Williams and Radu Sion. Usable PIR. In *Proceedings of NDSS 2008*, San Diego, CA, USA (February 2008).

BIOGRAPHICAL SKETCH

Ryan Henry is an assistant professor in the computer science department at Indiana University in Bloomington, Indiana. His research explores the systems challenges of applied cryptography, with an emphasis on using cryptography to build secure systems that preserve the privacy of their users. In addition to designing and analyzing privacy-enhancing systems, Professor Henry is interested in practical matters like implementing and working toward the deployment of such systems, as well as more theoretical matters like devising number-theoretic attacks against non-standard cryptographic assumptions and developing new models and theories to understand just how efficient "heavy-weight" cryptographic primitives can be. He received his MMath (2010) and Ph.D. (2014) from the University of Waterloo, where he held a Vanier Canada Graduate Scholarship (Vanier CGS), the most prestigious graduate scholarship in Canada. He has published several papers on PIR at top research venues (e.g., CCS, NDSS, and PETS), is a contributor to Percy++ (an open-source implementation of PIR protocols in C++), and two of his three active NSF grants heavily involve PIR research.

Acknowledgement: This material is based upon work supported by the National Science Foundation under Grant No. 1718475.

CCS'17 Tutorial Abstract / SGX Security and Privacy

Taesoo Kim   Zhiqiang Lin[†]   Chia-che Tsai[‡]

Georgia Institute of Technology   The University of Texas at Dallas[†]   Stony Brook University & UC Berkeley[‡]

ABSTRACT

In this tutorial, we will first introduce the basic concepts of Intel SGX, its development workflows, potential applications and performance characteristics. Then, we will explain known security concerns, including cache/branch side-channel attacks and memory safety issues, and corresponding defenses with various working demos. Last but not least, we will introduce various ways to quickly start writing SGX applications, especially by utilizing library OSes or thin shielding layers; we will explain the pros and cons of each approach in terms of security and usability.

CCS CONCEPTS

• **Security and privacy** → Systems security; Security in hardware;

KEYWORDS

Intel SGX; TEE; Library OS

1 INTRODUCTION

The Intel Software Guard Extensions (SGX)—a game-changing feature introduced in the recent Intel Skylake CPU—is a new technology likely to make secure and trustworthy computing in a hostile environment practical. At a high level, SGX consists of a set of new instructions that can be used to create secure regions (i.e., enclaves) to defeat attacks that aim to steal or tamper with the data within an enclave. Without a doubt, we expect that SGX will allow developers to protect sensitive code and data from unauthorized access or modification by software running at higher privilege levels such as an OS or a hypervisor.

However, SGX is merely a set of instructions; it lacks support from the OS and libraries. These deficiencies allow programmers to easily introduce naive yet preventable bugs that often lead to critical security holes in an enclave program [2]. Further, designing a correct and secure SGX infrastructure is also far from straightforward; enclave programs rely on the support of an underlying OS, but their security models exclude the OS from the TCB. This unconventional dependency makes various attack vectors, which are often considered impractical in a traditional setting, immediate and practical, especially in a cloud environment.

In this tutorial, we will first provide the basics of Intel SGX, covering workflows, potential applications and performance characteristics. Then, we will explain its security concerns, including cache/branch side-channel attacks [3], controlled-channel attacks [8], and traditional memory safety issues [2, 4], and potential defenses [5] with various demos. Last but not least, we will introduce various ways to quickly start writing SGX applications on Linux, especially by utilizing library OSes [7] or thin shielding layers [1, 6]; we will explain the pros and cons of each approach in terms of security and usability.

REFERENCES

[1] ARNAUTOX, S., TARCH, B., GREGOR, F., KNAUTH, T., MARTIN, A., PRIEBE, C., LIND, J., MUTHUKUMARAN, D., O'KEEFFE, D., STILLWELL, M. L., GOLTZSCHE, D., EYERS, D., KAPITZA, R., PIETZUCH, P., AND FETZER, C. SCONE: Secure Linux containers with Intel SGX. In *Proceedings of the 12th USENIX Symposium on Operating Systems Design and Implementation (OSDI)* (Savannah, GA, Nov. 2016).

[2] LEE, J., JANG, J., JANG, Y., KWAK, N., CHOI, Y., CHOI, C., KIM, T., PEINADO, M., AND KANG, B. B. Hacking in Darkness: Return-oriented Programming against Secure Enclaves. In *Proceedings of the 26th USENIX Security Symposium (Security)* (Vancouver, Canada, Aug. 2017).

[3] LEE, S., SHIH, M.-W., GERA, P., KIM, T., KIM, H., AND PEINADO, M. Inferring Fine-grained Control Flow Inside SGX Enclaves with Branch Shadowing. In *Proceedings of the 26th USENIX Security Symposium (Security)* (Vancouver, Canada, Aug. 2017).

[4] SEO, J., LEE, B., KIM, S., SHIH, M.-W., SHIN, I., HAN, D., AND KIM, T. SGX-Shield: Enabling Address Space Layout Randomization for SGX Programs. In *Proceedings of the 2017 Annual Network and Distributed System Security Symposium (NDSS)* (San Diego, CA, Feb. 2017).

[5] SHIH, M.-W., LEE, S., KIM, T., AND PEINADO, M. T-SGX: Eradicating Controlled-Channel Attacks Against Enclave Programs. In *Proceedings of the 2017 Annual Network and Distributed System Security Symposium (NDSS)* (San Diego, CA, Feb. 2017).

[6] SHINDE, S., TIEN, D. L., TOPLE, S., AND SAXENA, P. Panoply: Low-TCB Linux applications with SGX enclaves. In *Proceedings of the 2017 Annual Network and Distributed System Security Symposium (NDSS)* (San Diego, CA, Feb. 2017).

[7] TSAI, C.-C., PORTER, D. E., AND VIJ, M. Graphene-SGX: A practical library OS for unmodified applications on SGX. In *Proceedings of the 2017 USENIX Annual Technical Conference (ATC)* (Santa Clara, CA, July 2017).

[8] XU, Y., CUI, W., AND PEINADO, M. Controlled-channel attacks: Deterministic side channels for untrusted operating systems. In *Proceedings of the 36th IEEE Symposium on Security and Privacy (Oakland)* (San Jose, CA, May 2015).

Taesoo Kim. is an Assistant Professor in the School Computer Science at Georgia Tech. He also serves as the director of the Georgia Tech Systems Software and Security Center (GTS3). He is interested in building a system that has underline principles for why it should be secure. Those principles include the design of a system, analysis of its implementation, and clear separation of trusted components. His thesis work, in particular, focused on detecting and recovering from attacks on computer systems. He holds a BS from KAIST (2009), a SM (2011) and a Ph.D. (2014) from MIT in CS.

CCS '17, October 30-November 3, 2017, Dallas, TX, USA
© 2017 Copyright held by the owner/author(s).
ACM ISBN 978-1-4503-4946-8/17/10.
https://doi.org/10.1145/3133956.3136068

Zhiqiang Lin. is an Associate Professor of Computer Science at The University of Texas at Dallas. He earned his PhD from Computer Science Department at Purdue University in 2011. His primary research interests are systems and software security, with an emphasis on developing program analysis techniques and applying them to secure both application programs including mobile apps and the underlying system software such as Operating Systems and hypervisors. Dr. Lin is a recipient of the NSF CAREER Award and the AFOSR Young Investigator Award.

Chia-Che Tsai. is a PhD candidate at Stony Brook University, and will soon join the RISE Lab at UC Berkeley as a postdoc researcher. He is also joining the Computer Science and Engineering department of Texas A&M University in Fall 2018 as a faculty. He is interested in building OSes and runtimes with a balance between usability, security, and performance. He is the main contributor to the Graphene library OS, an open-source framework for reusing unmodified Linux applications on Intel SGX and other various host options.

Cliptography: Post-Snowden Cryptography

Qiang Tang
New Jersey Institute of Technology
qiang@njit.edu

Moti Yung
Snap. Inc, & Columbia University
moti@cs.columbia.edu

ABSTRACT

This tutorial covers a systematic overview of *kleptography*: stealing information subliminally from black-box cryptographic implementations; and *cliptography*: defending mechanisms that clip the power of kleptographic attacks via specification re-designs (without altering the underlying algorithms).

Despite the laudatory history of development of modern cryptography, applying cryptographic tools to reliably provide security and privacy in practice is notoriously difficult. One fundamental practical challenge, guaranteeing security and privacy without explicit trust in the algorithms and implementations that underlie basic security infrastructure, remains. While the dangers of entertaining adversarial implementation of cryptographic primitives seem obvious, the ramifications of such attacks are surprisingly dire: it turns out that – in wide generality – adversarial implementations of cryptographic (both deterministic and randomized) algorithms may leak private information while producing output that is statistically indistinguishable from that of a faithful implementation. Such attacks were formally studied in Kleptography.

Snowden revelations has shown us how security and privacy can be lost at a very large scale even when traditional cryptography seems to be used to protect Internet communication, when Kleptography was not taken into consideration.

We first explain how the above-mentioned Kleptographic attacks can be carried out in various settings. We then introduce several simple but rigorous immunizing strategies that were inspired by folklore practical wisdoms to protect different algorithms from implementation subversion. Those strategies can be applied to ensure security of most of the fundamental cryptographic primitives such as PRG, digital signatures, public key encryptions against kleptographic attacks when they are implemented accordingly. Our new design principles may suggest new standardization methods that help reducing the threats of subverted implementation. We also hope our tutorial to stimulate a community-wise efforts to further tackle the fundamental challenge mentioned at the beginning.

CCS CONCEPTS

• **Security and privacy** → **Cryptography**;

KEYWORDS

Kleptography, Cliptography, Cryptography, Backdoor resistance, Implementation subversion, Steganography

CCS '17, October 30-November 3, 2017, Dallas, TX, USA
© 2017 Copyright held by the owner/author(s).
ACM ISBN 978-1-4503-4946-8/17/10.
https://doi.org/10.1145/3133956.3136065

1 INTRODUCTION

In 1996, Young and Yung introduced the concept of *kleptography*, the study of cryptographic attacks in the setting where the fundamental cryptographic algorithms themselves are subject to adversarial subversion [13, 14]. Recent events have created a renewed urgency around the study of security in the kleptographic setting. In September 2013, the New York Times [10] reported the existence of a secret National Security Agency SIGINT Enabling Project designed to "make [systems] exploitable through SIGINT collection" by inserting vulnerabilities, collecting target network data, and influencing policies, standards and specifications for commercial public-key technologies. Beyond the immediate privacy concerns created by this activity, these efforts raise fears that cryptographic "backdoors" might be exploited by unauthorized parties. Indeed, there exists circumstantial evidence that this may have happened: In December 2015, Juniper Networks published a security advisory announcing that an undocumented NSA-designed random number generator within NetScreen Virtual Private Networking (VPN) devices had been modified by a state-sponsored attacker. This sophisticated modification allowed for passive decryption of all VPN connections terminated by a NetScreen device [3, 15].

The existence of well-funded kleptographic programs harms Internet security by reducing trust in cryptographic systems. However, this concern pales in comparison to the possibility that kleptographic efforts will be widely adopted and re-purposed by other threat actors, potentially rendering much of our infrastructure nonviable. In the context of cryptography, the technical ramifications of algorithm subversion are particularly concerning: this is because—in wide generality—*adversarial implementations of cryptographic algorithms may leak private information while producing output that is statistically and computationally indistinguishable from that of a faithful implementation* [1, 2, 7, 13]. This has implications for both cryptographic security and user privacy in general. Identifying these vulnerabilities and developing techniques to mitigate them has become a priority for the applied cryptographic research community [3–6, 8–12].

The goal of this tutorial is to give the audience a systematic overview of the kleptographic attacks, and more importantly, how recent progress of cliptography may provide robust security of cryptographic tools in the post-Snowden era. As the inventor of kleptography, Dr. Yung presents the evolution of kleptography from both theoretica perspectives and real-world attack examples. As the main contributor of cliptography, Dr. Tang explains how to leverage conventional security wisdom, such as nothing-up-my-sleeve numbers, and modular design principle, to re-consider the specification design of cryptographic tools to provide rigorous protection against kleptographic attacks. As a new direction, the tutorial covers both theoretical and practical open problems in the field, and also introduce some other security problems that are motivated by the new methodologies we have developed along the way. The outline of the tutorial is as follows:

- Introduction to Kleptography, including subliminal channel attacks in subverted algorithms, with real-world examples.
- Formal definitional framework of Cliptography.
- Mitigating the damage of subliminal channel attacks, using PRG as an example; defending mechanism that destroys the subliminal channel in subverted randomized algorithm, using encryption as an example; and self-correcting random oracles (hash functions) and its application to subversion-resistant digital signatures.
- Major remaining obstacles, important future directions in the field, and open problems motivated by our framework in related areas.

2 INTENDED AUDIENCES

All security researchers from academia, standardization organization and industry are welcome. We aim to provide (1.) introduction of Kleptography and Cliptography as a scientific subjects to academic researchers and discussion of important theoretical and practical questions; (2.) suggestions of specification design to standardization agencies that may alleviate subversion threats and such kind of undetectable attacks in deployed cryptographic tools; (3.) ideas for industry researchers, whose companies export or sell devices that may not be trusted, to re-consider the architecture of their device to convince the customers that their products can be used as faithfully implemented.

3 PREREQUISITE KNOWLEDGE

Basic knowledge about security notions of the standard cryptographic tools are helpful. Advanced knowledge of steganography, randomness extractor or self-correcting programs are not required, they will be explained in an intuitive level and the tutorial is mostly self-contained.

4 SPEAKER BIOGRAPHY

Qiang Tang is an assistant professor at the Department of Computer Science at New Jersey Institute of Technology (NJIT). Before joining NJIT, he was a postdoctoral associate at Cornell University and was also affiliated with the Initiative of CryptoCurrency and Contracts (IC3). He obtained his Ph.D from the University of Connecticut with a Taylor Booth Scholarship. He also held visiting researcher positions at various institutes including the University of Wisconsin, Madison, NTT Research, Tokyo and the University of Athens, Greece. His research interests are applied and theoretical cryptography, privacy and computer security. In particular, in accountability, post-Snowden cryptography, and blockchain technology. He has made contributions on using cryptocurrency to deter copyright infringement and to enforce key management policy, re-designing cryptographic specifications to defend against implementation subversion, as well as information theoretical security.

Moti Yung is a computer scientist whose main interests are in cryptography, security, and privacy. He is currently with Snap. Inc, and has been holding adjunct professor appointments at Columbia University where he has co-advised several Ph.D. students. He was

with IBM, CertCo, RSA Lab, and Google. Dr. Yung made extensive contributions on the foundation of modern cryptography as well as innovative secure industrial technology within actual large scale systems, including the Greek National Lottery system, the security and privacy aspects of Google's global systems such as the Ad Exchange (ADX) and the ephemeral ID efforts for Google's BLE beacons, and Snap's "my eyes only memories" cloud security. Also, his invention of Cryptovirology (including Kleptography) envisioned the explosion of ransomware, and algorithm subversion on crypto systems and standards such as the Dual_EC DRNG subversion. Dr. Yung has been giving distinguished and keynote speeches at numerous top-tier crypto/security/distributed computing conferences. He is a Fellow of ACM, IEEE, IACR, and EATCS.

REFERENCES

[1] Mihir Bellare, Joseph Jaeger, and Daniel Kane. 2015. Mass-surveillance without the State: Strongly Undetectable Algorithm-Substitution Attacks. In *ACM CCS 15*, Indrajit Ray, Ninghui Li, and Christopher Kruegel: (Eds.). ACM Press, 1431–1440.
[2] Mihir Bellare, Kenneth G. Paterson, and Phillip Rogaway. 2014. Security of Symmetric Encryption against Mass Surveillance. In *CRYPTO 2014, Part I (LNCS)*, Juan A. Garay and Rosario Gennaro (Eds.), Vol. 8616. Springer, Heidelberg, 1–19. https://doi.org/10.1007/978-3-662-44371-2_1
[3] Stephen Checkoway, Shaanan Cohney, Christina Garman, Matthew Green, Nadia Heninger, Jacob Maskiewicz, Eric Rescorla, Hovav Shacham, and Ralf-Philipp Weinmann. 2016. A Systematic Analysis of the Juniper Dual EC Incident. In *Proceedings of ACM CCS 2016*. Full version available at http://eprint.iacr.org/2016/376.
[4] Stephen Checkoway, Ruben Niederhagen, Adam Everspaugh, Matthew Green, Tanja Lange, Thomas Ristenpart, Daniel J. Bernstein, Jake Maskiewicz, Hovav Shacham, and Matthew Fredrikson. 2014. On the Practical Exploitability of Dual EC in TLS Implementations. In *Proceedings of the 23rd USENIX Security Symposium, San Diego, CA, USA, August 20-22, 2014*. 319–335.
[5] Jean Paul Degabriele, Kenneth G. Paterson, Jacob C. N. Schuldt, and Joanne Woodage. 2016. Backdoors in Pseudorandom Number Generators: Possibility and Impossibility Results. In *CRYPTO 2016, Part I (LNCS)*, Matthew Robshaw and Jonathan Katz (Eds.), Vol. 9814. Springer, Heidelberg, 403–432. https://doi.org/10.1007/978-3-662-53018-4_15
[6] Yevgeniy Dodis, Ilya Mironov, and Noah Stephens-Davidowitz. 2016. Message Transmission with Reverse Firewalls—Secure Communication on Corrupted Machines. In *CRYPTO 2016, Part I (LNCS)*, Matthew Robshaw and Jonathan Katz (Eds.), Vol. 9814. Springer, Heidelberg, 341–372. https://doi.org/10.1007/978-3-662-53018-4_13
[7] Nicholas J. Hopper, John Langford, and Luis von Ahn. 2002. Provably Secure Steganography. In *CRYPTO 2002 (LNCS)*, Moti Yung (Ed.), Vol. 2442. Springer, Heidelberg, 77–92.
[8] Jeff Larson, Nicole Perlroth, and Scott Shane. 2013. Revealed: The NSA's secret campaign to crack, undermine internet security. Pro-Publica. (2013). http://www.propublica.org/article/the-nsas-secret-campaign-to-crack-undermine-internet-encryption.
[9] Ilya Mironov and Noah Stephens-Davidowitz. 2015. Cryptographic Reverse Firewalls. In *EUROCRYPT 2015, Part II (LNCS)*, Elisabeth Oswald and Marc Fischlin (Eds.), Vol. 9057. Springer, Heidelberg, 657–686. https://doi.org/10.1007/978-3-662-46803-6_22
[10] Nicole Perlroth, Jeff Larson, and Scott Shane. 2013. N.S.A. able to foil basic safeguards of privacy on web. The New York Times. (2013). http://www.nytimes.com/2013/09/06/us/nsa-foils-much-internet-encryption.html.
[11] Alexander Russell, Qiang Tang, Moti Yung, and Hong-Sheng Zhou. 2016. Cliptography: Clipping the Power of Kleptographic Attacks. In *ASIACRYPT 2016, Part II (LNCS)*, Jung Hee Cheon and Tsuyoshi Takagi (Eds.), Vol. 10032. Springer, Heidelberg, 34–64. https://doi.org/10.1007/978-3-662-53890-6_2
[12] Alexander Russell, Qiang Tang, Moti Yung, and Hong-Sheng Zhou. 2017. Generic Semantic Security against a Kleptographic Adversary. In *Proceedings of the 24nd ACM SIGSAC Conference on Computer and Communications Security, Dallas, TX, USA, October 30-November 4, 2017*.
[13] Adam Young and Moti Yung. 1996. The Dark Side of "Black-Box" Cryptography, or: Should We Trust Capstone?. In *CRYPTO'96 (LNCS)*, Neal Koblitz (Ed.), Vol. 1109. Springer, Heidelberg, 89–103.
[14] Adam Young and Moti Yung. 1997. Kleptography: Using Cryptography Against Cryptography. In *EUROCRYPT'97 (LNCS)*, Walter Fumy (Ed.), Vol. 1233. Springer, Heidelberg, 62–74.
[15] Kim Zetter. 2015. Secret Code Found in Juniper's Firewalls Shows Risk of Government Backdoors. (December 2015).

Cache Side Channels:
State of the Art and Research Opportunities

Yinqian Zhang
Department of Computer Science and Engineering
The Ohio Sate University
yinqian@cse.ohio-state.edu

ABSTRACT

Cache side channels are a type of attack vectors through which an adversary infers secret information of a running program by observing its use of CPU caches or other caching hardware. The study of cache side channels, particularly access-driven cache side channels, is gaining traction among security researchers in recent years. A large volume of papers on cache side-channel attacks or defenses is being published in both security and computer architecture conferences each year. However, due to the diversity of the research goals, methods, and perspectives, it becomes much harder for researchers new to this field to keep track of the frontiers of this research topic. As such, in this tutorial, we will provide a high-level overview of the studies of cache side channels to help other security researchers to comprehend the state of the art of this research area, and to identify research problems that have not been addressed by the community. We also hope to bridge the gaps between the security community and the computer architecture community on this specific research topic by summarizing research papers from both sides.

ACM Reference Format:
Yinqian Zhang. 2017. Cache Side Channels: State of the Art and Research Opportunities. In *Proceedings of CCS '17*. ACM, New York, NY, USA, 3 pages. https://doi.org/10.1145/3133956.3136064

1 INTRODUCTION

Cache side channels are a type of attack vectors through which an adversary infers secret information of a running program by observing its use of CPU caches or other caching hardware. Attacks that exfiltrate sensitive data from CPU caches are called "side"-channel attacks, because the cache data cannot be read by the adversary directly, and the leakage is usually from indirect, "side" information. Prior studies have explored three types of cache side channels: time-driven, access-driven and trace-driven. They differ in their threat models. Time-driven attacks assume only the overall execution time of certain operation is observable by the adversary; trace-driven attacks assume the adversary is able to observe the power consumption traces of the execution; and access-driven attacks assume the adversary has logical access to a cache shared

with the victim and infers the victim program's execution through its own use of the shared cache.

This tutorial focuses on access-driven cache side-channel attacks. These attacks have been studied in the past 10 years in multiple contexts, most noticeably in desktop computers [1, 2, 20, 21, 21, 23, 40, 42, 44, 49], cloud servers and virtual machines [6, 25, 37, 61, 62, 67, 68], mobile devices [17, 33, 65], browsers [7, 41], and SGX-enabled Intel processors [8, 22, 47], where CPU caches are shared between mutually-distrusting software components. The exploited caches include not only CPU caches (*e.g.*, L1 data caches and per-core L2 unified caches [21, 23, 40, 42, 44, 49], instruction caches [1, 2, 67], and inclusive LLCs [6, 20, 24, 25, 27, 33, 37, 41, 61, 62, 65, 68]), but also hardware components that temporarily store data for speeding up the computation, such as TLBs [23], and Branch Prediction Units [3, 4, 16, 31]. Attacks on different micro-architectures, such as x86 and ARM, also differ because many of the characteristics of the attacks are CPU specific. Even distinct processors from the same vendors, such as Intel, may render cache side-channel attacks different. Targets of these attacks include cryptographic systems (*e.g.*, cryptographic keys), randomness in computer systems (*e.g.*, address space layout), user privacy (*e.g.*, passwords, private activities), *etc*.

Solutions to cache side channels are typically categorized into three types. First, some solutions are built into the victim programs. They are typically called software-based solutions. Prominent approaches include software transformation [10, 11, 18, 39, 46] and vulnerability detection [15, 53, 59]. Second, some solutions requires system software modifications. Hence they are called system-based defenses. Some of these work proposed to partition the shared caches [29, 35, 45, 48, 70], to eliminate fine-grained `rdtsc` instructions [52], to enforce coarse-grained context switches [50], to enforce deterministic execution [5, 32], to inject noise into the side channels [69], or to detect side-channel attacks at runtime using performance counters [12, 63]. Third, some solutions require new hardware designs, thus are called hardware-based defenses. Most prominent ideas are dynamic cache partitioning [14, 30, 43, 55, 57], cache allocation randomization [28, 36, 56, 57], coarse-grained time keeping [38], oblivious memory traces [34], relaxed inclusion caches [26]. These hardware solutions are typically effective, but are limited in that the time window required to have major processor vendors to incorporate them in commercial hardware is very long.

2 PURPOSES OF THE TUTORIAL

The study of cache side channels, particularly access-driven cache side channels, is gaining traction among security researchers in recent years. A large volume of papers on cache side-channel attacks or defenses is being published in both security and computer architecture conferences each year. Although these papers are all related to cache side channels, their research angles vary significantly: Among studies that develop new attacks, some explore new attack vectors (*i.e.*, new hardware resources that are shared and exploitable as side channels), some report new attack methods (*e.g.*, PRIME+ABORT [13], FLUSH+FLUSH [19]), some improve existing attacks under different micro-architectures (*e.g.*, ARM [17, 33, 65] vs. x86), some demonstrate attacks in new environments (*e.g.*, browsers [7, 41], Intel SGX [8, 22, 47]), and others exploit known methods and vectors against new targets (*e.g.*, userspace ASLR or kernel ASLR). Among the defense papers, the security community and the computer architecture community usually take different perspectives. The computer architecture community seeks for hardware solutions, or a combination of hardware and software solutions to address the issues. In contrast, the security community either enhances existing software systems to defeat side-channel attacks, by leveraging virtualization techniques or hardware features that are available on commodity processors, or transforms software applications to mitigate side-channel vulnerabilities. A recently emerging direction, however, is to conduct static or dynamic analysis on the software to detect vulnerabilities.

However, as the size of the literature grows, it becomes much harder to keep track of the frontiers of this research topic. Therefore, researchers who are new to the field will find it even more challenging to comprehend the state of the art of this research area, or to identify research problems that have not been addressed by the community. Therefore, in this tutorial, we will provide a high-level overview of the studies of cache side channels to help researchers to bootstrap their research.

The second purpose of this tutorial is to bridge the gap between the security community and the architecture community in the area of cache side channels. Cache side-channel research is an interdiscipline topic that is of interest in both communities. However, because the research angles from these two groups of researchers are different, cross-domain understanding and references are insufficient. Therefore, this tutorial also aims to serve as a bridge between the two communities and allow security researchers to learn more about the architecture side of the research.

Intended audience: The intended audience of this tutorial are security researchers with zero experience in cache side channels. It is expected that the audience have basic knowledge of computer architecture, operating systems and computer networking.

Duration: We expect the tutorial to last for 1.5 hours, with about 1 hour and 10 minutes for presentation and 20 minutes for questions.

3 SCOPE OF THE TUTORIAL

The tutorial will cover the following topics of cache side channels.

- *Background.* We will discuss the root causes of cache side channels, various attack vectors in computer micro-architectures, and basic methods to exploiting cache side channels for information extraction. We will try to make the description accessible to non-expert audience.

- *State of the arts.* We will guide the audience to review the literature of cache side-channel attacks and defenses. We will provide new perspectives to taxonomize related work in the field and discuss the state of the arts in each research category.

- *Research opportunities.* We will help the audience to identify key research problems in the field that have not been addressed, or inspire the audience to brainstorm opportunities to pursue innovation.

4 A SHORT BIO OF THE LECTURER

Dr. Yinqian Zhang is an assistant professor of the Department of Computer Science and Engineering at The Ohio State University. His research focuses on system security. His publication on side-channel attacks and defenses include those in the context of cloud computing [51, 60, 63, 64, 66–70], smartphones [58, 65], and Intel SGX [9, 54, 59]. Before joining OSU, Dr. Zhang receives his Ph.D. from University of North Carolina at Chapel Hill from Prof. Michael K. Reiter's research group.

Acknowledgement: This tutorial was supported in part by NSF 1566444.

REFERENCES

[1] Onur Aciiçmez. 2007. Yet another MicroArchitectural Attack: exploiting I-Cache. In *ACM workshop on Computer security architecture*.

[2] Onur Aciiçmez, Billy Bob Brumley, and Philipp Grabher. 2010. New results on instruction cache attacks. In *12th international conference on Cryptographic hardware and embedded systems*.

[3] Onur Aciiçmez, Shay Gueron, and Jean-Pierre Seifert. 2007. New branch prediction vulnerabilities in openSSL and necessary software countermeasures. In *11th international conference on Cryptography and coding*.

[4] Onur Aciiçmez, Çetin Kaya Koç, and Jean-Pierre Seifert. 2007. Predicting secret keys via branch prediction. In *7th Cryptographers' track at the RSA conference on Topics in Cryptology*.

[5] Amittai Aviram, Sen Hu, Bryan Ford, and Ramakrishna Gummadi. 2010. Determinating timing channels in compute clouds. In *ACM Workshop on Cloud Computing Security*.

[6] Naomi Benger, Joop van de Pol, Nigel P. Smart, and Yuval Yarom. 2014. "Ooh Aah... Just a Little Bit": A small amount of side channel can go a long way. In *Cryptology ePrint Archive*.

[7] Erik Bosman, Kaveh Razavi, Herbert Bos, and Cristiano Giuffrida. 2016. Dedup Est Machina: Memory Deduplication as an Advanced Exploitation Vector. In *IEEE Symposium on Security and Privacy*.

[8] Ferdinand Brasser, Urs Müller, Alexandra Dmitrienko, Kari Kostiainen, Srdjan Capkun, and Ahmad-Reza Sadeghi. 2017. Software Grand Exposure: SGX Cache Attacks Are Practical. In *11th USENIX Workshop on Offensive Technologies*.

[9] Sanchuan Chen, Xiaokuan Zhang, Michael Reiter, and Yinqian Zhang. 2017. Detecting Privileged Side-Channel Attacks in Shielded Execution with Déjà Vu. In *12th ACM Symposium on Information, Computer and Communications Security*.

[10] B. Coppens, I. Verbauwhede, K. De Bosschere, and B. De Sutter. 2009. Practical Mitigations for Timing-Based Side-Channel Attacks on Modern x86 Processors. In *30th IEEE Symposium on Security and Privacy*.

[11] S. Crane, A. Homescu, S. Brunthaler, P. Larsen, and M. Franz. 2015. Thwarting cache side-channel attacks through dynamic software diversity. In *ISOC Network and Distributed System Security Symposium*.

[12] John Demme, Matthew Maycock, Jared Schmitz, Adrian Tang, Adam Waksman, Simha Sethumadhavan, and Salvatore Stolfo. 2013. On the Feasibility of Online Malware Detection with Performance Counters. In *ACM Intl. Symp. on Computer Architecture*.

[13] Craig Disselkoen, David Kohlbrenner, Leo Porter, and Dean Tullsen. 2017. Prime+Abort: A Timer-Free High-Precision L3 Cache Attack using Intel TSX. In *26th USENIX Security Symposium*. USENIX Association.

[14] Leonid Domnitser, Aamer Jaleel, Jason Loew, Nael Abu-Ghazaleh, and Dmitry Ponomarev. 2012. Non-monopolizable caches: Low-complexity mitigation of cache side channel attacks. *ACM Trans. Archit. Code Optim.* 8, 4 (Jan. 2012).

[15] Goran Doychev, Dominik Feld, Boris Köpf, Laurent Mauborgne, and Jan Reineke. 2013. CacheAudit: A tool for the static analysis of cache side channels. In *22st USENIX Security Symposium*.

[16] Dmitry Evtyushkin, Dmitry Ponomarev, and Nael Abu-Ghazaleh. 2016. Jump over ASLR: Attacking branch predictors to bypass ASLR. In *49th Annual IEEE/ACM International Symposium on Microarchitecture*.

[17] Marc Green, Leandro Rodrigues-Lima, Andreas Zankl, Gorka Irazoqui, Johann Heyszl, and Thomas Eisenbarth. 2017. AutoLock: Why Cache Attacks on ARM Are Harder Than You Think. In *26th USENIX Security Symposium*.

[18] Daniel Gruss, Julian Lettner, Felix Schuster, Olya Ohrimenko, Istvan Haller, and Manuel Costa. 2017. Strong and Efficient Cache Side-Channel Protection using Hardware Transactional Memory. In *26th USENIX Security Symposium*.

[19] Daniel Gruss, Clémentine Maurice, Klaus Wagner, and Stefan Mangard. 2016. *Flush+Flush: A Fast and Stealthy Cache Attack*. Springer International Publishing.

[20] Daniel Gruss, Raphael Spreitzer, and Stefan Mangard. 2015. Cache Template Attacks: Automating Attacks on Inclusive Last-level Caches. In *24th USENIX Conference on Security Symposium*. USENIX Association.

[21] David Gullasch, Endre Bangerter, and Stephan Krenn. 2011. Cache games – Bringing access-based cache attacks on AES to practice. In *32nd IEEE Symposium on Security and Privacy*.

[22] Marcus Hähnel, Weidong Cui, and Marcus Peinado. 2017. High-Resolution Side Channels for Untrusted Operating Systems. In *2017 USENIX Annual Technical Conference*. USENIX Association.

[23] Ralf Hund, Carsten Willems, and Thorsten Holz. 2013. Practical Timing Side Channel Attacks Against Kernel Space ASLR. In *34th IEEE Symposium on Security and Privacy*.

[24] Mehmet Sinan Inci, Berk Gulmezoglu, Gorka Irazoqui, Thomas Eisenbarth, and Berk Sunar. 2015. Seriously, get off my cloud! Cross-VM RSA Key Recovery in a Public Cloud. Cryptology ePrint Archive. (2015).

[25] Gorka Irazoqui, Thomas Eisenbarth, and Berk Sunar. 2015. S$A: A Shared Cache Attack that Works Across Cores and Defies VM Sandboxing—and its Application to AES. In *IEEE Symposium on Security and Privacy*.

[26] Mehmet Kayaalp et al. 2017. RIC: Relaxed Inclusion Caches for Mitigating LLC Side-Channel Attacks. In *Design Automation Conference*.

[27] Mehmet Kayaalp, Nael Abu-Ghazaleh, Dmitry Ponomarev, and Aamer Jaleel. 2016. A High-resolution Side-channel Attack on Last-level Cache. In *53rd Annual Design Automation Conference*.

[28] G. Keramidas, A. Antonopoulos, D.N. Serpanos, and S. Kaxiras. 2008. Non deterministic caches: a simple and effective defense against side channel attacks. *Design Automation for Embedded Systems* 12 (2008), 221–230. Issue 3.

[29] T. Kim, M. Peinado, and G. Mainar-Ruiz. 2012. STEALTHMEM: system-level protection against cache-based side channel attacks in the cloud. In *21st USENIX Security Symposium*.

[30] Jingfei Kong, Onur Aciicmez, Jean-Pierre Seifert, and Huiyang Zhou. 2013. Architecting Against Software Cache-Based Side-Channel Attacks. *IEEE Trans. Comput.* 62, 7 (July 2013).

[31] Sangho Lee, Ming-Wei Shih, Prasun Gera, Taesoo Kim, Hyesoon Kim, and Marcus Peinado. 2017. Inferring Fine-grained Control Flow Inside SGX Enclaves with Branch Shadowing. In *26th USENIX Security Symposium*. USENIX Association.

[32] Peng Li, Debin Gao, and Michael K. Reiter. 2014. StopWatch: A Cloud Architecture for Timing Channel Mitigation. *ACM Trans. Inf. Syst. Secur.* 17, 2 (Nov. 2014).

[33] Moritz Lipp, Daniel Gruss, Raphael Spreitzer, Clémentine Maurice, and Stefan Mangard. 2016. ARMageddon: Cache Attacks on Mobile Devices. In *USENIX Security Symposium*.

[34] Chang Liu, Austin Harris, Martin Maas, Michael Hicks, Mohit Tiwari, and Elaine Shi. 2015. GhostRider: A Hardware-Software System for Memory Trace Oblivious Computation. In *20th International Conference on Architectural Support for Programming Languages and Operating Systems*. ACM.

[35] Fangfei Liu, Qian Ge, Yuval Yarom, Frank Mckeen, Carlos Rozas, Gernot Heiser, and Ruby B. Lee. 2016. CATalyst: Defeating Last-Level Cache Side Channel Attacks in Cloud Computing. In *22nd IEEE Symposium on High Performance Computer Architecture*.

[36] Fangfei Liu and Ruby B. Lee. 2014. Random Fill Cache Architecture. In *47th IEEE/ACM Symposium on Microarchitecture*.

[37] Fangfei Liu, Yuval Yarom, Qian Ge, Gernot Heiser, and Ruby B. Lee. 2015. Last-Level Cache Side-Channel Attacks are Practical. In *IEEE Symposium on Security and Privacy*.

[38] Robert Martin, John Demme, and Simha Sethumadhavan. 2012. TimeWarp: rethinking timekeeping and performance monitoring mechanisms to mitigate side-channel attacks. In *39th Annual International Symposium on Computer Architecture*.

[39] David Molnar, Matt Piotrowski, David Schultz, and David Wagner. 2005. The program counter security model: automatic detection and removal of control-flow side channel attacks. In *8th international conference on Information Security and Cryptology*.

[40] Michael Neve and Jean-Pierre Seifert. 2007. Advances on access-driven cache attacks on AES. In *13th international conference on Selected areas in cryptography*.

[41] Yossef Oren, Vasileios P. Kemerlis, Simha Sethumadhavan, and Angelos D. Keromytis. 2015. The Spy in the Sandbox: Practical Cache Attacks in JavaScript and Their Implications. In *22nd ACM SIGSAC Conference on Computer and Communications Security*.

[42] Dag Arne Osvik, Adi Shamir, and Eran Tromer. 2006. Cache attacks and countermeasures: the case of AES. In *6th Cryptographers' track at the RSA conference on Topics in Cryptology*.

[43] D. Page. 2005. Partitioned Cache Architecture as a Side-Channel Defence Mechanism. (2005). http://eprint.iacr.org/2005/280

[44] Colin Percival. 2005. Cache missing for fun and profit. In *2005 BSDCan*.

[45] Himanshu Raj, Ripal Nathuji, Abhishek Singh, and Paul England. 2009. Resource Management for Isolation Enhanced Cloud Services. In *ACM Cloud Computing Security Workshop*.

[46] Ashay Rane, Calvin Lin, and Mohit Tiwari. 2015. Raccoon: Closing Digital Side-Channels through Obfuscated Execution. In *24th USENIX Security Symposium*. USENIX Association.

[47] Michael Schwarz, Samuel Weiser, Daniel Gruss, Clémentine Maurice, and Stefan Mangard. 2017. *Malware Guard Extension: Using SGX to Conceal Cache Attacks*. Springer International Publishing.

[48] Jicheng Shi, Xiang Song, Haibo Chen, and Binyu Zang. 2011. Limiting cache-based side-channel in multi-tenant cloud using dynamic page coloring. In *41st International Conference on Dependable Systems and Networks Workshops*.

[49] Eran Tromer, Dag Arne Osvik, and Adi Shamir. 2010. Efficient Cache Attacks on AES, and Countermeasures. *J. Cryptol.* 23, 2 (Jan. 2010), 37–71.

[50] Venkatanathan Varadarajan, Thomas Ristenpart, and Michael Swift. 2014. Scheduler-based Defenses against Cross-VM Side-channels. In *23th USENIX Security Symposium*.

[51] Venkatanathan Varadarajan, Yinqian Zhang, Thomas Ristenpart, and Michael Swift. 2015. A Placement Vulnerability Study in Multi-Tenant Public Clouds. In *USENIX Security Symposium*.

[52] Bhanu C. Vattikonda, Sambit Das, and Hovav Shacham. 2011. Eliminating fine grained timers in Xen. In *3rd ACM Workshop on Cloud Computing Security*.

[53] Shuai Wang, Pei Wang, Xiao Liu, Danfeng Zhang, and Dinghao Wu. 2017. CacheD: Identifying Cache-Based Timing Channels in Production Software. In *26th USENIX Security Symposium*. USENIX Association.

[54] Wenhao Wang, Guoxing Chen, Xiaorui Pan, Yinqian Zhang, XiaoFeng Wang, Vincent Bindschaedler, Haixu Tang, and Carl A. Gunter. 2017. Leaky Cauldron on the Dark Land: Understanding Memory Side-Channel Hazards in SGX. In *ACM Conference on Computer and Communications Security*.

[55] Zhenghong Wang and Ruby B. Lee. 2006. Covert and Side Channels Due to Processor Architecture. In *22nd Annual Computer Security Applications Conference*.

[56] Zhenghong Wang and Ruby B. Lee. 2007. New cache designs for thwarting software cache-based side channel attacks. In *34th annual international symposium on Computer architecture*.

[57] Zhenghong Wang and Ruby B. Lee. 2008. A novel cache architecture with enhanced performance and security. In *41st annual IEEE/ACM International Symposium on Microarchitecture*.

[58] Qiuyu Xiao, Michael K. Reiter, and Yinqian Zhang. 2015. Mitigating storage side channels using statistical privacy mechanisms. In *22nd ACM Conference on Computer and Communications Security*.

[59] Yuan Xiao, Mengyuan Li, Sanchuan Chen, and Yinqian Zhang. 2017. Stacco: Differentially Analyzing Side-Channel Traces for Detecting SSL/TLS Vulnerabilities in Secure Enclaves. In *ACM Conference on Computer and Communications Security*.

[60] Yuan Xiao, Xiaokuan Zhang, Yinqian Zhang, and Radu Teodorescu. 2016. One Bit Flips, One Cloud Flops: Cross-VM Row Hammer Attacks and Privilege Escalation. In *USENIX Security Symposium*.

[61] Yuval Yarom and Naomi Benger. 2014. Recovering OpenSSL ECDSA Nonces Using the FLUSH+RELOAD Cache Side-channel Attack. In *Cryptology ePrint Archive*.

[62] Yuval Yarom and Katrina Falkner. 2014. FLUSH+RELOAD: A high resolution, low noise, L3 cache side-channel attack. In *23rd USENIX Security Symposium*. USENIX Association.

[63] Tianwei Zhang, Yinqian Zhang, and Ruby B. Lee. 2016. CloudRadar: A Real-Time Side-Channel Attack Detection System in Clouds. In *19th International Symposium on Research in Attacks, Intrusions and Defenses*.

[64] Tianwei Zhang, Yinqian Zhang, and Ruby B. Lee. 2017. DoS Attacks on Your Memory in Cloud. In *12th ACM on Asia Conference on Computer and Communications Security*. ACM, 253–265.

[65] Xiaokuan Zhang, Yuan Xiao, and Yinqian Zhang. 2016. Return-Oriented Flush-Reload Side Channels on ARM and Their Implications for Android Devices. In *ACM Conference on Computer and Communications Security*.

[66] Yinqian Zhang, Ari Juels, Alina Oprea, and Michael K. Reiter. 2011. Home-Alone: Co-residency Detection in the Cloud via Side-Channel Analysis. In *IEEE Symposium on Security and Privacy*.

[67] Yinqian Zhang, Ari Juels, Michael K. Reiter, and Thomas Ristenpart. 2012. Cross-VM Side Channels and Their Use to Extract Private Keys. In *ACM Conference on Computer and Communications Security*.

[68] Yinqian Zhang, Ari Juels, Michael K. Reiter, and Thomas Ristenpart. 2014. Cross-Tenant Side-Channel attacks in PaaS clouds. In *ACM Conference on Computer and Communications Security*.

[69] Yinqian Zhang and Michael K. Reiter. 2013. Düppel: retrofitting commodity operating systems to mitigate cache side channels in the cloud. In *ACM Conference on Computer and Communications Security*. 827–838.

[70] Ziqiao Zhou, Michael K. Reiter, and Yinqian Zhang. 2016. A Software Approach to Defeating Side Channels in Last-Level Caches. In *23rd ACM Conference on Computer and Communications Security*.

10th International Workshop on Artificial Intelligence and Security (AISec 2017)

Battista Biggio
University of Cagliari
battista.biggio@diee.unica.it

David Freeman
Facebook, Inc.
dfreeman@fb.com

Brad Miller
Google Inc.
bradmiller@google.com

Arunesh Sinha
University of Michigan
arunesh@umich.edu

KEYWORDS

Adversarial Learning, Secure Learning, Malware Detection

BACKGROUND

Artificial Intelligence (AI) and Machine Learning (ML) provide a set of useful analytic and decision-making techniques that are being leveraged by an ever-growing community of practitioners, including many whose applications have security-sensitive elements. However, while security researchers often utilize such techniques to address problems and AI/ML researchers develop techniques for Big Data analytics applications, neither community devotes much attention to the other. Within security research, AI/ML components are usually regarded as black-box solvers. Conversely, the learning community seldom considers the security/privacy implications entailed in the application of their algorithms when they are designing them. While these two communities generally focus on different directions, where these two fields do meet, interesting problems appear. Researchers working in this intersection have raised many novel questions for both communities and created a new branch of research known as secure learning. The AISec workshop has become the primary venue for this unique fusion of research.

In recent years, there has been an increase of activity within the AISec/secure learning community. There are several reasons for this surge. Firstly, machine learning, data mining, and other artificial intelligence technologies play a key role in extracting knowledge, situational awareness, and security intelligence from Big Data. Secondly, industry is increasingly exploring and deploying learning technologies to address Big Data problems for their customers. Finally, these trends are increasingly exposing companies and their customers/users to intelligent technologies. As a result, these learning technologies are being explored by researchers both as potential solutions to security/privacy problems and also

as a potential source of new vulnerabilities that need to be addressed. The AISec Workshop meets this need and serves as the sole long-running venue for this topic.

AISec, having been annually co-located with CCS for ten consecutive years, is the premier meeting place for researchers interested in the junction of security, privacy, AI, and machine learning. Its role as a venue has been to merge practical security problems with advances in AI and machine learning. In doing so, researchers also have been developing theory and analytics unique to this domain and have explored diverse topics such as learning in game-theoretic adversarial environments, privacy-preserving learning, and applications to spam and intrusion detection.

AISEC 2017

The tenth annual event in this series, AISec 2017 drew 36 submissions, of which eleven were selected for publication and presentation and approximately four were selected for presentation in a "lightning round." Paper topics included the following:

- **Malware and Intrusion Detection** including approaches to both evasion and improved classification and discovery.
- **Adversarial Learning** spanning evasive and causative attacks from both the attacker and defender perspectives.
- **ML-Powered Attacks** including techniques for defeating security challenges and CAPTCHAs.

The keynote address titled "Beyond Big Data: What Can We Learn from AI Models?" was given by Dr. Aylin Caliskan of Princeton University.

PROGRAM COMMITTEE

- Hyrum Anderson, Endgame, USA
- Sam Bretheim, Craigslist Inc., USA
- Michael Brückner, Amazon.com Inc., Germany
- Alvaro Cárdenas, University of Texas at Dallas, USA
- Nicholas Carlini, University of California, Berkeley, USA
- Clarence Chio, Kaitrust, USA
- Igino Corona, University of Cagliari, Italy
- Anupam Datta, Carnegie Mellon University, USA
- Milenko Drinic, Microsoft Corporation, USA

- Joseph Halpern, Cornell University, USA
- Alex Kantchelian, Google Inc., USA
- Davide Maiorca, University of Cagliari, Italy
- Pratyusa Manadhata, Hewlett Packard Labs, USA
- Patrick McDaniel, Pennsylvania State University, USA
- Katerina Mitrokotsa, Chalmers University, Sweden
- Luis Muñoz González, Imperial College, London, UK
- Michal Nánási, Facebook Inc., UK
- Blaine Nelson, Google, Inc., USA
- Damien Octeau, Google Inc., USA
- Roberto Perdisci, University of Georgia, USA
- Vasyl Pihur, Google Inc., USA
- Konrad Rieck, TU Braunschweig, Germany
- Fabio Roli, University of Cagliari, Italy
- Benjamin Rubinstein, University of Melbourne, Australia
- Tobias Scheffer, Universität Potsdam, Germany
- Michael Tschantz, ICSI, USA
- Doug Tygar, University of California, Berkeley, USA
- Eugene Vorobeychik, Vanderbilt University, USA
- Gang Wang, Virginia Tech, USA

ABOUT THE ORGANIZERS

Battista Biggio received the M.Sc. degree (Hons.) in Electronic Engineering and the Ph.D. degree in Electronic Engineering and Computer Science from the University of Cagliari, Italy, in 2006 and 2010, respectively. Since 2007 he has been with the Department of Electrical and Electronic Engineering, University of Cagliari, where he is currently an Assistant Professor. In 2011, he visited the University of Tübingen, Germany, where he studied the robustness of machine learning to training data poisoning. His research interests include secure machine learning, multiple classifier systems, kernel methods, biometrics, and computer security. Dr. Biggio has served as a reviewer and program committee member for several international conferences and journals, including several AISec editions. He is a senior member of the IEEE and member of the IAPR. He has been recently nominated Associate Editor of Pattern Recognition and chair of the IAPR Technical Committee 1 on Statistical Pattern Recognition Techniques.

David Freeman is a research scientist/engineer at Facebook working on spam and abuse problems. He previously led anti-abuse engineering and data science teams at LinkedIn, where he built statistical models to detect fraud and abuse and worked with the larger machine learning community at LinkedIn to build scalable modeling and scoring infrastructure. He is an author, presenter, and organizer at international conferences on machine learning and security, such as NDSS, WWW and AISec, and is currently writing (with Clarence Chio) a book on Machine Learning and Security to be published by O'Reilly. He holds a Ph.D. in mathematics from UC Berkeley and did postdoctoral research in cryptography and security at CWI and Stanford University.

Brad Miller holds a Ph.D. in Computer Science from the University of California, Berkeley, and has conducted research applying machine learning to problems in security and privacy. In 2015 he joined the SafeBrowsing team at Google, where he works to develop, launch, and land novel machine learning mechanisms to combat phishing and malware on the web. He has received a Best Student Paper award at Privacy Enhancing Technologies Symposium, has served on the program committee for AISec, and has been a reviewer for several journals.

Arunesh Sinha is an Assistant Research Scientist in the Computer Science and Engineering Department at the University of Michigan. He received his Ph.D. from Carnegie Mellon University, where he was advised by Prof. Anupam Datta, and was a postdoctoral scholar with Prof. Milind Tambe at the Computer Science Department of University of Southern California. He was awarded the Bertucci fellowship at CMU in appreciation of his novel research. Dr. Sinha has conducted research at the intersection of security, machine learning and game theory. His interests lie in the theoretical aspects of multi-agent interaction, machine learning, security and privacy, along with an emphasis on the real-world applicability of the theoretical models.

ASHES 2017— Workshop on Attacks and Solutions in Hardware Security

Chip Hong Chang
NTU Singapore
ECHChang@ntu.edu.sg

Marten van Dijk
University of Connecticut
vandijk@engr.uconn.edu

Farinaz Koushanfar
UC San Diego
farinaz@ucsd.edu

Ulrich Rührmair
Ruhr-University Bochum
ruehrmair@ilo.de

Mark Tehranipoor
University of Florida
tehranipoor@ece.ufl.edu

ABSTRACT

The workshop on **"attacks and solutions in hardware security"** (ASHES) deals with all aspects of hardware security, including any recent attacks and solutions in the area. Besides mainstream research in hardware security, it also covers new, alternative or emerging application scenarios, such as the internet of things, nuclear weapons inspections, satellite security, or consumer and supply chain security. It also puts some focus on special purpose hardware and novel methodological solutions, such as particularly lightweight, small, low-cost, and energy-efficient devices, or even non-electronic security systems. Finally, ASHES welcomes any theoretical works that systematize and structure the area, and so-called "Wild-and-Crazy" papers that describe and distribute seminal ideas at an early conceptual stage to the community.

CCS Concepts/ACM Classifiers

• CCS Concept: Hardware Security

Keywords

Hardware security; secure design; special purpose hardware; hardware attacks; internet of things; non-electronic security hardware; emerging application scenarios for security hardware

1 INTRODUCTION AND MOTIVATION

As predicted by Gartner in 2015, there will be around 21 billion hardware devices connected in the IoT by 2020, creating a spending of about 3,000 billion dollars per year. This makes the IoT and associated hardware security questions clearly one of the most massive and impactful endeavors of this century.

At the same time, the development of suitable hardware strategies seems to lag behind the actual spread of the IoT.

While the security community has long recognized that many of the established, classical recipes do not transfer easily (or not at all) to hardware in an IoT-setting, no fully convincing substitute strategies have been developed yet. This leads to a host of novel questions, which cannot be addressed by existing means and methods alone. One particular scientific challenge lies in the unprecedented threat landscape of the IoT, which will connect billions of pervasive, low-cost devices with no strong tamper-protection or even computational resources on board. Particularly pressing questions in this context include:

- How can we get individual cryptographic keys into billions of low-cost hardware devices?
- How can we securely identify low-cost hardware over digital channels, e.g., systems without digital signal processors or devices merely powered by scavenged energy?
- How can we protect against tampering and side-channels in low-cost hardware?
- How can we remotely verify the functionality and integrity of connected IoT-devices?
- How can we establish the long-term confidentiality of communications with resource-constrained hardware?
- How can we protect the IoT and its hardware against malware (viruses, Trojan horses, etc.) and network attacks?
- How can we enable secure physical data storage in lightweight hardware systems?
- How can we preserve the privacy of users in pervasive IoT-scenarios?

The purpose of this workshop is to foster solutions for these and other impending issues on hardware security, in particular with hindsight to new methods and application scenarios such as the IoT. It shall provide the CCS-community with a dedicated, specialized forum for this type of research. It is thereby meant not only to cover mainstream hardware security research, but also to support novel research and methods at an early stage, fostering innovation in the area.

2 TOPICS

ASHES deals with the entire range of established, mainstream hardware security research, but particularly tries to foster novel and innovative approaches, as well as emerging application areas.

This includes, but is not limited to:

- Tamper sensing and tamper protection
- Physical attacks (fault injection, side-channels, etc.), including new attack vectors or attack methods
- Biometrics and hardware security
- Physical unclonable functions (and new/emerging variants thereof)
- Device fingerprinting and hardware forensics
- Item tagging, secure supply chains and product piracy
- Use of emerging computing technologies in security (including quantum techniques)
- New designs and materials for secure hardware
- Nanophysics and nanotechnology in hardware security
- Hardware Trojans and countermeasures
- Lightweight security solutions, primitives and protocols
- Secure and efficient hardware implementation of cryptographic primitives
- Security of reconfigurable and adaptive hardware platforms
- Sensors and sensor networks
- Hardware security in emerging application scenarios: Internet of Things, smart home, automotive, wearable computing, pervasive and ubiquitous computing, etc.
- Scalable hardware solutions that work for particularly large numbers of players/endpoints
- Formal treatments, proofs, standardization, or categorization of the area (incl. surveys and systematization of knowledge papers)

3 PAPER CATEGORIES

To account for the special scope of the workshop, and for the particular nature of hardware security as a rapidly developing discipline, the workshop offers four different categories of papers:

- **Full papers**, with up to 10 pages in ACM double column format (including references and appendices), and a 25 min presentation timeslot at the workshop (including questions).
- **Short papers**, with up to 6 pages in ACM double column format (including references and appendices), and a 15 min presentation timeslot at the workshop (including questions).

- **Wild and Crazy (WaC) papers**, with 3 to 6 pages in ACM double column format, with additional appendices and references of up to 6 pages, and 15 min presentation timeslot at the workshop (including questions). WaC papers are meant to target groundbreaking new methods and paradigms for hardware security. Their focus lies on novelty and potential impact, and on the plausibility of their argumentation, but not on a full demonstration or complete implementation of their ideas. They are reviewed and assessed as such. Wild and crazy papers must bear the prefix "WaC:" in their title from the submission onwards.
- **Systematization of Knowledge (SoK) papers**, with up to 12 pages in ACM double column format (including appendices and references), and a 25 min presentation timeslot at the workshop (including questions). SoK papers shall evaluate, systematize, and contextualize existing knowledge. They should serve the community by fostering and structuring the development of a particular subarea within hardware security. Ideally, but not necessarily, they might provide a new viewpoint on an established, important subarea, support or challenge long-standing beliefs with compelling evidence, or present a convincing new taxonomy. They will be reviewed and assessed as such. Systematization of knowledge papers must bear the prefix "SoK:" in the title from the submission onwards.

4 PROGRAM

- 8:50 am - 9:00 am: *Welcome*
- 9:00 am - 10:00 am: *Invited Talk:*
  Srini Devadas (MIT)
  Secure Hardware and Cryptography: Contrasts, Synergies and Challenges
- 10:00 am - 10:25 am: *Coffee Break*
- 10:25 am - 11:25 pm: *Invited Talk:*
  Ahmad-Reza Sadeghi (TU Darmstadt):
  Hardware-Assisted Security: Promises, Pitfalls and Opportunities
- 11:25 am - 12:15 pm: *Session No. 1:*
  Solutions in Hardware Security
  - Giovanni Di Crescenzo (Vencore Labs), Jeyavijayan Rajendran (UT Dallas), Ramesh Karri (NYU), Nasir Memon (NYU) and Yevgenij Dodis (NYU): Boolean Circuit Camouflaging: Cryptographic Models, Limitations, Provable Results, and a Random Oracle Realization
  - Charles Suslowicz, Archanaa S Krishnan and Patrick Schaumont (all Virginia Tech): Optimizing Cryptography in Energy Harvesting Applications

- 12:15 pm – 2:00 pm: Lunch, Socializing
- 2:00 pm – 3:00 pm: *Invited Talk:*
  Ulfar Erlingsson (Google)
  Data-driven Software Security and its
  Hardware Support
- 3:00 pm – 3:30 pm: *Coffee Break*
- 3:30 pm - 4:10 pm: *Session No 2: WaC&SoK*
  - Yan Michalevsky and Yonatan Winetraub
    (both Stanford):
    WaC: SpaceTEE - Secure and Tamper-Proof
    Computing in Space using CubeSats
  - Hoda Maleki, Reza Rahaeimehr and Marten
    van Dijk (all University of Connecticut):
    SoK: A survey of Clone Detection approaches
    in RFID-based supply chains

- 4:10 pm – 5:00 pm: *Session No. 3:*
  Attacks in Hardware Security
  - Lars Tebelmann, Michael Pehl and Georg
    Sigl (all TU München):
    EM Attack on BCH-based Error Correction
    for PUF-based Key Generation
  - Varnavas Papaioannou and Nicolas Courtois
    (both University College London):
    On the Feasibility and Performance of
    Rowhammer Attacks

ACKNOWLEDGMENTS

Ulrich Rührmair acknowledges support by the German Ministry of Science and Education within the project *"PICOLA"*.

CCSW'17 — 2017 ACM Cloud Computing Security

Ghassan O. Karame
NEC Laboratories Europe
Heidelberg, Germany 69115
ghassan@karame.org

Angelos Stavrou
George Mason University
Fairdax, VA, USA 22030
astavrou@gmu.edu

ABSTRACT

The use and prevalence of cloud and large-scale computing infrastructures is increasing. They are projected to be a dominant trend in computing for the foreseeable future: major cloud operators are now estimated to house millions of machines each and to host substantial (and growing) fractions of corporate and government IT and web infrastructure. CCSW is a forum for bringing together researchers and practitioners to discuss the challenges and implications of current and future trends to the security of cloud operators, tenants, and the larger Internet community. Of special interest are the security challenges from the integration of cloud infrastructures with IoT and mobile application deployments. CCSW welcomes submissions on new threats, countermeasures, and opportunities brought about by the move to cloud computing, with a preference for unconventional approaches, as well as measurement studies and case studies that shed light on the security implications of cloud infrastructure and use cases.

KEYWORDS

Cloud Computing; Security.

1 MOTIVATION

No matter what the latest buzzword (grid, cloud, utility computing, SaaS, etc.), large-scale computing and cloud-like infrastructures are here to stay. How exactly they will look like tomorrow is still for the markets to decide, yet one thing is certain: clouds bring with them new untested deployment and associated adversarial models and vulnerabilities. Thus, it is essential that our community becomes involved. CCS is the ideal target for this workshop due to its often avant-garde position in the broader security landscape. According to Google Scholar (as of a year ago): 4 of the top 20 cited ACM CCS papers of the past five years come from CCSW.

2 TOPICAL COVERAGE

ACM CCSW is a forum for presenting novel research or empirical studies from academia, industry, and government on all theoretical and practical aspects of security, privacy, and data protection in cloud scenarios. Topics of interest include, but are not limited to: including:

- Secure cloud resource virtualization
- Secure data management outsourcing

CCS'17, October 30–November 3, 2017, Dallas, TX, USA
© 2017 Copyright held by the owner/author(s). ISBN 978-1-4503-4946-8/17/10.
DOI: http://dx.doi.org/10.1145/3133956.3137050

- Practical privacy and integrity mechanisms for outsourcing
- Cloud-centric threat models
- Secure outsourced computation
- Remote attestation mechanisms in clouds
- Sand-boxing and VM-based enforcements
- Trust and policy management in clouds
- Secure identity management mechanisms
- Cloud-aware web service security paradigms and mechanisms
- Cloud-centric regulatory compliance issues and mechanisms
- Business and security risk models for clouds
- Cost and usability models and their interaction with cloud security
- Scalability of secure clouds
- Trusted computing technology and clouds
- Analysis of software for remote attestation and cloud protection
- Network security (DoS, IDS etc.) mechanisms for clouds
- Security for cloud programming models
- Privacy-enhancing machine-learning in clouds
- Secure and privacy protecting IoT clouds
- Accountable Data Analytics for clouds

We would like to especially encourage novel paradigms and controversial ideas that are not on the above list. The workshop is to act as a fertile ground for creative debate and interaction in security-sensitive areas of computing impacted by clouds.

3 PROGRAM COMMITTEE

We are grateful to the members of our technical program committee:

- Frederik Armknecht, University of Mannheim
- Erik-Oliver Blass, Airbus Research
- Sherman Chow, Chinese University of Hong Kong
- Mihai Christodorescu, Qualcomm
- Mauro Conti, University of Padua
- Cas Cremers, Oxford University
- Reza Curtmola, NJIT
- Roberto Di Pietro, Roma Tre University of Rome
- Dario Fiore, IMDEA Software
- Sara Foresti, University of Milano
- Sotiris Ioannides, FORTH
- Vasileios P. Kemerlis, Brown University
- Florian Kerschbaum, SAP Research
- George Kesidis, Penn State University
- Ivan Martinovic, Oxford University
- Soumendra Nanda, BAE Systems
- Nick Nikiforakis, Stony Brook University
- Melek Onen, Eurecom

- Jason Polakis, University of Illinois
- Kasper Rasmussen, Oxford University
- Rei Safavi-Naini, University of Calgary
- Matthias Schunter, Intel Research
- Thomas Schneider, Technical University Darmstadt
- Elaine Shi, Cornell University
- Claudio Soriente, NEC
- Abhinav Srivastava, AT&T
- Nikos Triandopoulos, Stevens Institute of Technology
- Haining Wang, University of Delaware
- Yinqian Zhang, Ohio State University
- Fengwei Zhang, Wayne State University

4 PROGRAM CHAIRS

Ghassan Karame. is the Manager and Chief researcher of the Security Group of NEC Labs in Germany. Ghassan joined NEC Labs in April 2012. Prior to that, Ghassan was working as a postdoctoral researcher in the Institute of Information Security of ETH Zurich, Switzerland. He holds a Master of Science degree in Information Networking from Carnegie Mellon University (CMU), and a PhD degree in Computer Science from ETH Zurich.

Ghassan is interested in all aspects of security and privacy with a focus on cloud security, IoT security, network security, and Blockchain security.

Angelos Stavrou. is a full professor at George Mason University and the Director of the Center for Assurance Research and Engineering (CARE) at GMU. Stavrou has served as principal investigator on research awards from NSF, DARPA, IARPA, DHS, AFOSR, ARO, ONR, he is an active member of NIST's Mobile Security team and has written more than 90 peer-reviewed conference and journal articles.Stavrou received his M.Sc. in Electrical Engineering, M.Phil. andPh.D. (with distinction) in Computer Science all from Columbia University. He also holds an M.Sc. in theoretical Computer Science from University of Athens, and a B.Sc. in Physics with distinction from University of Patras, Greece.

Over the past few years, Dr. Stavrou's research has focused on two aspects of security: Systems' Security and Reliability with focus on large distributed systems and IoT.

CPS-SPC 2017: Third Workshop on Cyber-Physical Systems Security and PrivaCy

Rakesh B. Bobba
Oregon State University
Corvallis, Oregon, USA
rakesh.bobba@oregonstate.edu

Awais Rashid
Lancaster University
Lancaster, United Kingdom
a.rashid@lancaster.ac.uk

ABSTRACT

Cyber-Physical Systems (CPS) are becoming increasingly critical for the well-being of society (*e.g.,* electricity generation and distribution, water treatment, implantable medical devices *etc.*). While the convergence of computing, communications and physical control in such systems provides benefits in terms of efficiency and convenience, the attack surface resulting from this convergence poses unique security and privacy challenges. These systems represent the new frontier for cyber risk. CPS-SPC is an annual forum, in its 3rd edition this year, that aims to provide a focal point for the research community to begin addressing the security and privacy challenges of CPS in a comprehensive and multidisciplinary manner and, in tandem with other efforts, build a comprehensive research road map.

CCS CONCEPTS

• **General and reference** → **General literature**;

KEYWORDS

cyber-physical systems; security; privacy; workshop

1 INTRODUCTION

Cyber-Physical Systems (CPS) integrate computing and communication capabilities with monitoring and control of entities in the physical world. These systems are usually composed of a set of networked agents, including sensors, actuators, control processing units, and communication devices. While some forms of CPS are already in use, the widespread growth of wireless embedded sensors and actuators is creating several new applications in areas such as medical devices, autonomous vehicles, and smart infrastructure, and is increasing the role that the information infrastructure plays in existing control systems such as in the process control industry or the power grid.

Many CPS applications are safety-critical: their failure can cause irreparable harm to the physical system under control, and to the people who depend on it or use and operate it. In particular, critical cyber-physical infrastructures such as electric power generation,

CCS'17, , October 30–November 3, 2017, Dallas, TX, USA
© 2017 Association for Computing Machinery.
ACM ISBN ISBN 978-1-4503-4946-8/17/10...$15.00
https://doi.org/10.1145/3133956.3137051

transmission and distribution grids, oil and natural gas systems, water and waste-water treatment plants, and transportation networks play a fundamental and large-scale role in our society. Their disruption can have a significant impact on individuals, and nations at large. Securing these CPS infrastructures is, therefore, vitally important. Similarly because many CPS systems collect sensor data non-intrusively, users of these systems are often unaware of their exposure. Therefore, in addition to security, CPS systems must be designed with privacy considerations.

The challenges in securing CPS are many. But fundamentally, it is important to recognize that securing CPS differs from the traditional cyber security concerns of confidentiality, integrity and availability (CIA) that have dominated the security of information technology (IT) systems. At its core, CPS security must be approached and framed from the perspective of how attacks on CIA properties perturb control-theoretic properties such as controllability, observability and stability and consequently system safety. Like past editions, CPS-SPC 2017 aims to bring together a community around security and privacy challenges in CPS. It is held in conjunction with ACM Computer and Communications Security (CCS) conference, a flagship annual conference of ACM SIGSAC (Special Interest Group on Security, Audit and Control) and a premier security conference. The co-location of these two events brings advantages to both, as well as to the community itself.

2 SCOPE

CPS-SPC 2017 encourages participation from researchers and practitioners from diverse CPS domains and multiple disciplinary backgrounds representative of CPS, including but not limited to information security, control theory, embedded systems, and human factors. It provides a forum for researchers from these various CPS domains and backgrounds to share their ideas and results, to discuss emerging technologies and trends that impact CPS, to study differences and commonalities across different CPS domains, and to build a multidisciplinary body of knowledge in this sub-field that is still in its infancy.

This year's workshop builds on the foundations laid by the last two editions and invited submissions at the interface of control theory, information security, embedded and real-time systems, and human factors among others as applied to CPS. Specifically the topics of interest included but were not limited to:

- mathematical foundations for secure CPS
- control theoretic approaches to secure CPS
- high assurance security architectures for CPS
- security and resilience metrics for CPS
- metrics and risk assessment approaches for CPS
- privacy in CPS

- network security for CPS
- game theory applied to CPS security
- security of embedded systems, IoT and real-time systems in the context of CPS
- human factors and humans in the loop
- understanding dependencies among security and reliability
- and safety in CPS
- economics of security and privacy in CPS
- intrusion detection in CPS
- model-based security systems engineering
- experimental insights from real-world CPS or CPS testbeds

CPS domains of interest include but are not limited to:

- health care and medical devices
- manufacturing
- industrial control systems
- SCADA systems
- Robotics
- smart building environments
- unmanned aerial vehicles (UAVs)
- autonomous vehicles
- transportation systems and networks

Also of interest were papers that can point the research community to new research directions, and those that can set research agendas and priorities in CPS security and privacy.

3 PROGRAM

CPS-SPC 2017 is a one day workshop held on November 3rd 2017. The program comprises four technical sessions with talks on accepted short and regular length research papers. This year the workshop received 26 papers from 11 different countries and accepted 9 full and 4 short papers for presentation at the workshop.

4 WORKSHOP COMMITTEES

4.1 Program Committee

We are thankful to the members of our program committee without whose help and support this workshop wouldn't have been successful.

- Cristina Alcaraz, Universidad de Malaga, Spain
- Magnus Almgren, Chalmers University of Technology, Sweden
- Pauline Anthonysamy, Google
- Raheem Beyah, Georgia Institute of Technology, USA
- Alvaro Cardenas, University of Texas at Dallas, USA
- Gabriela Ciocarlie, SRI International, USA
- Simon Foley, IMT-Atlantique, France
- Sylvain Frey, University of Southampton, UK
- Benjamin Green, Fujitsu/Lancaster University, UK
- Adam Hahn, Washington State University, USA
- Wouter Joosen, KU Leuven, Belgium
- Marina Krotofil, Honeywell Industrial Cyber Security Lab
- Michail Maniatakos, New York University Abu Dhabi, UAE
- Daisuke Mashima, Advanced Digital Sciences Center, Singapore
- Aditya Mathur, Singapore University of Technology and Design, Singapore

- Sibin Mohan, University of Illinois at Urbana-Champaign, USA
- Xinming Ou, University of South Florida, USA
- Jose M. Such, King's College London, UK
- Roshan Thomas, MITRE, USA
- Nils Ole Tippenhauer, Singapore University of Technology and Design, Singapore
- Claire Vishik, Intel Corporation, UK
- Avishai Wool, Tel Aviv University, Israel
- Quanyan Zhu, New York University, USA

4.2 PC Co-Chairs

Rakesh B. Bobba is an Assistant Professor in the School of Electrical Engineering and Computer Science (EECS) at Oregon State University (OSU). He obtained his Ph.D. and M.S. in Electrical and Computer Engineering from the University of Maryland at College Park. Prior to joining OSU, Dr. Bobba was a Research Assistant Professor at the Information Trust Institute, University of Illinois, Urbana-Champaign. His research interests are in the design of secure and trustworthy networked and distributed computer systems, with a current focus on cyber-physical critical infrastructures, shared computing infrastructures and real-time systems. Together with Roshan K. Thomas and Alvaro C. Cardenas he initiated CPS-SPC in 2015 and served as a PC member.

Awais Rashid is Director of the Security-Lancaster Institute, comprising 100 researchers focusing on human and technical aspects of security. He leads multiple research projects on CPS, including a project as part of the UK Research Institute on Trustworthy Industrial Control Systems and an EU project (with KU Leuven and University College Cork) on adaptive security for CPS under attack. He also co-leads the Security and Safety Stream within the UK Research Hub on Cyber Security of the Internet of Things. He also organized and chaired the first workshop on security and resilience of cyber-physical infrastructures at the International Symposium on Engineering Secure Software and Systems (ESSoS) in 2016 and has served on the PC of the first two CPS-CPC workshops at CCS. Rashid is also leading a major project on developing a cyber-security body of knowledge (CyBOK).

ACKNOWLEDGMENTS

The co-chairs would like to thank members of the Program Committee and the external reviewers for their support and service to CPS-SPC and the community. We would also like to thank the CPS-SPC Steering Committee for their support in organizing the workshop. Thanks to Taesoo Kim and Cliff Wang, ACM CCS Workshop Co-Chairs; Matthew Wright and Apu Kapadia, ACM CCS Proceedings co-chairs; and Bhavani Thuraisingham ACM CCS General Chair. Last, but not least, we would like to thank all the authors who submitted their work to CPS-SPC 2017 and all the participants of the event.

CCS 2017 — Women in Cyber Security (CyberW) Workshop

Danfeng (Daphne) Yao
Virginia Tech
danfeng@vt.edu

Elisa Bertino
Purdue University
bertino@purdue.edu

ABSTRACT

The CyberW workshop is motivated by the significant gender imbalance in all security conferences, in terms of the number of publishing authors, PC members, organizers, and attendees. What causes this gender imbalance remains unclear. However, multiple research studies have shown that a diverse group is more creative, diligent, and productive than a homogeneous group. Achieving cyber security requires a diverse group. To maintain a sustainable and creative workforce, substantial efforts need to be made by the security community to broaden the participation from underrepresented groups in cyber security research conferences. We hope this workshop can attract all underrepresented cybersecurity professionals, students, and researchers to attend top security and privacy conferences, engage in cutting-edge security and privacy research, excel in cyber security professions, and ultimately take on leadership positions.

CCS Concepts/ACM Classifiers

• Social and Professional Topics

Keywords

Gender discrimination; gender gap; gender imbalance; gender bias; cyber security; underrepresented groups; leadership; female; women; technical competiveness; diversity; inclusive excellence; career;

1 INTRODUCTION

This past summer of 2017 was phenomenal. The discussion on the often shun away subject of gender discrimination was in full public display. Three established senior female scientists sued the prestigious Salk institute for Biological Studies at San Diego, CA for pervasive, long-standing gender discrimination [1, 2]. The infamous Google Manifesto was being hotly debated [3]. Adrienne Porter Felt's blog article articulated the severe gender imbalance issue in computer science conference program committees and how it may impact the fairness of the anonymous review process [4]. We could not ask for a better

time to boost people's interests in our CyberW workshop and engage in the discussion.

Despite the title, we encourage everyone to attend the workshop, regardless of the gender or race. The challenges faced by women and underrepresented groups are too complicated to be addressed by any single group on their own. It requires the collective effort of the community to understand the issues and commit to improving the situation.

CyberW complements the existing successful women in computing/security venues, in that CyberW aims to promote cutting edge research and technical leadership. CyberW is research- and technical-oriented. The field of cyber security needs women in leadership positions, well beyond entry-level positions. Observing and interacting face-to-face with successful technical role models will be inspiring for the attendees and encourage them in their career pursuit.

2 PROGRAM

This inaugural workshop consists of invited talks, a lightning talks session, and plenty of question-and-answers and networking opportunities.

We are excited to welcome Louis A. Beecherl, Jr. Distinguished Professor Bhavani Thuraisingham of University of Texas at Dallas and Professor David Evans of University of Virginia to give the opening the remarks to motivate the audience. Both of them have been strong advocates for women in computing for many years.

We are fortunate to have an outstanding group of researchers, professionals, and leaders in the cyber security field to give keynote speeches, including Regents Distinguished Professor Stephanie Forrest of University of New Mexico, Samuel Conte Term Professor Elisa Bertino of Purdue University, Professor Rebecca Wright of Rutgers University, Professor Ling Liu of Georgia Institute of Technology, Diane Staheli of MIT Lincoln Lab, Professor Alvaro Cardenas of University of Texas at Dallas. The topics of their keynote presentations cover various security areas. Besides the technical content, the keynote presentations share speakers' personal and professional experiences.

Keynote presentations are followed by Q&A sessions that allow attendees to interact with the invited speakers. The evening reception as part of the main CCS program provides additional networking opportunities for the workshop attendees.

The lightning talk session is open to the public. It gives every participant an opportunity to describe his or her work.

We believe that the workshop program will be conducive to an open and broad discussion on initiatives and actions that will lead to an increased involvement of a diverse community of researchers and practitioners in cyber security. Cyber security is today more critical than ever and we need complementary expertise and perspectives for effective solutions.

ACKNOWLEDGMENTS

The CyberW workshop has received generous funding and staff support from Computing Research Association Women (CRA-W)'s Discipline-specific mentoring workshops program (DSW). The funding from DSW made CyberW '17 possible. We thank DSW's Professor Russ Joseph and Claire Brady for their help, encouragement, and patience. We would also like to thank our other sponsors, including ACM Special Interest Group on Security, Audit, and Control (SIGSAC), Virginia Tech Department of Computer Science, University of Texas at Dallas, MIT Lincoln Lab, Virginia Tech Stack Center.

We would like to thank Professor Somesh Jha for embracing the idea of a workshop for women in cyber security, when we first mentioned it to him during CCS '16.

We would also like to thank our publicity chair and travel-grant co-chair Professor Hui (Wendy) Wang of Stevens Institute of Technology for being so committed to helping CyberW. We thank Stefan Nagy and Ya Xiao of Virginia Tech for maintaining the website and Twitter feeds. We thank Zachary Petricca for designing the cool logo for CyberW.

REFERENCES

[1] Meredith Wadman. Two female scientists sue Salk Institute, alleging discrimination at 'old boys club'. *Science.* July 14, 2017. http://www.sciencemag.org/news/2017/07/two-female-scientists-sue-salk-institute-alleging-discrimination-old-boys-club

[2] Meredith Wadman. Salk Institute hit with discrimination lawsuit by third female scientist. *Science.* July 20, 2017. http://www.sciencemag.org/news/2017/07/salk-institute-hit-discrimination-lawsuit-third-female-scientist

[3] John Hennessy, Maria Klawe, and David Patterson. What James Damore got wrong about gender bias in computer science. *WIRED.* September 1, 2017. https://www.wired.com/story/what-james-damore-got-wrong-about-gender-bias-in-computer-science/

[4] Adrienne Porter Felt. "Peer" review? Gender imbalance in program committees. June 18, 2017. https://techlady.haus/blog/2017/6/11/peer-review-gender-imbalance-in-program-committees

FEAST 2017: The Second Workshop on Forming an Ecosystem Around Software Transformation

Taesoo Kim
Georgia Institute of Technology
Atlanta, GA 30332, USA
taesoo@gatech.edu

Dinghao Wu
The Pennsylvania State University
University Park, PA 16802, USA
dwu@ist.psu.edu

ABSTRACT

The Second Workshop on Forming an Ecosystem Around Software Transformation (FEAST 2017) is held in conjunction with the 24th ACM Conference on Computer and Communications Security (CCS 2017) on November 3, 2017 in Dallas, Texas. The workshop is geared toward discussion and understanding of several critical topics surrounding software executable transformation for improving the security and efficiency of all software used in security-critical applications. The scope of discussion for this workshop includes topics that may be necessary to fully exploit the power and impact of late-stage software customization effort.

CCS CONCEPTS

• **Security and privacy** → **Software reverse engineering**; *Software security engineering*; • **Software and its engineering** → *Software maintenance tools*; *Software verification and validation*;

KEYWORDS

Software transformation, binary code, security, debloating

1 INTRODUCTION

Typical software engineering methodologies are largely focused on programmer productivity and their methods have been known to introduce significant execution inefficiency as a side effect. Recent work investigating efficient and timely software has attempted to enhance software execution efficiency while preserving the source code-level abstractions and object-orientation that enhance a programmer's productivity.

Such efforts seek to undo the side effects on security and performance overhead by reclaiming software execution efficiency and reducing indirection, as well as performing automatic program de-layering and program specialization (de-bloating). Several promising results from these efforts have demonstrated their viability in improving program execution efficiency as well as reduction of the cyber security attack surface. As a result, the community may benefit by investing in the development of tool ecosystems to take advantage of this recent progress, to mature the technologies, and determine how best to transparently deploy them.

CCS '17, October 30-November 3, 2017, Dallas, TX, USA
© 2017 Copyright held by the owner/author(s).
ACM ISBN 978-1-4503-4946-8/17/10.
https://doi.org/10.1145/3133956.3137052

Despite some early progress within the research community, software executable transformation is not a solved science. Some critical problems reverse engineering and binary understanding are, in the general case, undecidable. Various automated tools and ecosystems will need to be investigated and developed to guarantee the effectiveness and correctness of transformation efforts and to enhance and ensure the security of transformed software. The FEAST workshop aims at forming an ecosystem Around Software Transformation.

2 TOPICS

The FEAST workshop will provide a forum for researchers to share ideas and development on software transformation. It includes topics geared toward:

- Understanding issues of software executable transformation for various programming languages and environment, and the potential methods for alleviating those issues.
- Identification of tools to be investigated and developed for guaranteeing correctness, enhancing security, and enabling non-critical/undesired feature removal.
- Identification of layers and areas of computing systems that are suitable for and can benefit from software customization/transformation, along with identification of associated challenges and constraints, and the particular adaptation to the methodology needed to operate within the identified areas.
- Automated extraction of models from software executables that are amenable to formal methods analysis and verification.

3 FORMAT

Submissions should be in two-column, 10-point format, and can be up to 6 pages in length with as many additional pages as necessary for references.

4 REVIEW PROCESS

All accepted papers received two to three double-blind reviews. We would like to thank all PC members and external reviewers for their contributions.

5 INVITED SPEAKERS

The workshop has an invited talk. The keynote speaker is Vikram S. Adve from University of Illinois at Urbana-Champaign.

6 WORKSHOP ORGANIZATION

Program Committee Chairs

- Taesoo Kim, *Georgia Tech*
- Dinghao Wu, *Penn State University*

Program Committee Members

- Kevin Hamlen, *UT Dallas*
- Wenkee Lee, *Georgia Tech*
- Zhiqiang Lin, *UT Dallas*
- Mayur Naik, *UPenn*
- Mathias Payer, *Purdue University*
- Aravind Prakash, *Binghamton University*
- Binoy Ravindran, *Virginia Tech*

- Yan Shoshitaishvili, *Arizona State University*
- Gang Tan, *Penn State University*
- Jan Vitek, *Northeastern University*
- XiaoFeng Wang, *Indiana University*
- Dongyan Xu, *Purdue University*
- Harry Xu, *UC Irvine*
- Daphne Yao, *Virginia Tech*

ACKNOWLEDGMENTS

The FEAST Workshop is sponsored by Association for Computing Machinery (ACM), ACM SIGSAC, and Office of Naval Research (ONR).

MIST 2017: 9th International Workshop on Managing Insider Security Threats

Ilsun You
Department of Information Security Engineering
Soonchunhyang University
22 Soonchunhyangro, Asan-si, Chungnam-do, 336-745
Republic of Korea
ilsunu@gmail.com

Elisa Bertino
Department of Computer Science, Purdue University
305 N. University Street
West Lafayette, IN 47907
bertino@purdue.edu

ABSTRACT

This paper introduces the 9th International Workshop on Managing Insider Security Threats (MIST 2017), which takes place in conjunction with the 24th ACM Conference on Computer and Communications Security (ACM CCS 2017). Its objective is to present recent challenges and advanced technologies in managing insider security threats by publishing high-quality work that will be a trigger for further research related to this subject.

CCS Concepts

• **Security and privacy**

Keywords

Insider threats; Data leakage prevention; Cyber security and defense

1. INTRODUCTION

Insider threats refer to the jeopardise to operations caused by sanctioned users having adequate access to the system, data, or any other sensitive information of their organizations [1]. These threats are astronomically hazardous as these can result in access to confidential data, disclosing business information, defamation, embezzlement, etc [2, 3]. Such threats are more perplexed and difficult to identify than the ones caused by outsiders [4]. There have been a plethora of research in this direction, but still, this is one of the most arduous challenges in the areas of security.

The MIST workshop has been annually held since 2009 to assemble researchers from industry and academia to exchange incipient conceptions and approaches in the area of insider threats with practical paramountcy. We believe that this workshop has remarkably triggered further cognate research and technology amelioration.

The main topics of MIST 2017 include but not limited to:

• Theoretical foundations and algorithms for addressing insider threats

• Insider threat assessment and modeling

CCS '17, October 30-November 3, 2017, Dallas, TX, USA
© 2017 Copyright is held by the owner/author(s).
ACM ISBN 978-1-4503-4946-8/17/10.
https://doi.org/10.1145/3133956.3148525

• Security and cryptography technologies to prevent, detect and predict insider threats

• Cryptographic protocols against insider threats

• Validating the trustworthiness of staff

• Post-insider threat incident analysis

• Data breach modeling and mitigation techniques

• Registration, authentication and identification

• Certification and authorization

• Database security

• Device control system

• Digital forensic system

• Fraud detection

• Network access control system

• Intrusion detection

• Keyboard information security

• Information security governance

• Information security management systems

• Risk assessment and management

• Log collection and analysis

• Trust management

• IT compliance (audit)

• Continuous auditing

• Corporate ethics, accountability and integrity

2. HISTORY

The MIST workshop has the following history:

• **1st MIST** (in conjunction with IFIPTM 2009)
June 16, 2009, Purdue University, West Lafayette, USA

• **2nd MIST** (in conjunction with IFIPTM 2010)
June 15, 2010, Morioka, Iwate, Japan

• **3rd MIST** (in conjunction with InCos 2011)
December 1-2, 2011, Fukuoka Institute of Technology, Fukuoka, Japan

• **4th MIST**
November 8-9, 2012, Kyushu University, Fukuoka, Japan

• **5th MIST**
October 24-25, 2013, Pukyong National University, Busan, Rep. of Korea

- **6thMIST**
November 21-22, 2014, Konkuk University, Seoul,
Rep. of Korea

- **7thMIST** (in conjunction with ACM CCS 2015)
October 16, 2015, The Denver Marriot City Center, Denver, Colorado, USA

- **8thMIST** (in conjunction with ACM CCS 2016)
October 28, 2016, Hofburg Palace, Vienna, Austria

3. PROGRAM COMMITTEE

We are grateful to the members of the MIST 2017 program committee:

- Ioannis Agrafiotis (Oxford University, UK)

- Joonsang Baek (Khalifa University of Science, Technology and Research, UAE)

- William Casey (Software Engineering Institute - Carnegie Mellon University, USA)

- William R. Claycomb (Carnegie Mellon University, USA)

- Ing-Ray Chen (Virginia Tech, USA)

- Raymond Choo (The University of Texas at San Antonio, USA)

- Steven Furnell (University of Plymouth, UK)

- Florian Kammuelle (Middlesex University, UK)

- Fang-YieLeu (Tunghai University, Taiwan)

- Jason Nurse (Oxford University, UK)

- W. Michael Petullo (United States Military Academy, West Point, USA)

- Christian W. Probst (Technical University of Denmark, Denmark)

- Kyung-Hyune Rhee (Pukyong National University, South Korea)

- Malek Ben Salem (Accenture, USA)

- Fei Song (Beijing Jiaotong University, China)

- Hassan Takabi (University of North Texas, USA)

- Danfeng (Daphne) Yao (Virginia Tech, USA)

- Jeong Hyun Yi (Soongsil University, South Korea)

- Meng Yu (The University of Texas at San Antonio, USA)

- Quanyan Zhu (New York University, USA)

In addition, our thanks go to the following reviewer:

- Gökhan Kul (The State University of New York at Buffalo, USA)

- Vishal Sharma (Soonchunhyang University, South Korea)

4. WORKSHOP PROGRAM

MIST 2017 is held on October 30, 2017 as one day. It is composed of presentations for the 7 full and 5 short accepted papers. In addition, we invite one keynote, where Dr. Kim-Kwang Raymond Choo from The University of Texas at San Antonio talks about "Research Challenges and Opportunities in Big Digital Forensic Data".

5. WORKSHOP ORGANIZERS

Ilsun You (general co-chair) received his M.S. and Ph.D. degrees in Computer Science from Dankook University, Seoul, Korea in 1997 and 2002, respectively. Also, he obtained his second Ph.D. degree from Kyushu University, Japan in 2012. Now, he is working as an associate professor at Soonchunhyang University, Republic of Korea. Dr. You has published more than 120 papers and 30 special issues in his main areas including internet security, formal security analysis, and insider threats. He is now serving as EiC of Journal of Journal of Wireless Mobile Networks, Ubiquitous Computing, and Dependable Applications (JoWUA). He is a Fellow of the IET and a Senior member of the IEEE.

Elisa Bertino(general co-chair)is professor of computer science at Purdue University, and serves as Director of the Purdue Cyber Space Security Lab (Cyber2SLab). She is also an adjunct professor of Computer Science & Info Tech at RMIT. Prior to joining Purdue in 2004, she was a professor and department head at the Department of Computer Science and Communication of the University of Milan. She has been a visiting researcher at the IBM Research Laboratory (now Almaden) in San Jose, at the Microelectronics and Computer Technology Corporation, at Rutgers University, at Telcordia Technologies. Her recent research focuses on data security and privacy, digital identity management, policy systems, and security for drones and embedded systems. She is a Fellow of ACM and of IEEE. She received the IEEE Computer Society 2002 Technical Achievement Award, the IEEE Computer Society 2005 Kanai Award and the 2014 ACM SIGSAC outstanding contributions award. She is currently serving as EiC of IEEE Transactions on Dependable and Secure Computing.

6. ACKNOWLEDGMENTS

We would like to extend our sincere thanks to all authors who submitted papers as well as the program committee members for their timely and nice review work.

7. REFERENCES
[1] I. Agrafiotis, A. Erola, M. Goldsmith, and S. Creese, 2017, Formalising policies for insider-threat detection: A tripwire grammar. Journal of Wireless Mobile Networks, Ubiquitous Computing, and Dependable Applications. 8, 1, (March 2017), 26-43.

[2] F. Kammüller, M. Kerber, and C. W. Probst, 2017, Insider Threats and Auctions: Formalization, Mechanized Proof, and Code Generation. Journal of Wireless Mobile Networks, Ubiquitous Computing, and Dependable Applications. 8, 1, (March 2017), 44-78.

[3] C.L. Huth, D.W. Chadwick, W.R. Claycomb, and I. You, 2013, Guest editorial: A brief overview of data leakage and insider threats. Information Systems Frontiers. 15, 1 (March 2013), 1-4.

[4] C. W. Probst, I. You, D. Shin, and K. Sakurai, 2011, Journal of Wireless Mobile Networks, Ubiquitous Computing, and Dependable Applications, Guest Editorial: Addressing Insider Threats and Information Leakage, 2, 1 (March 2011), 1-3.

MTD 2017: Fourth ACM Workshop on Moving Target Defense (MTD)

Hamed Okhravi
MIT Lincoln Laboratory
Lexington, MA, USA
hamed.okhravi@ll.mit.edu

Xinming Ou
University of South Florida
Tampa, FL, USA
xou@usf.edu

ABSTRACT

The fourth ACM Workshop on Moving Target Defense (MTD) is held in Dallas, Texas, USA on October 30, 2017, co-located with the 24th ACM Conference on Computer and Communications Security (CCS). The main objective of the workshop is to discuss novel randomization, diversification, and dynamism techniques for computer systems and networks, new metric and analysis frameworks to assess and quantify the effectiveness of MTD, and discuss challenges and opportunities that such defenses provide. We have constructed an exciting and diverse program of nine refereed papers and two invited keynote talks that will provide the participant with a vibrant and thought-provoking set of ideas and insights.

CCS Concepts/ACM Classifiers
• Security and privacy~Systems security
• Security and privacy~Network security
• Security and privacy~Software and application security
• Security and privacy~Formal security models

Keywords
Moving Target Defenses (MTD), Randomization, Diversification, Dynamism, Cyber Agility, Adaptive Defenses

1 INTRODUCTION

The static nature of current computing systems has made them easy to attack and hard to defend. Adversaries have an asymmetric advantage in that they have the time to study a system, identify its vulnerabilities, and choose the time and place of attack to gain the maximum benefit. The idea of moving-target defense (MTD) is to impose the same asymmetric disadvantage on attackers by making systems dynamic and therefore harder to explore and predict [1, 2]. With a constantly

changing system and its ever adapting attack surface, attackers will have to deal with a great amount of uncertainty just like defenders do today. The ultimate goal of MTD is to increase the attackers' workload so as to level the cybersecurity playing field for both defenders and attackers - hopefully even tilting it in favor of the defender.

The MTD'2017 workshop aims to provide a forum for researchers and practitioners in this area to exchange their novel ideas, findings, experiences, and lessons learned.

2 SCOPE
Randomization, diversification, and dynamism can be applied to many different components of a computer system/network and to different layers of its software stack [3]. As a result, MTD covers a broad spectrum of techniques and their associated metrics and analysis frameworks.

Topics of interest include, but not limited to:

• System randomization
• Artificial diversity
• Cyber maneuver and agility
• Software diversity
• Dynamic network configuration
• Moving target in the cloud
• System diversification techniques
• Dynamic compilation techniques
• Adaptive defenses
• MTD quantification methods and models
• MTD evaluation and assessment frameworks
• MTD analytics
• Large-scale MTD (using multiple techniques)
• Moving target in software coding and application API
• Autonomous technologies for MTD
• Theoretical studies on trade-offs of MTD approaches
• Human, social, and usability aspects of MTD
• Other related areas

3 WORKSHOP OBJECTIVES

This workshop will bring together researchers from academia, government, and industry to report on the latest research efforts on MTD, and to have productive discussions and constructive debates on this topic.

The fourth MTD workshop will also have a focus on the lessons learned from the past years of research in the area of moving target, and the challenges and opportunities faced by the community moving forward.

4 MTD PROGRAM

The fourth MTD workshop is a one-day pre-conference workshop that will happen in conjunction with the ACM CCS conference. We have two invited keynote speakers. Prof. Paul Van Oorschot (Carleton University, Canada) will talk about science of security and what can be learned from the history of academic literature. Prof. Ahmad-Reza Sadeghi (Technische Universität Darmstadt, Germany) will talk about the effectiveness of system randomization. We will also have an exciting set of nine refereed full papers and two short papers, covering a broad range of topics from code/network/policy/web randomization techniques, to metrics and analysis frameworks, to botnet detection. The presentations will be grouped based on topics.

5 ORGANIZERS

Hamed Okhravi (PC co-chair) is a Senior Staff member at the Cyber Security and Information Sciences Division of MIT Lincoln Laboratory, where he leads programs and conducts research in the area of systems security. His research interests include cyber security, science of security, security evaluation, and operating systems. He is the recipient of 2014 MIT Lincoln Laboratory Early Career Technical Achievement Award and 2015 Team Award for his work on cyber moving target research. He is also the recipient of an honorable mention (runner-up) at the 2015 NSA's 3rd Annual Best Scientific Cybersecurity Paper Competition. He has served as a program committee member for many academic conferences and workshops including ACM Computer and Communications Security (CCS), Network and Distributed Systems Security (NDSS), IEEE Secure Development Conference (SecDev), ACM Asia Conference on Computer and Communications Security (AsiaCCS), Symposium on Research in Attacks, Intrusions, and Defenses (RAID), and International Conference on Applied Cryptography and Network Security (ACNS), among others. Dr. Okhravi earned his MS and PhD in electrical and computer engineering from University of Illinois at Urbana-Champaign in 2006 and 2010, respectively. More

information about him can be found at http://okhravi.mit.edu/index.

Xinming (Simon) Ou (PC co-chair) is currently associate professor of Computer Science and Engineering at University of South Florida. He received his PhD from Princeton University in 2005. Before joining USF in fall 2015, he had been a faculty member at Kansas State University since 2006. Dr. Ou's research is primarily in cyber defense technologies, with focuses on human-centered approach to addressing this challenge problem. He also has broad interest and on-going work in cyber-physical system security, intrusion/forensics analysis, moving-target defense, and mobile system security. He is the author of the MulVAL attack graph tool which has been used by Idaho National Laboratory, Defence Research and Development Canada -- Ottawa, NATO, NIST, Thales Groups, General Dynamics, Johns Hopkins University Applied Physics Lab, Swedish Defence Research Agency, Army Research Laboratory, and researchers from numerous academic institutions. Dr. Ou's research has been funded by U.S. National Science Foundation, Department of Defense, Department of Homeland Security, Department of Energy, National Institute of Standards and Technology (NIST), HP Labs, and Rockwell Collins. He is a recipient of 2010 NSF Faculty Early Career Development (CAREER) Award, a three-time winner of HP Labs Innovation Research Program (IRP) award, and 2013 Kansas State University Frankenhoff Outstanding Research Award.

ACKNOWLEDGMENTS

This material is based upon work supported by the Department of Defense under Air Force Contract No. FA8721-05-C-0002 and/or FA8702-15-D-0001. Any opinions, findings, conclusions or recommendations expressed in this material are those of the author(s) and do not necessarily reflect the views of the Department of Defense.

REFERENCES

[1] Hamed Okhravi, Thomas Hobson, David Bigelow, and William Streilein. "Finding focus in the blur of moving-target techniques." IEEE Security & Privacy 12, no. 2, pp: 16-26, 2014.

[2] Sushil Jajodia, Anup K. Ghosh, Vipin Swarup, Cliff Wang, and X. Sean Wang, eds. Moving target defense: creating asymmetric uncertainty for cyber threats. Vol. 54. Springer Science & Business Media, 2011.

[3] Hamed Okhravi, Mark Rabe, Travis Mayberry, William Leonard, Thomas Hobson, David Bigelow, and William Streilein. "Survey of cyber moving target techniques." MIT Lincoln Lanoratory, Technical Report No. MIT/LL-TR-1166, 2013.

PLAS 2017 – ACM SIGSAC Workshop on Programming Languages and Analysis for Security

Nataliia Bielova
INRIA
nataliia.bielova@inria.fr

Marco Gaboardi
University at Buffalo, The State University of New York
gaboardi@buffalo.edu

ABSTRACT

The 12th ACM SIGSAC Workshop on Programming Languages and Analysis for Security (PLAS 2017) is co-located with the ACM Conference on Computer and Communications Security (CCS). Over its now more than ten-year history, PLAS has provided a unique forum for researchers and practitioners to exchange ideas about programming language and program analysis techniques with the goal of improving the security of software systems.

PLAS aims to provide a forum for exploring and evaluating ideas on using programming language and program analysis techniques to improve the security of software systems. Strongly encouraged are proposals of new, speculative ideas, evaluations of new or known techniques in practical settings, and discussions of emerging threats and important problems.

CCS CONCEPTS

• **Security and privacy** → **Software and application security**;

KEYWORDS

programming languages; security

1 INTRODUCTION

PLAS aims to provide a forum for exploring and evaluating ideas on the use of programming language and program analysis techniques to improve the security of software systems. Strongly encouraged are proposals of new, speculative ideas, evaluations of new or known techniques in practical settings, and discussions of emerging threats and important problems. We are especially interested in position papers that are radical, forward-looking, and likely to lead to lively and insightful discussions that will influence future research that lies at the intersection of programming languages and security.

2 SCOPE

The scope of PLAS includes, but is not limited to:

- Compiler-based security mechanisms (e.g. security type systems) or runtime-based security mechanisms (e.g. inline reference monitors)
- Program analysis techniques for discovering security vulnerabilities

- Automated introduction and/or verification of security enforcement mechanisms
- Language-based verification of security properties in software, including verification of cryptographic protocols
- Specifying and enforcing security policies for information flow and access control
- Model-driven approaches to security
- Security concerns for Web programming languages
- Language design for security in new domains such as cloud computing and IoT
- Applications, case studies, and implementations of these techniques

3 WORKSHOP FORMAT

This year, PLAS received a good number of submissions attesting the continued vitality of the community whose work sits at the intersection of programming languages and security.

PLAS 2017 welcomed the submission of both long research papers as well as short papers presenting preliminary or exploratory work aiming at generating lively discussions at the workshop. PLAS 2017 attracted 16 submissions—of which, 6 were short papers—from 9 countries (Australia, France, Germany, India, Singapore, Sweden, Taiwan, UK, USA), with authors spanning both academia and industry.

PLAS 2017 is delighted to have two excellent invited talks:

- Authorization Contracts, Stephen Chong (Harvard University)
- Languages for Oblivious Computation, Michael Hicks (University of Maryland)

4 PROGRAM COMMITTEE MEMBERS

- Mario Alvim, Universidade Federal de Minas Gerais, Brazil
- Aslan Askarov, Aarhus University, Denmark
- Lujo Bauer, Carnegie Mellon University, USA
- Nataliia Bielova, INRIA, France, Co-chair
- Marco Gaboardi, University at Buffalo, SUNY, USA, Co-chair
- Deepak Garg, MPI Software Systems, Germany
- Kevin Hamlen, University of Texas at Dallas, USA
- Boris Koepf, IMDEA Software Institute, Spain
- Steve Kremer, Loria & Inria, France
- Scott Moore Galois Inc, USA
- Frank Piessens, DistriNet, Katholieke Universiteit Leuven, Belgium
- Omer Tripp, Google, USA
- Danfeng Zhang, Penn State University, USA

CCS'17, , October 30–November 3, 2017, Dallas, TX, USA
© 2017 Copyright held by the owner/author(s).
ACM ISBN ISBN 978-1-4503-4946-8/17/10.
https://doi.org/http://dx.doi.org/10.1145/3133956.3137045

5   WORKSHOP ORGANISERS

Nataliia Bielova (PC co-chair) is a Research Scientist in the Secure Diffuse Programming group at Inria (French Institute for Research in Computer Science and Automation). Nataliia's research examines how to apply programming language analysis to security and privacy of web applications. In her latest work, Nataliia has been focusing on merging language-based information flow control with runtime monitoring to detect web tracking scripts. Nataliia is organising a Dagstuhl seminar on Online Privacy and Web Transparency and participated multiple times in the program committees of the major conferences and journals in formal methods and security (ACM TISSEC, IEEE CSF, POST), where she herself has a number of publications.

Marco Gaboardi (PC co-chair) is an Assistant Professor in the Department of Computer Science and Engineering at the University at Buffalo, SUNY. Previously, he was a faculty at the University of Dundee, Scotland. Marco's research is in programming language design and implementation, and in differential privacy. In particular, he has been developing different language-based techniques for the verification of differential privacy. Marco has been involved in the organization of two Dagstuhl seminars, a NII Shonan meeting, a NII Shonan school. He has been the PC chair of four international workshops and has been on the program committees of major conferences in programming languages and security.

6   ACKNOWLEDGMENTS

We would like to thank all the authors who has submitted contributions to PLAS and the program committee members who have helped in reviewing. Thanks also to the invited speakers Stephen Chong and Michael Hicks who have kindly accepted our invitation. Finally, we would like to thank INRIA for financial support.

SafeConfig'17: Applying the Scientific Method to Active Cyber Defense Research

Nicholas J. Multari
Pacific Northwest National Lab,
Richland, WA, USA
nick.multari@pnnl.gov

Anoop Singhal
National Inst for Standards and
Technology, Rockville, MD, USA
anoop.singhal@nist.gov

Erin Miller
Pacific Northwest National Lab,
Richland, WA, USA
erin.miller@pnnl.gov

ABSTRACT

The focus of this workshop is the application of scientific practices to cyber security research. The objective of this workshop is examine the implementation of science practices in cyber defense research and understand the ramification of tradeoffs between simplifications to obtain interpretable results vs. observational studies of systems in the wild where the results can lead to ambiguous interpretations. The research papers accepted addressed a wide variety of technical questions in the cyber domain and the maturity of the work spanned the range of initial ideas and proofs of concept to mature work that is ready for operational implementation. Papers were evaluated for the reproducibility of the work as represented by the documentation of methods and testing environments.

CCS CONCEPTS

· **General and reference~Experimentation** · **Security and privacy** · **Networks~Network security** · **Networks~ Network experimentation** · **Software and its engineering~Software verification and validation**

KEYWORDS

SafeConfig; Testing; Validation; Security; Resilience; cyber; testbeds; metrics; cyber experimentation; science of cybersecurity

1 INTRODUCTION

Recently, there has been a great deal of interest about the science of cybersecurity[1,2,3,4]. In order to be considered scientific, the processes from concept through testing must follow a series of steps to ensure repeatable, reproducible and therefore verifiable results.

These steps include:
- Define a tractable problem.
- Ensure falsifiability

- Obtain ground truth
- Document assumptions and test them
- Start with simple experiments
- Assess progress to the larger problem

Upon completing this cycle, the process repeats with previous results incorporated into the problem and assumptions.

The focus of this workshop is the application of scientific practices to cyber security research. The objective of this workshop is examine the implementation of science practices in cyber defense research and understand the ramification of tradeoffs between simplifications to obtain interpretable results vs. observational studies of systems in the wild where the results can lead to ambiguous interpretations.

2 TOPICS

This workshop will consist of papers, presentations, and a panel discussing cyber security research and the means of applying the scientific processes to that research. To obtain a broad swath of areas in which these process could be applied, the following topics are of interest of this workshop:

- Configuration testing, forensics, debugging and evaluation.;
- Continuous monitoring and response;
- Cyber resiliency, agility and moving target defense;
- Cost effectiveness;
- Resilience/ agility effectiveness;
- Testbeds;
- Research Infrastructure;
- Verification techniques;
- Validation techniques;
- Testing & evaluation methods;
- Cyber-physical systems security;
- Security configuration verification and economics;
- Security metrics including adversarial and user measures;
- Security policy management;
- Theory of defense-of-depth;
- Mission metrics to include mission assurance, mission measures, and conflicting mission management.

3 PROGRAM

The workshop will consist of a combination of peer-reviewed and invited papers, a keynote presentation and a panel.

The keynote presentation will be given by Dr. William (Bill) Sanders. Bill is the Department Head of the Electrical and Computer Engineering Department at the University of Illinois at Urbana/Champaign. His presentation will discuss the processes in going from good science to good engineering in the context of cyber security and cyber resilience. The panel will consist of Bill and professors from University of Texas at Dallas, the University of Colorado at Boulder, and at least one other panellist to be named shortly. In addition, each of the panellist will present their introductory remarks as invited talks.

The remainder of the program will consist of 15 and 30 minute presentations by the authors of accepted papers. Full papers authors will receive the 30 minutes each while the short paper authors will get 15 minutes each.

4 PROGRAM COMMITTEE

Steering Committee

Ehab Al-Shaer, UNC Charlotte, USA
Chris Oehmen, Pacific Northwest National Lab, USA
Krishna Kant, Temple University, USA

Technical Committee

Michael Atifhetchi, Raytheon Corp BBN, USA
Salman Baset, IBM, USA
Steve Borbash, US Department of Defense, USA
Eric Burger, Georgetown University, USA
Seraphin Calo, IBM, USA
Thomas Carroll, Pacific Northwest National Lab, USA
Andrea Ceccarelli, Universita degli Studi di Firenze, IT
Yung Ryn Choe, Sandia National Lab, USA
Naranker Dulay, Imperial College, UK
Thomas Edgar, Pacific Northwest National Lab, USA
Alwyn Goodloe, NASA Langley Research Center, USAYong Guan, Iowa State University, USA
Krishna Kant, Temple University, USA
DongSeong Kim, University of Canterbury, NZ
Richard Kuhn, National Institute of Standards & Technology, USA
Alex Liu, Michigan State University, USA
Peng Liu, Penn State University, USA
Emil Lupu, Imperial College, UK
Luigi Mancini, Universita di Roma La Sapienza, Italy
Mohammad Rahman, Tennessee Tech, USA
Walid Saad, Virginia Tech, USA
Mahesh Tripunitara, University of Waterloo, CA
Carlos Westphall, Federal University of Santa Catarina, BR
Geoffrey Xie, Naval Postgraduate School, USA
Jeff Yan, Lancaster University, UK
Daphne Yao, Virginia Tech, USA

5 WORKSHOP CHAIRS

Nicholas J. Multari provides programmatic and technical guidance to cybersecurity research programs at the Pacific Northwest National Lab (PNNL). Prior to joining PNNL, he led the trusted cyber technology research at Boeing Research and Technology in Seattle, Washington. In 2008, he served as a consultant to the USAF Scientific Advisory Board (SAB) investigating the effects of the contested cyber environment on the USAF mission. Other positions held include five years as a Senior Security Engineer with Scitor Corporation in Northern Virginia, and 20 years as a computer scientist in the Air Force retiring as a Lt. Col. He is a member of external advisory boards at University of Washington and Iowa State University and is an associate editor of the Data and Knowledge Engineering Journal by Elsevier. He received his PhD in computer science from the University of Texas at Austin.

Anoop Singhal, is currently a Senior Computer Scientist in the Computer Security Division at the National Institute of Standards and Technology (NIST) in Gaithersburg, MD. He received his Ph.D. in Computer Science from Ohio State University, Columbus, Ohio. His research interests are in network security, network forensics, cloud computing security and data mining systems. He is a member of ACM, senior member of the IEEE and he has co-authored over 50 technical papers in leading conferences and journals. He has two patents in the area of attack graphs and he has also co-edited a book on Secure Cloud Computing.

Erin Miller is the current chair of PNNL's Science Council, a group consisting of empirical researchers whose purpose is bringing science-based practices to cyber security research. She is a research scientist in the Radiation Detection & Nuclear Sciences group at PNNL, and the Technical Team Lead for Radiation Imaging and Materials Science. She has lead projects developing methods for gratings-based x-ray imaging for explosives detection; gamma emission tomography for verification of nuclear fuel; and inverse problems in radiation detection: localizing and describing radioactive sources in aerial survey, pedestrian search, and in combination with radiographic data in cargo containers. She holds a PhD in Physics from the University of Washington.

REFERENCES
[1] Tardiff et al., "Applying the Scientific Method to Cybersecurity Research" (2016), *in* Proceedings of the 2016 IEEE International Symposium on Technologies for Homeland Security, Boston, MA.
[2] https://www.afcea.org/committees/cyber/documents/ScienceofSecurityFinal_000.pdf
[3] https://www.nsf.gov/news/news_summ.jsp?cntn_id=190444
[4] http://webhost.laas.fr/TSF/IFIPWG/Workshops&Meetings/67/index.htm

16th Workshop on Privacy in the Electronic Society (WPES 2017)

Adam J. Lee
University of Pittsburgh
Pittsburgh, Pennsylvania
adamlee@cs.pitt.edu

ABSTRACT

The 16th Workshop on Privacy in the Electronic Society was held on October 30, 2017 in conjunction with the 24th ACM Conference on Computer and Communications Security (CCS 2017) in Dallas, Texas, USA. The goal of WPES is to bring together a diverse group of privacy researchers and practitioners to discuss privacy problems that arise in global, interconnected societies, and potential solutions to them. The program for the workshop contains 14 full papers and 5 short papers selected from a total of 56 submissions. Specific topics covered in the program include but are not limited to: de-anonymization, fingerprinting and profiling, location privacy, and private memory systems.

CCS CONCEPTS

• **Security and privacy;**

KEYWORDS

Privacy protection

ACM Reference Format:
Adam J. Lee. 2017. 16th Workshop on Privacy in the Electronic Society (WPES 2017). In *Proceedings of CCS '17*. ACM, New York, NY, USA, Article 4, 2 pages. https://doi.org/10.1145/3133956.3137047

1 INTRODUCTION

The increased power and interconnectivity of computer systems available today create the ability to store and process large amounts of data, resulting in networked information accessible from anywhere at any time. It is becoming easier to collect, exchange, access, process, and link information. This global scenario has inevitably resulted in an increasing degree of awareness with respect to privacy. Privacy issues have been the subject of public debates, and the need for privacy-aware policies, regulations, and techniques has been widely recognized.

The goal of this workshop is to discuss the problems of privacy in global interconnected societies, as well as possible solutions to these types of problems. The workshop seeks submissions from academia and industry presenting novel research on all theoretical and practical aspects of electronic privacy, as well as experimental studies of fielded systems. We encourage submissions from other communities such as law and business that present these communities' perspectives on technological issues. Topics of interest include, but are not limited to:

- anonymization and transparency
- crowdsourcing for privacy and security
- data correlation and leakage attacks
- data security and privacy
- data and computations integrity in emerging scenarios
- electronic communication privacy
- economics of privacy
- information dissemination control
- models, languages, and techniques for big data protection
- personally identifiable information
- privacy-access control
- privacy and anonymity on the web
- privacy in biometric systems
- privacy in cloud and grid systems
- privacy and confidentiality management
- privacy and data mining
- privacy in the Internet of Things
- privacy in the digital business
- privacy in the electronic records
- privacy enhancing technologies
- privacy and human rights
- privacy in health care and public administration
- privacy metrics
- privacy in mobile systems
- privacy in outsourced scenarios
- privacy policies
- privacy vs. security
- privacy of provenance data
- privacy in social networks
- privacy threats
- privacy and virtual identity
- user profiling
- wireless privacy

2 PROGRAM

The program for the workshop contains 14 full papers and 5 short papers selected from a total of 56 submissions. Specific topics covered in the program include but are not limited to: de-anonymization, fingerprinting and profiling, location privacy, and private memory systems. The selection of these papers was made by a program committee consisting of 37 researchers whose backgrounds include a diverse array of topics related to privacy:

- Adam J. Lee (*Chair*), University of Pittsburgh, USA
- Mahdi Nasrullah Al-Ameen, Clemson University, USA
- Vijay Atluri, Rutgers University, USA

- Carlo Blundo, Università degli Studi di Salerno, Italy
- Nikita Borisov, University of Illinois at Urbana-Champaign, USA
- Sherman S. M. Chow, Chinese University of Hong Kong
- Omar Chowdhury, University of Iowa, USA
- Daniel Cullina, Princeton University, USA
- Sabrina De Captitani di Vimercati, Università degli Studi di Milano, Italy
- Josep Domingo-Ferrer, Universitat Rovira i Virgili, Spain
- Sara Foresti, Università degli Studi di Milano, Italy
- Roberto Hoyle, Oberlin College
- Sushil Jajodia, George Mason University, USA
- Limin Jia, Carnegie Mellon University, USA
- Aaron Johnson, NRL, USA
- Apu Kapadia, Indiana University at Bloomington, USA
- Aniket Kate, Purdue University, USA
- Florian Kerschbaum, University of Waterloo, Canada
- Changchang Liu, Princeton University, USA
- Giovanni Livraga, Università degli Studi di Milano, Italy
- Catherine Meadows, NRL, USA
- Pradeep Kumar Murukannaiah, Rochester Institute of Technology, USA
- Mohamed Nabeel, Qatar Computing Research Institute, Qatar
- Samir Patil, Indiana University at Bloomington, USA
- Gerardo Pelosi, Politecnico di Milano, Italy
- Indrakshi Ray, Colorado State University, USA
- Pierangela Samarati, Università degli Studi di Milano, Italy
- Nitesh Saxena, University of Alabama at Birmingham, USA
- Paul Syverson, NRL, USA
- Vicenc Torra, U. Skovd, Sweden
- Blase Ur, University of Chicago, USA
- Kami Vaniea, University of Edinburgh, UK
- Eugene Vasserman, Kansas State University, USA

- Meng Yu, University of Texas at San Antonio, USA
- Ting Yu, Qatar Computing Research Institute, Qatar
- Moti Yung, Snapchat and Columbia University, USA
- Nan Zhang, The George Washington University, USA

3 ORGANIZERS

WPES 2017 was organized by the following individuals:

- *General chair:* Bhavani Thuraisingham, The University of Texas at Dallas
- *Workshop chairs:*
  - Taesoo Kim, Georgia Tech
  - Cliff Wang, Army Research Office
- *Program chair:* Adam J. Lee, University of Pittsburgh
- *Publicity chair:* William C. Garrison III, University of Pittsburgh
- *Steering committee:*
  - Sabrina De Capitani di Vimercati, Università degli Studi di Milano
  - Sushil Jajodia, George Mason University
  - Pierangela Samarati (*Chair*), Università degli Studi di Milano
  - Paul Syverson, Naval Research Laboratory

4 ACKNOWLEDGMENTS

I would like to thank the members of the program committee for their insightful reviews and thoughtful discussion, which were central to the selection of the program for this year's workshop. The WPES steering committee was a useful source of guidance and advice along the way, especially Pierangela Samarati. And, of course, I must thank all of the authors who chose to submit papers to WPES, as well as everyone who attended and participated in the workshop.

Workshop on Multimedia Privacy and Security*

Roger Hallman
US Navy SPAWAR Systems Center
Pacific
San Diego, California
roger.hallman@navy.mil

Kurt Rohloff
New Jersey Institute of Technology
Newark, New Jersey
rohloff@njit.edu

Victor Chang
Xian Jiaotong Liverpool University
Suzhou, China
ic.victor.chang@gmail.com

CCS CONCEPTS

• **Security and privacy** → *Information accountability and usage control*; *Software security engineering*;

KEYWORDS

Security,Privacy,Multimedia

This workshop addresses the technical challenges arising from our current interconnected society. Multitudes of devices and people can be connected to each other by intelligent algorithms, apps, social networks, and the infrastructure set by Internet of Things (IoT). As more people and their devices are connected without much restriction, the issues of security, privacy, and trust remain a challenge. Multimedia in IoT services should provide a robust and resilient security platforms and solutions against any unauthorized access. Recent literature shows increased concerns about hacking, security breaches, data manipulation, social engineering, and new attack methods. Malware can be hidden within multimedia files and visiting infected websites can trigger its download to victims machines. There are a multitude of techniques to steal personal information and other sensitive media for unauthorized dissemination; imposters/identity thefts are common in social networks. In order to demonstrate the effectiveness of resilient security and privacy solutions, methods such as new standards, advance cryptography, improved algorithms for intrusion detection, personalized privacy, and isolation of questionable or malicious files can be used independently or all together to minimize the threats.

Multimedia has expanded beyond the scope its original definition. With the rise of social media, large quantities of multimedia (e.g., pictures, videos, data, analytics and personal information) can be created in a short period of time. When all these data are stored in a cloud environment, many people can connect to these services for viewing, sharing, commenting, and storing information. IoT represents a collection of devices, platforms, and software that allow people to store and share data in the cloud and also connects different

*Co-Located Workshops Chairs Summary Abstract

types of clouds altogether. Hence, multimedia in the IoT serves a significant purpose as many peoples updates, status, locations, and live actions can be seen, disseminated, tracked, commented on, and monitored in near real time. IoT opens up many possibilities since more people can broadcast themselves and allow their networks to view and share in their lives. There are also increased fraudulent activities, cybercrimes, unauthorized access, malicious attacks, phishing, and impersonating/stealing identities. This presents challenges for existing areas such as access control, authentication, data leakage, permission, social engineering, denial of service, and identity management for the attackers to impose identity, steal information, and manipulate data in the IoT environment. Challenges also include new problems such as large scale attacks and prevention, the strength of security protection (e.g., common encryption algorithms), hiding malware with multimedia, location-based privacy with high accuracy and anonymity, underground criminal networks, and hidden security breaches.

Our workshopl, The 1st International Workshop on Multimedia Privacy and Security (MPS), as part of CCS 2017, focuses on these concerns, specific to the IoT ecosystem. We solicited submissions on new and innovative methods, techniques, and proofsofconcepts supported by strong theory/algorithms and simulation/experiments to submit papers for this workshop. We accepted 5 submissions, and organized the workshop around talks for these publications with a keynote from Dr. Jeremy Epstein of the NSF and a panel discussion. Accepted papers include:

(1) "Unwinding Ariadne's Identity Thread: Privacy Risks with Fitness Trackers and Online Social Networks" by Angeliki Aktypi, Jason Nurse, and Michael Goldsmith (University of Oxford, UK)
(2) "A Study on Autoencoder-based Reconstruction Method for Wi-Fi Location Data with Erasures" by Tetsushi Ohki (Shizuoka University, Japan) and Akira Otsuka (Institute of Information Technology, Japan)
(3) "Attacking Automatic Video Analysis Algorithms: A Case Study of Google Cloud Video Intelligence API" by Hossein Hosseini, Baicen Xiao, and Radha Poovendran (University of Washington, USA), Andrew Clark (Worcester Polytechnic Institute, USA)
(4) "Approximate Thumbnail Preserving Encryption" by Byron Marohn (Intel; Portland State University, USA), Charles Wright and Wu-Chi Feng (Portland State University, USA), Mike Rosulek and Rakesh B. Bobba (Oregon State University, USA)

(5) "Detecting Spying and Fraud Browser Extensions" by
    Gaurav Varshney and Manoj Misra (Indian Institute
    of Technology, Roorkee, India), and Pradeep K. Atrey
    (State University of New York at Albany, USA)

The Keynote is entitled "An NSF View of Multimedia Privacy
and Security", and the panel is entitled "Multimedia Security
and Privacy with IoT and Social Networks".

IoT S&P 2017: First Workshop on Internet of Things Security and Privacy

Theophilus Benson
Brown University
tabenson@cs.brown.edu

Srikanth Sundaresan
Princeton University
srikanths@princeton.edu

Peng Liu
Penn State University
pliu@ist.psu.edu

Yuqing Zhang
University of Chinese Academy of Sciences, China
zhangyq@ucas.ac.cn

ABSTRACT

The First Workshop on Internet of Things Security and Privacy is held in Dallas, TX, USA on November 3, 2017, co-located with the ACM Conference on Computer and Communications Security (CCS). The workshop aims to address the security and privacy challenges of the emerging Internet-of-Things landscape. The workshop aims to bring together academic and industrial researchers, and to that end, we have put together an exciting program offering a a mix of current and potential challenges. The workshop will also features 12 papers, 4 posters, and an invited keynote.

KEYWORDS

Internet-of-Things; Security; Privacy

ACM Reference Format:
Theophilus Benson, Peng Liu, Srikanth Sundaresan, and Yuqing Zhang. 2017. IoT S&P 2017: First Workshop on Internet of Things Security and Privacy. In *Proceedings of CCS '17, October 30-November 3, 2017, Dallas, TX, USA, ,* 2 pages.
https://doi.org/10.1145/3133956.3137053

1 INTRODUCTION

The future of the Internet-of-Things is already upon us — a variety of sensors and devices are already available in the market, ranging from smart light bulbs to juicers, barbecues, and security systems. This has implications for privacy — what sort of information are these sensors collecting about users? — and security, with recent Internet-scale DDoS attacks caused by thousands of cheap, poorly patched devices.

Motivated by an increasing number of attacks and information leaks, IoT device manufactures, cloud providers, and researchers are working to design systems to secure to control the flow of information between devices, to detect new vulnerabilities; and to provide security and privacy within the context of user and the devices. While researchers continue to tackle IoT security and privacy, many questions remain open.

Further, with the growing adoption of IoT devices, we will see a growth in the number of security and privacy issues. The goal of the First ACM CCS Workshop on IoT S&P is to bring together academic and industry researchers from the security and communication communities to design, measure, and analyze secure and privacy enhancing systems for IoT devices.

2 SCOPE OF THE WORKSHOP

IoT S&P'17 encouraged the submission of previously unpublished, work-in-progress papers in the area of design, implementation, management, and deployment of secure and private IoT frameworks as well as measurement and analysis of the privacy and security of existing IoT devices and packages. The topics included the following:

- Security and privacy issues in IoT
- Network architectures and protocols for scalable, robust, secure, and privacy enhancing IoT
- Network services and management for IoT
- Measurement of IoT privacy leakage
- Measurement of Industrial IoT
- Usable security and privacy frameworks for home networks
- Threat Models and Attack Strategies in IoT
- Intrusion and Malware Detection
- Security Architectures for the IoT Stack
- System and Data Integrity
- Identity and access management in IoT
- Trustworthiness in IoT
- Secure Operating Systems in IoT
- Automated armoring and patching
- Cross-layer IoT security
- IoT ecosystem-level security analysis
- Clean-slate IoT security design

3 THE WORKSHOP

We received 30 submissions, of which we accepted 12 papers; a further four were invited to be presented as posters. The program was divided into four sessions; two for discussing existing IoT systems that requires urgent attention, one for defense against IoT hacks, and one discussing building blocks for next-gen defense. The workshop, held over one day, also included a keynote by Earlence Fernandes, a research associate at the University of Washington. Earlence's keynote, titled "Computer Security and Privacy for the

Physical World", discussed recent results in securing emerging IoT systems, and outlined directions of future research.

4 ORGANIZERS

Theophilus Benson, TPC co-chair, (Brown University, USA): received his BS from Tufts University, and his MS and PhD degrees from University of Wisconsin – Madison in 2012. Dr. Benson is an Assistant Professor of Computer Science at Brown University. Dr Benson's research focuses on solving practical networking and systems problems, with a focus on Software Defined Networking, data centers, clouds, and configuration management. To this end, his group works on developing abstractions, algorithms and frameworks for using programmable data planes (Software-Defined Networking) to improve the reliability, performance and security of enterprise, ISP, home networks, and networks in developing regions. Dr Benson has served on program committee for multiple workshops/conferences (SIGCOMM, IMC, CoNext, SoSR, SoCC, Usenix ATC, HotCloud, HotMB), the publicity chair for several workshops/conferences (CoNext'14 Workshop, SoSR'17) and as the Workshop Co-Chair for several successful workshops (HotMB'16, CoNext Workshop'15).

Peng Liu, General co-chair, (Penn State University, USA): received his BS and MS degrees from the University of Science and Technology of China, and his PhD from George Mason University in 1999. Dr. Liu is a Professor of Information Sciences and Technology, founding director of the Center for Cyber-Security, Information Privacy, and Trust, and founding director of the Cyber Security Lab at Penn State University. His research interests are in all areas of computer and network security. He has published a monograph and over 260 refereed technical papers. His research has been sponsored by NSF, ARO, AFOSR, DARPA, DHS, DOE, AFRL, NSA, TTC, CISCO, and HP. He has served as a program (co-)chair or general (co-)chair for over 10 international conferences (*e.g.* Asia CCS 2010) and workshops (*e.g.*, MTD 2016). He chaired the Steering Committee of SECURECOMM during 2008-14. He has served on over 100 program committees and reviewed papers for numerous journals. He is an associate editor for IEEE TDSC.

Srikanth Sundaresan, TPC co-chair, (Princeton University, USA): Srikanth's research interests include the design and measurements of networked systems with a focus on quality of experience for end users—including performance, privacy, and security. He has experience building large-scale IoT systems at Samsara Networks, and successful academic network monitoring systems, including BISmark and Lumen Privacy Monitor. He has served on program committees for IMC 2017, PAM 2016, and several workshops.

Yuqing Zhang, General co-chair, (University of Chinese Academy of Sciences, China) received his PhD in Cryptography from Xidian University, China. Dr. Zhang is a Professor of Computer Sciences and the Director of the National Computer Network Intrusion Protection Center at University of CAS. His research interests include network and system security, cryptography, and networking. He has published more than 100 research papers in many international journals and conferences, such as ACM CCS, IEEE Transactions on Parallel and Distributed Systems, and IEEE Transactions on Dependable and Secure Computing. His research has been sponsored by NSFC, Huawei, Qihu360 and Google. He has served as a program chair for over 5 international workshops (*e.g.*, SMCN-2017). He has been the PC member for more than 10 international conferences in networking and security, such as IEEE Globecom 16/17, IEEE CNS 17, and IFIP DBSec 17.

ACKNOWLEDGMENTS

We would like to acknowledge the authors who submitted their research to the conference, and also the program committee members who contributed to putting together the exciting program. We would also like to thank the keynote speakers, and the organizers of the CCS conference.

Author Index

Acar, Gunes 2021
Acar, Yasemin 1065, 2187
Acer, Mustafa Emre.....................1407
Agrawal, Shashank 665
Agrawal, Shweta 2277
Ahmed, Muhammad Ejaz...........2467
Ahmed, Shabbir 2531
Aldweesh, Amjad 211
Allodi, Luca 1483
Almeida, José Bacelar 1807, 1989
Alwen, Joel 1001
Ambrona, Miguel 647
Ames, Scott 2087
Andriesse, Dennis 1675
Antonakakis, Manos 569, 1125
Appel, Andrew W.......................2007
Araujo, Frederico 2523
Arden, Owen 1875, 1893
Arrowood, James 2575
Asghar, Hassan Jameel.................2555
Ashraf, Mohammed 1601
Asokan, N. 619
Ateniese, Giuseppe 603
Aviv, Adam 507
Backes, Michael 1037, 1065,
                1757, 1943, 2187
Bahri, Leila 2603
Bai, Xiaolong 829
Barbosa, Manuel 1807, 1989
Barcellos, Marinho 2495
Barrett, Jacob 1421
Barron, Timothy 957
Barthe, Gilles 647, 1807, 1989
Bauer, Lujo 295
Bellare, Mihir 891, 923, 1515
Benson, Theophilus 2647
Beringer, Lennart 2007
Berndt, Sebastian 1649
Bertino, Elisa 2631, 2635
Beurdouche, Benjamin 1789
Bhargava, Radhika 1407
Bhargavan, Karthikeyan 1789
Bhattacherjee, Sanjay 2277
Bian, Pan 2139
Bielova, Nataliia 2607, 2639
Biggio, Battista 2621
Bijlani, Ashish 2169
Bilge, Leyla 1299

Bindschaedler, Vincent 2421
Biswas, Priyam 2373
Blocki, Jeremiah 1001
Blot, Arthur 1807
Blumberg, Andrew J.....................2071
Bobba, Rakesh B.......................2629
Böhme, Marcel 2329
Böhme, Rainer 553
Boit, Christian 1661
Bonawitz, Keith 1175
Boneh, Dan 765, 983
Bos, Herbert 1675
Bost, Raphaël 1465
Bourquard, Aurélien 2595
Boyle, Elette 2105
Braithwaite, Matt 1407
Bruinderink, Leon Groot............1843
Bugiel, Sven 1037, 2187
Buiras, Pablo 1893
Bursztein, Elie 1421
Butler, Kevin R. B. 2245
Cai, Zixi 2471
Cain, Noah 2559
Camenisch, Jan 683
Campanelli, Matteo 229
Cao, Shaosheng 2475
Cao, Yinzhi 163
Cao, Yulong 941
Cao, Zigang 2471, 2487
Carmer, Brent 747
Carr, Scott 2373
Cassel, Darion 245
Cecchetti, Ethan 701, 1875
Cerulli, Andrea 1583
Cha, Sang Kil 2345
Chandran, Nishanth 277
Chang, Chip Hong.....................2623
Chang, Ee-Chien 119
Chang, Victor 2645
Chase, Melissa 665, 1825
Chatterjee, Rahul 329
Chen, Bo 2217
Chen, Chaochao 2543
Chen, Guoxing 2421
Chen, Hao (UC Davis) 135
Chen, Hao (Microsoft)............... 1243
Chen, Jia 875
Chen, Kai 815, 829, 2139

Chen, Li 2479
Chen, Qi Alfred.....................941
Chen, Sanchuan 859
Chen, Tanghui 2491
Chen, Tao 2535, 2543
Chen, Xi 1675
Chen, Yan 1375
Chen, Yi 815
Chen, Yingying 73
Chen, Yizheng 569, 1125
Chen, Zhanhao 163
Cheng, Long 2483
Cheng, Yueqiang 2491
Chhotaray, Animesh 1533
Cho, Kyong-Tak 1109
Choi, Seung Geol 507
Chong, Stephen 1893
Choudhuri, Arka Rai.....................719
Chowdhury, Anusha 329
Christin, Nicolas 295
Cline, Daren B.H.....................971
Comanescu, Oxana 1421
Cook, Kyle 2575
Corina, Jake 2123
Cortier, Véronique 409
Couteau, Geoffroy 2105
Cranor, Lorrie Faith 295
Cremers, Cas 1773
Crosser, Corey 2389
Cryan, Jenna 1143
Cui, Jinhua 89
Cui, Mingxin 2487
Cvrcek, Dan 1583
Dai, Wei 923
Danezis, George 1583
Dang, Hung 119
Danilova, Anastasia 311
Datta, Anupam 1193
Dechand, Sergej 311
del Pino, Rafaël 1565
Dell'Amico, Matteo 1299
Derler, David 1825
Derr, Erik 2187
Dev, Bhanu 1407
Devadas, Srinivas 2435
Diaz, Claudia 2021
Dillig, Isil 875
Ding, Xuhua 89

Ding, Yu 2491
Doerner, Jack 523
Dong, Changyu 211
Döttling, Nico 2263
Downing, Evan 377
Dresel, Lukas 347
Drijvers, Manu 683
Du, Kun 537
Du, Min 1285
Duan, Haixin 537
Duan, Ran 2491
Duan, Ruian 2169
Dubovitskaya, Maria 683
Dumitraş, Tudor 1435
Dupressoir, François 1989
Egelman, Serge 295
Eranti, Vijay 1421
Espitau, Thomas 1857
Etigowni, Sriharsha 1095
Fahl, Sascha 1065, 1407, 2187
Fazzini, Mattia 377
Felt, Adrienne Porter 1407
Feng, Qian 363
Feng, Yu 875
Fenske, Ellis 2295
Ferber, Aaron 2463
Fernandez, José 1159
Finkbeiner, Bernd 633
Fisch, Ben 765
Flynn, Cheryl 1389
Forget, Alain 295
Forte, Domenic 1533
Fouque, Pierre-Alain 1857
Fowze, Farhaan 2245
Frassetto, Tommaso 2405
Fredrikson, Matthew 1193
Freeman, David 2621
Freire, Lucas 2495
Gaboardi, Marco 2639
Gamero-Garrido, Alexander 1501
Garay, Juan A. 277
Gay, Romain 647
Gehr, Timon 391
Genkin, Daniel 845
Gennaro, Rosario 229
Gens, David 2405
Gérard, Benoît 1857
Gervais, Arthur 439
Ghosh, Satrajit 2263
Gilboa, Niv 2105
Giuffrdia, Cristiano 1675

Goldfeder, Steven 229, 1825
Gorbunov, Sergey 765
Goto, Shigeki 2587
Green, Matthew 473, 719, 2007
Greenlee, Elliot 2463
Greenstadt, Rachel 2021
Grégoire, Benjamin 1807, 1989
Grimm, Niklas 409
Groß, Samuel 1709
Guajardo, Jorge 491
Guarnieri, Marco 391
Gueron, Shay 1019
Gunter, Carl A. 2421
Habib, Hana 295
Hafiz, Syed Mahbub 1361
Hale, John 2575
Halevi, Shai 783
Halevi, Tzipora 783
Hallman, Roger 2645
Hamlen, Kevin W. 1909
Han, HyungSeok 2345
Han, Xinhui 829
Han, Yi 1095
Han, Yufei 1299
Hao, Shuang 2123
Harsha, Ben 1001
Hartung, Gunnar 1925
Hay, Michael 1375
Hayashi, Yu-ichi 2587
Hazay, Carmit 2087
He, Xi 1389, 1051
Henry, Ryan 1361, 2611
Hernandez, Grant 2245
Herold, Gottfried 1547
Herzog, Marco 311
Hitaj, Briland 603
Ho, Jun-Won 2499
Hoang, Thang 491
Hoang, Viet Tung 1515
Hoffmann, Max 1547, 1925
Holland, Jordan 2503
Honarmand, Nima 149
Horvat, Marko 1773
Hoyland, Jonathan 1773
Huang, Jian 2231
Huang, Jie 1037
Huang, Yan 245
Huang, Yue 119
Humbert, Mathias 1943
Invernizzi, Luca 1421

Ishai, Yuval 2087, 2105
Islam, Mohammad A. 1079
Ivanov, Vladimir 1175
Jaeger, Joseph 891
Jaeger, Trent 2359
Jain, Abhishek 719
Jana, Suman 2155
Jeon, Yuseok 2373
Ji, Xiaoyu 103
Ji, Yan 701
Ji, Yang 377
Ji, Ye 2071
Jia, Shijie 2217
Jing, Jiwu 1051
Johns, Martin 1709, 1757
Johnson, Aaron 2295
Joosen, Wouter 553, 957
Juarez, Mark 2021
Juels, Ari 701
Juliato, Marcio 2531
Juuti, Mika 619
Kaafar, Moahmed Ali 2555
Kanich, Chris 179
Kantarcioglu, Murat 1211
Kaptchuk, Gabriel 719
Kar, Diptendu Mohan 2507
Karame, Ghassan O. 2627
Kashyap, Sanidhya 2313
Kate, Aniket 455
Katz, Jonathan 21, 39
Keromytis, Angelos D. 2155
Kersten, Rody 2511
Khalil, Issa 425
Khalil, Rami 439
Khan, Latifur 1211
Kim, Dohyun 195, 1435
Kim, Hyoungshick 2467
Kim, Jee Sun 2499
Kim, Kee Sung 1449
Kim, Minkyu 1449
Kim, Seungyeon 2515
Kim, Taesoo 377, 2169,
2313, 2613, 2633
Kim, Woo-Hwan 1449
Kim, Yongdae 195
Kintis, Panagiotis 569
Kinugawa, Masahiro 2587
Klein, Amit 2519
Klinec, Dusan 1583, 1631
Klooß, Michael 1547
Ko, Gihyuk 1193

Koch, Simon 1757
Kogan, Dmitry 983
Kohlbrenner, Anne 2523
Kohno, Tadayoshi 1741
Kolesnikov, Vladimir 3, 1257
Korczynski, David 1691
Korczyński, Maciej 553
Kosba, Ahmed 701
Kotowicz, Krzysztof 1709
Kountouras, Athanasios 1125
Koushanfar, Farinaz 2623
Kravtsov, Vladimir 2519
Kreuter, Ben 1175
Kruegel, Christopher ...347, 1159, 2123
Kučera, Martin 391
Kvasnicka, Michael 2575
Kwon, Bum Jun 1435
Kwon, Taekyoung 2515, 2527
Kwon, Yujin 195
Labrèche, Francois 1159
Laine, Kim 1243
Lallemand, Joseph 409
Laporte, Vincent 1807, 1989
Lazrig, Ibrahim 2507
Lebedev, Ilia 2435
Lee, Adam J. 2643
Lee, Byoungyoung 2373
Lee, Dongsoo 1449
Lee, Hoyeon 2515
Lee, Sangho 377
Lee, Wenke 377, 2169
Lee, Yeonjoon 815
Lee, Youngjoo 2527
Lee, Youngseok 2571
Lei, Lingguang 1051
Lekies, Sebastian 1709
Len, Julia 891
Lerner, Ada 1741
Levchenko, Kirill 1501
Lever, Charles 569
Li, Feifei 1285
Li, Frank 1421, 2201
Li, Huaxin 2531
Li, Long 2491
Li, Longfei 2535, 2599
Li, Mengyuan 859
Li, Qi 1051
Li, Song 163
Li, Tongxin 829
Li, Xiaolong ... 2475, 2535, 2543, 2599
Li, Yong 1343

Li, Zhen 2471
Li, Zhou 537
Li, Zhoujun 89
Liang, Bin 2139
Liao, Xiaojing 2139
Liebchen, Christopher 2405
Ligatti, Jay 2567
Lin, Guanjun 2539
Lin, Zhiqiang ..799, 1211, 2389, 2613
Lindell, Yehuda 259, 1019
Liśkiewicz, Maciej 1649
Liu, Baojun 537
Liu, Chang 363
Liu, Daiping 537
Liu, Hongyu 2389
Liu, Hua 1095
Liu, Jian 73, 619
Liu, Peng 2217, 2231, 2647
Liu, Shen 2359
Liu, Tongping 2389
Liu, Yujiang 2599
Liu, Ziqi 2543
Loguinov, Dmitri 971
Lohrke, Heiko 1661
Lu, Pei-Hsuan 2547
Lu, Yao 619
Luckow, Kasper 2511
Luo, Meng 149
Luo, Wei 2539
Lyubashevsky, Vadim 1565
Machanavajjhala, Ashwin ..1375, 1389
Machiry, Aravind 2123
Maffei, Matteo 409, 455
Malavolta, Giulio 455
Malozemoff, Alex J......................747
Mani, Akshaya 2295
Manohar, Nathan 983
Mao, Z. Morley 941
Marcedone, Antonio 1175
Mardziel, Piotr 1193
Margolis, Daniel 1421
Markov, Yarik 1421
Maruyama, Seita 2551, 2587
Masood, Rahat 2555
Matania, Naor 1257
Matyas, Vashek 1631
Mavroudis, Vasilios 1583
Mayberry, Travis 507
Mazumdar, Arya 2053
McConky, Katie 2563
McCorry, Patrick 211

McMahan, H. Brendan 1175
Memon, Nasir 1273
Meng, Dongyu 135
Miers, Ian 473, 719
Miklau, Gerome 1375
Miller, Brad 2621
Miller, Erin 2641
Min, Changwoo 2313
Minaud, Brice 1465
Miramirkhani, Najmeh 569
Mittal, Prateek 2583
Mohassel, Payman 277
Monrose, Fabian 1125
Moore, Tyler 553
Moreno-Sanchez, Pedro 455
Mori, Tatsuya 2551, 2587
Moscicki, Angelika 1421
Mukherjee, Subhojeet 2559
Müller, Christian 633
Multari, Nicholas J.....................2641
Myers, Andrew C. 1875
Nabeel, Mohammed Thari 1601
Nadji, Yacin 1125
Naeini, Pardis Emami 295
Nagel, Matthias 1925
Nahiyan, Adib 1533
Naiakshina, Alena 311
Nasr, Milad 2037, 2053
Nemec, Matus 1631
Neven, Gregory 1565
Neves, Miguel 2495
Nguyen, Duc Cuong.....................1065
Nguyen, Manh-Dung 2329
Nguyen, Tam 491
Nielsen, Jesper Buus.............. 3, 2263
Nikiforakis, Nick 149, 569, 957
Nilges, Tobias 2263
Nilizadeh, Shirin 1159
Nizzardo, Luca 229
Nof, Ariel 259
Noroozian, Arman 553
Ohrimenko, Olga 1465
Okhravi, Hamed 2637
Okutan, Ahmet 2563
Oliveira, Tiago 1807
Orlandi, Claudio 1825
Orrù, Michele 2105
Orso, Alessandro 377
Osterweil, Eric 941
Ou, Xinming 2637
Overdorf, Rebekah 2021

Oya, Simon 1959
Ozkaptan, Ceyhun D.....................491
Pacheco, Hugo 1807
Palombo, Hernan M. 2567
Pan, Lei 2539
Pan, Xiaorui 2421
Pang, Jun 1943
Park, Je Hong 1449
Park, Jonghyeon 2571
Păsăreanu, Corina S. 2511
Patel, Sarvar 1175
Paxson, Vern 1421, 2201
Payer, Mathias 2373
Pearman, Sarah 295
Pellegrino, Giancarlo 1757
Perdisci, Roberto 1125
Pereira, Vitor 1989
Perez-Cruz, Fernando 603
Pérez-González, Fernando 1959
Perlmuter, Alon 2519
Pessl, Peter 1843
Petcher, Adam 2007
Petropulu, Athina 1095
Petsios, Theofilos 2155
Pham, Van-Thuan 2329
Phan, Duong Hieu 2277
Piessens, Frank 1313
Pinkas, Benny 1257
Pitropakis, Nikolaos 569
Pnueli, Yuval 329
Protzenko, Jonathan 1789
Pu, Calton 1725
Qi, Yuan (Alan)............................2475
Qin, Zhan 425
Qureshi, Moinuddin K. 2231
Ràfols, Carla 1547
Rajendran, Jeyavijayan (JV) 1601
Ramacher, Sebastian 1825
Ramage, Daniel 1175
Ranellucci, Samuel 21, 39
Ranieri, Juri 1421
Rashid, Awais 2629
Ravi, Srivatsan 455
Ray, Indrajit 2507, 2559
Ray, Indrakshi 2507, 2559
Raykova, Mariana 747
Rechberger, Christian 1825
Ren, Kui 425
Ren, Shaolei 1079
Rindal, Peter 1229, 1243
Ristenpart, Thomas 329, 587

Roche, Daniel S. 507
Roesner, Franziska 1741
Rohloff, Kurt 2645
Romero-Gómez, Rosa 569
Rossow, Christian 1757
Rosulek, Mike 3, 1229, 1257
Roychoudhury, Abhik 2329
Rührmair, Ulrich 2623
Rupp, Andy 1547, 1925
Russell, Alexander 907
Russo, Alejandro 1893
Sadeghi, Ahmad-Reza 2405
Sahita, Ravi 2479
Salls, Christopher 347, 2123
Sanguansin, Naphat 2007
Sastry, Manoj R. 2531
Savage, Stefan 1501
Saxena, Nitesh 73, 1329
Schaeffer-Filho, Alberto 2495
Schäge, Sven 1343
Schmidt, Benedikt 1807
Schranz, Oliver 1037
Schuchard, Max 2503
Scott, Sam 1773
Sedighian, Alireza 1159
Segal, Aaron 1175
Seidl, Helmut 633
Seifert, Jean-Pierre 1661
Seiler, Gregor 1565
Sen, Shayak 1193
Sengupta, Abhrajit 1601
Seshia, Sanjit A. 2435
Seth, Karn 1175
Shamsi, Zain 971
Shan, Huasong 1725
Shaon, Fahad 1211
Shaw, Thomas 2575
Shelat, Abhi 523, 2071
Sherr, Micah 2295
Shi, Elaine 701
Shi, Junzheng 2487
Shin, Kang G. 1109
Shirvanian, Maliheh 1329
Shmatikov, Vitaly 587
Shoshitaishvili, Yan 347, 2123
Shoup, Victor 783
Shrimpton, Thomas 1533
Shulman, Haya 2519
Siadati, Hossein 1273
Silvestro, Sam 2389
Sinanoglu, Ozgur 1601

Singh, Abhishek 2579
Singhal, Anoop 2641
Sinha, Arunesh 2621
Sinha, Rohit 2435
Slamanig, Daniel 1825
Sleevi, Ryan 1407
Smith, Jared M.............................2463
Smith, Matthew 311
Snoeren, Alex C. 1501
Snyder, Peter 179
Son, Yunmok 195
Song, Congzheng 587
Song, Dawn 363
Song, Le 363, 2543
Song, Liwei 2583
Srikumar, Vivek 1285
Srivastava, Divesh 1389
Stamatogiannakis, Manolis 1675
Stark, Emily 1407
Starov, Oleksii 149
Stavrou, Angelos 2627
Stehlé, Damien 2277
Stephens-Davidowitz, Noah 783
Stoecklin, Marc Ph.......................2523
Stringhini, Gianluca 1159
Strub, Pierre-Yves 1807
Subramanyan, Pramod 2435
Sun, Kun 1051
Sundaresan, Srikanth 2647
Svenda, Petr 1583, 1631
Sys, Marek 1631
Tabriz, Parisa 1407
Tajalizadehkhoob, Samaneh 553
Tajik, Shahin 1661
Tan, Gang 2359
Tan, Sheng 57
Tang, Haixu 2421
Tang, Qiang 907, 2615
Taylor, Cynthia 179
Taylor, Shay 2575
Taylor, Teryl 2523
Tehranipoor, Mark 1533, 2623
Thaler, Justin 2071
Thomas, Jeremy 295
Thomas, Kurt 1421
Thomas, Matthew 941
Tian, Dave (Jing) 2245
Tian, Ke 2483
Tibouchi, Mehdi 1857
Tiefenau, Christian 311
Trieu, Ni 3, 1257

Trifiletti, Roberto 3, 2263
Troncoso, Carmela 1959
Tsai, Chia-che 2613
Tsai, Ming-Hsien 1973
Tsankov, Petar 391
Tsudik, Gene 89
Valenta, Luke 845
van der Merwe, Thyla 1773
van der Veen, Victor 1675
van Dijk, Marten 2623
van Eeten, Michel 553
Van Goethem, Tom 553, 957
van Moorsel, Aad 211
Vanhoef, Mathy 1313
Vasiloglou, Nikolaos 1125
Vasserman, Eugene 195
Vechev, Martin 391
Vela Nava, Eduardo A.............1709
Venkitasubramaniam,
Muthuramakrishnan 2087
Vigna, Giovanni 347, 1159, 2123
Vinayagamurthy, Dhinakaran 765
Vissers, Thomas 957
Viswanath, Bimal 1143
Vusirikala, Satyanarayana 277
Wagner, David 1
Wahby, Riad S. 2071
Waidner, Michael 2519
Wakabayashi, Satohiro 2551, 2587
Walfish, Michael 2071
Walker, Jacob 2559
Wang, Baosheng 2591
Wang, Bow-Yaw 1973
Wang, Chen 73
Wang, Haining 537
Wang, Huibo 2491
Wang, Qingyang 1725
Wang, Ruoyu 347
Wang, Weiren 377
Wang, Wenhao 1909, 2421
Wang, Xiao 21, 39
Wang, XiaoFeng 815, 829,
                          2139, 2421, 2591
Wang, Xueqiang 829
Wang, Yilei 211
Wang, Yuewu 1051
Waye, Lucas 1893

Wee, Hoeteck 647
Wei, Tao 2491
Weir, Charles 1065
Weissbacher, Michael 347
Weng, Jian 1051
Wermke, Dominik 1065
Werner, Gordon 2563
White, David 2559
Wierman, Adam 1079
Wies, Thomas 2071
Won, KyungRok 2499
Woodage, Joanne 329
Wu, Dinghao 2633
Wu, Shujiang 163
Xia, Luning 2217
Xia, Wei 2471
Xiang, Yang 2539
Xiao, Kai 2475
Xiao, Xiaokui 425
Xiao, Yuan 859
Xing, Luyi 829
Xing, Qianqian 2591
Xing, Xinyu 2231
Xiong, Gang 2471, 2487
Xu, Feng 2543
Xu, Jun 2231
Xu, Meng 2169
Xu, Wen 2313
Xu, Wenyuan 103
Xu, Xiaojun 363
Xu, Xiaoyang 1909
Yamada, Shota 2277
Yan, Chen 103
Yan, Jeff 2595
Yang, Bo-Yin 1973
Yang, Chih-yuan 2479
Yang, Jie 57
Yang, Lily L. 2531
Yang, Shanchieh Jay.................2563
Yang, WonSeok 2527
Yang, XinXing 2475
Yang, Yin 425
Yao, Danfeng (Daphne)....2483, 2631
Yao, Yuanshun 1143
Yarom, Yuval 845, 1843
Yasin, Muhammad 1601
Yavuz, Attila A. 491

Yavuz, Tuba 2245
Ye, Katherine Q........................2007
Yin, Heng 363, 1691
You, Ilsun 2635
You, Jie 941
You, Wei 815, 2139
Yu, Chia-Mu 2547
Yu, Ting 425
Yung, Moti 907, 2615
Zălinescu, Eugen 633
Zand, Ali 1159, 1421
Zaverucha, Greg 1825
Zha, Mingming 829
Zhang, Fan 701
Zhang, Guoming 103
Zhang, Jun 2539
Zhang, Linghan 57
Zhang, Mingwei 2479
Zhang, Nan 829
Zhang, Taimin 103
Zhang, Tianchen 103
Zhang, Ya-Lin 2599
Zhang, Yang 1943
Zhang, Yinqian 859, 2421, 2617
Zhang, Yuanchao 2599
Zhang, Yulong 2491
Zhang, Yuqing 2647
Zhang, Zhangkai 89
Zhao, Ben Y............................1143
Zhao, Benjamin Zi Hao 2555
Zhao, Jason 2155
Zhao, Li 2531
Zhao, Qingchuan 799
Zheng, Guineng 1285
Zheng, Haitao 1143
Zheng, Hao 2567
Zhou, Hong-Sheng 907
Zhou, Jun 2475, 2535, 2543, 2599
Zhou, Zhi-Hua 2599
Zhu, Ruiyu 245
Zinzindohoué, Jean-Karim 1789
Zolfaghari, Hadi 2037
Zong, Peiyuan 2139
Zonouz, Saman 1095
Zou, Wei 815
Zuo, Chaoshun 799